SQL Qu

2012 Joes 2 Pros®
Volume 5

XML Querying Techniques for SQL Server 2012

(SQL Exam Prep Series 70-461 Volume 5 of 5)

By

Rick A. Morelan
MCDBA, MCTS, MCITP, MCAD, MOE, MCSE, MCSE+I

Pinal Dave
Founder of SQLAuthority.com

EAN: 978-1-939666-04-8
Info@Joes2Pros.com

Table of Contents

About the Authors

We write each book in this series to help anyone seeking knowledge about SQL Server - whether an intermediate looking to fill gaps in their knowledge, an expert looking for new features in the 2012 version of SQL Server, or even a developer picking up SQL Server as their second or third programming language. At the heart of the mission as an educator remains the dedication to helping people with the power of SQL Server. The goal of education is action.

Rick A Morelan

In 1994, you could find Rick Morelan braving the frigid waters of the Bering Sea as an Alaskan commercial fisherman. His computer skills were non-existent at the time, so you might figure such beginnings seemed unlikely to lead him down the path to SQL Server expertise at Microsoft. However, every computer expert in the world today woke up at some point in their life knowing nothing about computers.

Making the change from fisherman seemed scary and took daily schooling at Catapult Software Training Institute. Rick got his lucky break in August of 1995, working his first database job at Microsoft. Since that time, Rick has worked more than 10 years at Microsoft and has attained over 30 Microsoft technical certifications in applications, networking, databases and .NET development.

His books are used the world over by individuals and educators to help people with little experience learn these technical topics and gain the ability to earn a Microsoft certification or have the confidence to do well in a job interview with their new found knowledge.

Rick's speaking engagements have included SQL Saturdays and SQL Server Intelligence Conferences. In addition to these speaking engagements Rick gives back to the community by personally teaching students at both Bellevue College and MoreTechnology in Redmond, WA.

Pinal Dave

Pinal Dave is a technology enthusiast and avid blogger. Prior to joining Microsoft, his outstanding community service helped to earn several awards, including the Microsoft Most Valuable Professional in SQL Server Technology (3 continuous years) and the Community Impact Award as an Individual Contributor for 2010. Playing an active role in the IT industry for over eight years, his career has taken him across the world working in both India and the US, primarily with SQL

Server Technology, from version 6.5 to its latest form. His early work experience includes being a Technology Evangelist with Microsoft and a Sr. Consultant with SolidQ, and he continues to work on performance tuning and optimization projects for high transactional systems.

Pinal's higher education degrees include a Master of Science from the University of Southern California, and a Bachelor of Engineering from Gujarat University. In addition to his degrees, Pinal holds multiple Microsoft certificates and helps to spread his knowledge as a regular speaker for many international events like TechEd, SQL PASS, MSDN, TechNet and countless user groups.
At the time of this writing, Pinal has co-authored three SQL Server books:

- SQL Server Programming
- SQL Wait Stats
- SQL Server Interview Questions and Answers

Pinal's passion for the community drives him to share his training and knowledge and frequently writes on his blog http://blog.SQLAuthority.com covering various subjects related to SQL Server technology and Business Intelligence. As a very active member of the social media community it is easy to connect with him using one of these services:

- Twitter: http://twitter.com/pinaldave
- Facebook: http://facebook.com/SQLAuth

When he is not in front of a computer, he is usually travelling to explore hidden treasures in nature with his lovely daughter, Shaivi, and very supportive wife, Nupur.

Acknowledgements from Rick Morelan

As a book with a supporting web site, illustrations, media content and software scripts, it takes more than the usual author, illustrator and editor to put everything together into a great learning experience. Since my publisher has the more traditional contributor list available, I'd like to recognize the core team members:

Editor: Lori Stow

Technical Review: Tony Smithlin

User Acceptance Testing: Sandra Howard

Index: Tony Smithlin

Thank you to all the teachers at Catapult Software Training Institute in the mid-1990s. What a great start to open my eyes. It landed me my first job at Microsoft by August of that year. A giant second wind came from Koenig-Solutions, which gives twice the training and attention for half the price of most other schools. Mr. Rohit Aggarwal is the visionary founder of this company based in New Delhi, India. Rohit's business model sits students down one-on-one with experts. Each expert dedicates weeks to help each new IT student succeed. The numerous twelve-hour flights I took to India to attend those classes were pivotal to my success. Whenever a new generation of software was released, I got years ahead of the learning curve by spending one or two months at Koenig.

Dr. James D. McCaffrey at Volt Technical Resources in Bellevue, Wash., taught me how to improve my own learning by teaching others. You'll frequently see me in his classroom because he makes learning fun. McCaffrey's unique style boosts the self-confidence of his students, and his tutelage has been essential to my own professional development. His philosophy inspires the *Joes 2 Pros* curriculum.

Preface

Many years ago I was in an advanced training with another SQL expert, Gary, who worked for the defense industry. At the time, I was a Microsoft employee. With just the two of us taking a Koenig class in Goa (India), we covered a lot of ground as we prepared for the SQL 2005 certification. Needless to say, we both passed our test with very little worry. Then we proceeded to prepare for our MCITP exam in SQL Server. At the time, I didn't see any significance in my scores being about 100 points higher than Gary's - he was equally as competent as I was and it seemed luck was just on my side. However, Gary had an excellent observation. He said he thought our SQL skills were about the same, but in today's world, *what SQL touches* matters almost as much as what you can do with SQL itself.

At the time, I didn't realize the big jump start I'd received from doing a SQL-XML project, as well as my MCSE experience. Rather than sheer luck, this additional exposure was responsible for my 100 point advantage. The power of new tools and languages is an opportunity for SQL to become more powerful by interoperating with these technologies. As time goes on, these powerful touch points become even more useful, and now you need to know this very well if one of your goals is to pass the Microsoft 70-461 certification.

Introduction

As a kid, I liked listening to the radio before falling asleep. One funny radio spot (i.e., commercial advertisement) featured a TV and Newspaper arguing over which type of media is better. The TV proudly says, "You can't change channels on a newspaper." The newspaper voice came up and said, "You can't put a TV set in the bottom of a bird cage." It was a funny way of pointing out that each type of mainstream media has its own unique advantages and uses and its own disadvantages.

I often remember that radio ad when jokingly arguing with my good friend, Fayyaz. We have a running gag, because he loves C# and knows SQL, while the opposite is true for me. He might hear me say that C# is a good language but that SQL is the real language. His witty comebacks are themed around how C# is "way cool" and SQL is "just OK." One day we were teaching a class together and a student wanted to know which was true. Fayyaz said that, all kidding aside, these two languages do different things and we need both in a good enterprise. For extracting data, SQL is king. For complex functions and calculations, C# runs circles around SQL. *By interoperating you can have the best of both worlds.*

I don't intend to say that you should become an expert at many other languages. Rather, you likely will want to stay specialized in SQL and have just a working knowledge of other languages in order to benefit from their power in SQL Server.

Each lesson and chapter builds sequentially until you know how to use interoperability with XML, C#, and PowerShell. The good news is that we don't assume you know a single thing about any of these languages. All the basics and terminology will be taught in the first chapter of each language and build from there into how SQL can use them. The labs have been created and delivered by me over several years of teaching SQL. The labs in this book are the end result, and each one consistently elicits "ah-ha" moments in my classes.

Downloadable files help make this book a true learning experience. Answer keys, quiz games, and setup scripts will prepare you and your instance of SQL Server for practices that will hone your skills. The files can be found at www.Joes2Pros.com. After you have run the right code several times, you are ready to write code and help others do the same by spotting errors in code samples. Each chapter's interactive Bug Catcher section highlights common mistakes people make and improves your code literacy.

This book is an essential tool. When used correctly, you can determine how far and fast you can go. It has been polished and tuned for your use and benefit. In fact, this is the book I really wish I could have read years ago when I was learning about SQL Server. What took me years of struggle to learn can now be yours in only months in the form of efficient, enjoyable and rewarding study.

Skills Needed for this Book

This book assumes a high level of SQL query and programming knowledge. If you have no SQL coding experience, then you will need to read and cover the first four volumes in this series.

If you have less SQL coding knowledge, then I recommend you first get into the groove of the first four volumes of *SQL queries 2012 Joes 2 Pros* book series. I have carefully sequenced the chapters and topics to build upon each other.

About this Book

This book follows what students told me worked for them and launched their careers. This curriculum has helped many people achieve their career goals. If you would like to gain the confidence that comes with really knowing how to get things done, this book is your ticket.

For those of you who have read my 2008 series for the 70-433 exam you will find a lot of the same material from the 2008 series in this series. This is because much of the 70-461 exam covers the same material as the 70-433. I have added material that is new to the exam and removed material that is no longer relevant. If you have already read this series or have already passed the 70-433 exam you may choose to read my book *SQL 2012 Querying What's New and Cool* which covers only the changes from 70-433 to 70-461. This book will be released in December 2012.

How to Use this Book

There is a video on the Joes2Pros website that can be watched while online, or downloaded and watched offline that demonstrates how to install SQL Server on a computer. If SQL Server 2012 is already installed on a computer, then open your favorite web browser and type www.Joes2Pros.com to be taken directly to the website for this book series *and follow the download instructions.*
Taking the practice quizzes is another great use of this book. Some multiple choice questions may only have one answer, while others will require multiple answers. There is a standard that most tests have adopted that is good for you to know as you study and prepare.

Here is an example of a question with a single answer:

1.) What is the result of the equation: 2 + 3?

O a. 2
O b. 3
O c. 5

The correct answer to question #1 is (c). Notice that each choice has a round bubble symbol to the left of the letter selection. This symbol means that there will only be a single answer for this question.

Sometimes a question will have more than one correct answer, and for these multiple-answer types of questions, a square box symbol is shown to the left of the letter selection. An example of this is shown in question #2.

2.) Which numbers in the following list are greater than 2?

□ a. 0
□ b. 2
□ c. 3
□ d. 4

The correct answers to question #2 are (c) and (d). Notice that each choice has a square box symbol to the left of the letter selection. This symbol means that there will be more than one answer for this question.

I'm often asked about the Points to Ponder feature, which is popular with both beginners and experienced developers. Some have asked why I don't simply call it a Summary Page. While it's true that the Points to Ponder page generally captures key points from each section, I frequently include options or technical insights not contained in the section. Often these are points which my students have found helpful and will likely enhance your understanding of SQL Server. These books are also available as video books. To see the latest in this learning format visit the www.Joes2Pros.com website and click on Videos. Many of our students find that using the text and video together often help in their learning.

How to Use and Download Companion Files

To help get you started, the first three chapters are in video format for free downloading. Videos show labs, demonstrate concepts, and review Points to Ponder along with tips from the appendix. Ranging from 3-15 minutes in length, they use special effects to highlight key points. You can go at your own pace and pause or replay within these lessons as needed. To make knowing where to start even easier, the videos are numbered. You don't even need to refer to the book to know what order they should be viewed in. There is even a "Setup" video that shows you how to download and use all other files.

Clear content and high-resolution multimedia videos coupled with code samples will make learning easy and fun. To give you all this and save printing costs, all supporting files are available with a free download from www.Joes2Pros.com. The breakdown of the offerings from these supporting files is listed below:

Answer keys: The downloadable files also include an answer key. All exercise lab coding answers are available for peeking if you get really stuck.

Resource files: If you are asked to import a file into SQL, you will need that resource file. Located in the resources sub-folder from the download site are your practice lab resource files. These files hold the few non-SQL script files needed for certain labs.

Lab setup files: SQL Server is a database engine and we need to practice on a database. The Joes 2 Pros Practice Company database is a fictitious travel booking company that has been shortened to the database name of JProCo. The scripts to set up the JProCo database can be found here.

Chapter review files: Ready to take your new skills out for a test drive? We have the ever popular Bug Catcher game located here.

What this Book is Not

This is not a memorization book. Rather, this is a skills book to make part of preparing for the 70-461 certification test a familiarization process. This book prepares you to apply what you have learned to answer SQL questions in the job setting. The highest hopes are that your progress and level of SQL knowledge will soon have business managers seeking your expertise to provide the reporting and information vital to their decision making. It's a good feeling to achieve and to help others at the same time. Many students commented that the training method used in *Joes 2 Pros* was what finally helped them achieve their goal of certification.

When you go through the *Joes 2 Pros* series and really know this material, you deserve a fair shot at SQL certification. Use only authentic testing engines to measure your skill. Show you know it for real. At the time of this writing, MeasureUp® at http://www.measureup.com provides a good test preparation simulator. The company's test pass guarantee makes it a very appealing option.

DVD or Videos as a Companion

Training videos: These books are also available for sale as video books. In these videos I guide you through the lessons of each section of the book. Every lab of every chapter of this book series has multimedia steps recorded into videos. The content of the five book series fits into 10 DVDs. When comparing prices, you will find the costs are much less than the existing ad-hoc options on the market today.

If you have done some shopping around you will have noticed there are video training sets that cost over $300. You might also have seen single certification books for $60 each. Do the math and you see one book from other leading publishers will set you back nearly $400.

Chapter 1. Introduction to XML

XML stands for **Ex**tensible **M**arkup **L**anguage. No matter what your programming level or job experience, if you've had any degree of exposure to the IT world in the last decade, you probably have heard of XML. At its simplest level, it is a file format consumable by nearly all browsers and programs. It is also very readable by humans.

SQL Server 2000 was the first version to include XML support, including streaming XML. Its flexibility rapidly accelerated adoption of the XML standard by the IT world, generally, and by SQL Server, specifically. SQL Server's next version (SQL Server 2005) included a significantly larger degree of XML support and functionality, including SQL Server's launch of the **XML data type**.

The first seven chapters of this volume are an extended review of XML and its interoperability with SQL Server. The goals of this chapter are to introduce you to XML and enable you to begin working hands-on with XML data.

READERNOTE:*Please run the script SQLQueries2012Vol5Chapter1.0-4.2Setup.sql in order to follow along with the examples in the first section of Chapter 1. You only need to run this script once for all examples in Chapters 1 through 4. All scripts mentioned in this chapter may be found at* ***www.Joes2Pros.com****. Also, on our site there is a selection of free videos to watch to help you get started. Our entire video instruction library is available via online subscription and DVD.*

What is XML?

A common observation by people seeing XML for the first time is that it looks like just a bunch of data inside a text file. XML files are text-based documents, which makes them easy to read. All of the data is literally spelled out in the document and relies on just a few characters (<, >, =) to convey relationships and structure of the data. XML files can be used by any commonly available **text editor**, such as Notepad and WordPad.

Much like a book's Table of Contents, your first glance at well-written XML will tell you the subject matter of the data and its general structure. Hints appearing within the data help you to quickly identify the main theme (similar to a book's subject), its headers (similar to chapter titles or sections of a book), data elements (similar to a book's characters or chief topics), and so forth.

Later in this chapter we'll learn to recognize and use the structural "hints," which are XML's markup components (e.g., XML tags, root elements). Applications and websites scan XML and read these components to understand the organization and structure of the data. Additionally, XML can include instructions for how a program should consume its data. To understand how this works, we first must discuss the concept of data and metadata.

Data

In the opening pages of *SQL Queries 2012 Joes 2 Pros Volume 1*, the first concept distinguishes between "data" and "information." That discussion helps us get clear on the idea of **data** - the raw numbers and most granular components that you store in a database. **Information** is what you find in a report and is the end result when raw data undergoes value-added processing (e.g., aggregations, calculations, data being combined with or compared to other data, etc.) in order for it to appear in a format consumable by decision makers.

List A (on the lefthand side of Figure 1.1, next page) contains raw data in a single list. When we look closely at the data values (i.e., the names of the items in the list), we can see a few words that hint at a possible hierarchy. However, there's no outline or formatting to help impart clues about the hierarchical relationships contained within the data.

Metadata

In short, **metadata** is data about data. A timestamp, a row number, a column name, the name of table, a data type - these are examples of metadata, because they help characterize and describe your data but aren't actually part of the raw data itself. **Metadata** describes your data, including relationships within your data.

Indentation is a simple formatting cue used to show structure, such as subtopics belonging to a topic (*Examples:* A class outline or a book's Table of Contents). In Data List B (Figure 1.1, right hand side), indentation serves as metadata because it helps us understand the relationships between the items in the list. Later we will see the layout of an XML document includes fairly simple cues, like indentation and tags to help distinguish one hierarchical level from another.

Since the heading "Veggies" appears below the title "Food" and is indented once, we know Veggies is a category belonging to Food. "Meat" and "Fruit" appear at the same level as Veggies, so they are a peer of Veggies and also a type of Food. Below each type sits a further indented level, which indicates that these items (Carrots, Chicken, Banana, etc.) are types of Veggies, Meat, and Fruit and are sub-types of Food (Figure 1.1).

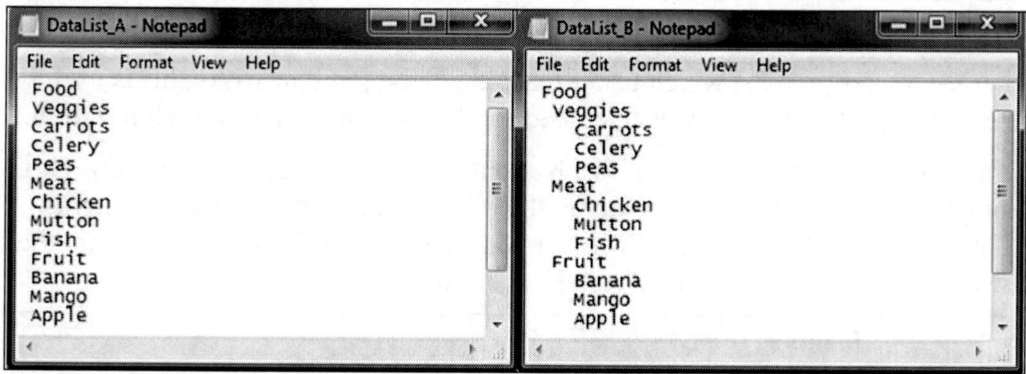

Figure 1.1 List A and List B: Two versions of the same Food list.

XML is comprised of two components:

1) Data
2) Metadata - the description of the data, including relationships and properties of the data

Let's first consider the data component of XML with a look at the following list of countries (Figure 1.2). When we look at the countries included in the list, we detect countries which we know are related. For example, Spain and Finland are both located in Europe. Let's recognize that nothing appearing in the list or its structure tells us these are two European countries - it's just an observation we can make since we are familiar with the items contained in the list.

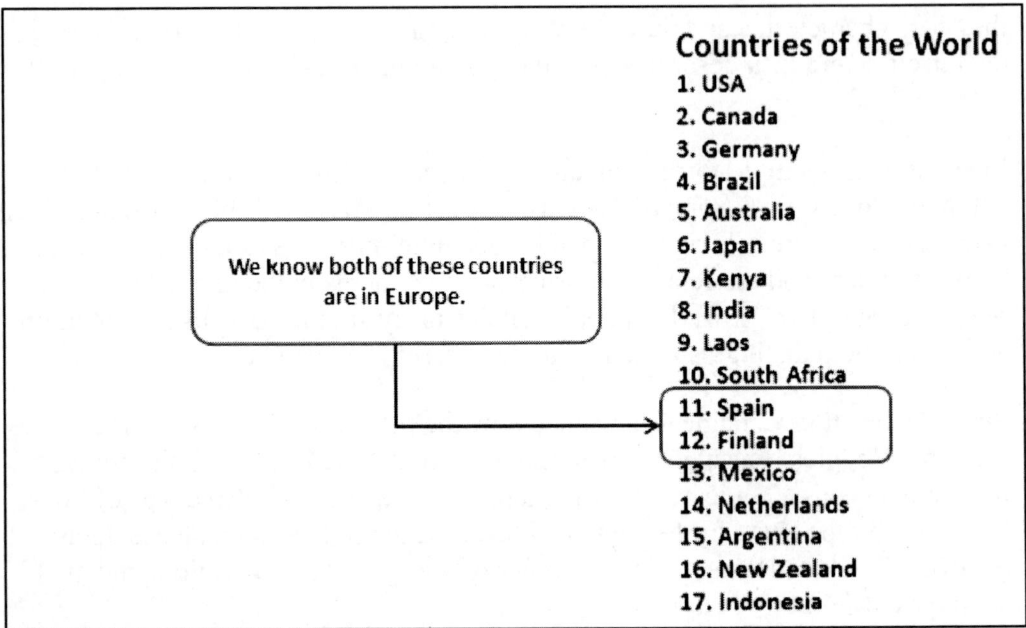

Figure 1.2 List of countries.

Let's next look at a list which fewer readers will be familiar with. This is useful because it will better allow us to appreciate the concept of **self-describing data**.

These are the teams of the NFL, the National Football League (Figure 1.3). This simple list doesn't tell us much about the relationships between these 32 items. Later on, we will see that the XML version of this list will tell us more about the structure of the NFL and how these 32 teams are related.

Teams of the NFL

1. Buffalo Bills
2. Miami Dolphins
3. New England Patriots
4. New York Jets
5. Baltimore Ravens
6. Cincinnati Bengals
7. Cleveland Browns
8. Pittsburgh Steelers
9. Houston Texans
10. Indianapolis Colts
11. Jacksonville Jaguars
12. Tennessee Titans
13. Denver Broncos
14. Kansas City Chiefs
15. Oakland Raiders
16. San Diego Chargers
17. Dallas Cowboys
18. New York Giants
19. Philadelphia Eagles
20. Washington Redskins
21. Chicago Bears
22. Detroit Lions
23. Green Bay Packers
24. Minnesota Vikings
25. Atlanta Falcons
26. Carolina Panthers
27. New Orleans Saints
28. Tampa Bay Buccaneers
29. Arizona Cardinals
30. San Francisco 49ers
31. Seattle Seahawks
32. St. Louis Rams

Figure 1.3 The 32 teams of the NFL. Later we will see this data organized in an XML document.

Text Data

Text files are useful for some things. The Notepad program is included with every version of Windows, so it's widely available and requires no additional purchase, installation, or training. You can easily fit lots of data into a text (.txt) file, which you can then pump into a SQL table. You can also take the data from a table and pump it into a text file. We used **BCP** to perform both of these operations in *SQL SQL Queries 2012 Joes 2 Pros Volume 1*. When importing data into SQL Server from a text file, you need to take extra care and examine the contents of the file to ensure that the right data goes into the right field. This is because a text file lacks programmatic features to support metadata or to help you recognize the true meaning or intended destination of the data. A little research on your part is necessary to make this work. In short, text data is just data (no metadata).

On occasion, a text file can be a handy way of looking at relatively small quantities of data. Even without the field headers, we would be able to look at many of JProCo's tables in a text file and be able to comfortably recognize data from the Employee or Grant table. Viewing raw table data in a text file is a trick used by data experts to find unexpected spaces or delimiters (e.g., an extra tab or carriage return) hidden in your Excel or Access data. These cause problems when you need to export your table data to another program (e.g., SQL Server).

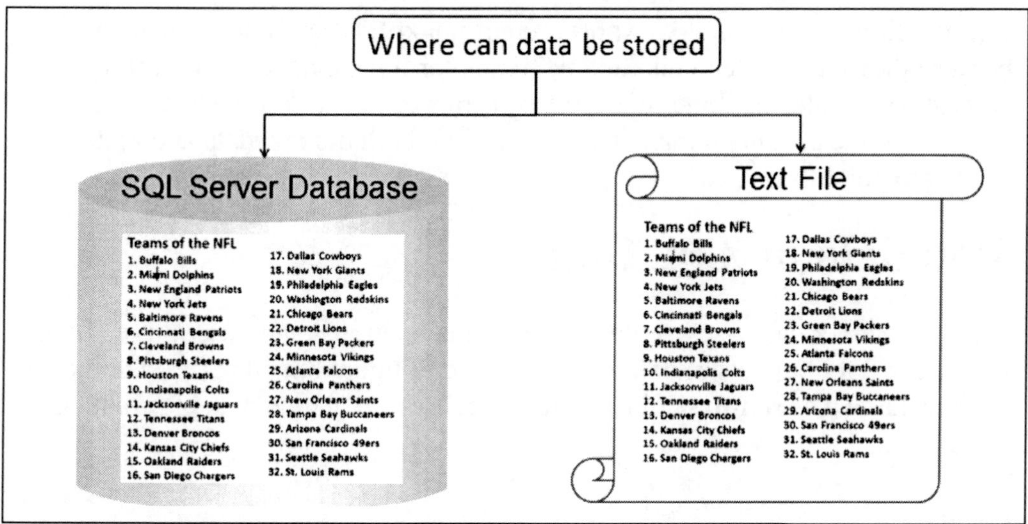

Figure 1.4 Think of a list of data stored in SQL Server versus the same list stored as a text file.

Relational Data

We know SQL Server is an **RDBMS**, a relational database management system. The power of an RDBMS is its ability to programmatically track, store, and organize your data and metadata. Throughout the *Joes 2 Pros* series, we see that using relational database design (e.g., normalized data to minimize data redundancy, primary and foreign key relationships, lookup tables) to store and maintain data improves the efficiency and scalability of your database systems.

If we use SQL Server's programmatic capabilities to store the NFL list efficiently, our database users will be able to discern quite a bit about the NFL. Just by looking at how the data is stored in tables and lookup tables, users can see how the 32 teams are organized into conferences and regional divisions. However, the same data exported from SQL Server to a text file will simply store a flat version of this list and, therefore, will not be able to tell users about the data or relationships within the data.

Let's consider the same scenario, except with two frequently used tables in the JProCo database. The Employee table has seven columns and the Location table has four columns. If you wanted to export all of this data from SQL Server into a single text file, you would need some sort of marker for where the Employee data ends and the Location table begins.

The text file can't win in this export scenario: text files can't describe data, because they have no features capable of supporting metadata. They can't describe one table, let alone two. However, this can be accomplished using XML. An XML file can contain many tables, meaning both the raw data and metadata needed to build the tables.

Metadata in XML Data

In a SQL Server database, we know the data is relational and descriptive. Text files are simply flat lists of data, and you have to figure out what the data means. XML is known as **self-describing data**, because you get the data plus metadata.

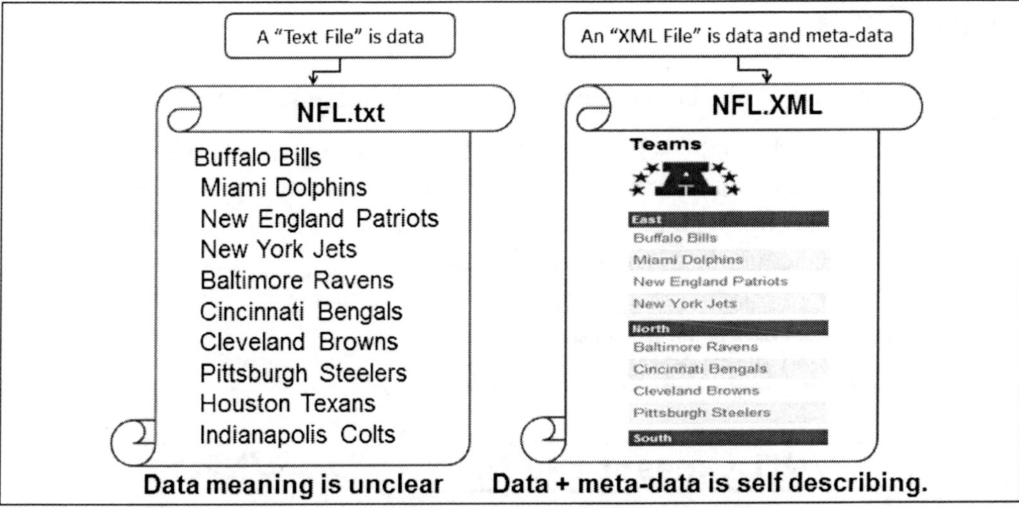

Figure 1.5 XML is self-describing, meaning that you get data and metadata.

An XML file reads more like an outline. Notice how seeing the list of 32 NFL teams in outline form (raw data plus some metadata) helps us understand quite a bit more about the data relationships (Figure 1.6).

AFC Teams	NFC Teams
East	East
Buffalo Bills	Dallas Cowboys
Miami Dolphins	New York Giants
New England Patriots	Philadelphia Eagles
New York Jets	Washington Redskins
North	North
Baltimore Ravens	Chicago Bears
Cincinnati Bengals	Detroit Lions
Cleveland Browns	Green Bay Packers
Pittsburgh Steelers	Minnesota Vikings
South	South
Houston Texans	Atlanta Falcons
Indianapolis Colts	Carolina Panthers
Jacksonville Jaguars	New Orleans Saints
Tennessee Titans	Tampa Bay Buccaneers
West	West
Denver Broncos	Arizona Cardinals
Kansas City Chiefs	San Francisco 49ers
Oakland Raiders	Seattle Seahawks
San Diego Chargers	St. Louis Rams

Figure 1.6 Seeing list data in outline form helps illustrate the relationships between the elements.

XML's capabilities allow it to serve much like a self-describing relational database stored as a file (i.e., an XML document) or a stream (i.e., a tabular view of XML data produced by a program like SQL Server). All data-aware applications can interact with XML.

XML Tags

XML utilizes tags < > to create the data "outline." These tags can also be nested.

Here (Figure 1.7) the first "NFL" shown is the **beginning tag**. It sits between brackets and contains no slash. The lower "NFL" is the **ending tag**. It appears identical to the beginning tag, except it contains a forward slash. Ending tags must follow the same sequence as the beginning tags.

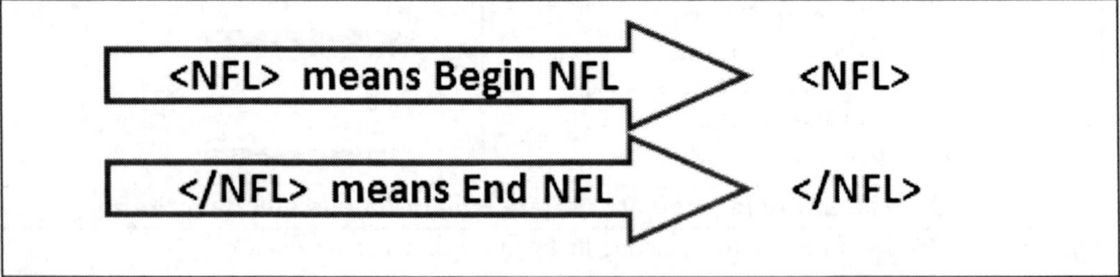

Figure 1.7 Example of a beginning tag and an ending tag.

XML Elements

Elements are actually the tags themselves. Element data is the data which sits between tags. For example, Seahawks is element data. It is data belonging to the element, Team.

```
<Team>Seahawks</Team>
```

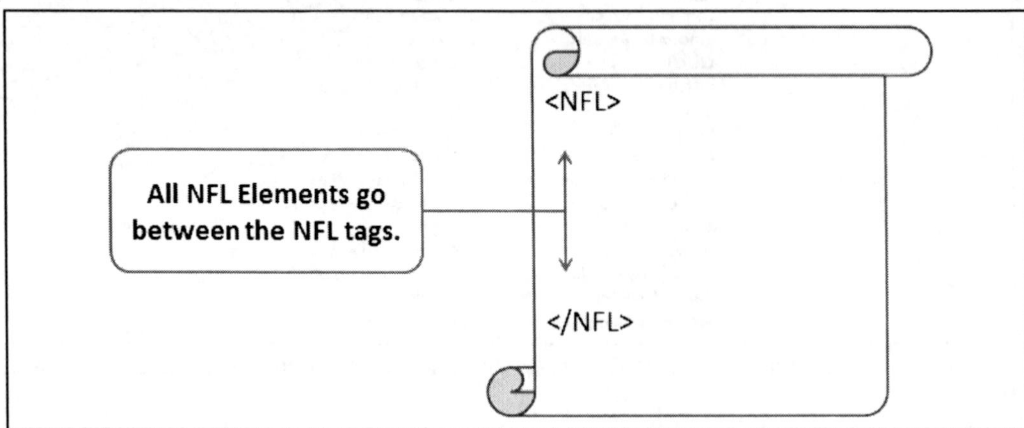

Figure 1.8 Seahawks belongs to the Team element.

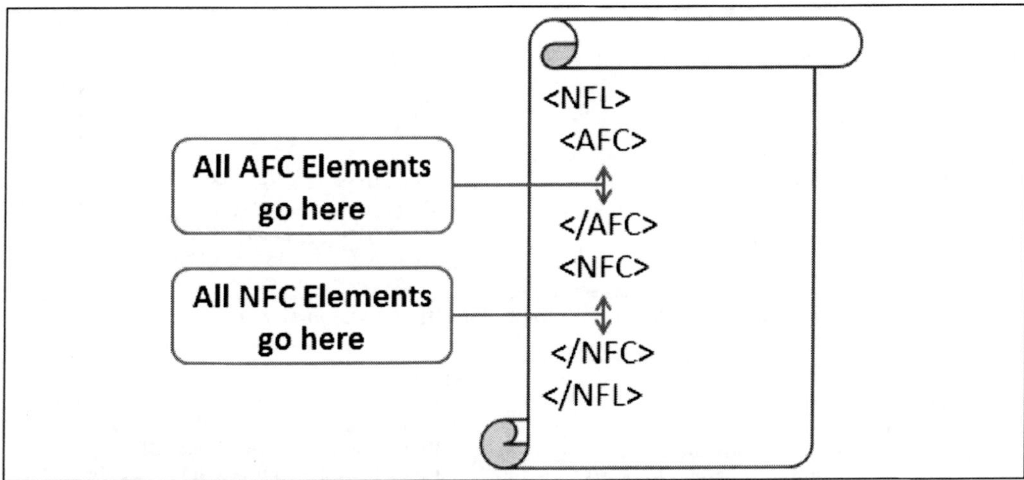

Figure 1.9 The NFL consists of two conferences, AFC and NFC.

Two elements belonging to the <NFL> element are <AFC> and <NFC> (Figure 1.9). All of the data belong to the <AFC> and <NFC> must sit between the respective beginning and ending tags. Each division element (e.g., <West>, <North>, <South>, and <East>) must also include a beginning and ending tag (Figure 1.10).

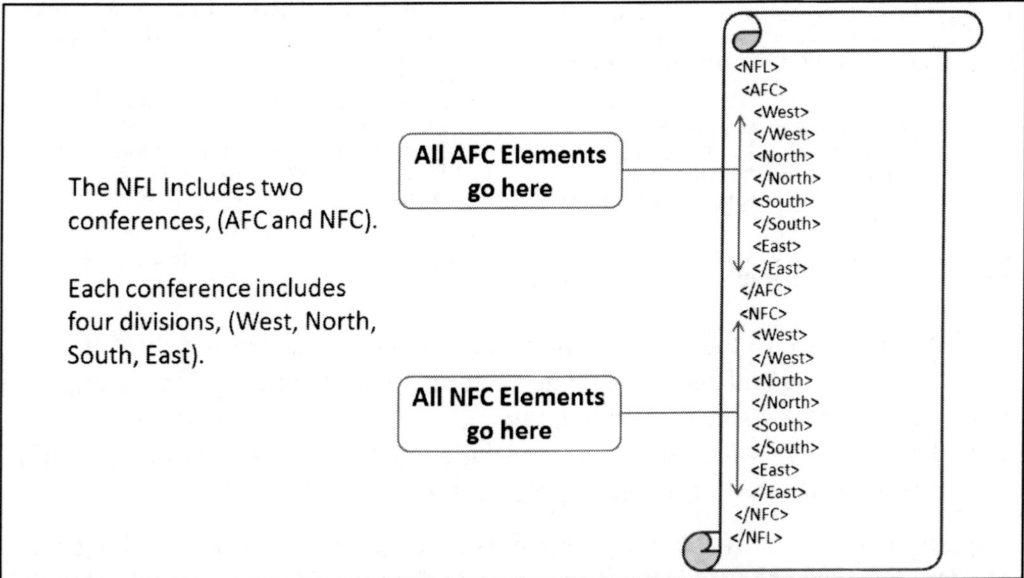

Figure 1.10 All AFC data goes between the AFC tags; the same is true for NFC data, which goes between the NFC tags.

Each of the four divisions belonging to a conference contains multiple teams. The <AFC> East division consists of four teams: the Buffalo Bills, the Miami Dolphins, the New England Patriots, and the New York Jets (Figure 1.11).

The NFL Includes two conferences, (AFC and NFC).

Each conference includes four divisions, (West, North, South, East).

Each division has many teams.

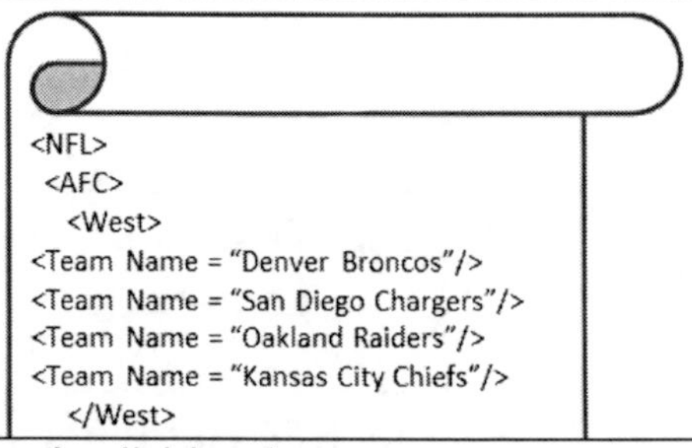

```
<NFL>
 <AFC>
   <West>
<Team Name = "Denver Broncos"/>
<Team Name = "San Diego Chargers"/>
<Team Name = "Oakland Raiders"/>
<Team Name = "Kansas City Chiefs"/>
   </West>
```

Figure 1.11 The team elements appear with their respective division element.

```
<NFL>
 <AFC>
  <East>
   <Team Name = "Buffalo Bills"/>
   <Team Name = "Miami Dolphins" />
   <Team Name = "New England Patriots"/
   <Team Name = "New York Jets" />
  </East>
  <North>
   <Team Name = "Baltimore Ravens"/>
   <Team Name = "Cincinnati Bengals"/>
   <Team Name = "Cleveland Browns"/>
   <Team Name = "Pittsburgh Steelers"/>
  </North>
  <South>
   <Team Name = "Houston Texans"/>
   <Team Name = "Indianapolis Colts"/>
   <Team Name = "Tennessee Titans"/>
   <Team Name = "Jacksonville Jaguars"/>
  </South>
  <West>
   <Team Name = "Denver Broncos"/>
   <Team Name = "San Diego Chargers"/>
   <Team Name = "Oakland Raiders"/>
   <Team Name = "Kansas City Chiefs"/>
  </West>
 </AFC>
 <NFC>
  <East>
   <Team Name = "Dallas Cowboys"/>
   <Team Name = "New York Giants" />
   <Team Name = "Philadelphia Eagles" />
   <Team Name = "Washington Redskins" />
  </East>
  <North>
   <Team Name = "Chicago Bears"/>
   <Team Name = "Detroit Lions"/>
   <Team Name = "Green Bay Packers"/>
   <Team Name = "Minnesota Vikings"/>
  </North>
  <South>
   <Team Name = "Atlanta Falcons"/>
   <Team Name = "Carolina Panthers"/>
   <Team Name = "New Orleans Saints"/>
   <Team Name = "Tampa Bay Buccaneers"/>
  </South>
  <West>
   <Team Name = "Arizona Cardinals"/>
   <Team Name = "St. Louis Rams"/>
   <Team Name = "San Francisco 49ers"/>
   <Team Name = "Seattle Seahawks"/>
  </West>
 </NFC>
</NFL>
```

Figure 1.12 The NFL teams shown by conference & division.

Notice in Figure 1.12 that if a tag contains no element data, or element children, then the beginning and ending tag may be combined into one tag. For example we don't see a <Team Name> beginning tag and a </Team Name> ending tag. We see <Team Name/> which serves as the single tag. Since <East> has many child elements, it needs an </East> ending element to mark the end.

Suppose hypothetically that the South division contained no teams. In that case, we could choose either to leave it as shown in Figure 1.11, or we could show it as <South/>.

An XML file is a lot like a mini-database stored inside a file. The XML file contains data and the accompanying metadata needed to interpret the relationships amongst the data. If you were to put all 32 teams in their divisions and in proper

XML, it would look quite a bit this like (Figure 1.12). Due to space constraints, three AFC teams aren't shown here. However, this is the way the actual XML document appears - one long column enclosed with an <NFL> opening tag at the top and a closing tag </NFL> at the bottom.

Supposed we are asked a question, such as, "What division are the Denver Broncos in?" We can answer it by looking at the XML document. Even if we don't really know much about football or the NFL, we can easily see they are in the AFC West division (Figure 1.13).

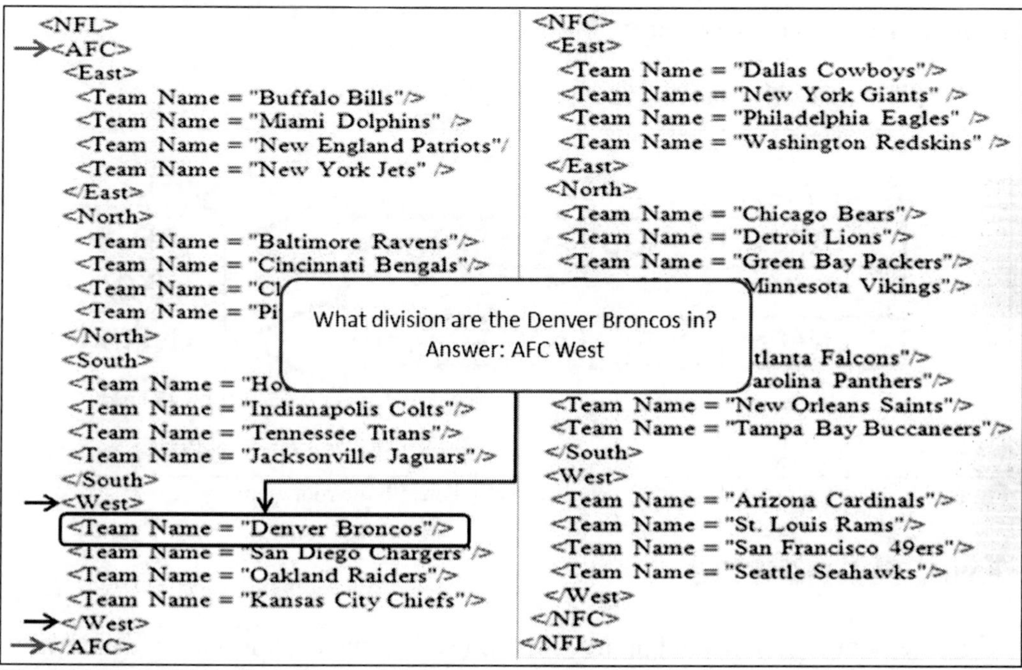

Figure 1.13 An XML file is like a mini-database stored inside of a file. The self-describing nature of XML allows us to answer questions, even when we aren't very familiar with the subject matter.

Here, the <NFL> is known as the **root element** (also known as the **root node**). The entire list of 32 teams is encompassed within the <NFL>. In other words, all data in this XML appears beneath the **root element** of <NFL>.

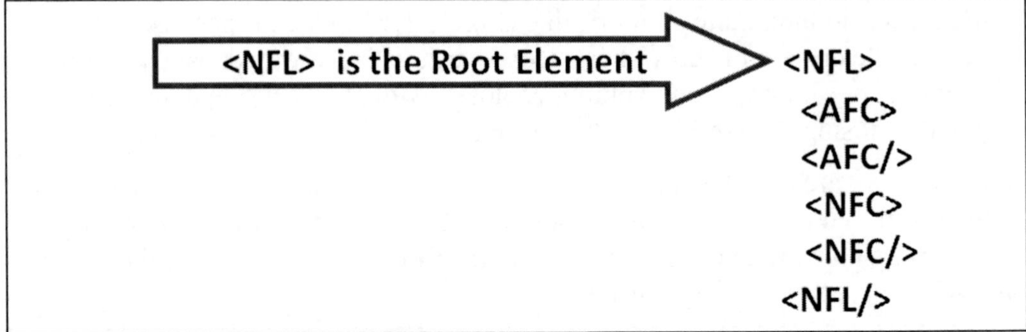
<NFL> is the Root Element
<NFL>
<AFC>
<AFC/>
<NFC>
<NFC/>
<NFL/>

Figure 1.14 The <NFL> is the root element of our XML data.

The <AFC> and <NFC> are known as **top-level elements**.

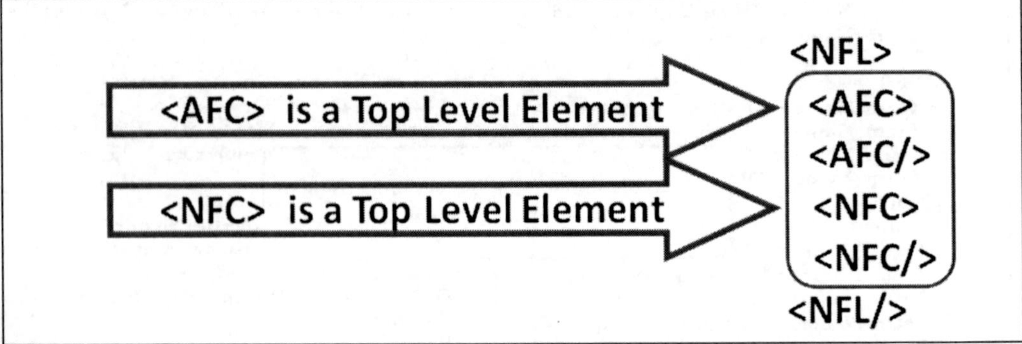
<AFC> is a Top Level Element
<NFC> is a Top Level Element
<NFL>
<AFC>
<AFC/>
<NFC>
<NFC/>
<NFL/>

Figure 1.15 The top-level element(s) appear directly beneath the root element.

XML Attributes

XML element tags may contain information within the tags providing descriptive information about the element or its properties. These are known as **attributes**.

Attribute data appears with the opening tag name and is enclosed in quotation marks:

```
<Team Name = "Seahawks"></Team>
```

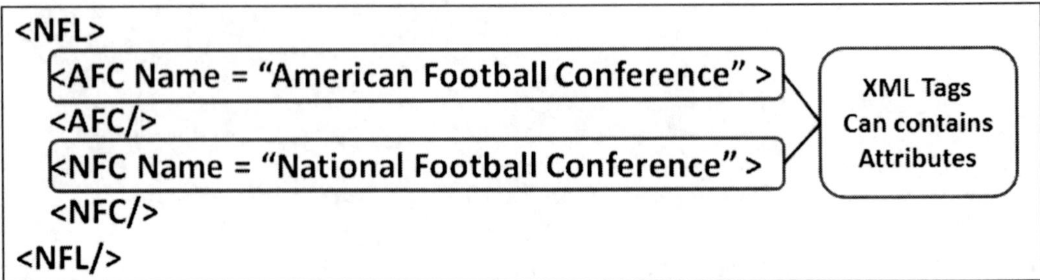
<NFL>
<AFC Name = “American Football Conference” >
<AFC/>
<NFC Name = “National Football Conference” >
<NFC/>
<NFL/>
XML Tags
Can contains
Attributes

Figure 1.16 XML element tags can contain attributes describing the element or its properties.

Lab 1.1: What is XML

Lab Prep: Each lab has one or more Skill Checks. Start with Skill Check 1 and proceed until reaching the Points to Ponder section.

Before beginning this lab, verify that SQL Server 2012 is properly installed and operating. Before running the lab setup script for resetting the database (SQLQueries2012Vol5Chapter1.0-4.2Setup.sql), please make sure to close all query windows within SSMS. An open query window pointing to a database context can lock that database preventing it from updating when the script is executing. A simple way to assure all query windows are closed, is to exit out of SSMS, then open a new instance of SSMS, and lastly run the setup script.

Skill Check 1: Based on the XML in the right half of the following figure, answer the questions in the left side of the figure.

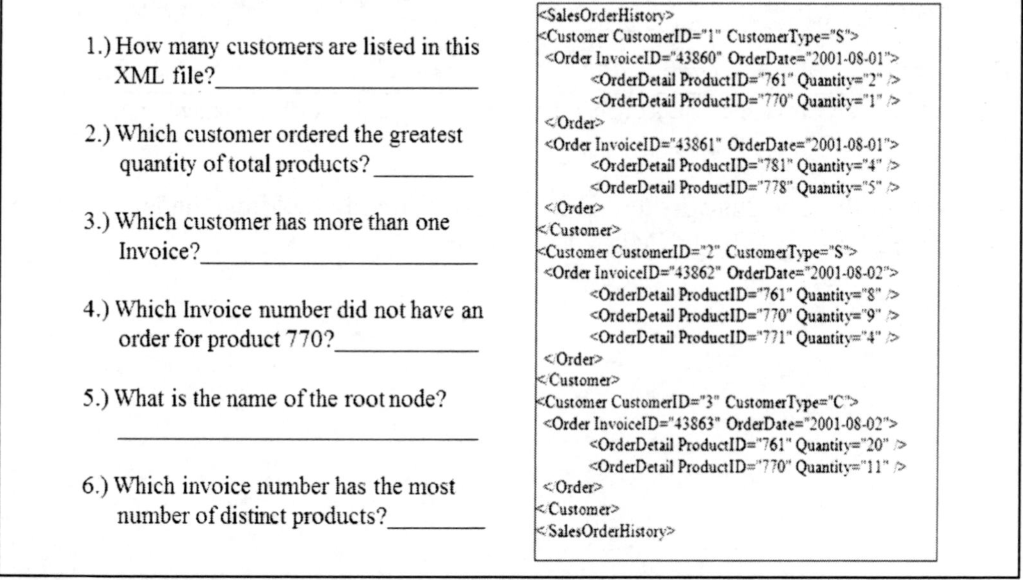

1.) How many customers are listed in this XML file?____________________

2.) Which customer ordered the greatest quantity of total products?________

3.) Which customer has more than one Invoice?____________________

4.) Which Invoice number did not have an order for product 770?____________

5.) What is the name of the root node?

____

6.) Which invoice number has the most number of distinct products?________

```
<SalesOrderHistory>
<Customer CustomerID="1" CustomerType="S">
 <Order InvoiceID="43860" OrderDate="2001-08-01">
     <OrderDetail ProductID="761" Quantity="2" />
     <OrderDetail ProductID="770" Quantity="1" />
 </Order>
 <Order InvoiceID="43861" OrderDate="2001-08-01">
     <OrderDetail ProductID="781" Quantity="4" />
     <OrderDetail ProductID="778" Quantity="5" />
 </Order>
</Customer>
<Customer CustomerID="2" CustomerType="S">
 <Order InvoiceID="43862" OrderDate="2001-08-02">
     <OrderDetail ProductID="761" Quantity="8" />
     <OrderDetail ProductID="770" Quantity="9" />
     <OrderDetail ProductID="771" Quantity="4" />
 </Order>
</Customer>
<Customer CustomerID="3" CustomerType="C">
 <Order InvoiceID="43863" OrderDate="2001-08-02">
     <OrderDetail ProductID="761" Quantity="20" />
     <OrderDetail ProductID="770" Quantity="11" />
 </Order>
</Customer>
</SalesOrderHistory>
```

Figure 1.17 Skill Check 1 consists of six questions regarding the XML document in the right panel.

Skill Check 2: Based on the XML in the right half of Figure 1.18, answer the questions in the left side of the figure.

1.) Which song title has only been sung by One band?__________________

2.) From question 1.) what is the TitleID?

____

3.) Bands sing songs. Which songs were sung and written by the same person?

____

4.) Which song(s) was never sung by it's writer?__________________

5.) What is the name of the root node?

____

6.) How many different bands sang "Red Red Wine"?______________

```
<Music>
  <Song TitleID="13159">
    <WriterName>Niel Diamond</WriterName>
    <Title>Red Red Wine</Title>
    <Singer OrderID="1">
      <BandName>Neil Diamond</BandName>
    </Singer>
    <Singer OrderID="2">
      <BandName>UB40</BandName>
    </Singer>
  </Song>
  <Song TitleID="13160">
    <WriterName>Prince</WriterName>
    <Title>Manic Monday</Title>
    <Singer OrderID="1">
      <BandName>Bengals</BandName>
    </Singer>
  </Song>
  <Song TitleID="13161">
    <WriterName>Roy Orbison</WriterName>
    <Title>Pretty Woman</Title>
    <Singer OrderID="1">
      <BandName>Roy Orbison</BandName>
    </Singer>
    <Singer OrderID="2">
      <BandName>Van Halen</BandName>
    </Singer>
  </Song>
</Music>
```

Figure 1.18 Skill Check 2 consists of six questions regarding the XML document in the right panel.

Answer Code: The answers to this lab can be found in the downloadable files in a file named Lab1.1_WhatIsXML.sql.

Points to Ponder - What is XML

1. Metadata is data about your data. Metadata is information which helps to describe the properties and relationships of data.
2. SQL Server is relational and therefore supports data and keeps track of its metadata, too.
3. Text files only contain data (no metadata). It's up to you to understand what the data means.
4. XML is self-describing data, as it contains both data and metadata.
5. XML holds its data and metadata in a hierarchical set of tags.
6. A beginning and ending tag always have the same name. You can tell them apart because the ending tag starts with a forward slash.
7. The ending tag for <Joes2Pros> would be </Joes2Pros>.
8. The data in XML can be in the form of attributes or elements.
9. Element data is stored between the beginning and ending element tag.
10. Attribute data is stored inside of a beginning tag.
11. Any data-aware application can interact with XML.
12. XML is case-sensitive.
13. XML tag names cannot have spaces between them.
14. Each element or attribute has exactly one parent (except for the root element).
15. Any node that is two or more levels above is called an Ancestor.
16. Any node that is two or more levels below is called a Descendant.
17. An attribute is data that is inside an element.

Streams

In the IT world, the term **stream** signifies the output of information by a program or process.

Don't feel badly if that definition doesn't immediately register with you. It took me years to understand the "streams" concept. A colleague finally sat me down and explained it. It's understandable if you're picturing a flowing bed of water running past a mountain cabin, but XML streams are really nothing like that. Let me save you years of bewilderment on this funny geek-speak term.

Instead of water, these days I think "result set" when I hear the term **stream**. As we know, the form of a result set can change slightly depending on the context.

In SQL Server terms, a **stream** resembles a table: the grid like presentation of rows and columns that you get when you run a query. This is because SQL Server prefers to present data in a grid shape. SQL Server even produces spatial data first as a grid, although we humans prefer to view the result shaped as a sphere or map. However, XML does not set things up in rows and columns.

Tabular Stream

Let's look at a simple SELECT statement from JProCo's Location table and notice we get a table-like result set, also known as a tabular result set (Figure 1.19). As noted above, the tabular stream is SQL Server's preferred mode of streaming output from its data engine to your display.

```
SELECT LocationID, City
FROM Location
```

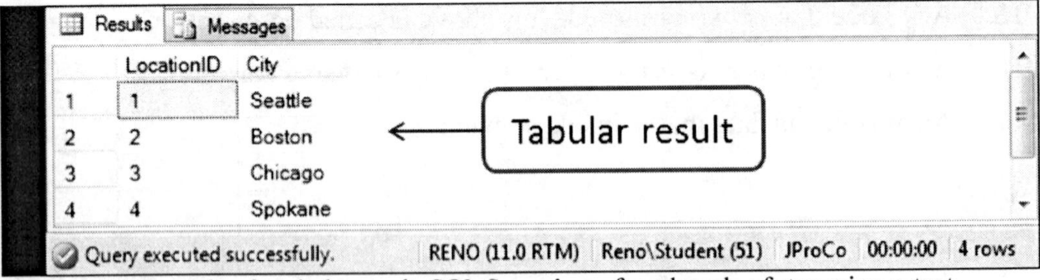

	LocationID	City
1	1	Seattle
2	2	Boston
3	3	Chicago
4	4	Spokane

Figure 1.19 Example of a tabular result, SQL Server's preferred mode of streaming output.

XML Streams

Unlike SQL Server, XML actually has many modes of streaming output. You can instruct SQL Server to stream your XML result using the mode you prefer.

Let's look again at the data we queried from the Location table (Figure 1.19). In the next section we will have the output appear as an XML stream, rather than a tabular result.

XML Raw Mode

To our base query, we need to add the keywords "FOR XML" in order for our results to appear as XML. We also need to specify the mode, which in this case is RAW (Figure 1.20).

```
SELECT LocationID, City
FROM Location
FOR XML RAW
```

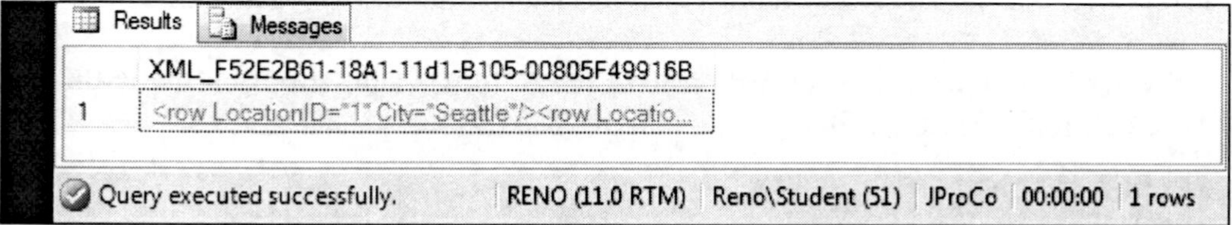

Figure 1.20 Adding keywords FOR XML RAW will make our output appear as an XML stream.

Raw is the easiest type of XML to run. We would say this result set now appears in an XML raw dataformat. Notice the result is a hyperlink, which you click to view your results. The XML raw mode is the only mode we will explore in this beginning chapter. In subsequent chapters, we will see many other modes.

Notice that the default tag label is "row" for each row of our result set. And the data appear as attributes (Figure 1.21).

```
XML_F52E2B61-18A...00805F49916B1.xml*  SQLQuery2.sql - RE...(Reno\Student (51))*
<row LocationID="1" City="Seattle" />
<row LocationID="2" City="Boston" />
<row LocationID="3" City="Chicago" />
<row LocationID="4" City="Spokane" />
```

Figure 1.21 XML creates a <row> tag for each row.

XML will allow you to override the default name <row> and set it to something more descriptive. The syntax shown here will change the name for each attribute tag to "RowLocation" (Figure 1.23).

```
SELECT LocationID, City
FROM Location
FOR XML RAW('RowLocation')
```

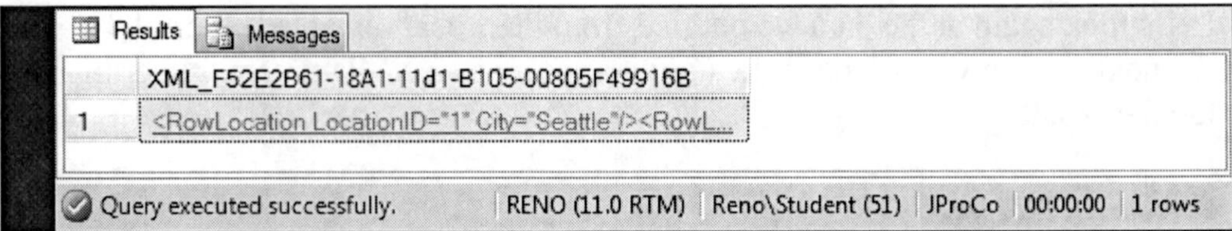

Figure 1.22 We've changed our code to override the default label for each row attribute.

XML_F52E2B61-18A...00805F49916B2.xml* × SQLQuery2.sql - RE...(Reno\Student (51))*

Object Explorer

```
<RowLocation LocationID="1" City="Seattle" />
<RowLocation LocationID="2" City="Boston" />
<RowLocation LocationID="3" City="Chicago" />
<RowLocation LocationID="4" City="Spokane" />
```

Figure 1.23 "RowLocation" now appears as the default label for each row attribute.

Let's see what happens when we remove the term row and simply rename the tag as "Location" (Figure 1.24).

```
SELECT LocationID, City
FROM Location
FOR XML RAW('Location')
```

Results | Messages

XML_F52E2B61-18A1-11d1-B105-00805F49916B

1 <Location LocationID="1" City="Seattle"/><Locatio...

Query executed successfully. | RENO (11.0 RTM) | Reno\Student (51) | JProCo | 00:00:00 | 1 rows

Figure 1.24 This syntax will change the name for each row element tag to "Location."

Observe the red IntelliSense underline and mouseover tag appearing in the result Figure 1.25 ("XML document cannot contain multiple root level elements"). Also notice we have four (4) top-level nodes and no root (Figure 1.25). SQL Server would prefer that we have a root element appearing in our data.

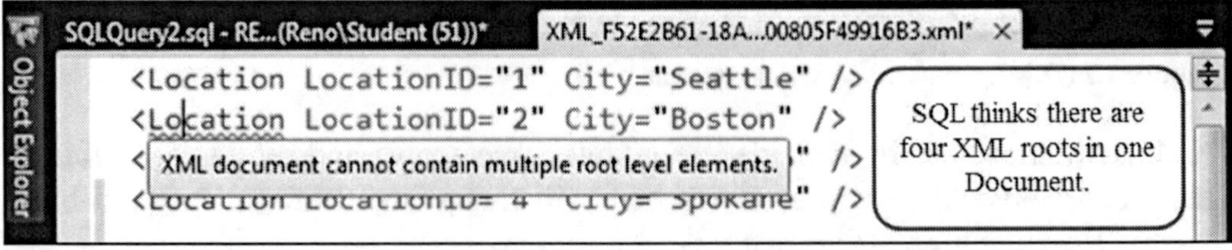

Figure 1.25 SQL Server interprets our XML RAW result as having multiple root level elements.

Raw is the simplest mode where all data is considered to be at the same level with no nesting. The XML RAW command by default does not create a root.

Next, we'll see how we can alter our code to add a root element to our XML.

Root Element Option

XML is considered complete (known as **well-formed XML**) only if it has a root tag which encompasses all other tags. Adding the keyword **ROOT** to our code specifies the ROOT element option (Figure 1.26).

Adding the ROOT command to our code will add root tags in our XML data.

```
SELECT LocationID, City
FROM Location
FOR XML RAW('Location'), ROOT
```

Results | Messages

XML_F52E2B61-18A1-11d1-B105-00805F49916B
1 <root><Location LocationID="1" City="Seattle"/><L...

Query executed successfully. | RENO (11.0 RTM) | Reno\Student (51) | JProCo | 00:00:00 | 1 rows

Figure 1.26 Our code now specifies the ROOT element option.

And now instead of just an **XML fragment**, our code produces an entire XML stream. This output is a well-formed XML document.

XML_F52E2B61-18A...00805F49916B4.xml* × SQLQuery3.sql - RE...(Reno\Student (51))*

Object Explorer

```
<root>
  <Location LocationID="1" City="Seattle" />
  <Location LocationID="2" City="Boston" />
  <Location LocationID="3" City="Chicago" />
  <Location LocationID="4" City="Spokane" />
</root>
```

Figure 1.27 Our result is no longer an XML fragment. It is a well-formed XML document.

We will add a name for our root tag to our code. In the code below, you can see we've added the name JProCo (Figure 1.28).

```
SELECT LocationID, City
FROM Location
FOR XML RAW('Location'), ROOT('JProCo')
```

Figure 1.28 We've modified our code to provide a name for our root tag.

Our result shows the root is now called JProCo (Figure 1.29).

SQLQuery3.sql - RE...(Reno\Student (51))* XML_F52E2B61-18A...00805F49916B5.xml*

```
<JProCo>
  <Location LocationID="1" City="Seattle" />
  <Location LocationID="2" City="Boston" />
  <Location LocationID="3" City="Chicago" />
  <Location LocationID="4" City="Spokane" />
</JProCo>
```

Figure 1.29 Our XML RAW result now shows one root level element.

Notice the data appears as attributes inside of the tag. Next we will make all this data display as sub-elements of the top element, Location.

Elements Option

The raw mode likes to store all of its data as attributes. You can choose whether data appears as attributes or as elements. If you prefer elements, then you can append the ELEMENTS option to the XML Raw mode (Figure 1.30).

```
SELECT LocationID, City
FROM Location
FOR XML RAW('Location'), ROOT('JProCo'), ELEMENTS
```

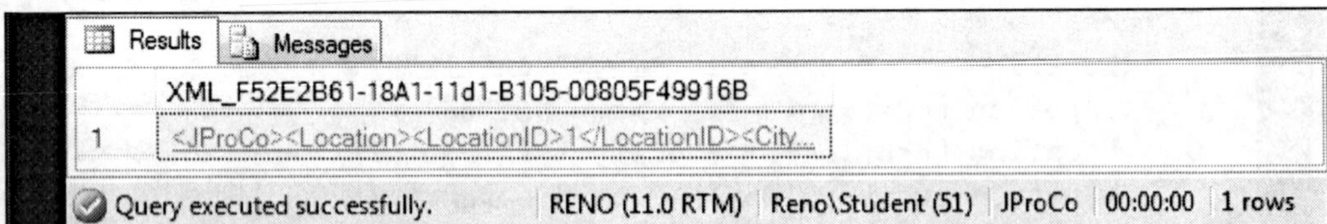

Figure 1.30 Adding the keyword ELEMENTS will make our output display as elements.

Look closely at the XML output, and you'll recognize the values for Records 1, 2, 3, and 4 from the Location table (Figure 1.31).

```
<JProCo>
  <Location>
    <LocationID>1</LocationID>
    <City>Seattle</City>
  </Location>
  <Location>
    <LocationID>2</LocationID>
    <City>Boston</City>
  </Location>
  <Location>
    <LocationID>3</LocationID>
    <City>Chicago</City>
  </Location>
  <Location>
    <LocationID>4</LocationID>
    <City>Spokane</City>
  </Location>
</JProCo>
```

Figure 1.31 Our same data now appears as elements.

Let's look at another example from the Employee table. If you ran the reset script for this chapter, you should see 13 JProCo employees showing in your Employee table (Figure 1.32).

```
SELECT FirstName, LastName, LocationID
FROM Employee
```

Results | Messages

	FirstName	LastName	LocationID
1	Alex	Adams	1
2	Barry	Brown	1
3	Lee	Osako	2
4	David	Kennson	1
5	Eric	Bender	1
6	Lisa	Kendall	4

Query executed successfully. | RENO (11.0 RTM) | Reno\Student (51) | JProCo | 00:00:00 | 13 rows

Figure 1.32 Our next example uses the Employee table, which currently shows 14 employees.

Next we will add FOR XML RAW to view the result from the Employee table as an XML output and using the raw mode (Figure 1.33).

```
SELECT FirstName, LastName, LocationID
FROM Employee
FOR XML RAW
```

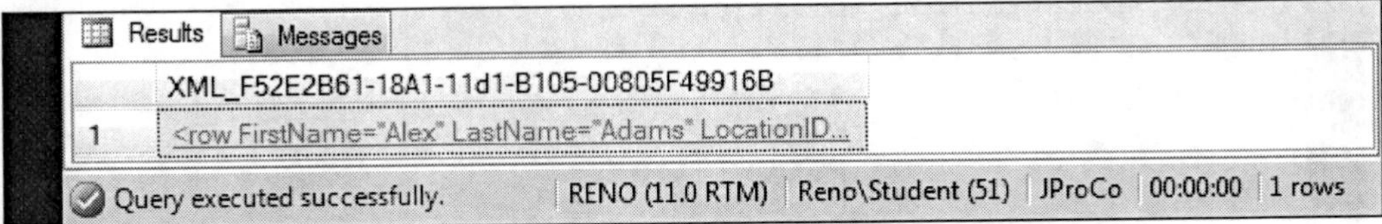

Figure 1.33 We have changed our Employee table result to output as XML RAW.

Notice that every row of our XML RAW output is labeled "row" by default.

```
XML_F52E2B61-18A...00805F49916B8.xml*   SQLQuery3.sql - RE...(Reno\Student (51))*
<row FirstName="Alex" LastName="Adams" LocationID="1" />
<row FirstName="Barry" LastName="Brown" LocationID="1" />
<row FirstName="Lee" LastName="Osako" LocationID="2" />
<row FirstName="David" LastName="Kennson" LocationID="1" />
<row FirstName="Eric" LastName="Bender" LocationID="1" />
<row FirstName="Lisa" LastName="Kendall" LocationID="4" />
<row FirstName="David" LastName="Lonning" LocationID="1" />
<row FirstName="John" LastName="Marshbank" />
<row FirstName="James" LastName="Newton" LocationID="2" />
<row FirstName="Terry" LastName="O'Haire" LocationID="2" />
<row FirstName="Sally" LastName="Smith" LocationID="1" />
<row FirstName="Barbara" LastName="O'Neil" LocationID="4" />
<row FirstName="Phil" LastName="Wilconkinski" LocationID="1" />
```

Figure 1.34 Each row of an XML RAW output is labeled "row" by default.

We next will add a root to our output. We will add the keyword ROOT to our existing code (Figure 1.35) and then look at our revised output (Figure 1.38).

```
SELECT FirstName, LastName, LocationID
FROM Employee
FOR XML RAW, ROOT
```

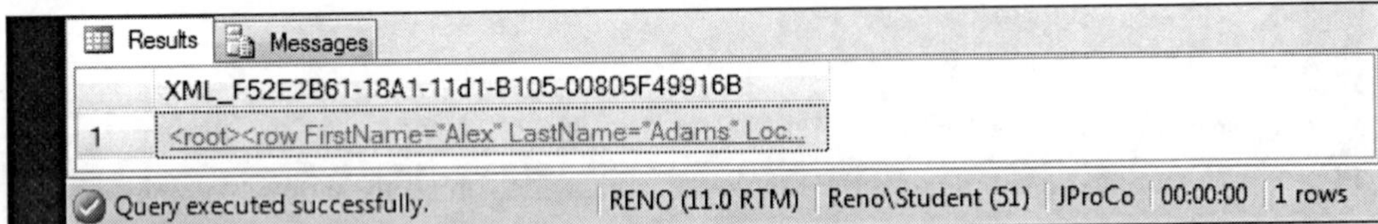

Figure 1.35 We are adding the keyword ROOT in order to see a root node in our XML output.

We now see the root node (a.k.a., the root element). Not only is our output more readable and organized, but this is considered "well-formed XML" (Figure 1.36).

SQLQuery3.sql - RE...(Reno\Student (51))* | XML_F52E2B61-18A...0805F49916B10.xml*

```
<root> <--
  <row FirstName="Alex" LastName="Adams" LocationID="1" />
  <row FirstName="Barry" LastName="Brown" LocationID="1" />
  <row FirstName="Lee" LastName="Osako" LocationID="2" />
  <row FirstName="David" LastName="Kennson" LocationID="1" />
  <row FirstName="Eric" LastName="Bender" LocationID="1" />
  <row FirstName="Lisa" LastName="Kendall" LocationID="4" />
  <row FirstName="David" LastName="Lonning" LocationID="1" />
  <row FirstName="John" LastName="Marshbank" />
  <row FirstName="James" LastName="Newton" LocationID="2" />
  <row FirstName="Terry" LastName="O'Haire" LocationID="2" />
  <row FirstName="Sally" LastName="Smith" LocationID="1" />
  <row FirstName="Barbara" LastName="O'Neil" LocationID="4" />
  <row FirstName="Phil" LastName="Wilconkinski" LocationID="1" />
</root> <--
```

Figure 1.36 Adding the root node makes our XML output well-formed XML.

Now let's with the query in a way where the XML stream will have its data put into elements (Figure 1.37).

```
SELECT FirstName, LastName, LocationID
FROM Employee
FOR XML RAW, ROOT, ELEMENTS
```

Figure 1.37 We have added the keyword ELEMENTS in order to see our data as elements.

We can see each employee now has three sub-elements under the top element, which is "row" (Figure 1.38).

Figure 1.38 Each employee now has three sub-elements beneath the top element, "row."

The exception is John Marshbank, who only has two elements (Figure 1.39).

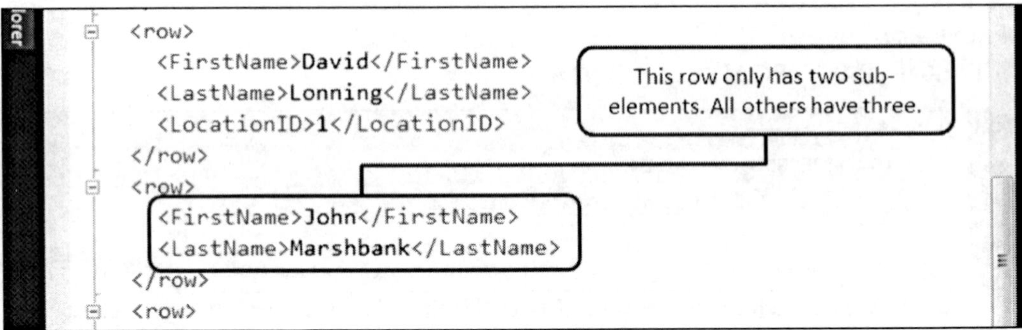

Figure 1.39 John Marshbank has just two sub-elements beneath the top element, "row".

If we query the Employee table, we quickly see the reason for this is that John Marshbank is the only one with a NULL LocationID (Figure 1.40).

Results | Messages

	FirstName	LastName	LocationID
6	Lisa	Kendall	4
7	David	Lonning	1
8	John	Marshb...	NULL ←
9	James	Newton	2
10	Terry	O'Haire	2
11	Sally	Smith	1

Query executed successfully. | RENO (11.0 RTM) | Reno\Student (51) | JProCo | 00:00:00 | 13 rows

Figure 1.40 Recall that John Marshbank is the only employee with a NULL LocationID.

Our mystery is solved - we understand that John Marshbank having just two data sub-elements is caused by his LocationID value being a NULL. Suppose the program which needs to consume our result requires three data sub-elements. Or suppose company policy specifies that each employee record must contain three data sub-elements. John Marshbank's record doesn't meet the criteria and would thus be in violation of the policy.

XSINIL

The **XSINIL** option allows you to force a tag(s) to be present, even if the underlying data is NULL. Our next example will show us how to make a LocationID tag appear for John Marshbank.

For fields in SQL Server which include a null value for some records but are populated with regular values in the other records, you will seem to have missing tags for the null record. Often this is alright, as missing tags are presumed to be null. However, if you require all tags to be present (even if they have no data), then you can specify the XSINIL option for your XML stream. The XSINIL option will force tags to be present for all records, including those which contain null values. Let's rerun our prior code and add the XSINIL option (Figure 1.41).

```
SELECT FirstName, LastName, LocationID
FROM Employee
FOR XML RAW, ROOT, ELEMENTS XSINIL
```

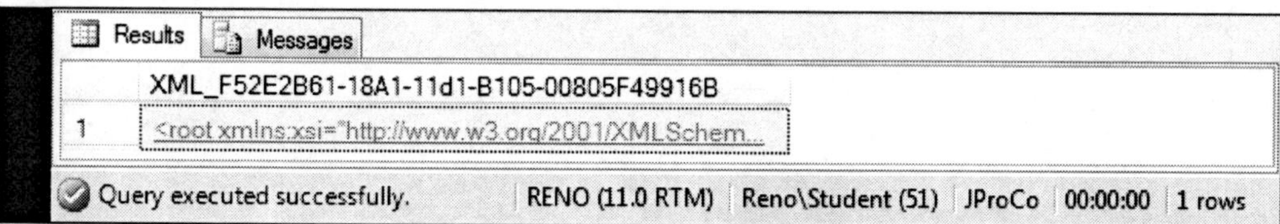

Figure 1.41 We are re-running our previous code with the XSINIL option.

We now see a third sub-element for John Marshbank. The LocationID tag is no longer missing. It is present and shows the value xsi:nil="true" in place of a LocationID (Figure 1.42).

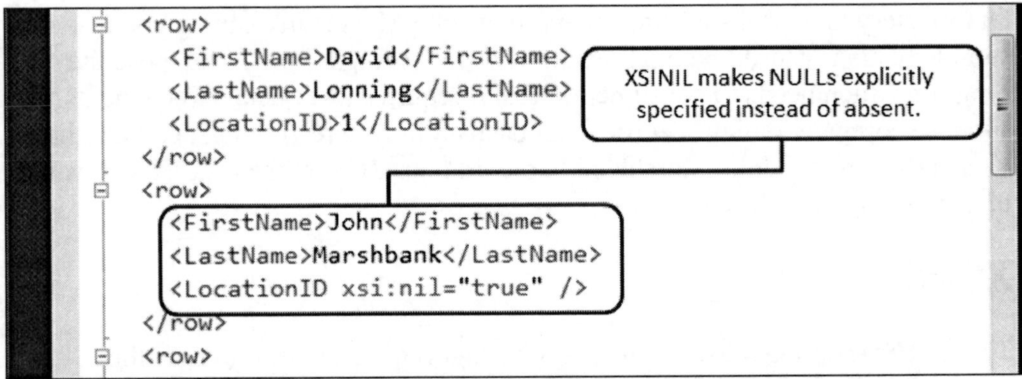
<row>
<FirstName>David</FirstName>
<LastName>Lonning</LastName>
<LocationID>1</LocationID>
</row>
<row>
<FirstName>John</FirstName>
<LastName>Marshbank</LastName>
<LocationID xsi:nil="true" />
</row>
<row>
XSINIL makes NULLs explicitly specified instead of absent.

Figure 1.42 Our objective has been met: John Marshbank's record now includes three data elements thanks to XSINIL.

Lab 1.2: XML Streams

Lab Prep: Each lab has one or more Skill Checks. Start with Skill Check 1 and proceed until reaching the Points to Ponder section.

Before beginning this lab, verify that SQL Server 2012 is properly installed and operating. Before running the lab setup script for resetting the database (SQLQueries2012Vol5Chapter1.0-4.2Setup.sql), please make sure to close all query windows within SSMS. An open query window pointing to a database context can lock that database preventing it from updating when the script is executing. A simple way to assure all query windows are closed, is to exit out of SSMS, then open a new instance of SSMS, and lastly run the setup script.

Skill Check 1: Create an XML stream using the RAW option to get the ClassID and ClassName fields from the MgmtTraining table. Each top-level element should be named after the table. When you're done, your screen should resemble Figure 1.43.

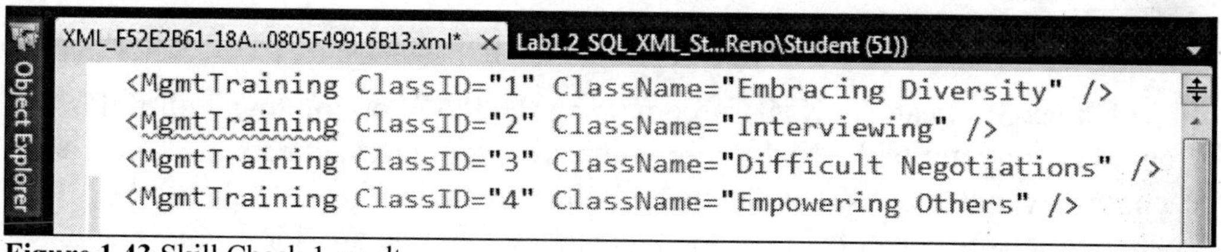

XML_F52E2B61-18A...0805F49916B13.xml* × Lab1.2_SQL_XML_St...Reno\Student (51))

Object Explorer

```
<MgmtTraining ClassID="1" ClassName="Embracing Diversity" />
<MgmtTraining ClassID="2" ClassName="Interviewing" />
<MgmtTraining ClassID="3" ClassName="Difficult Negotiations" />
<MgmtTraining ClassID="4" ClassName="Empowering Others" />
```

Figure 1.43 Skill Check 1 result.

Skill Check 2: Create an XML stream using the RAW option to get the GrantName and Amount fields from the [Grant] table. Make sure you have a root element named <root> and each top-level element should be named after the table. All the data should be in Attributes inside the top-level element. When you are done, your result should resemble Figure 1.44 below.

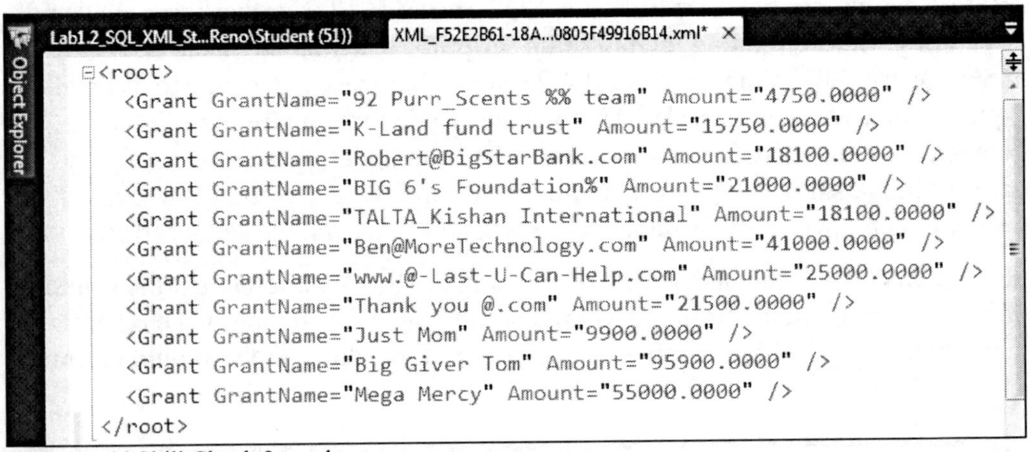

Lab1.2_SQL_XML_St...Reno\Student (51)) | XML_F52E2B61-18A...0805F49916B14.xml* ×

Object Explorer

```
<root>
  <Grant GrantName="92 Purr_Scents %% team" Amount="4750.0000" />
  <Grant GrantName="K-Land fund trust" Amount="15750.0000" />
  <Grant GrantName="Robert@BigStarBank.com" Amount="18100.0000" />
  <Grant GrantName="BIG 6's Foundation%" Amount="21000.0000" />
  <Grant GrantName="TALTA_Kishan International" Amount="18100.0000" />
  <Grant GrantName="Ben@MoreTechnology.com" Amount="41000.0000" />
  <Grant GrantName="www.@-Last-U-Can-Help.com" Amount="25000.0000" />
  <Grant GrantName="Thank you @.com" Amount="21500.0000" />
  <Grant GrantName="Just Mom" Amount="9900.0000" />
  <Grant GrantName="Big Giver Tom" Amount="95900.0000" />
  <Grant GrantName="Mega Mercy" Amount="55000.0000" />
</root>
```

Figure 1.44 Skill Check 2 result.

Skill Check 3: Create an XML stream using the RAW option to get all fields from the contractor table. Make sure you have a root element named <root> and each top-level element should be named after the table. The data should be contained in sub elements of the top element. When you are done, your result should resemble Figure 1.45 below.

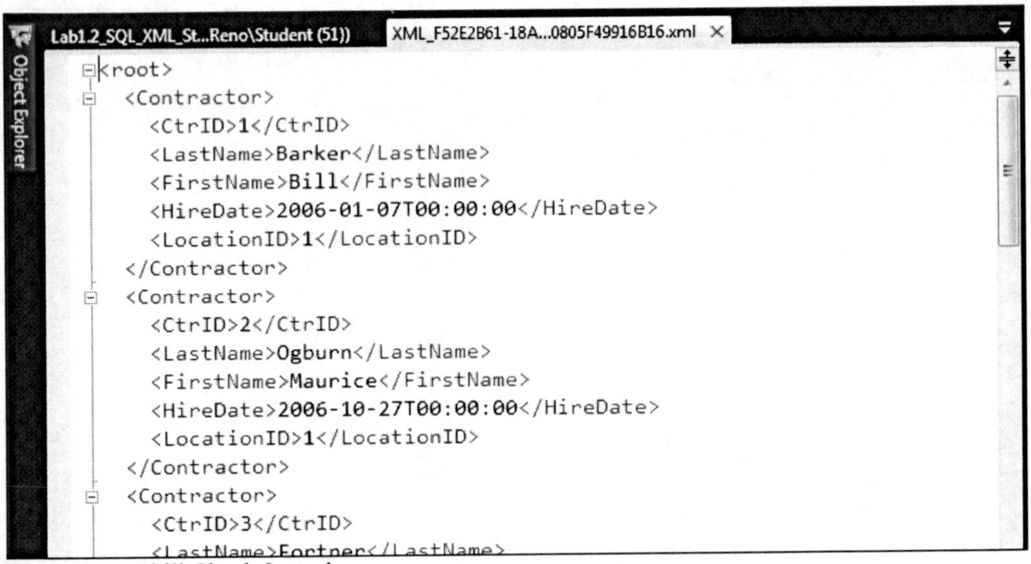

Lab1.2_SQL_XML_St...Reno\Student (51)) | XML_F52E2B61-18A...0805F49916B16.xml ×

Object Explorer

```
<root>
  <Contractor>
    <CtrID>1</CtrID>
    <LastName>Barker</LastName>
    <FirstName>Bill</FirstName>
    <HireDate>2006-01-07T00:00:00</HireDate>
    <LocationID>1</LocationID>
  </Contractor>
  <Contractor>
    <CtrID>2</CtrID>
    <LastName>Ogburn</LastName>
    <FirstName>Maurice</FirstName>
    <HireDate>2006-10-27T00:00:00</HireDate>
    <LocationID>1</LocationID>
  </Contractor>
  <Contractor>
    <CtrID>3</CtrID>
    <LastName>Fortner</LastName>
```

Figure 1.45 Skill Check 3 result.

Skill Check 4: Create an XML stream using the RAW option to get all fields from the PayRates table. Make sure you have a root element named <root> and each top-level element should be named <PR>. The data should be contained in sub elements of the top element. Elements must be present even if their value is null. When you are done, your result should resemble Figure 1.46.

```
XML_F52E2B61-18A...0805F49916B17.xml  X  Lab1.2_SQL_XML_St...Reno\Student (51))
<root xmlns:xsi="http://www.w3.org/2001/XMLSchema-instance">
  <PR>
    <EmpID>1</EmpID>
    <YearlySalary>76000.0000</YearlySalary>
    <MonthlySalary xsi:nil="true" />
    <HourlyRate xsi:nil="true" />
  </PR>
  <PR>
    <EmpID>2</EmpID>
    <YearlySalary>79000.0000</YearlySalary>
    <MonthlySalary xsi:nil="true" />
    <HourlyRate xsi:nil="true" />
  </PR>
  <PR>
    <EmpID>3</EmpID>
```

Figure 1.46 Skill Check 4 result.

READERNOTE: As shown above (Figure 1.46), your XML stream will likely contain an xmlns declaration in the root element. While common, XML declarations are a deep subject and fall outside the scope of this book.

Answer Code: The T-SQL code to this lab can be found in the downloadable files in a file named Lab1.2_SQL_XML_Streams.sql.

Points to Ponder - XML Streams

1. The FOR XML clause instructs SQL Server to return data as an XML stream rather than a rowset.
2. The FOR XML clause is appended at the end of your SELECT statement.
3. Two common reasons why you might want to retrieve data as XML instead of a SQL Server table could be:
    - Publishing data to a website.
    - Retrieving data to exchange with a trading partner who should not have direct access to your SQL Server.
4. FOR XML has four mode options and RAW is just one of them.
5. The RAW option can be used with the ROOT or ELEMENTS keywords or both to customize your expected XML stream.
6. The ROOT and ELEMENTS keywords are optional.
7. FOR XML RAW defaults to making a <row> tag. You can change this to anything you like by using the optional parentheses () after the word RAW.
    - FOR XML RAW - - Results in <row…>
    - FOR XML RAW('emp') - - Results in <emp…>

Chapter Glossary

Attributes: Data stored inside of a beginning tag.

BCP (bulk copy program)**:** A utility used to export data into/out of a SQL Server table.

Beginning tag: This sits between brackets and contains no slash.

Data: The raw numbers and most granular components that you store in a database.

Elements: XML node storing data between the beginning and ending element tags.

ELEMENTS: Optional keyword used to customize the XML stream.

Ending tag: This appears identical to the beginning tag, except it contains a forward slash. Ending tags must follow the same sequence as the beginning tags.

FOR XML: Clause which instructs SQL to return data as an XML stream rather than a rowset. The FOR XML clause is appended at the end of the SELECT statement.

Information: The end result after data undergoes value-added processing (e.g., aggregations, calculations, data combined with or compared to other data).

Metadata: Data about data; describes your data, including relationships within your data.

RAW: The simplest mode where data is all considered to be at the same level with no nesting. The FOR XML RAW command by default does not create a root. The raw mode likes to store all of its data as attributes.

RDBMS: A relational database management system, such as SQL Server.

ROOT: Optional keyword which specifies the ROOT element option.

Root element: Also known as the **root node**; the element which begins and ends a well-formed XML stream.

Self-describing data: Data and metadata presented together.

Stream: The forming of the data in the way which a program or process prefers to output information. In SQL Server terms, a stream resembles a table: the grid like presentation of rows and columns that you get when you run a query.

Text editor: Text-based program often used to write code (e.g., for use by HTML); Notepad and WordPad are examples of simple text editors.

Top-level element: Appears directly beneath the root element.

Well-formed XML: XML is considered complete (known as well-formed XML) only if it has a root tag which encompasses all other tags.

XML: Extensible **M**arkup **L**anguage.

XML fragment: Any XML document, or partial document, that doesn't meet the criteria of well-formed XML.

XSINIL: Option which allows you to force a tag(s) to be present even if the underlying data is NULL.

Review Quiz - Chapter One

1.) What do text files, XML streams, and SQL databases all have in common?

O a. They all run only on Windows servers.

O b. They all contain data.

O c. They all contain metadata.

2.) Your root tag is named <Joes2Pros> in your well-formed XML stream. How should the ending root tag be named?

O a. </Joes2Pros>

O b. <\Joes2Pros>

O c. <--Joes2Pros>

O d. <Joes2Pros/>

O e. <Joes2Pros\>

3.) What do you call data inside of a tag like the example seen below?
<Team Name = “Vikings”>

O a. Data fragment

O b. XML fragment

O c. Element

O d. Attribute

4.) RAW is the only XML mode.

O a. True

O b. False

5.) RAW automatically adds the root element tag in SQL Server.

O a. True

O b. False

6.) If you don’t specify any option, then XML RAW will have your data streamed in as:

O a. Element text.

O b. Attributes.

7.) Without XSINIL, what happens to null values from your result set?

O a. They error out since XSINIL does not allow nulls.

O b. They appear as empty tags.

O c. No tags are present for null values.

8.) You are using FOR XML RAW to get your relational data. After testing this, you notice that not all items from the query appear in the XML stream. You notice that this is happening when fields have a NULL value. Only those employees who have values for all elements appear. You need to modify your T-SQL statement so that all employees' tags appear in the XML document. What should you do?

O a. Add a HAVING clause to the query.

O b. Remove the RAW option and let SQL pick the default.

O c. Add the XSINIL argument to the ELEMENTS option in the query.

O d. Add the replace value to the clause of the query.

Answer Key

1.) Because Text files and XML streams do not run on Windows servers (a) is incorrect. Text files do not contain metadata therefore (c) is incorrect. Because text files, XML streams and SQL databases all contain data (b) is the correct answer.

2.) A valid opening tag is between < > and a valid closing tag will always be between</ >Therefore (a) is the correct answer.

3.) The data contained is data, not a data fragment, so (a) is an incorrect answer. An XML fragment is an XML string that is not well formed, so (b) is incorrect. An Element describes what it contains and is not the content, making (c) an incorrect answer. An attribute cannot contain other elements and provides information about the element and will always be in quotation marks, so (d) is the correct answer.

4.) XML RAW is only one of several modes including XML AUTO and XML Path. The answer is (b), False.

5.) RAW is the simplest mode where data is all considered to be at the same level with no nesting. The FOR XML RAW command by default does not create a root. The answer is (b), False.

6.) XML RAW will store its data as attributes by default, so (b) is the correct answer.

7.) XSINIL allows you to force a tag(s) to be present even if the underlying data is NULL, so (a) and (b) are incorrect. Without XSINIL no tags are present for null values, making (c) the correct answer.

8.) To force a tag(s) to be present even if the underlying data is NULL the XSINIL must be added to the element option in the query. This means (c) is the correct answer.

Bug Catcher Game

To play the Bug Catcher game run the SQLQueries2012Vol5BugCatcher1.pps from the BugCatcher folder of the companion files found at www.Joes2Pros.com.

Chapter 2. XML Modes

In the last chapter, we covered creating the XML RAW stream. This chapter will introduce additional XML modes, including XML AUTO and XML PATH. These modes are more commonly used than RAW. We will also explore some additional options to further customize your XML stream.

As noted in Chapter 1, XML is case-sensitive. In order for your examples and exercises to run properly in Chapters 1 through 7, be sure that your XML fragments precisely match the figures with respect to uppercase and lowercase.

READERNOTE:*Please run the script SQLQueries2012Vol5Chapter1.0-4.2Setup.sqlin order to follow along with the examples in the first section of Chapter 2. You only need to run this script once for all examples in Chapters 1 through 4. All scripts mentioned in this chapter may be found at* ***www.Joes2Pros.com****.*

XML Auto Mode

By way of contrast, let's first review some features of the Raw mode before we look at Auto. We then will compare the output streams produced by these two XML modes.

In the last chapter, we used the following code to create an XML stream using the Raw mode (Figure 2.1, Figure 2.2). This code generates one element for each record which appears in the tabular result set. The data appear as attributes, and the default tag is named <row>.

```
SELECT * FROM Location
FOR XML RAW
```

Results | Messages
XML_F52E2B61-18A1-11d1-B105-00805F49916B
1 <row LocationID="1" Street="111 First ST" City="S...
Query executed successfully. | RENO (11.0 RTM) | Reno\Student (51) | JProCo | 00:00:00 | 1 rows

Figure 2.1 This code creates an XML stream using the Raw mode.

XML_F52E2B61-18A...0805F49916B18.xml* × SQLQuery4.sql - RE...(Reno\Student (51))*

```
<row LocationID="1" Street="111 First ST" City="Seattle" state="WA" />
<row LocationID="2" Street="222 Second AVE" City="Boston" state="MA" />
<row LocationID="3" Street="333 Third PL" City="Chicago" state="IL" />
<row LocationID="4" Street="444 Ruby ST" City="Spokane" state="WA" />
```

Figure 2.2 The XML stream produced by the Raw mode (code appears in Figure 2.1).

When selecting from a single table, the Auto mode resembles the Raw mode with one exception. Whereas the Raw mode defaults each tag to <row>, the Auto mode names each tag according to the table name (or table alias) listed in the FROM clause of the query.

The code for the Auto mode is similar to the code for Raw.

```
SELECT * FROM Location
FOR XML AUTO
```

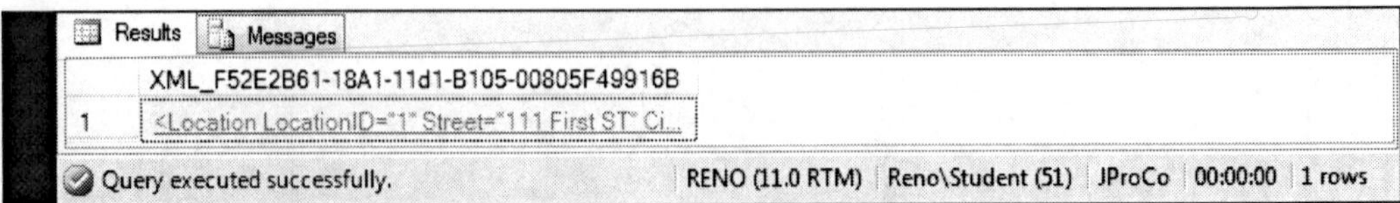

Figure 2.3 This code creates an XML stream using the Auto mode.

The resulting XML is also quite similar to the Raw mode. The data appear as attributes, and by default there is no root element. However, note that the Auto mode has defaulted the row tags to the table name as it appears in the FROM clause. The tag <Location> is named for the Location table.

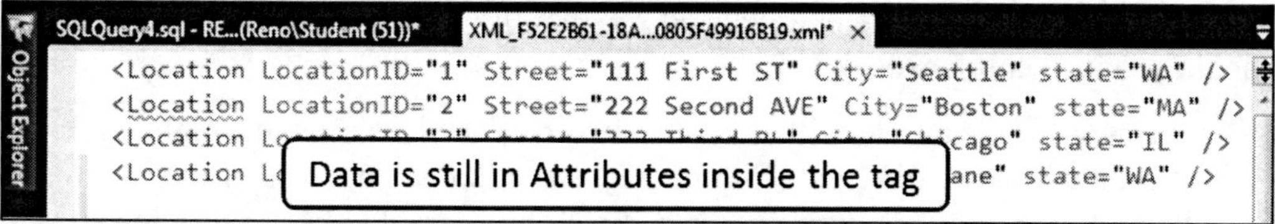

Figure 2.4 The XML stream produced by the Auto mode (code appears in Figure 2.3).

If we specify "Location" in our XML Raw code, then the stream resulting from our Raw query would be identical to our Auto query (Figure 2.25 and Figure 2.26).

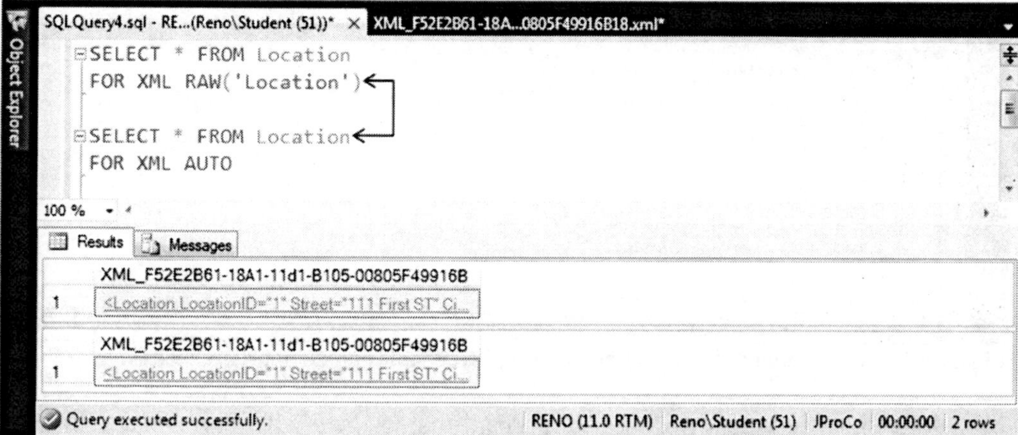

Figure 2.5 These queries will produce an identical result.

```
<Location LocationID="1" Street="111 First ST" City="Seattle" state="WA" />
<Location LocationID="2" Street="222 Second AVE" City="Boston" state="MA" />
<Location LocationID="3" Street="333 Third PL" City="Chicago" state="IL" />
<Location LocationID="4" Street="444 Ruby ST" City="Spokane" state="WA" />
```

RAW mode was overridden to have the Location name for top level element.

Figure 2.6 This stream will be the result from both queries (Raw and Auto) shown in Figure 2.5.

Our Raw query overrode the default top-level element name <row> with <Location>. Because we added this tag name specification to our Raw code, both the Raw and Auto queries produced the same result. This will always be the case, so long as you are selecting from a single table.

Multiple Table XML Queries

Next we will query multiple tables and see that the Raw and Auto modes will again produce similar results.

The query in this example will be an inner join of the Location and Employee tables on the LocationID field (Figure 2.7). Note that we have 13 records in our result set. Since we've chosen an inner join, John Marshbank's record does not appear in our result.

```
SELECT City, FirstName, LastName
FROM Location INNER JOIN Employee
ON Location.LocationID = Employee.LocationID
```

Results | Messages

	City	FirstName	LastName
1	Seattle	Alex	Adams
2	Seattle	Barry	Brown
3	Boston	Lee	Osako
4	Seattle	David	Kennson
5	Seattle	Eric	Bender
6	Spok...	Lisa	Kendall

Query executed successfully. | RENO (11.0 RTM) | Reno\Student (51) | JProCo | 00:00:00 | 12 rows

Figure 2.7 An inner join of the Location and Employee tables producing 12 records.

Now let's view the query above and its result using the XML Raw mode (Figure 2.8 and Figure 2.9). The result is straightforward and consistent with the other streams we've seen thus far in this chapter - the data are contained in attributes, there is no <root> element, and each record has the default tag name of <row>.

```
SELECT City, FirstName, LastName
FROM Location
INNER JOIN Employee
ON Location.LocationID = Employee.LocationID
FOR XML RAW
```

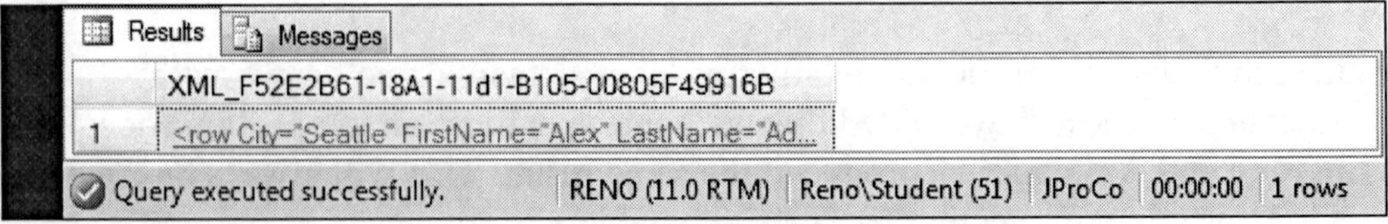

Figure 2.8 Our same inner join query, now adding the XML Raw mode.

```
XML_F52E2B61-18A...0805F49916B23.xml  X  SQLQuery4.sql - RE...(Reno\Student (51))*
<row City="Seattle" FirstName="Alex" LastName="Adams" />
<row City="Seattle" FirstName="Barry" LastName="Brown" />
<row City="Boston" FirstName="Lee" LastName="Osako" />
<row City="Seattle" FirstName="David" LastName="Kennson" />
<row City="Seattle" FirstName="Eric" LastName="Bender" />
<row City="Spokane" FirstName="Lisa" LastName="Kendall" />
<row City="Seattle" FirstName="David" LastName="Lonning" />
<row City="Boston" FirstName="James" LastName="Newton" />
<row City="Boston" FirstName="Terry" LastName="O'Haire" />
<row City="Seattle" FirstName="Sally" LastName="Smith" />
<row City="Spokane" FirstName="Barbara" LastName="O'Neil" />
<row City="Seattle" FirstName="Phil" LastName="Wilconkinski"
```

Figure 2.9 The XML stream produced by the Raw mode (code appears in Figure 2.8).

Add Location to specify that we want the row tag to be named <Location>.

```
SELECT City, FirstName, LastName
FROM Location
INNER JOIN Employee
ON Location.LocationID = Employee.LocationID
FOR XML RAW('Location')
```

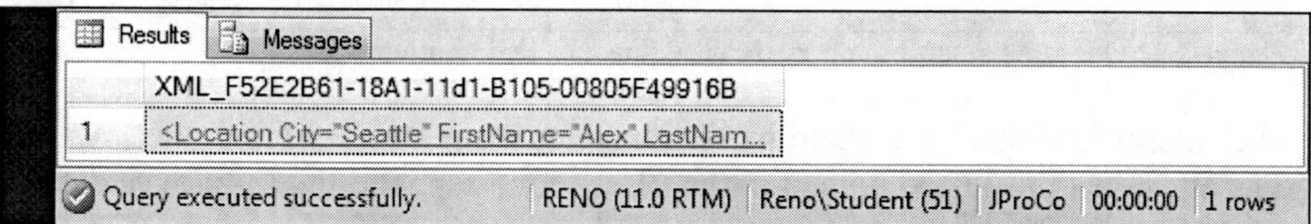

Figure 2.10 This code specifies that each row tag should be named <Location>.

```
XML_F52E2B61-18A...0805F49916B24.xml*  X  SQLQuery4.sql - RE...(Reno\Student (51))*
<Location City="Seattle" FirstName="Alex" LastName="Adams" />
<Location City="Seattle" FirstName="Barry" LastName="Brown" />
<Location City="Boston" FirstName="Lee" LastName="Osako" />
<Location City="Seattle" FirstName="David" LastName="Kennson" />
<Location City="Seattle" FirstName="Eric" LastName="Bender" />
<Location City="Spokane" FirstName="Lisa" LastName="Kendall" />
<Location City="Seattle" FirstName="David" LastName="Lonning" />
<Location City="Boston" FirstName="James" LastName="Newton" />
<Location City="Boston" FirstName="Terry" LastName="O'Haire" />
<Location City="Seattle" FirstName="Sally" LastName="Smith" />
<Location City="Spokane" FirstName="Barbara" LastName="O'Neil" />
<Location City="Seattle" FirstName="Phil" LastName="Wilconkinski" />
```

Figure 2.11 The XML stream produced by the Raw mode (code appears in Figure 2.10.

Now let's turn our attention to the Auto mode. Since the Auto mode names the tag after the table, how would you expect the result to appear in a multi-table query? Will the tag be named after the Location table or after the Employee table?

```
SELECT City, FirstName, LastName
FROM Location
INNER JOIN Employee
ON Location.LocationID = Employee.LocationID
FOR XML RAW('Location')
```

Question: If AUTO mode were to be used and it names the tag after the table what do queries with 2 tables names get?

Let's test this out by changing our query to include the Auto mode.

```
SELECT City, FirstName, LastName
FROM Location INNER JOIN Employee
ON Location.LocationID = Employee.LocationID
FOR XML AUTO
```

```
Results | Messages
   XML_F52E2B61-18A1-11d1-B105-00805F49916B
1  <Location City="Seattle"><Employee FirstName="Al...
Query executed successfully. | RENO (11.0 RTM) | Reno\Student (51) | JProCo | 00:00:00 | 1 rows
```

Figure 2.12 Our same inner join query, now adding the XML Auto mode.

The answer is "both." The Auto mode generates a tag for each table: the Location data attribute (City) is contained in the <Location> tag, and the Employee data attributes (FirstName, LastName) are contained in the <Employee> tag (Figure 2.13).

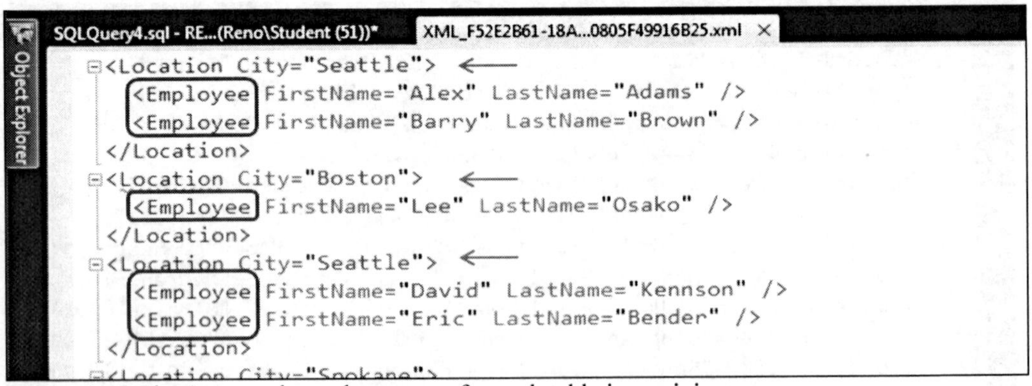

```
SQLQuery4.sql - RE...(Reno\Student (51))*   XML_F52E2B61-18A...0805F49916B25.xml
<Location City="Seattle">
  <Employee FirstName="Alex" LastName="Adams" />
  <Employee FirstName="Barry" LastName="Brown" />
</Location>
<Location City="Boston">
  <Employee FirstName="Lee" LastName="Osako" />
</Location>
<Location City="Seattle">
  <Employee FirstName="David" LastName="Kennson" />
  <Employee FirstName="Eric" LastName="Bender" />
</Location>
<Location City="Spokane">
```

Figure 2.13 The Auto mode produces a tag for each table in our join query.

So this demonstrates a difference between the Auto mode and the Raw mode. The Auto mode will nest the results, but the Raw mode will not.

Look back to our query (Figure 2.14) and note that the Auto mode placed the tags in the order in which the tables appeared in our query. In this example, the Location table becomes the top-level element tag because the first field in the SELECT list is City which is from the Location table (Figure 2.12). The second (nested) table is Employee which appears beneath as a child element.

```
SQLQuery4.sql - RE...(Reno\Student (51))*    XML_F52E2B61-18A...0805F49916B25.xml
<Location City="Seattle">
  <Employee FirstName="Alex" LastName="Adams" />
  <Employee FirstName="Barry" LastName="Brown" />
</Location>
<Location City="Boston">
  <Employee FirstName="Lee" LastName="Osako" />
</Locat
<Locati
  <Empl                                        son" />
  <Empl                                        r" />
</Locati
```

Auto mode will nest child elements based on the order of your field Select list.

Figure 2.14 The Auto mode produces a tag for each table in our join query.

If you were to list any field from the Employee table first, rather than a field from the Location table, then the <Employee> element would have the <Location> element nested inside of it (Figure 2.15).

```
SQLQuery4.sql - RE...(Reno\Student (51))*    XML_F52E2B61-18A...0805F49916B25.xml
SELECT City, FirstName, LastName
FROM Location
INNER JOIN Employee
ON Location.LocationID = Employee.LocationID
FOR XML AUTO
```

Figure 2.15 The order of fields in your SELECT list determines how elements are nested.

If you switch the field SELECT list and have FirstName appear before City (Figure 2.16) this will cause your XML stream to have <Employee> as the parent element even though the Location table is listed before the Employee table in the join.

```
SELECT FirstName, City, LastName
FROM Location INNER JOIN Employee
ON Location.LocationID = Employee.LocationID
FOR XML AUTO
```

```
SELECT FirstName, City, LastName

<Employee FirstName="Alex" LastName="Adams">
  <Location City="Seattle" />
</Employee>
<Employee FirstName="Barry" LastName="Brown">
  <Location City="Seattle" />
</Employee>
<Employee FirstName="Lee" LastName="Osako">
  <Location City="Boston" />
</Employee>
<Employee FirstName="David" LastName="Kennson">
  <Location City="Seattle" />
```

Figure 2.16 The Employee table is the parent element shown here.

Using Root with Auto

Next we'll add a root element (also called *root node*), so that our stream will be well-formed XML.

Using the ROOT keyword in combination with the Auto mode produces the same result as it does with the Raw mode: your XML stream will contain a root (named <root> by default). To specify a name for the root, put this name in the parentheses inside single quotes right after the ROOT keyword in your code (shown in Figure 2.19).

Now let's add a ROOT to our code, because we want to have well-formed XML.

```
SELECT City, FirstName, LastName
FROM Location INNER JOIN Employee
ON Location.LocationID = Employee.LocationID
FOR XML AUTO, ROOT
```

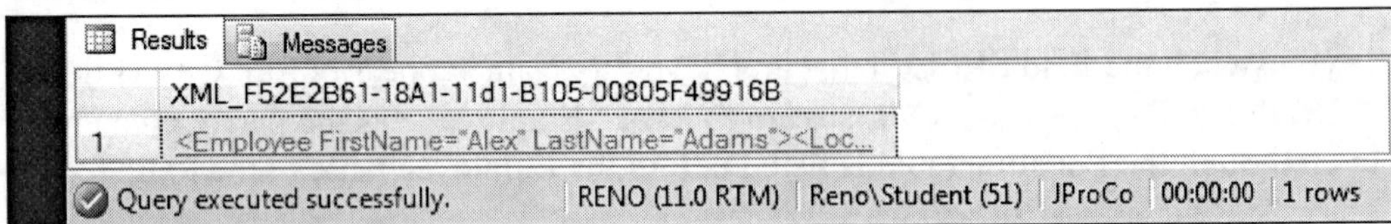

Figure 2.17 We are adding a root element, in order to achieve well-formed XML.

Our XML result appears the same as in the prior result, except that now all of our data is enclosed within the opening and closing tags named <root>.

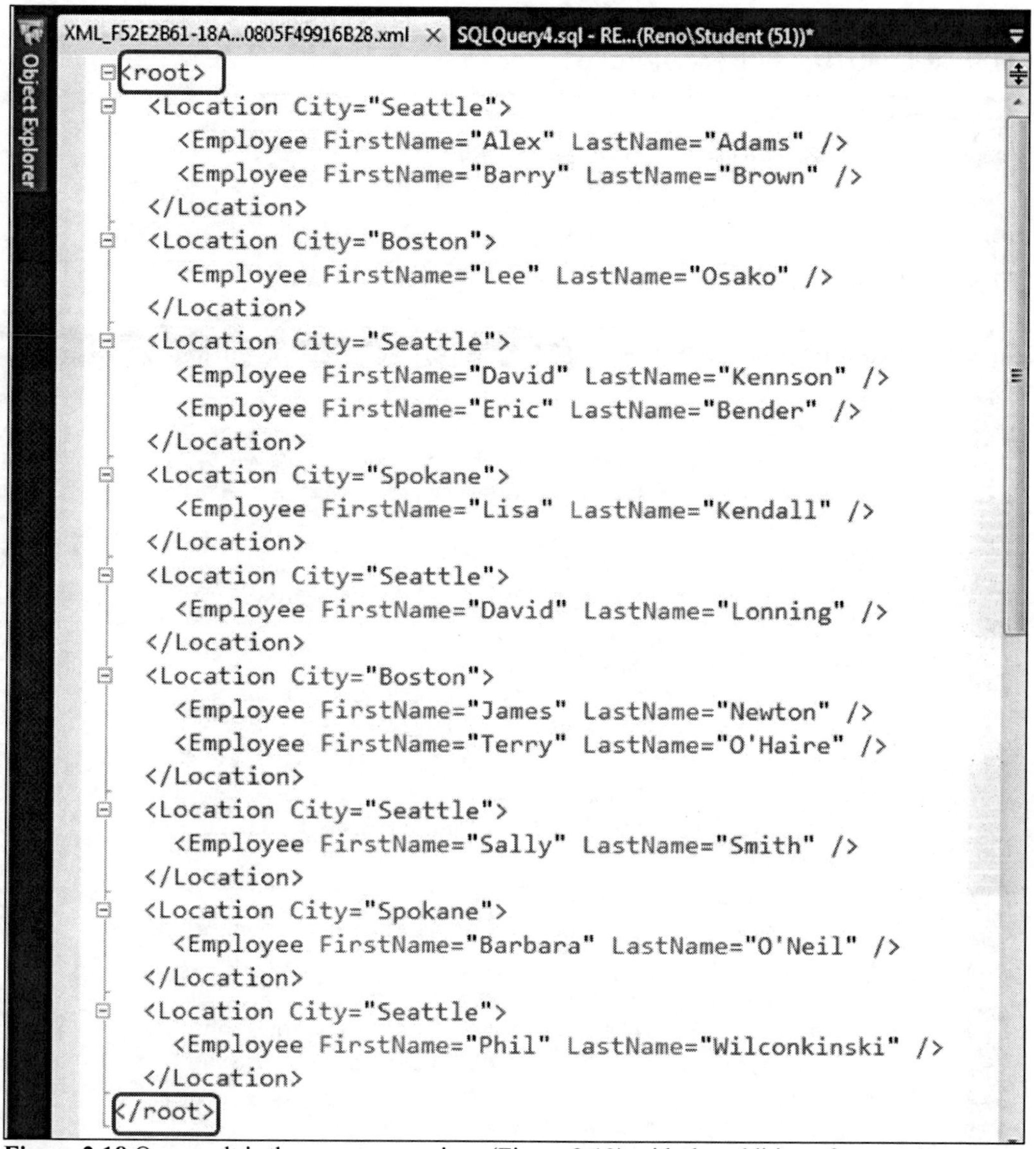

XML_F52E2B61-18A...0805F49916B28.xml × SQLQuery4.sql - RE...(Reno\Student (51))*

Object Explorer

```
<root>
  <Location City="Seattle">
    <Employee FirstName="Alex" LastName="Adams" />
    <Employee FirstName="Barry" LastName="Brown" />
  </Location>
  <Location City="Boston">
    <Employee FirstName="Lee" LastName="Osako" />
  </Location>
  <Location City="Seattle">
    <Employee FirstName="David" LastName="Kennson" />
    <Employee FirstName="Eric" LastName="Bender" />
  </Location>
  <Location City="Spokane">
    <Employee FirstName="Lisa" LastName="Kendall" />
  </Location>
  <Location City="Seattle">
    <Employee FirstName="David" LastName="Lonning" />
  </Location>
  <Location City="Boston">
    <Employee FirstName="James" LastName="Newton" />
    <Employee FirstName="Terry" LastName="O'Haire" />
  </Location>
  <Location City="Seattle">
    <Employee FirstName="Sally" LastName="Smith" />
  </Location>
  <Location City="Spokane">
    <Employee FirstName="Barbara" LastName="O'Neil" />
  </Location>
  <Location City="Seattle">
    <Employee FirstName="Phil" LastName="Wilconkinski" />
  </Location>
</root>
```

Figure 2.18 Our result is the same as previous (Figure 2.13) with the addition of a root element.

Let's take our same code and give the root a more meaningful name. To specify a name for the root, put the name inside single quotes, within parentheses, right after the ROOT keyword in your code. We'll name it <JProCo> after the database which both of our tables come from (please see the code in Figure 2.19 and the result stream in Figure 2.20).

```
SELECT City, FirstName, LastName
FROM Location INNER JOIN Employee
```

```
ON Location.LocationID = Employee.LocationID
FOR XML AUTO, ROOT('JProCo')
```

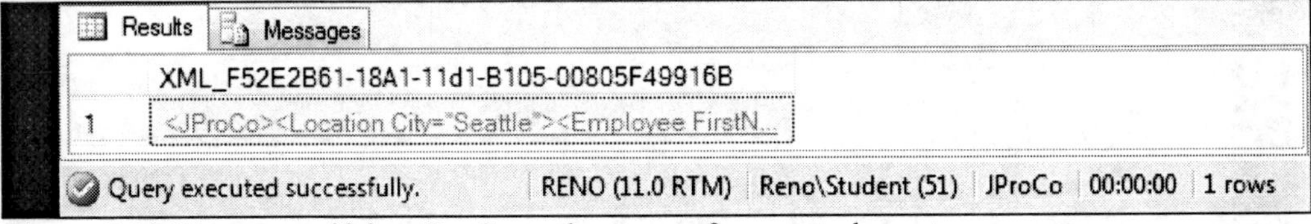

Figure 2.19 We are specifying JProCo as the name of our root element.

```
XML_F52E2B61-18A...0805F49916B29.xml  ×  SQLQuery4.sql - RE...(Reno\Student (51))*
<JProCo>
  <Location City="Seattle">
    <Employee FirstName="Alex" LastName="Adams" />
    <Employee FirstName="Barry" LastName="Brown" />
  </Location>
  <Location City="Boston">
    <Employee FirstName="Lee" LastName="Osako" />
  </Location>
  <Location City="Seattle">
    <Employee FirstName="David" LastName="Kennson" />
    <Employee FirstName="Eric" LastName="Bender" />
  </Location>
  <Location City="Spokane">
    <Employee FirstName="Lisa" LastName="Kendall" />
  </Location>
  <Location City="Seattle">
    <Employee FirstName="David" LastName="Lonning" />
  </Location>
  <Location City="Boston">
    <Employee FirstName="James" LastName="Newton" />
    <Employee FirstName="Terry" LastName="O'Haire" />
  </Location>
  <Location City="Seattle">
    <Employee FirstName="Sally" LastName="Smith" />
  </Location>
  <Location City="Spokane">
    <Employee FirstName="Barbara" LastName="O'Neil" />
  </Location>
  <Location City="Seattle">
    <Employee FirstName="Phil" LastName="Wilconkinski" />
  </Location>
</JProCo>
```

Figure 2.20 The root element of our well-formed XML has been re-named <JProCo>.

Sorting Nested Elements

XML offers a great deal of flexibility in how you can choose to organize your result output. For example, since eight JProCo employees are listed under Seattle, then there is really no need to see Seattle listed multiple times. By sorting on the higher level element, you can put all related child elements under the same parent. This way you don't have to repeatedly list the parent element.

Let's combine our results together in a more efficient and readable manner by grouping the Seattle employees together.(Figure 2.21)

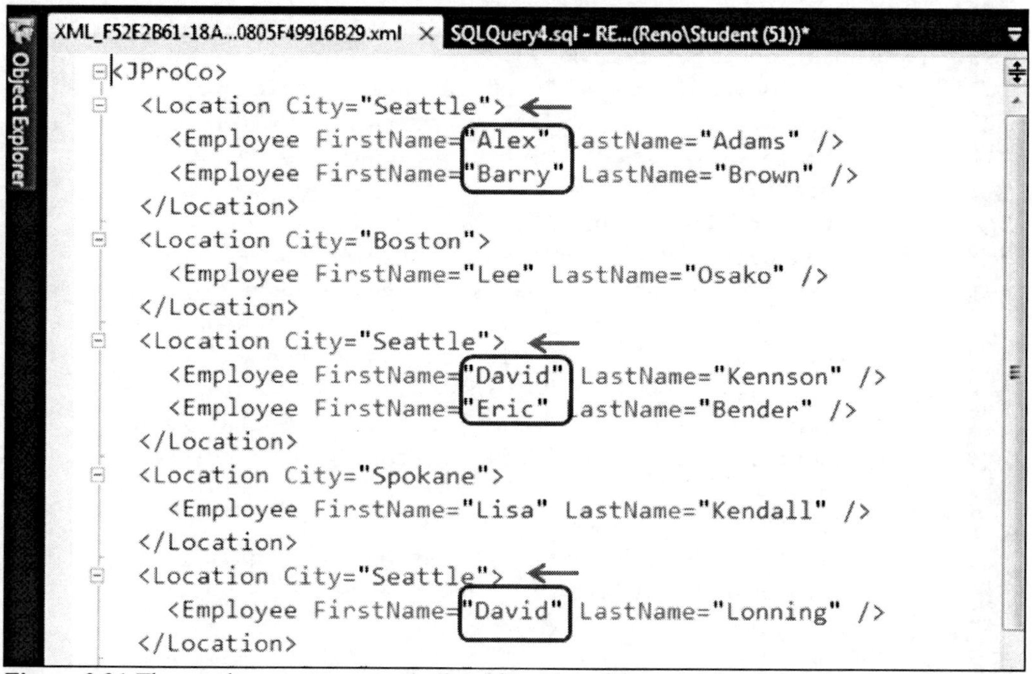

XML_F52E2B61-18A...0805F49916B29.xml × SQLQuery4.sql - RE...(Reno\Student (51))*

Object Explorer

```
<JProCo>
  <Location City="Seattle">
    <Employee FirstName="Alex" LastName="Adams" />
    <Employee FirstName="Barry" LastName="Brown" />
  </Location>
  <Location City="Boston">
    <Employee FirstName="Lee" LastName="Osako" />
  </Location>
  <Location City="Seattle">
    <Employee FirstName="David" LastName="Kennson" />
    <Employee FirstName="Eric" LastName="Bender" />
  </Location>
  <Location City="Spokane">
    <Employee FirstName="Lisa" LastName="Kendall" />
  </Location>
  <Location City="Seattle">
    <Employee FirstName="David" LastName="Lonning" />
  </Location>
```

Figure 2.21 The employees are currently listed in order of the natural sort (on EmployeeID).

Instead of grouping the results by the natural sort of the table (i.e., by EmployeeID), we would prefer to have the the results grouped by city. An ORDER BY clause will help achieve our goal.

```
SELECT City, FirstName, LastName
FROM Location INNER JOIN Employee
ON Location.LocationID = Employee.LocationID
ORDER BY City
FOR XML AUTO, ROOT('JProCo')
```

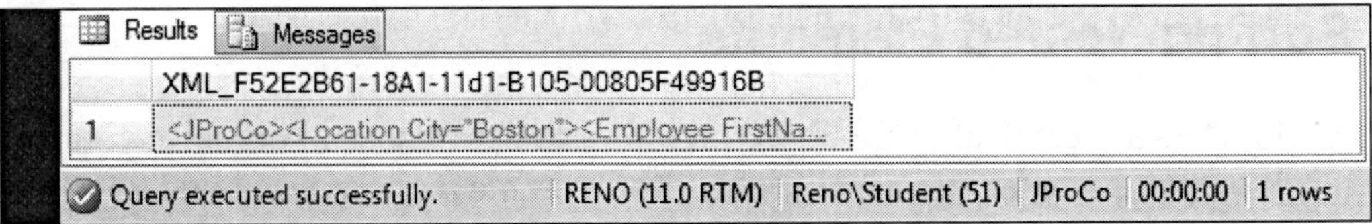

Figure 2.22 We are adding an ORDER BY clause to our code.

This result is very readable. We now see each city (Boston, Seattle and Spokane) listed once along with the employees working in each one.

SQLQuery4.sql - RE...(Reno\Student (51))* XML_F52E2B61-18A...0805F49916B30.xml

```
<JProCo>
  <Location City="Boston">
    <Employee FirstName="Lee" LastName="Osako" />
    <Employee FirstName="James" LastName="Newton" />
    <Employee FirstName="Terry" LastName="O'Haire" />
  </Location>
  <Location City="Seattle">
    <Employee FirstName="Alex" LastName="Adams" />
    <Employee FirstName="Barry" LastName="Brown" />
    <Employee FirstName="David" LastName="Kennson" />
    <Employee FirstName="Eric" LastName="Bender" />
    <Employee FirstName="David" LastName="Lonning" />
    <Employee FirstName="Sally" LastName="Smith" />
    <Employee FirstName="Phil" LastName="Wilconkinski" />
  </Location>
  <Location City="Spokane">
    <Employee FirstName="Lisa" LastName="Kendall" />
    <Employee FirstName="Barbara" LastName="O'Neil" />
  </Location>
</JProCo>
```

Figure 2.23 The ORDER BY clause has reorganized and tidied up our XML stream.

Each of the JProCo employees from Boston is listed as a child element below the top-level element <Location> which has a City attribute with a value of “Boston”. We similarly see the Seattle employees nested beneath the <Location> with a City attribute of “Seattle”.

Lab 2.1: XML Auto Mode

Lab Prep: Each lab has one or more Skill Checks. Start with Skill Check 1 and proceed until reaching the Points to Ponder section.

Before beginning this lab, verify that SQL Server 2012 is properly installed and operating. Before running the lab setup script for resetting the database (SQLQueries2012Vol5Chapter1.0-4.2Setup.sql), please make sure to close all query windows within SSMS. An open query window pointing to a database context can lock that database preventing it from updating when the script is executing. A simple way to assure all query windows are closed, is to exit out of SSMS, then open a new instance of SSMS, and lastly run the setup script.

Skill Check 1: Write a query from the Employee table and join it to the Grant table. Your field SELECT list should include the Employee LastName, FirstName, GrantName and Amount. Use the correct FOR XML AUTO option and ORDER BY clause to achieve the following output (Figure 2.24).

Lab2.1_XML_AUTO_...eno\Student (51))   XML_F52E2B61-18A...0805F49916B32.xml ×

Object Explorer

```
<Charity>
  <Employee LastName="Bender" FirstName="Eric">
    <Grant GrantName="Just Mom" Amount="9900.0000" />
  </Employee>
  <Employee LastName="Brown" FirstName="Barry">
    <Grant GrantName="K-Land fund trust" Amount="15750.0000"
  </Employee>
  <Employee LastName="Kennson" FirstName="David">
    <Grant GrantName="BIG 6's Foundation%" Amount="21000.0000
  </Employee>
  <Employee LastName="Lonning" FirstName="David">
    <Grant GrantName="Robert@BigStarBank.com" Amount="18100.0
    <Grant GrantName="92 Purr_Scents %% team" Amount="4750.00
    <Grant GrantName="www.@-Last-U-Can-Help.com" Amount="2500
    <Grant GrantName="Big Giver Tom" Amount="95900.0000" />
  </Employee>
  <Employee LastName="Newton" FirstName="James">
    <Grant GrantName="Mega Mercy" Amount="55000.0000" />
  </Employee>
  <Employee LastName="O'Haire" FirstName="Terry">
    <Grant GrantName="Ben@MoreTechnology.com" Amount="41000.0
```

Figure 2.24 The result produced by Skill Check 1.

Skill Check 2: Write a query from the Location table and join it to the Employee table. Your field SELECT list should include [State], FirstName and LastName. Make sure the results cluster the employees by state. Also make sure each employee within each state is listed alphabetically by last name. Use the FOR XML AUTO option and ORDER BY clause. The XML stream should be well-formed and include the root called <EmpLocReport>. Your result should resemble Figure 2.25.

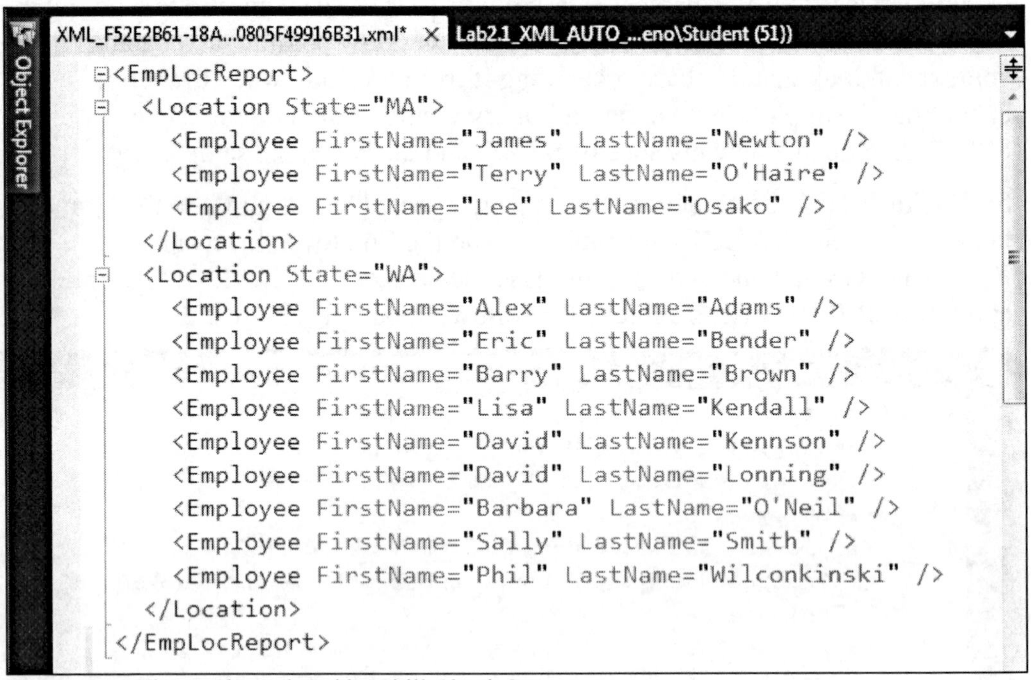

XML_F52E2B61-18A...0805F49916B31.xml* × Lab2.1_XML_AUTO_...eno\Student (51))

Object Explorer

```
<EmpLocReport>
  <Location State="MA">
    <Employee FirstName="James" LastName="Newton" />
    <Employee FirstName="Terry" LastName="O'Haire" />
    <Employee FirstName="Lee" LastName="Osako" />
  </Location>
  <Location State="WA">
    <Employee FirstName="Alex" LastName="Adams" />
    <Employee FirstName="Eric" LastName="Bender" />
    <Employee FirstName="Barry" LastName="Brown" />
    <Employee FirstName="Lisa" LastName="Kendall" />
    <Employee FirstName="David" LastName="Kennson" />
    <Employee FirstName="David" LastName="Lonning" />
    <Employee FirstName="Barbara" LastName="O'Neil" />
    <Employee FirstName="Sally" LastName="Smith" />
    <Employee FirstName="Phil" LastName="Wilconkinski" />
  </Location>
</EmpLocReport>
```

Figure 2.25 The result produced by Skill Check 2.

Points to Ponder - XML Auto Mode

1. The FOR XML clause instructs SQL Server to return data as an XML stream rather than a rowset.
2. Each row in XML Auto is named after the table (or the table alias).
3. Raw does not nest the result of multi-table queries, whereas Auto does.
4. When you use Auto mode with a JOIN query, SQL Server nests the resulting values in the order in which the tables appear in the SELECT list.
5. Auto mode also enables you to specify whether columns are mapped as elements or attributes within the XML stream:
   - If you specify the ELEMENTS option, then your Auto data will appear as elements.
   - If you leave the ELEMENTS option off, then Auto will default to showing your data as attributes.
6. You can use Auto to organize your data into either elements or attributes, but you cannot mix them. Your XML result must contain either all elements or all attributes.

XML Path Mode

The XML Raw and Auto modes are great for displaying data as all attributes or all elements - but not both at once. If you want your XML stream to have some of its data shown in attributes and some shown as elements, then you can use the XML Path mode.

The following Select statement shows us all locations and the employees who work in each location. There are 13 matching records in this inner join between the Location and Employee tables. The Location table is aliased "Loc", and the Employee table is aliased "Emp." Recall that in SQL the AS keyword is recommended when aliasing tables, but it is optional (Figure 2.26).

```
SELECT *
FROM location AS loc INNER JOIN employee AS emp
ON loc.LocationID = emp.LocationID
```

Results | Messages

	LocationID	Street	City	state	EmpID	LastName	FirstName	HireDate
1	1	111 First ST	Seattle	WA	1	Adams	Alex	2001-01
2	1	111 First ST	Seattle	WA	2	Brown	Barry	2002-08
3	2	222 Second AVE	Boston	MA	3	Osako	Lee	1999-09
4	1	111 First ST	Seattle	WA	4	Kennson	David	1996-03
5	1	111 First ST	Seattle	WA	5	Bender	Eric	2007-05
6	4	444 Ruby ST	Spokane	WA	6	Kendall	Lisa	2001-11

Query executed successfully. | RENO (11.0 RTM) | Reno\Student (51) | JProCo | 00:00:00 | 12 rows

Figure 2.26 An inner join query between the Location and Employee tables.

Let's stream this query in an XML mode, called Path.

```
SELECT *
FROM location AS loc INNER JOIN employee AS emp
ON loc.LocationID = emp.LocationID
FOR XML PATH
```

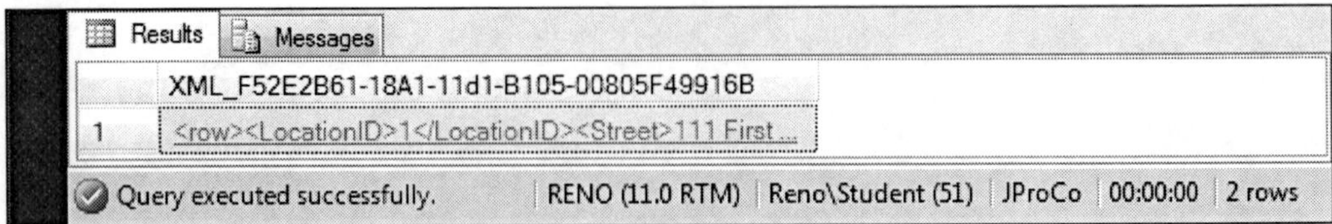

Figure 2.27 We will stream our query in the XML Path mode.

Much like Raw and Auto, each top-level element has a tag named "row" and by default there is no <root> element. However, unlike the previous modes we've seen, the Path mode defaults to putting all its data in elements.

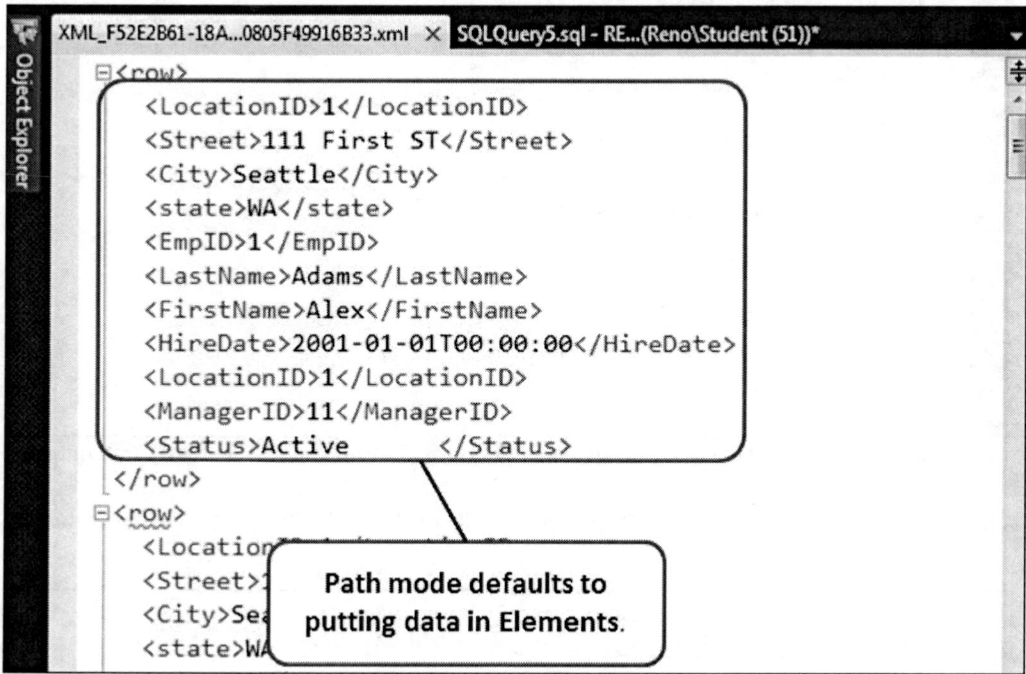

Figure 2.28 Our inner join query streamed as an XML Path output.

Now we'll itemize the fields in our query.

```
SELECT City, FirstName, LastName
FROM location AS loc INNER JOIN employee AS emp
ON loc.LocationID = emp.LocationID
FOR XML PATH
```

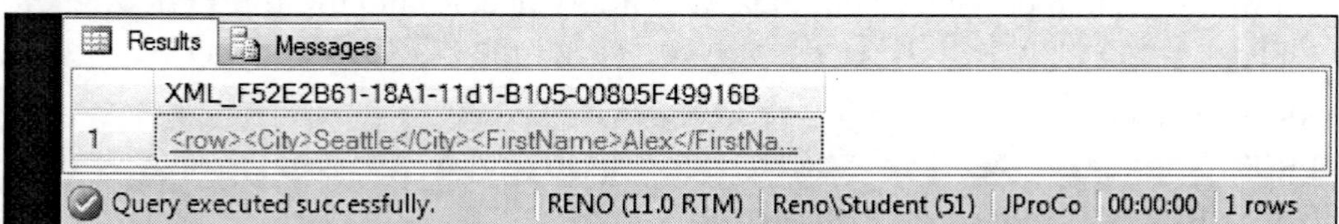

Figure 2.29 We've itemized our field list and will look at the revised XML Path stream.

The result appears much the same. We see "row" as the default name of the opening and closing tags. We also see nested within each "row", elements for each of the three fields we itemized in our query (City, FirstName, LastName).

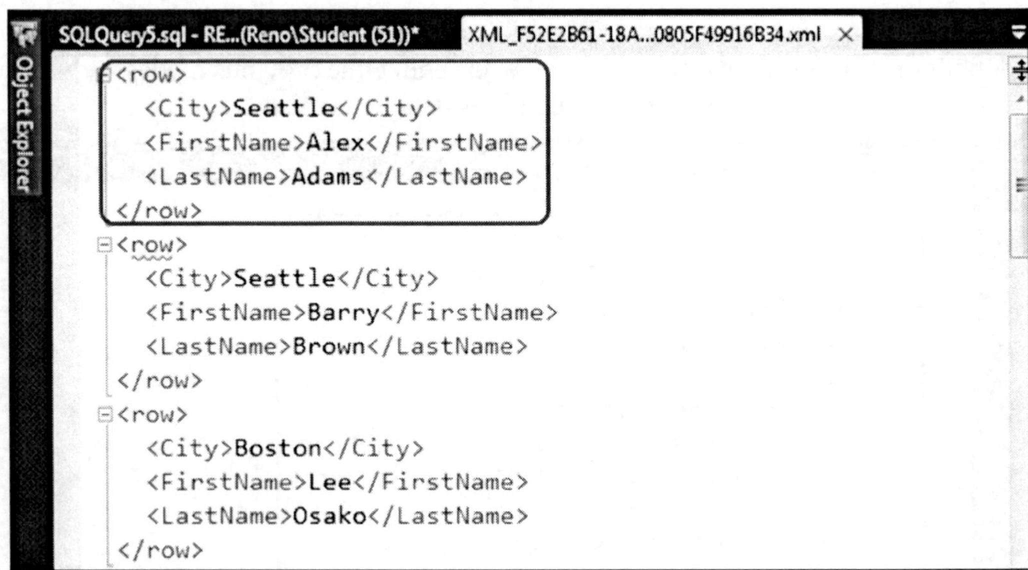

Figure 2.30 Our itemized query (code appears in Figure 2.29) streamed as an XML Path output.

Our next goal is to modify our SQL query, so that our XML result will include an <Employees> root tag.

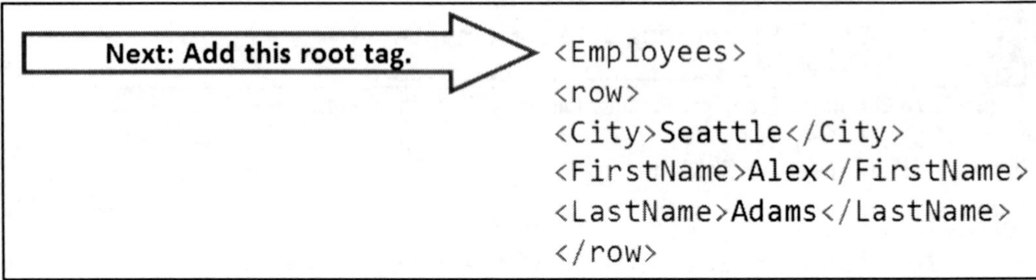

Figure 2.31 Our next goal is to add an <Employees> root tag to our XML Path output.

As we've seen in previous examples, we simply need to modify our FOR XML Path clause to include ROOT('Employees') after the FOR XML PATH.

```
SELECT City, FirstName, LastName
FROM location AS loc INNER JOIN employee AS emp
ON loc.LocationID = emp.LocationID
FOR XML PATH, ROOT('Employees')
```

Figure 2.32 Our code now includes the root element <Employees>.

In the result, we see that we now have our root, which is called "<Employees>" (Figure 2.33).

```
XML_F52E2B61-18A...0805F49916B35.xml   SQLQuery5.sql - RE...(Reno\Student (51))*
<Employees>
  <row>
    <City>Seattle</City>
    <FirstName>Alex</FirstName>
    <LastName>Adams</LastName>
  </row>
  <row>
    <City>Seattle</City>
    <FirstName>Barry</FirstName>
    <LastName>Brown</LastName>
  </row>
  <row>
    <City>Boston</City>
    <FirstName>Lee</FirstName>
    <LastName>Osako</LastName>
  </row>
```

Figure 2.33 The root element <Employees> is now visible in our XML Path stream.

Let's change our current stream (code in Figure 2.32, output shown in Figure 2.33) to have each top-level element tagged as <Employee> instead of <row>.

```
SELECT City, FirstName, LastName
FROM location AS loc INNER JOIN employee AS emp
ON loc.LocationID = emp.LocationID
FOR XML PATH('Employee'), ROOT('Employees')
```

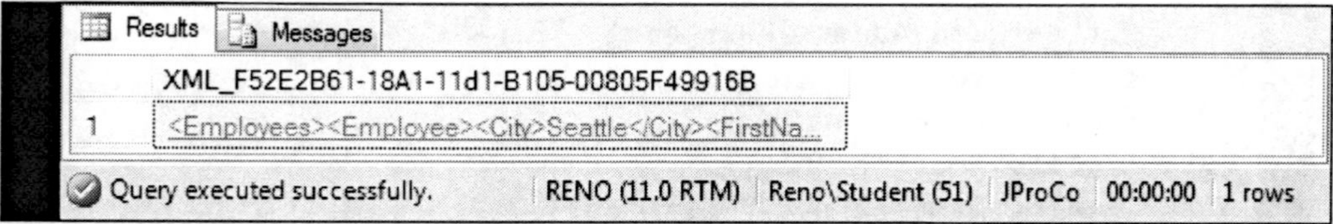

Figure 2.34 Our code will tag each top-level element as <Employee> instead of <row>.

Our stream is looking much more readable and organized. Each top-level element is now called <Employee> instead of <row> (Figure 2.35).

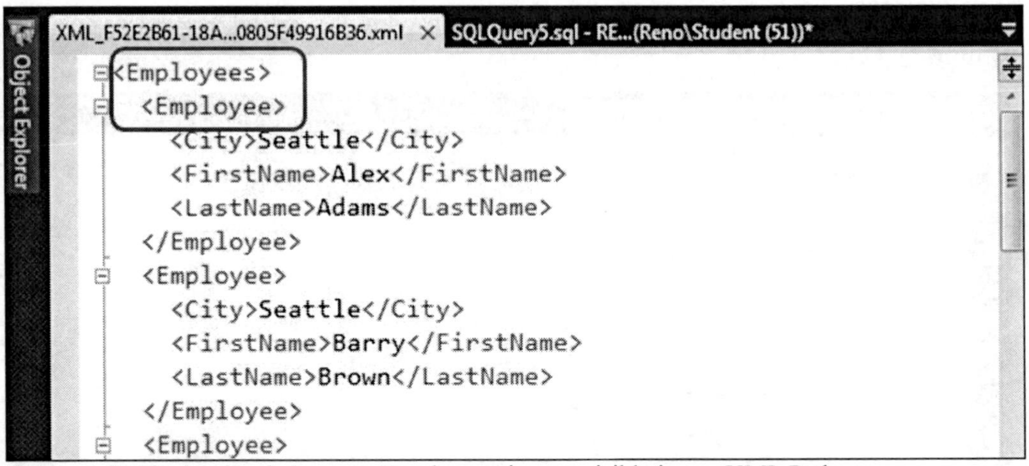

```
XML_F52E2B61-18A...0805F49916B36.xml   SQLQuery5.sql - RE...(Reno\Student (51))*
<Employees>
  <Employee>
    <City>Seattle</City>
    <FirstName>Alex</FirstName>
    <LastName>Adams</LastName>
  </Employee>
  <Employee>
    <City>Seattle</City>
    <FirstName>Barry</FirstName>
    <LastName>Brown</LastName>
  </Employee>
  <Employee>
```

Figure 2.35 The top-level element <Employee> is now visible in our XML Path stream.

Custom Attributes

If you are using an XML Path stream, then by default all of the values will be shown as elements. However, you can pick one or more of your elements to instead be shown as an attribute(s). Use the [@Fieldname] syntax to do this.

Our next goal is to move City inside the <Employee> tag as an attribute. The [@Fieldname] construct will help us accomplish this.

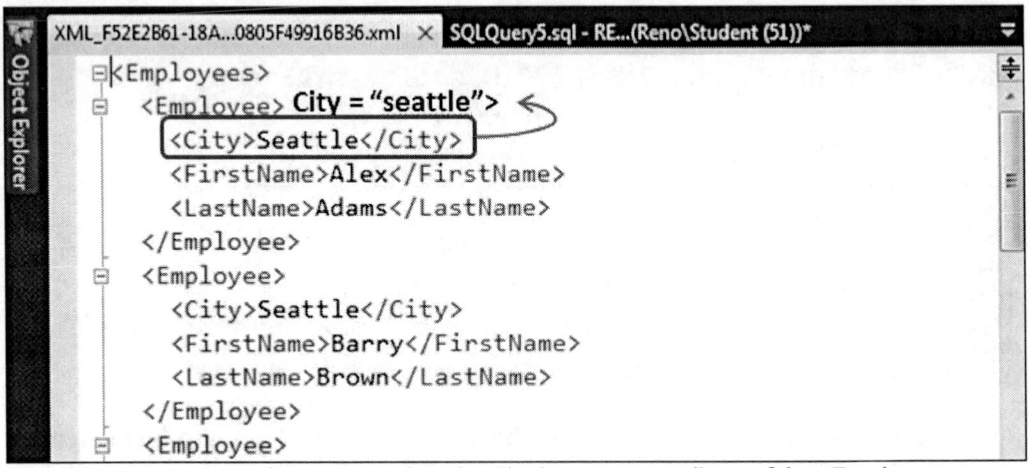

```
XML_F52E2B61-18A...0805F49916B36.xml   SQLQuery5.sql - RE...(Reno\Student (51))*
<Employees>
  <Employee City = "seattle">
    <City>Seattle</City>
    <FirstName>Alex</FirstName>
    <LastName>Adams</LastName>
  </Employee>
  <Employee>
    <City>Seattle</City>
    <FirstName>Barry</FirstName>
    <LastName>Brown</LastName>
  </Employee>
  <Employee>
```

Figure 2.36 A mockup of our next goal: make City become an attribute of the <Employee> tag.

To make our code reflect this change, all we need to do is alias the City field as @City (For illustrative purposes, we will alias the attribute as "CityName" instead of "City"). Just as when we have previously aliased fields and tables in our SQL queries, with our XML queries we also have the freedom to alias the field City using any name we choose.) One easy way to think of this code syntax is to remember that @ (a.k.a., the "at" sign) goes with "ATtributes".

```
SELECT City AS [@CityName], FirstName, LastName
FROM location AS loc INNER JOIN employee AS emp
ON loc.LocationID = emp.LocationID
FOR XML PATH('Employee'), ROOT('Employees')
```

Results | Messages

	XML_F52E2B61-18A1-11d1-B105-00805F49916B
1	<Employees><Employee CityName="Seattle"><FirstNam...

Query executed successfully. | RENO (11.0 RTM) | Reno\Student (51) | JProCo | 00:00:00 | 1 rows

Figure 2.37 We have aliased the City field to become an attribute of the top-level element.

City is now an attribute of <Employee>, instead of a separate element.

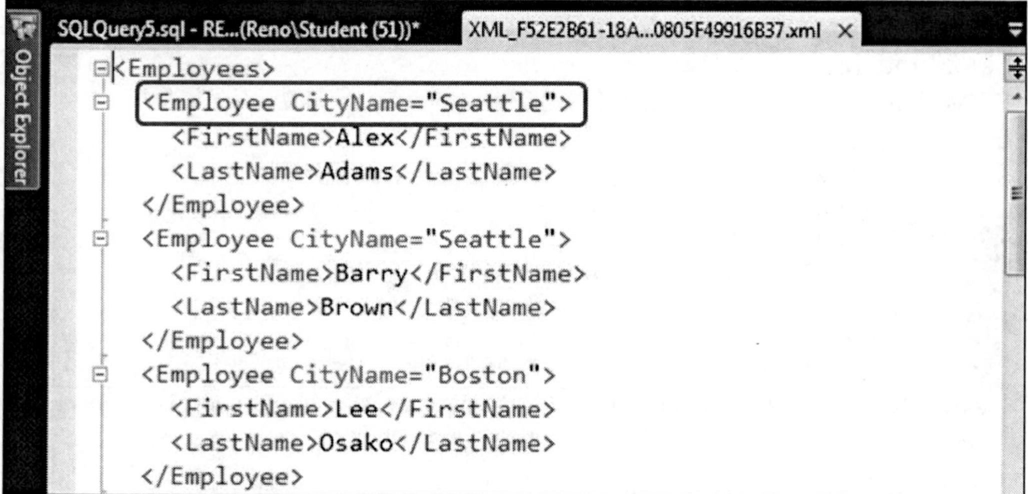

Figure 2.38 Our XML Path output shows CityName as an attribute of the Employee element.

Custom Elements

The element's name does not need to be named after the field from the table. You can set it to anything you want by specifying a field alias.

For our next goal, we want the <FirstName> element to instead be called <First> and the <LastName> element to instead be called <Last>. In other words, we will rename (or alias) these two XML elements.

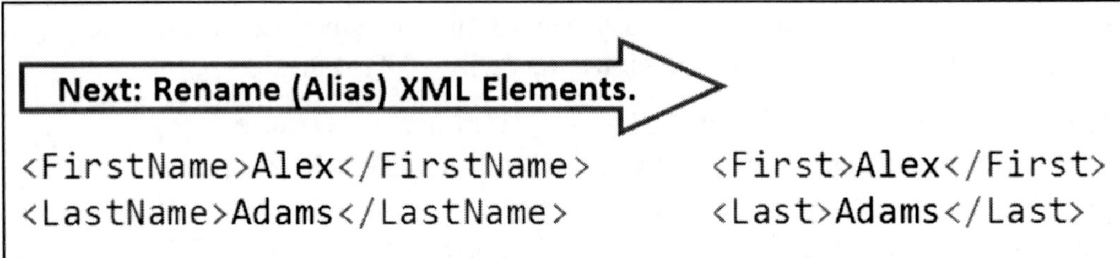

Figure 2.39 A mockup of our next goal: rename two elements (FirstName and LastName).

When we changed the <City> element into the attribute CityName, recall we needed to prefix the alias with the @ sign (our mnemonic device reminds us we need an "at" sign when turning an element into an "ATtribute"). However, the XML Path mode defaults to representing data as elements (as shown earlier in Figure 2.28). So all we need to do here is alias the fields using the AS [ElementName] syntax.

```
SELECT City AS [@CityName], FirstName AS [First],
LastName AS [Last]
FROM location AS loc INNER JOIN employee AS emp
ON loc.LocationID = emp.LocationID
FOR XML PATH('Employee'), ROOT('Employees')
```

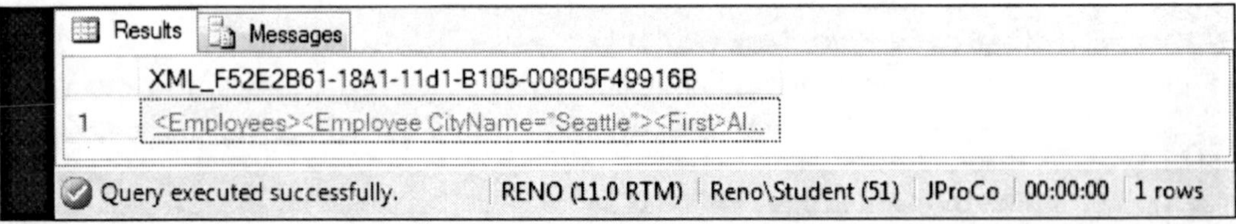

Figure 2.40 We have aliased (renamed) the FirstName and LastName elements. The keyword AS is optional but is highly recommended for your code's readability.

Our result (Figure 2.41) is similar to our previous stream (shown in Figure 2.38). Data previously shown as attributes are still attributes, and all the elements are still elements. The only change is that the original element names (FirstName and LastName) have changed (To First and Last, respectively).

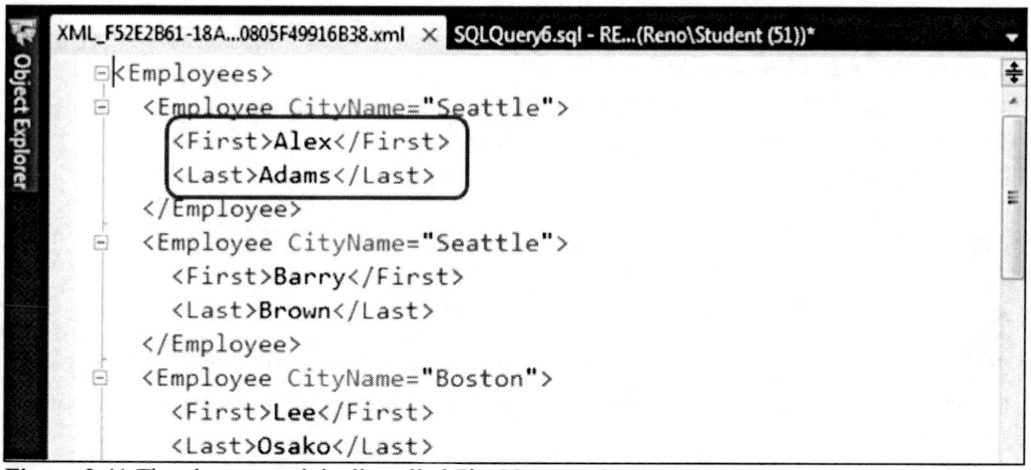

XML_F52E2B61-18A...0805F49916B38.xml × SQLQuery6.sql - RE...(Reno\Student (51))*

```
<Employees>
  <Employee CityName="Seattle">
    <First>Alex</First>
    <Last>Adams</Last>
  </Employee>
  <Employee CityName="Seattle">
    <First>Barry</First>
    <Last>Brown</Last>
  </Employee>
  <Employee CityName="Boston">
    <First>Lee</First>
    <Last>Osako</Last>
```

Figure 2.41 The elements originally called FirstName and LastName are now First and Last.

Custom Level and Nesting

The Path mode also nests elements within other elements. The nesting order is based on the order of fields in your SELECT list.

Our final Path example will introduce a custom element <Name> just beneath the top-level element <Employee>. We will nest this element above the elements <First> and <Last>.

```
<Employees>
<Employee CityName="Seattle">
<Name>
<First>Alex</First>
<Last>Adams</Last>
</Name>
</Employees>
```

Figure 2.42 A mockup of our next goal: add and nest the custom element <Name>.

Specify a custom level by adding a / (forward slash) before each element that you want nested immediately below the new level. The name of the custom level precedes the forward slash.

```
SELECT City AS [@CityName],FirstName AS [Name/First],
LastName AS [Name/Last]
FROM location AS loc INNER JOIN employee AS emp
ON loc.LocationID = emp.LocationID
FOR XML PATH('Employee'), ROOT('Employees')
```

Figure 2.43 We have added a custom level "Name" nested just above the child-level elements, <First> and <Last>.

Our goal has been achieved. A new child-level element <Name> appears beneath <Employee> and includes our aliased elements, <First> and <Last>.

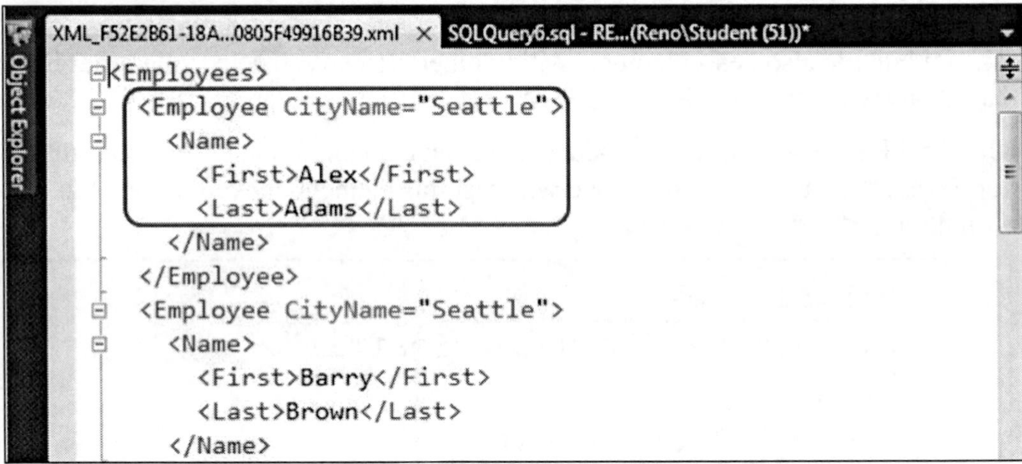

Figure 2.44 Our final Path stream includes a custom level nested beneath the top-level element and above our custom elements, <First> and <Last>.

Lab 2.2: XML Path Mode

Lab Prep: Each lab has one or more Skill Checks. Start with Skill Check 1 and proceed until reaching the Points to Ponder section.

Before beginning this lab, verify that SQL Server 2012 is properly installed and operating. Before running the lab setup script for resetting the database (SQLQueries2012Vol5Chapter1.0-4.2Setup.sql), please make sure to close all query windows within SSMS. An open query window pointing to a database context can lock that database preventing it from updating when the script is executing. A simple way to assure all query windows are closed, is to exit out of SSMS, then open a new instance of SSMS, and lastly run the setup script.

Skill Check 1: Create an XML stream by selecting the EmpID, FirstName and LastName fields from the Employee table. Call your root <HR> and your top-level element <Employee>. The EmpID field and its value should be an attribute of the <Employee> element. The tags should be <FName> for the FirstName field and <LName> for LastName. Your result will match Figure 2.45.

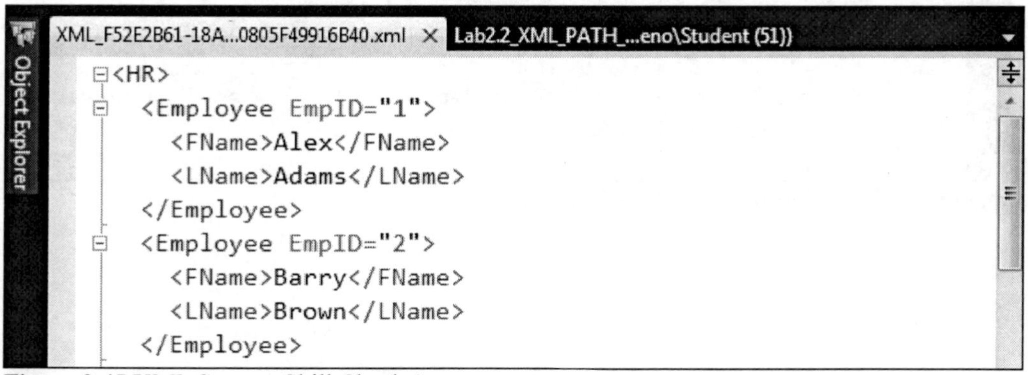

XML_F52E2B61-18A...0805F49916B40.xml × Lab2.2_XML_PATH_...eno\Student (51))

```
<HR>
  <Employee EmpID="1">
    <FName>Alex</FName>
    <LName>Adams</LName>
  </Employee>
  <Employee EmpID="2">
    <FName>Barry</FName>
    <LName>Brown</LName>
  </Employee>
```

Figure 2.45 XML Stream, Skill Check 1.

Skill Check 2: Create an XML stream by selecting the GrantID, GrantName and Amount fields from the [Grant] table. Make sure your root is called <Charity> and your top-level element is called <Grants>. The GrantID and GrantName fields and their values should be attributes of the Grants element. The value of the Amount field should be an element under the <Grants> element. When done, your result should resemble the Figure 2.46.

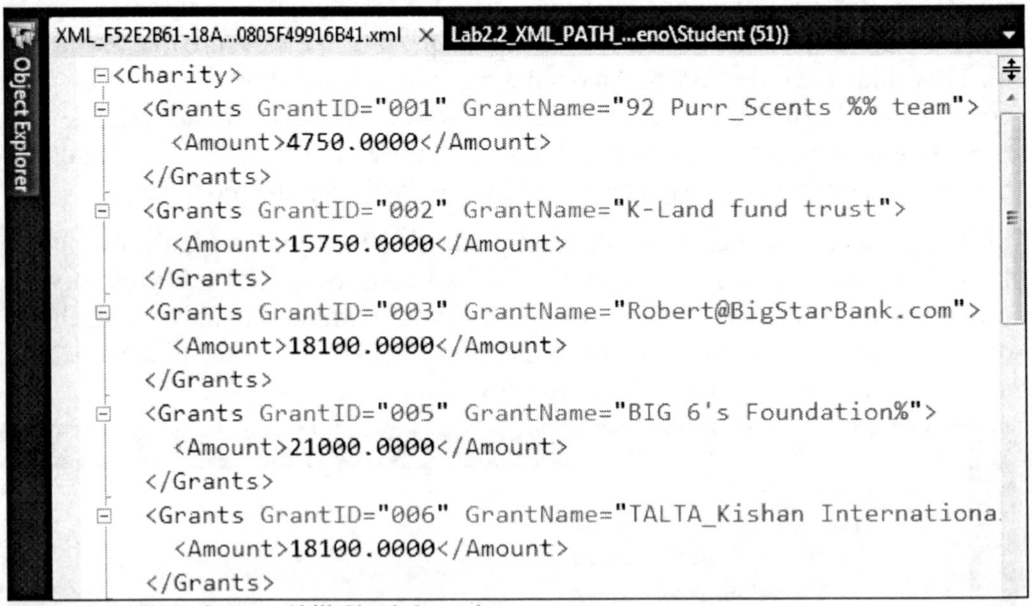

```
XML_F52E2B61-18A...0805F49916B41.xml   Lab2.2_XML_PATH_...eno\Student (51))
<Charity>
  <Grants GrantID="001" GrantName="92 Purr_Scents %% team">
    <Amount>4750.0000</Amount>
  </Grants>
  <Grants GrantID="002" GrantName="K-Land fund trust">
    <Amount>15750.0000</Amount>
  </Grants>
  <Grants GrantID="003" GrantName="Robert@BigStarBank.com">
    <Amount>18100.0000</Amount>
  </Grants>
  <Grants GrantID="005" GrantName="BIG 6's Foundation%">
    <Amount>21000.0000</Amount>
  </Grants>
  <Grants GrantID="006" GrantName="TALTA_Kishan Internationa
    <Amount>18100.0000</Amount>
  </Grants>
```

Figure 2.46 XML Stream, Skill Check 2 result.

Skill Check 3: Create an XML stream using the CurrentProducts table's fields ProductID, ProductName, Category and RetailPrice. Call your root <Products> and your top-level element <Product>. The ProductID and Price fields' values should be inside the <Product> element as two attributes. The value for the ProductName field should be an element under the <Product> element and named PName. The value for the ProductCategory field should be an element under the <Product> element and named <PCat>. When you're done, your result will resemble this Figure 2.47.

XML_F52E2B61-18A...0805F49916B42.xml × Lab2.2_XML_PATH_...eno\Student (51))

Object Explorer

```
<Products>
  <Product ID="1" Price="61.4830">
    <PName>Underwater Tour 1 Day West Coast</PName>
    <PCat>No-Stay</PCat>
  </Product>
  <Product ID="2" Price="110.6694">
    <PName>Underwater Tour 2 Days West Coast</PName>
    <PCat>Overnight-Stay</PCat>
  </Product>
  <Product ID="3" Price="184.4490">
    <PName>Underwater Tour 3 Days West Coast</PName>
    <PCat>Medium-Stay</PCat>
  </Product>
  <Product ID="4" Price="245.9320">
    <PName>Underwater Tour 5 Days West Coast</PName>
    <PCat>Medium-Stay</PCat>
  </Product>
```

Figure 2.47 XML Stream, Skill Check 3 result.

Skill Check 4: Create an XML stream by selecting the EmpID, ManagerID, FirstName and LastName fields from the Employee table. The root should be called <JProCo> and the top-level element called <Employee>. Set the EmpID as an attribute called ID in the top-level element. The ManagerID should appear below the top-level element and be called BossID. FirstName and LastName should appear under a custom element named <Name>. Your result will resemble Figure 2.48.

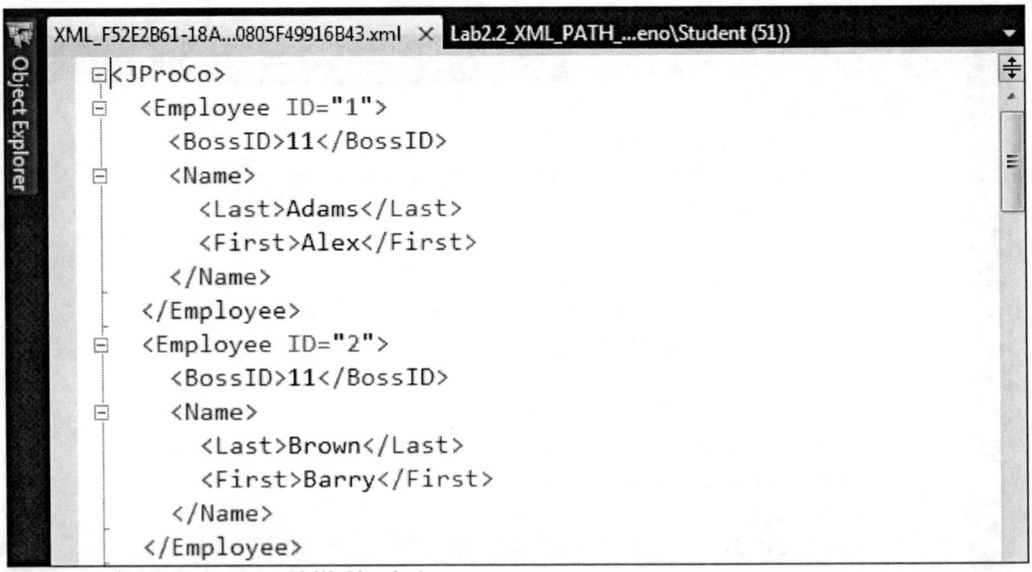

XML_F52E2B61-18A...0805F49916B43.xml × Lab2.2_XML_PATH_...eno\Student (51))

Object Explorer

```
<JProCo>
  <Employee ID="1">
    <BossID>11</BossID>
    <Name>
      <Last>Adams</Last>
      <First>Alex</First>
    </Name>
  </Employee>
  <Employee ID="2">
    <BossID>11</BossID>
    <Name>
      <Last>Brown</Last>
      <First>Barry</First>
    </Name>
  </Employee>
```

Figure 2.48 XML Stream, Skill Check 4.

Answer Code: The T-SQL code to this lab can be found in the downloadable files in a file named Lab2.2_XML_Path_Mode.sql.

Points to Ponder - XML Path Mode

1. Raw and Auto modes both can use the ELEMENTS option. If ELEMENTS is not used, then both Raw and Auto will display your XML stream in attributes.
2. Path mode queries can produce customized XML layouts of mixed attributes and elements which can't be achieved by AUTO or RAW.
3. Path mode queries recognize a syntax called XPath to easily customize the layout.
4. Using @ ("at" symbol) at the beginning of your XPath statement tells SQL to make this data part of an attribute.
5. Leaving off @ ("at" symbol) means you want the data in an element.
6. The XPath command allows syntax (like EmployeeID "@EmpID", FirstName "EmpName/First") to put data in both elements and attributes.
7. In XPath you can delimit the field names with ' ' or [ ].
8. The FOR XML Path clause supports the addition of a root element by appending a ROOT clause at the end of your statement.
9. If you don't specify the ROOT keyword then there won't be a root tag set.
10. If you don't specify a top-level element name after the Path clause, then each record's element will have the <row> tag.

XML Nameless Fields

A nameless field belongs to no tag in your XML file. This can be useful for manipulating your XML stream for readability. In the examples we will see, an element tag will be rendered "nameless" by using a wildcard to alias the tag in our XML.

Begin with this simple query which returns two fields from all 14 records of the Employee table.

```
SELECT EmpID, FirstName
FROM Employee
```

Results | Messages

	EmpID	FirstName
1	1	Alex
2	2	Barry
3	3	Lee
4	4	David
5	5	Eric
6	6	Lisa

Query executed successfully. | RENO (11.0 RTM) | Reno\Student (51) | JProCo | 00:00:00 | 13 rows

Figure 2.49 Begin with this query from the Employee table.

```
SELECT EmpID, FirstName
FROM Employee
FOR XML PATH
```

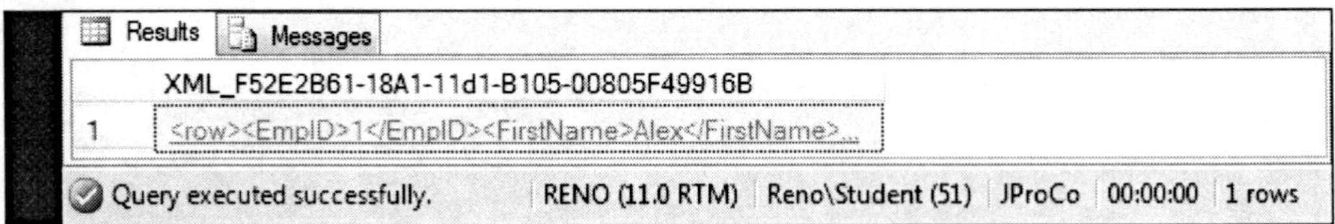

Figure 2.50 Stream this query as an XML Path output.

Since we know XML Path doesn't include a root by default, and we haven't specified a root, this is not well-formed XML.

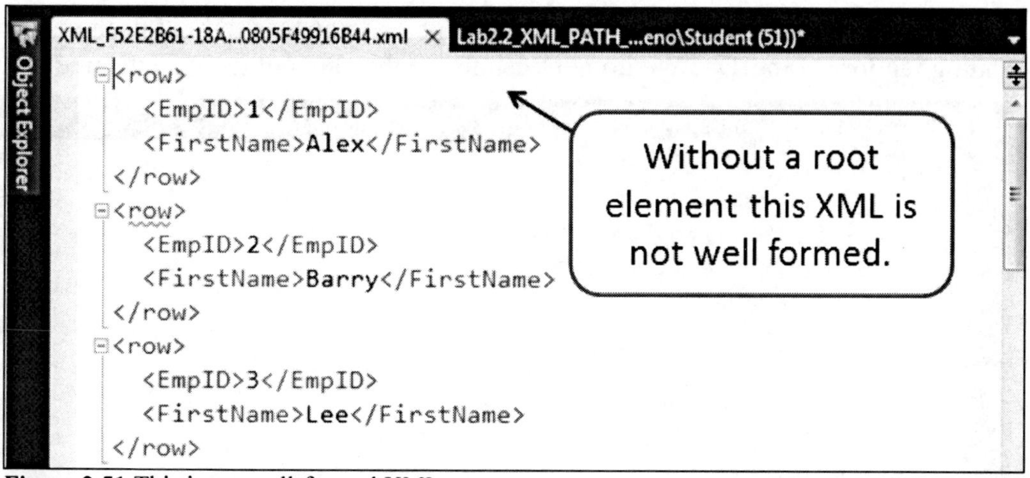

```
<row>
  <EmpID>1</EmpID>
  <FirstName>Alex</FirstName>
</row>
<row>
  <EmpID>2</EmpID>
  <FirstName>Barry</FirstName>
</row>
<row>
  <EmpID>3</EmpID>
  <FirstName>Lee</FirstName>
</row>
```


Figure 2.51 This is not well-formed XML.

Add a root and name each top-level element <Employee>.

```
SELECT EmpID, FirstName
FROM Employee
FOR XML PATH('Employee'), ROOT
```

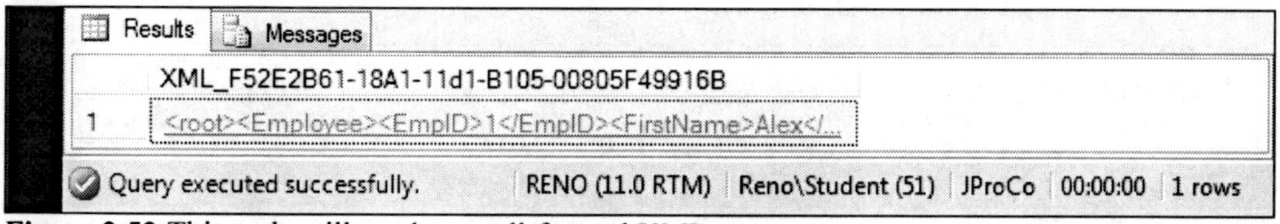

Figure 2.52 This code will produce well-formed XML.

Our code has produced a well-formed XML document.

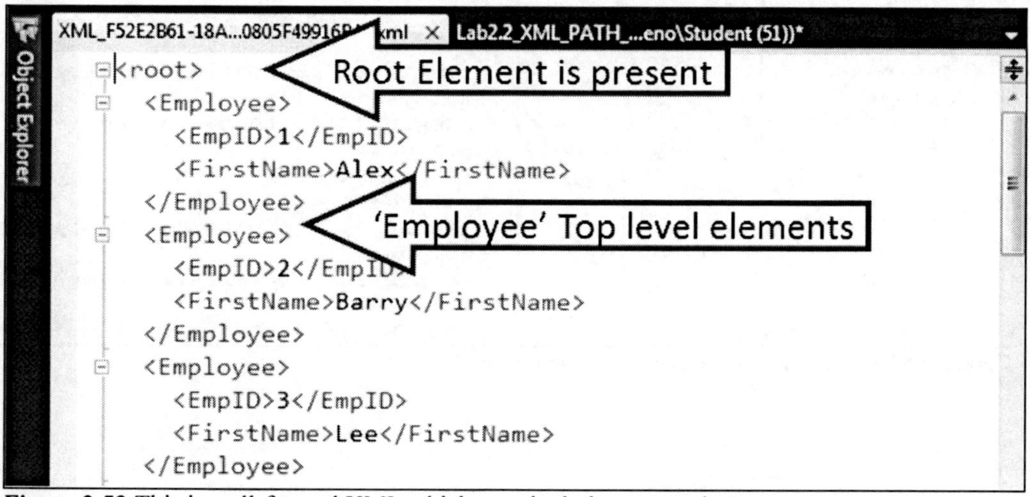

```
<root>
  <Employee>
    <EmpID>1</EmpID>
    <FirstName>Alex</FirstName>
  </Employee>
  <Employee>
    <EmpID>2</EmpID>
    <FirstName>Barry</FirstName>
  </Employee>
  <Employee>
    <EmpID>3</EmpID>
    <FirstName>Lee</FirstName>
  </Employee>
```


Figure 2.53 This is well-formed XML which now includes a root element.

Our goal will be to move each employee's name up to appear right after the ending tag for </EmpID>. We do not wish to see the element tag <FirstName>.

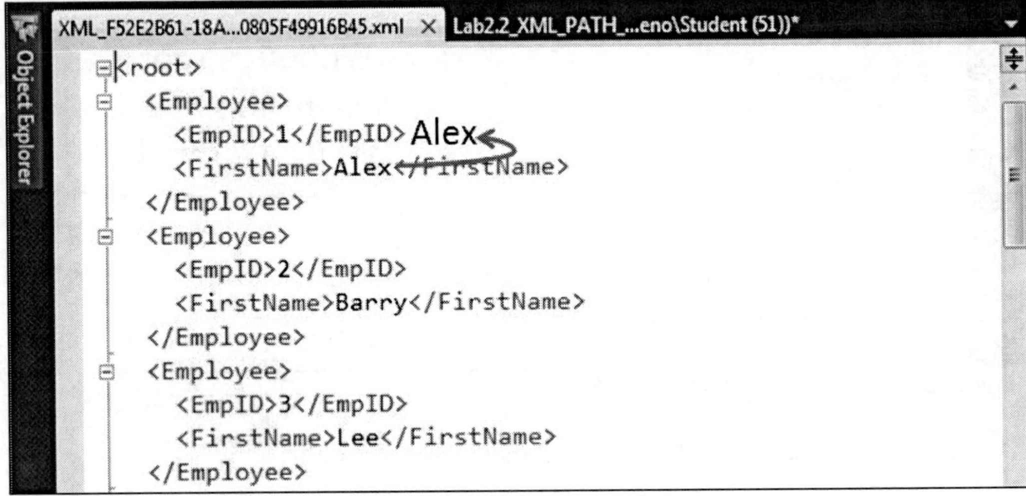

Figure 2.54 The mockup of our next goal.

If we use a wildcard to accomplish this goal, then our XML stream will appear just like the right hand panel shown here.

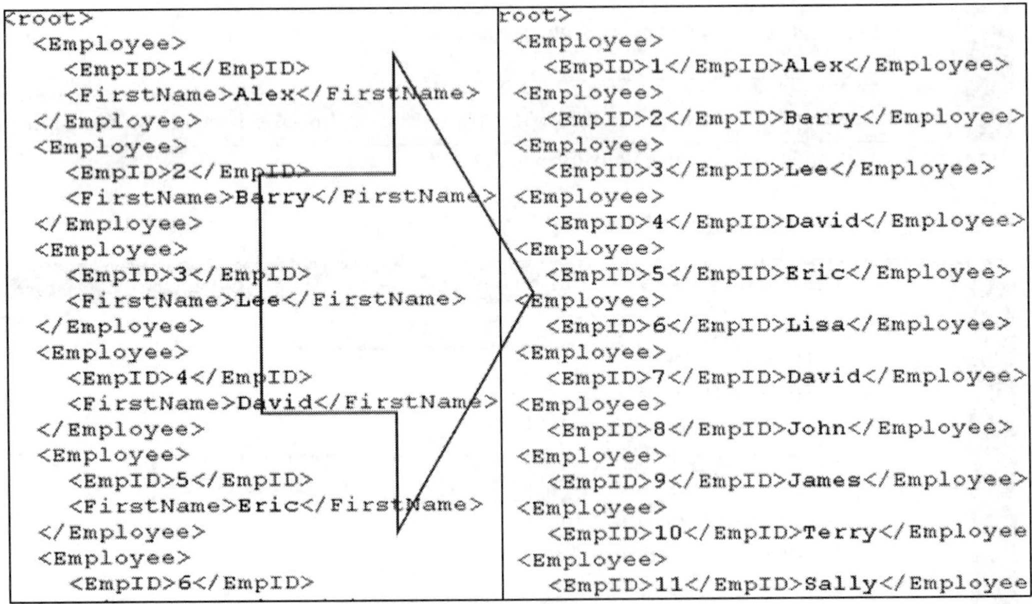

Figure 2.55 A wildcard will help accomplish our goal.

```
SELECT EmpID, FirstName AS [*]
FROM Employee
FOR XML PATH('Employee'), ROOT
```

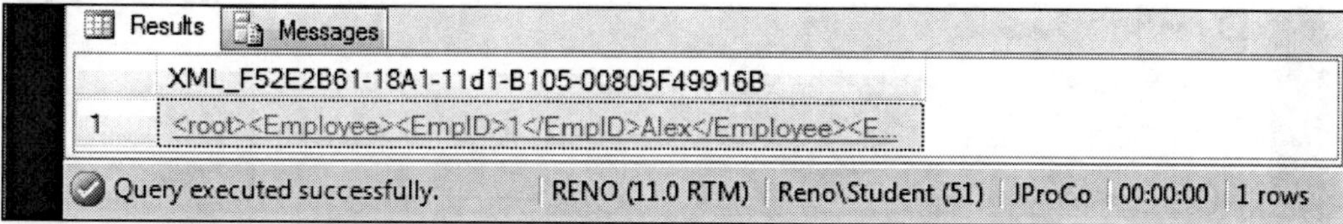

Figure 2.56 The revised code, including the wildcard.

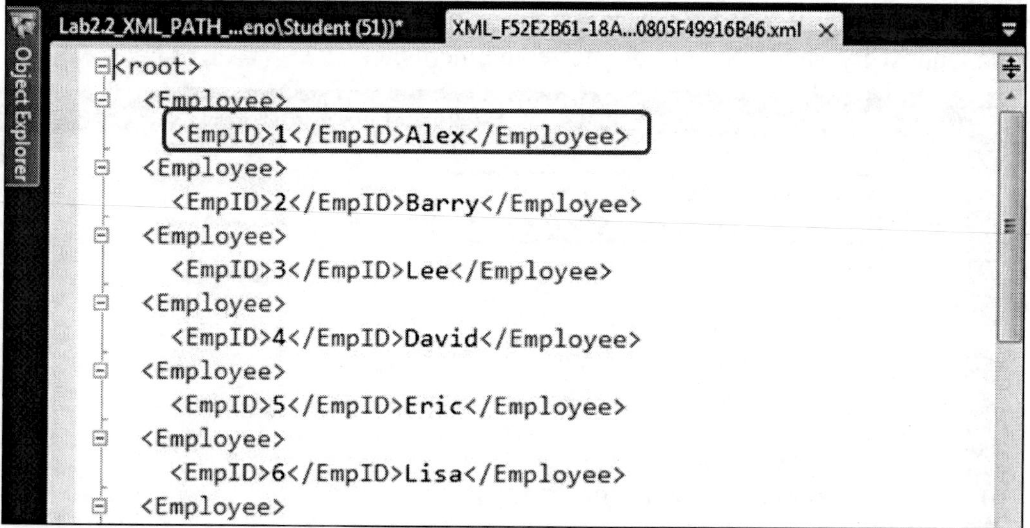

Figure 2.57 Our XML Path query, including the wildcard, has accomplished our desired output.

XML Nameless Fields recap

Let's see that step again, this time with two fields from the Location table.

```
SELECT city, Street
FROM Location
```

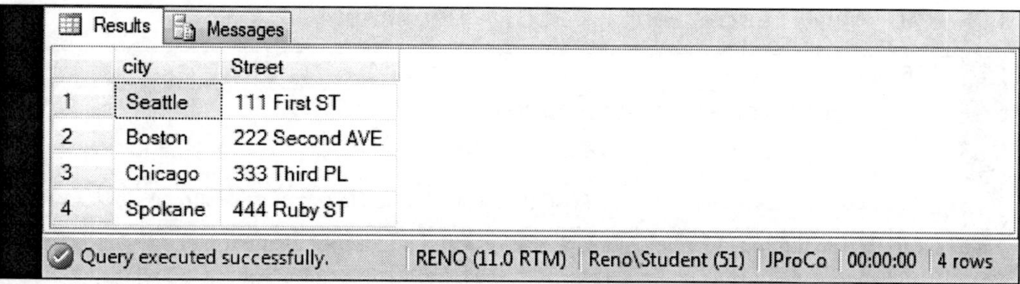

	city	Street
1	Seattle	111 First ST
2	Boston	222 Second AVE
3	Chicago	333 Third PL
4	Spokane	444 Ruby ST

Figure 2.58 Begin with this query from the Location table.

```sql
SELECT city, Street
FROM Location
FOR XML PATH
```

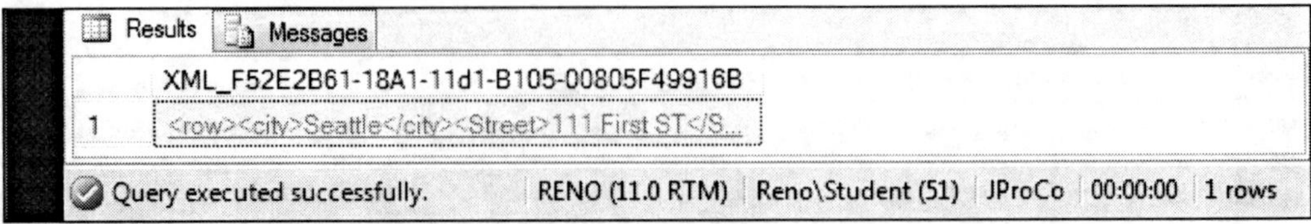

Figure 2.59 Stream the query as an XML Path output.

Here is our output thus far. There is no root, each record has the default <row> tag, and <City> and <Street> are nested elements.

```xml
<row>
  <city>Seattle</city>
  <Street>111 First ST</Street>
</row>
<row>
  <city>Boston</city>
  <Street>222 Second AVE</Street>
</row>
<row>
  <city>Chicago</city>
  <Street>333 Third PL</Street>
</row>
<row>
```

Figure 2.60 The preliminary output produced by our query.

We will name our top-level element <Location> and add a root element named <Geography>.

```sql
SELECT city, Street
FROM Location
FOR XML PATH('Location'), ROOT('Geography')
```

```
XML_F52E2B61-18A1-11d1-B105-00805F49916B
1  <Geography><Location><city>Seattle</city><Street>...
```

Figure 2.61 Name the top- level element <Location> and add a root element named <Geography>.

```
XML_F52E2B61-18A...0805F49916B49.xml  SQLQuery8.sql - RE...(Reno\Student (51))*
<Geography>
  <Location>
    <city>Seattle</city>
    <Street>111 First ST</Street>
  </Location>
  <Location>
    <city>Boston</city>
    <Street>222 Second AVE</Street>
  </Location>
  <Location>
    <city>Chicago</city>
    <Street>333 Third PL</Street>
  </Location>
  <Location>
    <city>Spokane</city>
```

Figure 2.62 We see our <Geography> root element and our <Location> top-level element.

Similar to our previous example, our next goal will move the second element <Street> up and have it appear next to the first element, <city>.

```
XML_F52E2B61-18A...0805F49916B49.xml  SQLQuery8.sql - RE...(Reno\Student (51))*
<Geography>
  <Location>
    <city>Seattle</city> 111 First ST
    <Street>111 First ST</Street>
  </Location>
  <Location>
    <city>Boston</city>
```

Figure 2.63 The mockup of our next goal.

As we saw previously, the use of an asterisk wildcard [*] will help accomplish our goal.

```
SELECT city, Street AS [*]
FROM Location
FOR XML PATH('Location'), ROOT('Geography')
```

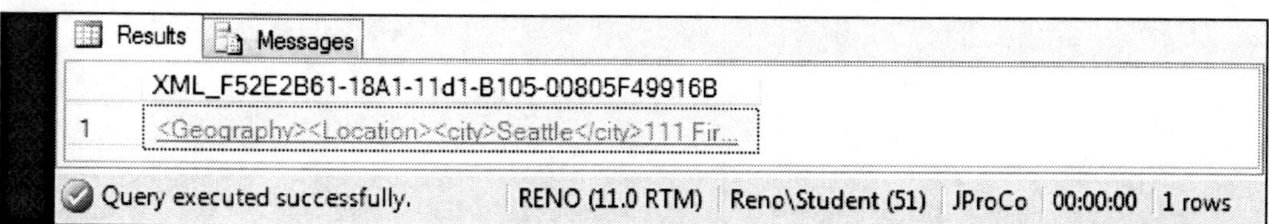
	XML_F52E2B61-18A1-11d1-B105-00805F49916B
1	<Geography><Location><city>Seattle</city>111 Fir...

Figure 2.64 Our revised code, including the wildcard.

Since the wildcard character makes the field "nameless" in the XML stream, the element tag <Street> will not appear in our output.(Figure 2.65)

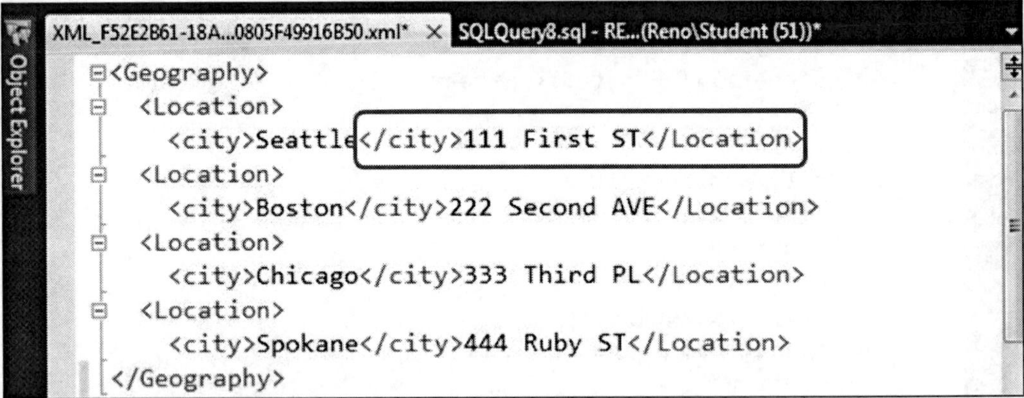

Figure 2.65 The "nameless" Street field value is now to the right of the <city> element.

Lab 2.3: XML Nameless Fields

Lab Prep: Each lab has one or more Skill Checks. Start with Skill Check 1 and proceed until reaching the Points to Ponder section.

Before beginning this lab, verify that SQL Server 2012 is properly installed and operating. Before running the lab setup script for resetting the database (SQLQueries2012Vol5Chapter1.0-4.2Setup.sql), please make sure to close all query windows within SSMS. An open query window pointing to a database context can lock that database preventing it from updating when the script is executing. A simple way to assure all query windows are closed, is to exit out of SSMS, then open a new instance of SSMS, and lastly run the setup script.

Skill Check 1: Write a query that shows the CustomerID and CustomerType fields from the Customer Table. Turn this query into an XML Path stream. Name the root <SalesData> and the top-level element <Cust>. The CustomerID field should be an element. The CustomerType field should be nameless and be placed directly after the ending <CustomerID> tag.

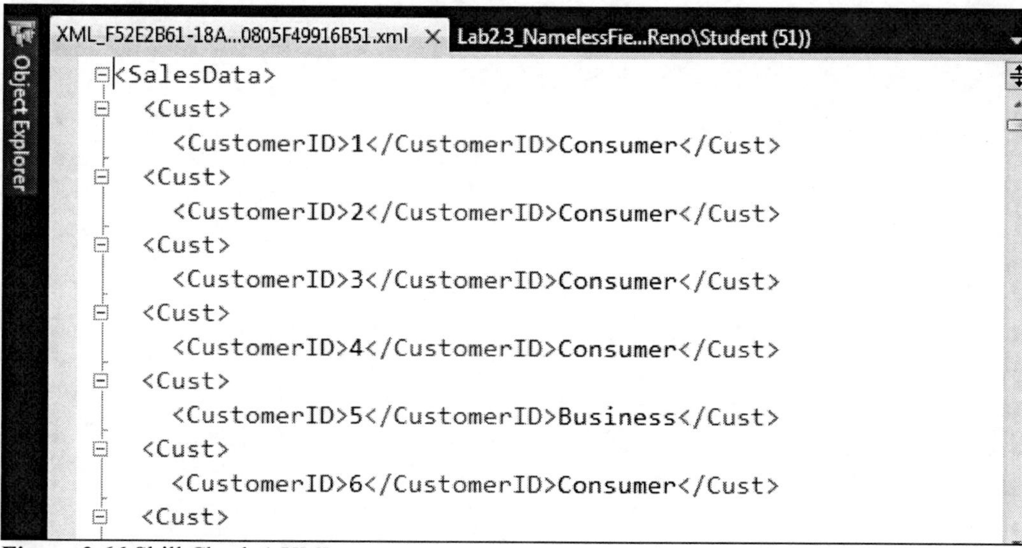
XML_F52E2B61-18A...0805F49916B51.xml
Lab2.3_NamelessFie...Reno\Student (51))
Object Explorer
<SalesData>
<Cust>
<CustomerID>1</CustomerID>Consumer</Cust>
<Cust>
<CustomerID>2</CustomerID>Consumer</Cust>
<Cust>
<CustomerID>3</CustomerID>Consumer</Cust>
<Cust>
<CustomerID>4</CustomerID>Consumer</Cust>
<Cust>
<CustomerID>5</CustomerID>Business</Cust>
<Cust>
<CustomerID>6</CustomerID>Consumer</Cust>
<Cust>

Figure 2.66 Skill Check 1 XML stream.

Skill Check 2: Write a query that shows the ProductName and RetailPrice fields from the CurrentProducts Table. Turn this query into an XML Path stream. Name the root ProductFeed and the top-level element <Product>. The RetailPrice field should be named Price and should appear as an attribute of the top-level element. The ProductName field should be nameless.

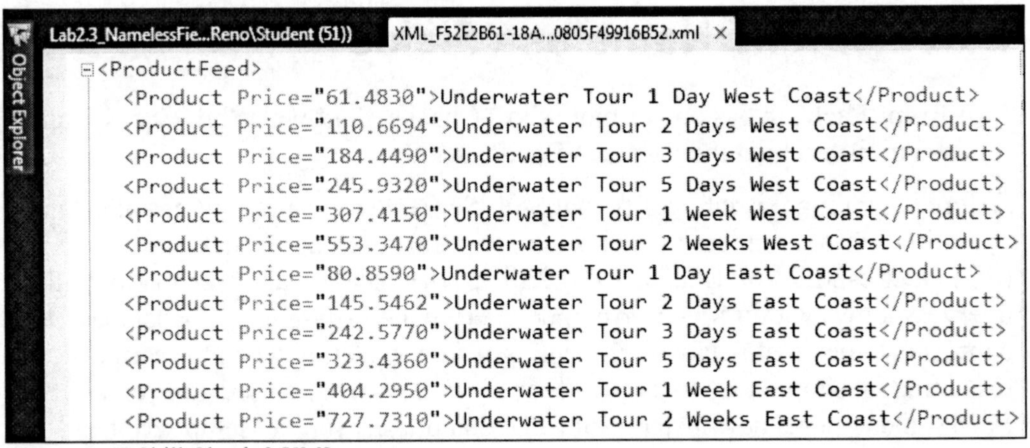

Lab2.3_NamelessFie...Reno\Student (51)) XML_F52E2B61-18A...0805F49916B52.xml

```
<ProductFeed>
  <Product Price="61.4830">Underwater Tour 1 Day West Coast</Product>
  <Product Price="110.6694">Underwater Tour 2 Days West Coast</Product>
  <Product Price="184.4490">Underwater Tour 3 Days West Coast</Product>
  <Product Price="245.9320">Underwater Tour 5 Days West Coast</Product>
  <Product Price="307.4150">Underwater Tour 1 Week West Coast</Product>
  <Product Price="553.3470">Underwater Tour 2 Weeks West Coast</Product>
  <Product Price="80.8590">Underwater Tour 1 Day East Coast</Product>
  <Product Price="145.5462">Underwater Tour 2 Days East Coast</Product>
  <Product Price="242.5770">Underwater Tour 3 Days East Coast</Product>
  <Product Price="323.4360">Underwater Tour 5 Days East Coast</Product>
  <Product Price="404.2950">Underwater Tour 1 Week East Coast</Product>
  <Product Price="727.7310">Underwater Tour 2 Weeks East Coast</Product>
```

Figure 2.67 Skill Check 2 XML stream.

Answer Code: The T-SQL code to this lab can be found in the downloadable files in a file named Lab2.3_NamelessFields.sql

Points to Ponder - XML Nameless Fields

1. If the column name is aliased with the wildcard character [*], then the content will have no named XML element or attribute.
2. The wildcard character * should be surrounded by square brackets.
3. The wildcard character makes the field nameless in your XML stream.
4. If you have multiple columns with the wildcard [*] then they will be concatenated together in the same nameless field.

Chapter Glossary

Auto mode: XML Auto mode; defaults to display data as nested XML elements.

Nameless fields: Aliasing a field within the SELECT list "AS [*]" ensures that the field will have no named XML attribute or element; the wildcard character makes the field nameless in the XML stream.

Path mode: XML Path mode; defaults to display data as elements; Path mode queries can produce customized XML layouts of mixed attributes and elements which cannot be achieved by using AUTO or RAW.

Review Quiz - Chapter Two

1.) What is the only XML mode that will not nest elements of multi-table queries according to the order of fields in the SELECT list?

O a. XML RAW

O b. XML AUTO

O c. XML PATH

2.) What is the only XML mode which defaults to element without using the Elements option?

O a. XML RAW

O b. XML AUTO

O c. XML PATH

3.) What alias will cause the EmpID field to become an attribute?

O a. EmpID as [@EmpID]

O b. EmpID as @EmpID

O c. EmpID as [Employee/EmpID]

O d. EmpID @ [EmpID]

4.) Which two XML modes allow you to choose attributes or elements but can't use both at the same time? (Choose two)

□ a. FOR XML AUTO

□ b. FOR XML RAW

□ c. FOR XML PATH

5.) What XML wildcard can make a field nameless in the XML?

O a. [null]

O b. [xsinull]

O c. [xsinil]

O d. [*]

O e. [@]

6.) You want to create an XML stream which is attribute-based and has each row called <row>. Which code do you append to the FOR XML?

O a. AUTO

O b. RAW

7.) You have a table named Location and want to produce the following XML stream.

```
<JProCo>
 <Site LocationID="1"><CityName>Seattle</CityName></Site>
 <Site LocationID="2"><CityName>Boston</CityName></Site>
 <Site LocationID="3"><CityName>Chicago</CityName></Site>
 <Site LocationID="4"><CityName>Spokane</CityName></Site>
</JProCo>
```

Which query will achieve this result?

O a.
```
SELECT LocationID AS [@LocationID], City AS [CityName]
FROM Location
FOR XML PATH('Site'), ROOT('JProCo')
```

O b.
```
SELECT LocationID AS [LocationID], City AS [@CityName]
FROM Location
FOR XML PATH('Site'), ROOT('JProCo')
```

O c.
```
SELECT LocationID AS [@LocationID], City AS [@CityName]
FROM Location
FOR XML PATH('Site'), ROOT('JProCo')
```

8.) You are selecting the LocationID, City and [State] fields from the Location table. Your XML output is seen below.

```
<JProCo>
 <Site LocationID="1"><City>Seattle</City>WA</Site>
 <Site LocationID="2"><City>Boston</City>MA</Site>
 <Site LocationID="3"><City>Chicago</City>IL</Site>
 <Site LocationID="4"><City>Spokane</City>WA</Site>
</JProCo>
```

Which field is using the [*] wildcard?

O a. LocationID

O b. City

O c. State

9.) You have a Customers and an Invoices table in your database. You need to stream the data as a valid, well-formed XML document with attributes. The XML stream must have the invoices data nested in the customer data. Which T-SQL code will meet all objectives?

O a.
```
SELECT c.ContactName, o.OrderDate, o.ExpectedDate
FROM Customers c
INNER JOIN Invoices o
ON c.CustomerID = o.CustomerID
FOR XML RAW('Contact'), ROOT('ContactOrderDate')
```

O b.
```
SELECT c.ContactName, o.OrderDate, o.ExpectedDate
FROM Customers c
INNER JOIN Invoices o
ON c.CustomerID = o.CustomerID
FOR XML PATH('ContactOrderDate')
```

O c.
```
SELECT c.ContactName, o.OrderDate, o.ExpectedDate
FROM Customers c
INNER JOIN Invoices o
ON c.CustomerID = o.CustomerID
FOR XML AUTO
```

O d.
```
SELECT c.ContactName, o.OrderDate, o.ExpectedDate
FROM Customers c
INNER JOIN Invoices o
ON c.CustomerID = o.CustomerID
FOR XML AUTO, ROOT('ContactOrderDate')
```

10.) You want to create an XML stream from a query that uses two tables in an INNER JOIN. You do NOT want any nesting in your XML in the result set. Which code do you append in the FOR XML clause?

O a. AUTO

O b. RAW

11.) If you don't put ROOT after the XML AUTO clause, then what happens?

O a. You get well-formed XML.

O b. You don't get well-formed XML.

12.) You have a query which joins tables. You want to create a well-formed XML stream, which is attribute-based and nests the results in the table from the first field of the SELECT list. Which code do you append to the SQL statement?

O a. FOR XML AUTO
O b. FOR XML RAW
O c. FOR XML AUTO, ROOT
O d. FOR XML RAW, ROOT

13.) You have a table named Location and want to produce the following XML stream:

```
<JProCo>
 <Site LocationID="1">
  <Area><City>Seattle</City>
   <State>WA</State>
  </Area>
 </ Site >
 <Site LocationID="2">
  <Area>
   <City>Boston</City>
   <State>MA</State>
  </Area>
 </ Site >
</JProCo>
```

Which query will achieve this result?

O a.
```
SELECT LocationID [@LocationID], City [Area], [City], State
[State]
FROM Location
FOR XML PATH('Site'), ROOT('JProCo')
```
O b.
```
SELECT LocationID [@LocationID] , City [Area/City], State
[Area/State]
FROM Location
FOR XML PATH('Site'), ROOT('JProCo')
```
O c.
```
SELECT LocationID [@LocationID] , City [City/Area], State
[State/Area]
FROM Location
FOR XML PATH('Site'), ROOT('JProCo')
```

14.) You need to generate the following XML document from your CurrentProducts table:

```
<ProductExport>
 <Product Price="99">Product1</Product>
 <Product Price="199">Product2</Product>
 <Product Price="299">Product3</Product>
 <Product Price="399">Product4</Product>
</ProductExport>
```

Which query should you use?

O a.
```
SELECT Price, ProductName
FROM CurrentProducts AS ProductExport
FOR XML PATH('Product')
```

O b.
```
SELECT Price, ProductName
FROM CurrentProducts
FOR XML AUTO, ROOT('ProductExport')
```

O c.
```
SELECT Price [@Price], ProductName AS [*]
FROM CurrentProducts AS ProductExport
FOR XML AUTO, ELEMENTS
```

O d.
```
SELECT Price [@Price], ProductName AS [*]
FROM CurrentProducts
FOR XML PATH('Product'), ROOT('ProductExport')
```

Answer Key

1.) XML Auto returns results as nested XML elements, so (b) is incorrect. XML PATH will return both elements and attributes, so (c) is incorrect.XML RAW will not return nested elements, so (a) is the correct answer.

2.) XML RAW will store all of it data by default as attributes, so (a) is incorrect. XML Auto mode defaults to display data as nested XML elements, so (b) is incorrect. XML Path mode defaults to display data as elements, so (c) is the correct answer.

3.) Answer (b) will cause EmpID to become a variable and is incorrect. Answer (c) will cause EmpID to become an element and is incorrect. The syntax in answer (d) will cause an error and is incorrect. The literal brackets around '@EmpID' will cause it to become an attribute, so (a) is correct.

4.) XML PATH can be customized to return both elements and attributes, so (c) is incorrect. (a) and (b) are the correct answers.

5.) To ensure that the field will have no named XML attribute or element, alias the field within the SELECT list "AS [*]"; the wildcard character makes the field nameless in the XML stream, so (d) is correct.

6.) The Auto mode names each tag according to the table name (or table alias) listed in the FROM clause of the query, so (a) is incorrect. The Raw mode defaults each tag to <row>, so (b) is correct.

7.) Answer (b) will return a nested element named LocationID and is incorrect. Answer (c) will return CityName as an attribute rather than a nested element. The correct answer is (a).

8.) LocationID is an attribute of the <Site> element, so (a) is incorrect. The city name is wrapped in the <City> tags, so (b) is incorrect. The [*] wildcard character makes the field nameless in the XML stream, since State is nameless (c) is the correct answer.

9.) XML RAW does not support nested elements, so (a) is incorrect. Answer (b) does not specify a <root> and will not be well formed, so (b) is incorrect. XML AUTO returns its data by default as attributes inside tags named after the table the data is pulled from and will not be well formed unless specified, so (c) is incorrect. Answer (d) will return a well-formed XML document with attributes. The XML stream will have the invoices data nested in the customer data, so (d) is correct.

10.) XML Auto returns results as nested XML elements, so (a) is incorrect. RAW will not return nested elements, so (b) is correct.

11.) XML AUTO does not return a <root> tag by default, so (b) is correct.

12.) Answer (a) will return attribute based nested results but will not be well formed, so (a) is incorrect. XML RAW cannot return nested data, so (b) and (d) are incorrect. Answer (c) will return attribute based nested results in well-formed XML, so (c) is correct.

13.) Answer (a) will return <Area>, <City> and <State> as elements at the same level, so (a) is incorrect. Answer (c) will return <Area> as a nested element inside both <City> and <State>, so (c) is incorrect. The only answer that will return <City> and <State> as nested elements inside <Area> tag is (b), so (b) is the correct answer.

14.) Answer (a) will create a <root> named <Product>, so (a) is incorrect. Answer (b) will create a <root> element named <ProductExport> but the next level element will be named after the table <CurrentProducts> rather than <Product>, so (b) is incorrect. Answer (c) will return the correct <root> but the first level element will named by the @Price variable. So (c) is incorrect. Answer (d) will return well-formed XML with the properly named <root> and sub elements containing the Price and ProductName attributes, so (d) is correct.

Bug Catcher Game

To play the Bug Catcher game run the SQLQueries2012Vol5BugCatcher2.pps from the BugCatcher folder of the companion files found at www.Joes2Pros.com.

Chapter 3. Shredding XML

At the opening of this book, we mentioned the rapid adoption and popularity of the XML standard. Within just a few years of its debut, its flexibility and ability to work between a variety of platforms quickly made XML the "go-to" method for sharing data between programs, as well as with web applications. While SQL Server has provided XML support since its 2000 version, each subsequent version has consistently stepped up SQL Server's capabilities and options for utilizing and interacting with XML. It should be no surprise that your preparation for SQL certification includes XML. No matter what your intended role (Analyst, Developer, or DBA), any serious work in the database world will invariably include XML data.

Our introduction to XML thus far has focused on seeing tabular data taken from SQL Server and streamed into well-formed XML instead of the rowset data we typically work with. The next two chapters will focus on the reverse process. Our starting point will be data which is already in XML and which we will turn into table data, or which we will query in order to answer questions.

Operations which parse and consume XML data are known collectively by the term **shredding XML**. This chapter will focus on the steps to prepare an XML stream so you can turn it into a table or some other tabular result set.

As noted in Chapter 1, XML is case-sensitive. In order for your examples and exercises to run properly in Chapters 1 through 7, be sure that your XML fragments precisely match the figures with respect to uppercase and lowercase.

READERNOTE:*Please run the script SQLQueries2012Vol5Chapter1.0-4.2Setup.sqlin order to follow along with the examples in the first section of Chapter 3. You only need to run this script once for all examples in Chapters 1 through 4. All scripts mentioned in this chapter may be found at* ***www.Joes2Pros.com****.*

Consuming XML

Anytime you turn XML into another data format (e.g., into a SQL Server table) that process is called **shredding XML**. Before you can shred your XML, you must first prepare it. **Preparing XML** for SQL means storing the XML in a memory space where a query can retrieve and make use of the data.

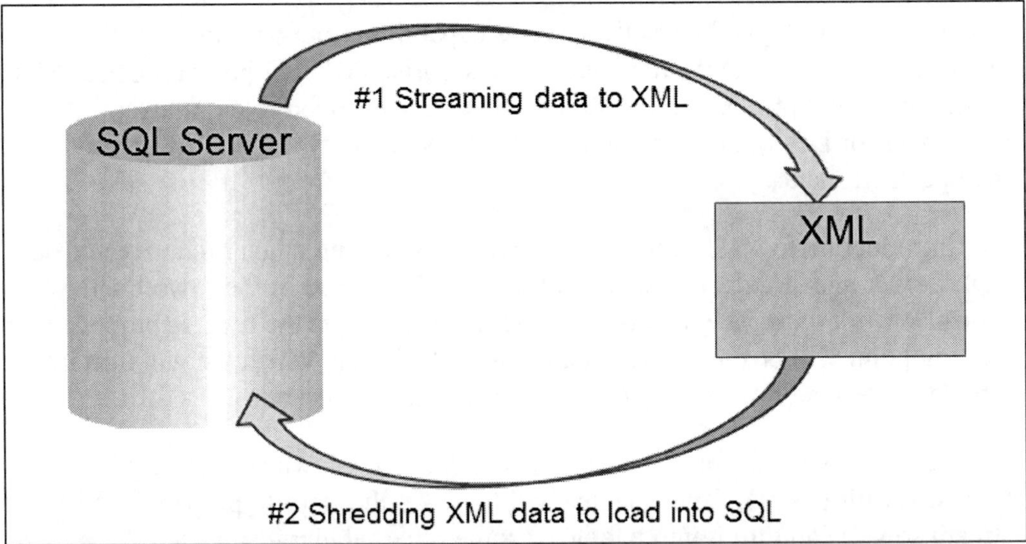

Figure 3.1 SQL Server 2008 provides native XML support to make streaming and shredding XML more robust.

Notice we need to devote an entire chapter to the preparation steps necessary before SQL Server can consume XML. This chapter is being written at the approach of the North American Thanksgiving holiday, which may provide us with a helpful analogy: *think of XML as a big meal for SQL.* While we essentially added just one line of code to our SELECT query to turn tabular data into an XML document, going the other direction is more complex. Behind the scenes, SQL Server uses additional memory when consuming XML. Our preparation will include a step to parse and store the XML document in memory. Finally, the same way a big feast requires additional cleanup, we should include a step to remove the XML document from the memory cache once it is no longer needed.

In earlier chapters, we produced XML using the modes Raw, Auto and Path. We used familiar data from the JProCo database (Employee, Location, Grant and Customer data). We refined and manipulated our XML queries in order for the XML result to appear according to our precise specifications (Figure 3.2).

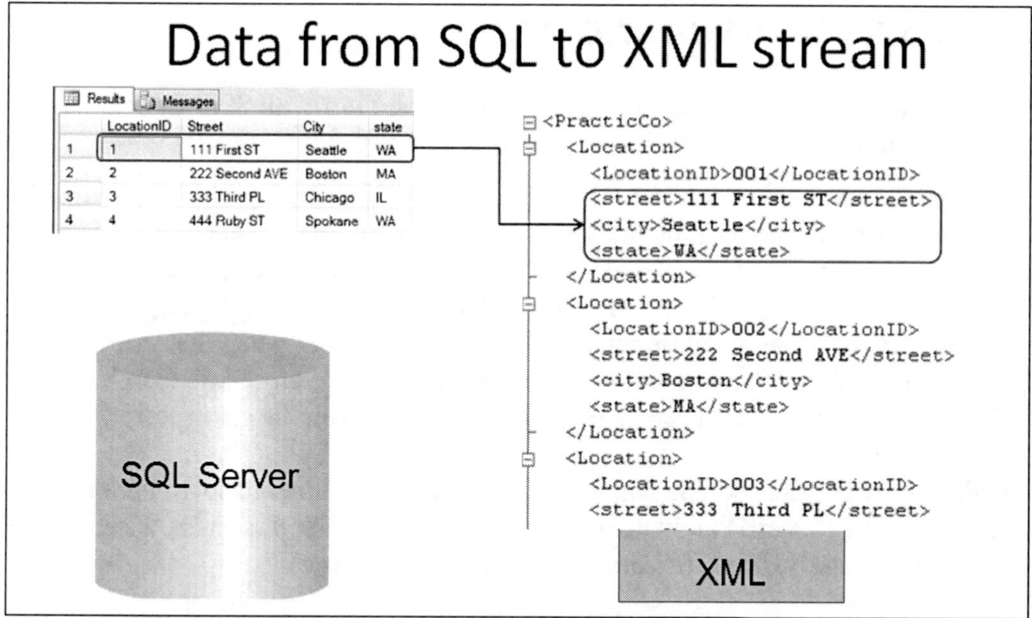

Figure 3.2 Our initial work focused on streaming data into XML.

Now that we understand the essential rules and components of well-formed XML documents, we will turn our attention toward consuming XML data (as shown in Figure 3.3). In Chapter 7 we will see an advanced method (nodes) for shredding XML.

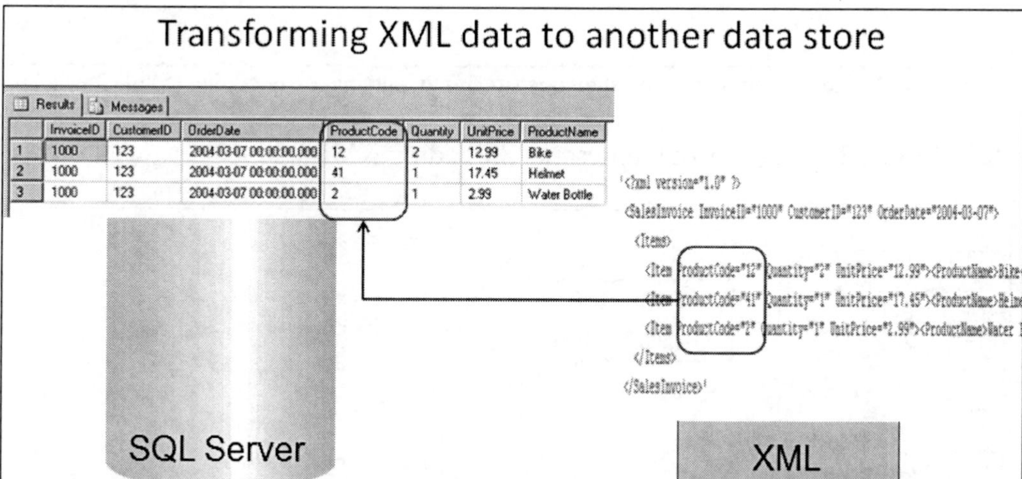

Figure 3.3 Next we will examine the processes for sending data the other direction: from XML into data consumable by SQL Server.

Lab 3.1: Consuming XML

Lab Prep: Each lab has one or more Skill Checks. Start with Skill Check 1 and proceed until reaching the Points to Ponder section.

Before beginning this lab, verify that SQL Server 2012 is properly installed and operating. Before running the lab setup script for resetting the database (SQLQueries2012Vol5Chapter1.0-4.2Setup.sql), please make sure to close all query windows within SSMS. An open query window pointing to a database context can lock that database preventing it from updating when the script is executing. A simple way to assure all query windows are closed, is to exit out of SSMS, then open a new instance of SSMS, and lastly run the setup script.

Skill Check 1: Suppose you want to take the XML document shown here and send just the ProductID and Quantity into a result set in SQL server. What type of operation would this be? (Streaming | Parsing | Shredding)

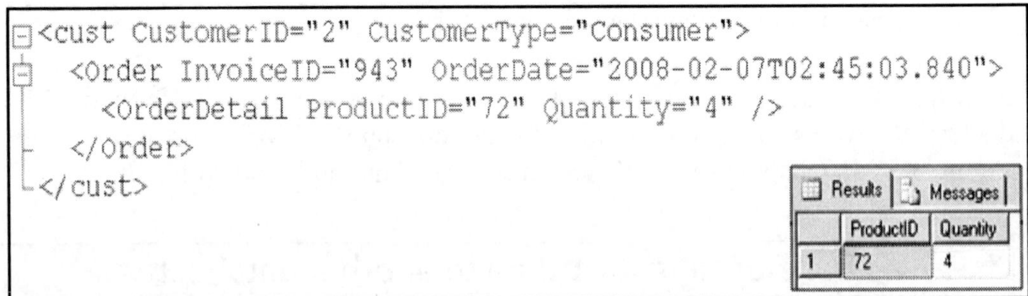

Figure 3.4 Decide whether the action shown is streaming, parsing, or shredding (Skill Check 1).

Skill Check 2: Which arrow represents Shredding XML?

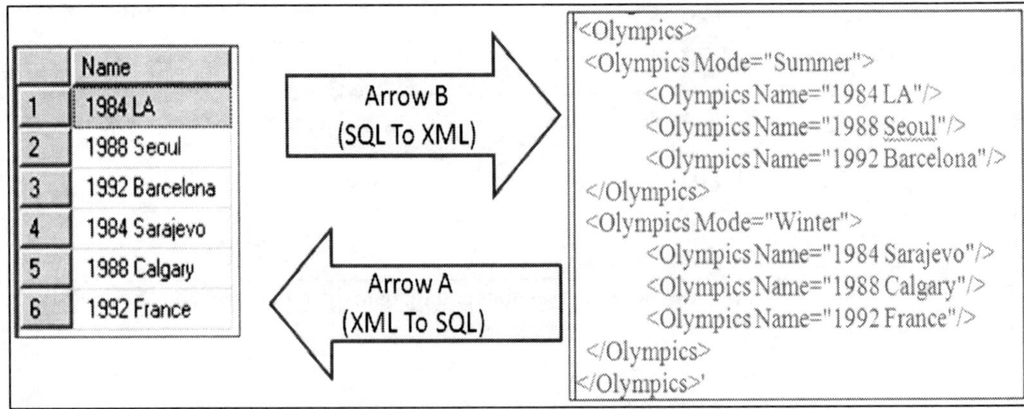

Figure 3.5 Select the arrow which depicts XML being shredded (Skill Check 2).

Points to Ponder - Consuming XML

1. SQL Server can turn table data into XML data.
2. SQL Server can turn XML data into tabular data.
3. XML shredding is the process of extracting data from XML streams and turning them into a tabular stream (e.g., a table)/

Preparing XML in Memory

If you want to take XML data and create a result set in SQL Server, you must first store the XML in memory. The process of preparing XML in SQL includes storing the XML in memory and processing the XML so that all the data and metadata is ready and available for you to query.

> Preparing XML for SQL Server is similar to how you prepare anything. If you were preparing a Thanksgiving dinner, you would take the necessary ingredients and follow a process to assemble and present them as a meal - that is, in a way your guests can readily identify and consume them. The internal cache prepares your XML and all the data and metadata so you can consume just the records or fields you want.

XML Levels

We will begin by creating an XML document for use in our example. Begin with this SELECT query before adding the FOR XML Auto clause (Figure 3.6 & Figure 3.7).

```
SELECT cust.CustomerID, cust.CustomerType,
[Order].InvoiceID, [Order].OrderDate,
OrderDetail.ProductID, OrderDetail.Quantity
FROM Customer AS cust
INNER JOIN SalesInvoice AS [Order]
ON Cust.CustomerID = [Order].CustomerID
INNER JOIN SalesInvoiceDetail AS OrderDetail
ON [Order].InvoiceID = OrderDetail.InvoiceID
WHERE Cust.CustomerID = 2
```

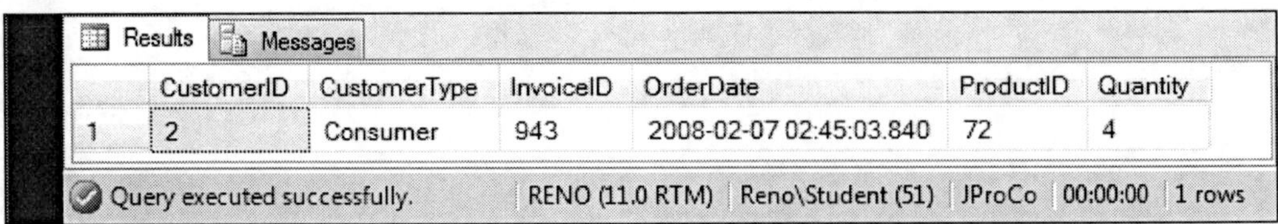

	CustomerID	CustomerType	InvoiceID	OrderDate	ProductID	Quantity
1	2	Consumer	943	2008-02-07 02:45:03.840	72	4

Figure 3.6 The base query joining the Customer, SalesInvoice, and SalesInvoiceDetail tables.

```
SELECT Cust.CustomerID, cust.CustomerType,
[Order].InvoiceID, [Order].OrderDate,
OrderDetail.ProductID, OrderDetail.Quantity
FROM Customer AS cust
INNER JOIN SalesInvoice AS [Order]
ON Cust.CustomerID = [Order].CustomerID
INNER JOIN SalesInvoiceDetail AS OrderDetail
ON [Order].InvoiceID = OrderDetail.InvoiceID
WHERE cust.CustomerID = 2
FOR XML AUTO
```

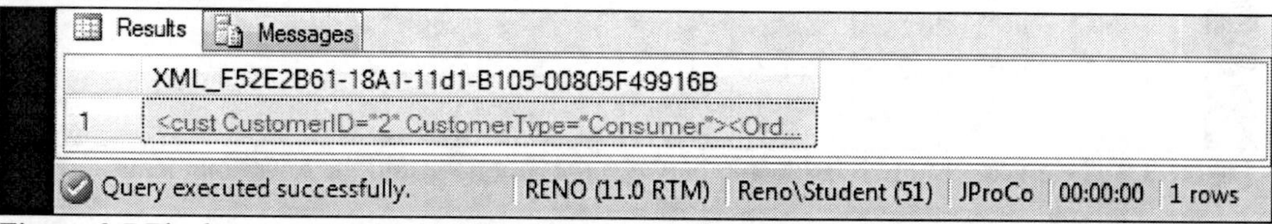

Figure 3.7 The base query with the FOR XML Auto clause.

Recall that element levels in your XML document appear in the same order that tables appear in your SELECT list and are named according to any aliases you may have chosen (e.g., cust, Order, OrderDetail).

```
XML_F52E2B61-18A...00805F49916B1.xml  SQLQuery1.sql - RE...(Reno\Student (51))*
<cust CustomerID="2" CustomerType="Consumer">
  <Order InvoiceID="943" OrderDate="2008-02-07T02:45:03.840">
    <OrderDetail ProductID="72" Quantity="4" />
  </Order>
</cust>
```

Levels are named after your table aliases.

Figure 3.8 The XML stream resulting from running the code in Figure 3.7.

A related query (showing the purchases for CustomerID 1, see Figure 3.9) helps to illustrate our root element (<cust>) having a top-level element (<Order>) and a child-level element (<OrderDetail>). There is a 1:Many (One-to-Many) relationship between the root node and the lower elements.

```
SQLQuery1.sql - RE...(Reno\Student (51))*    XML_F52E2B61-18A...00805F49916B2.xml
<cust C          ROOT LEVEL    erType="Consumer">
  <Order In  oiceID="824" OrderDate="2007-11-09T11:23:51.043">
    <OrderDetai  ProductID="61" Quantity="4" />
  </Order>       TOP LEVEL
  <Order Invoi  ID="1027" OrderDate="2008-04-17T16:13:59.480">
    <OrderDetail ProductID="49" Quantity="4" />
  </Order>
  <Order InvoiceID="1401" OrderDate="2009-01-31T07:21:03.997">
    <OrderDetail ProductID="69" Quantity="1" />
    <OrderDetail ProductID="60" Quantity="5" />
    <OrderDetail ProductID="15" Quantity="2" />
    <OrderDetail ProductID="53" Quantity="4" />
    <OrderDetail ProductID="63" Quantity="4" />
```

Figure 3.9 There is a 1:Many relationship between the root node and the lower elements.

Using sp_XML_PrepareDocument

Copy your XML result (shown in Figure 3.8 and produced by our query shown in Figure 3.7) into a brand new query window and enclose it in single quotes (Figure 3.10).

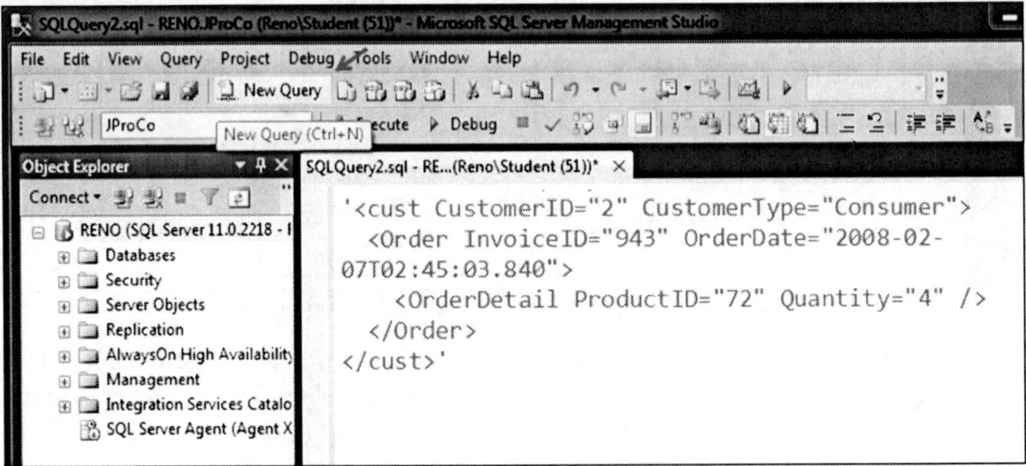

Figure 3.10 Copy the XML into a brand new query window.

Let's briefly digress for another comparison which may be helpful for our next step. Preparing to have your XML document shredded by SQL Server is a bit like the steps you take when having your tailor create a custom garment for you. One of my students recently underwent this process. Her favorite tailor, Kim, had the design for a poncho she liked. The tailor sent my student to the fabric store to select the particular fabric and trim she wanted for her poncho.

When she brought the fabric and trim to Kim's shop, Kim took the fabric, wrote up an order slip, and then gave my student a claim ticket and said her poncho would be done in a week. This tailor runs a small neighborhood shop but is always very busy due to the high quality of her work. While Kim could eventually have located the order without the benefit of the claim ticket, my conscientious student made very sure to bring her ticket when she returned the following week. She submitted her claim ticket and in exchange she was handed her lovely new hand-made garment.

Much the same way, when you send an XML document into memory, SQL Server gives you a number (called a handle) which you need later when referring to that document. In Figure 3.14, we will see the "claim ticket" created: we will send our XML document into memory and in exchange we will get back the handle in the form of an integer.

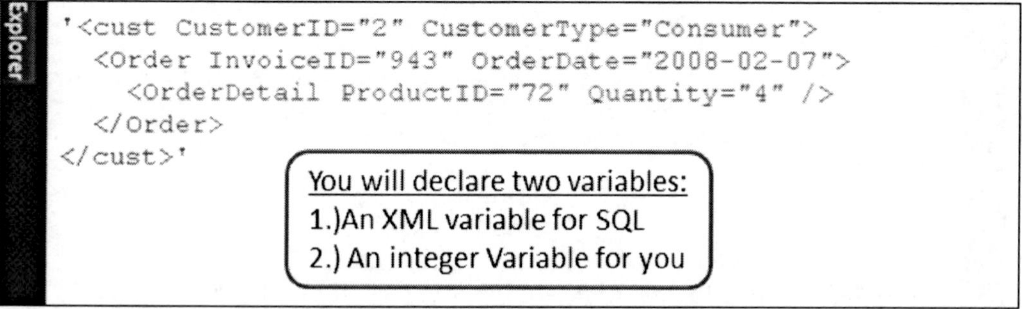
Explorer
'<cust CustomerID="2" CustomerType="Consumer">
<Order InvoiceID="943" OrderDate="2008-02-07">
<OrderDetail ProductID="72" Quantity="4" />
</Order>
</cust>'
You will declare two variables:
1.)An XML variable for SQL
2.) An integer Variable for you

Figure 3.11 Two variables are needed when sending our XML document into memory.

To send our document into memory, we first need to declare an XML variable. In order for this variable to contain our XML document, we will set it equal to our XML (Figure 3.12).

```
DECLARE @Doc xml

SET @Doc = '<cust CustomerID="2" CustomerType="Consumer">
  <Order InvoiceID="943" OrderDate="2008-02-07T02:45:03.840">
    <OrderDetail ProductID="72" Quantity="4" />
  </Order>
</cust>'
```

Figure 3.12 The @Doc variable's data type is XML.

Next we will declare the variable @hDoc, which we know will be an integer because it is the variable which will act as our document handle (i.e., our "claim ticket"). We will also use sp_XML_PrepareDocument, a system-supplied stored procedure which reads our XML document (@Doc), parses it, and makes it available for SQL's use (Figure 3.13).

```
DECLARE @hDoc int
EXEC SP_xml_prepareDocument @hDoc OUTPUT, @Doc
```

Figure 3.13 The syntax to declare our handle variable and execute sp_XML_PrepareDocument.

When we send our XML to SQL Server's internal cache, we will receive a number which functions as our "claim ticket." Run all of the code together, including a SELECT statement to display the document handle (i.e., our "claim ticket" which SQL Server provides in exchange for the XML document) (Figure 3.14).

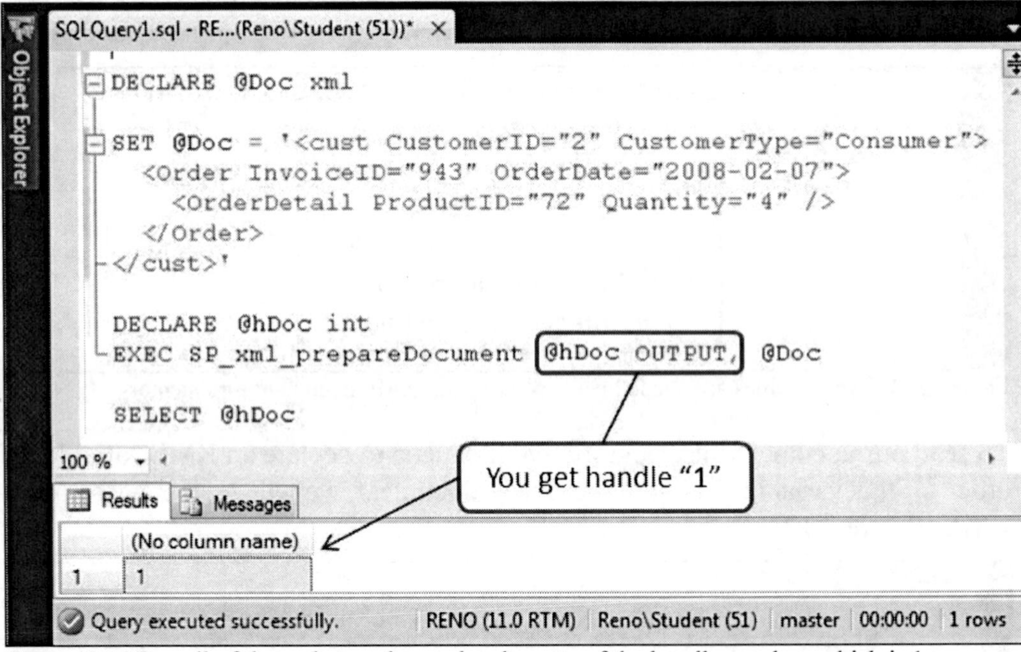

Figure 3.14 Run all of the code together and make note of the handle number, which is 1.

Be sure to run this code only once, otherwise you will create multiple handles and instances of your XML document.

```
DECLARE @hDoc int
EXEC SP_xml_prepareDocument @hDoc OUTPUT, @Doc

SELECT @hDoc
```

Don't run this again or it will create 2 handles in memory with identical data

Figure 3.15 Avoid accidentally creating unneeded instances of your document and handle.

Using the OPENXML Function

We just sent our prepared XML into the SQL Server's internal cache so that we may pull out the data we want. The OPENXML function provides a rowset view of your XML data. It works with the in-memory copy of the XML document you've stored and provides a view of the data, no longer formatted as XML but with all its parts separated into a large grid. This allows you to query just the data that you need.

Rowpattern

We know the key to accessing the stored XML document is the document handle or "claim ticket." The first argument needed by the OPENXML function is this value expressed as an integer. The second argument is the *rowpattern* hint for the data we wish to see.

After declaring an integer variable and setting it equal to 1 (i.e., the value of our document handle, see Figure 3.14), we can use a SELECT statement to query the result set of the OPENXML function. The variable @iNum is the first parameter. The second parameter '/cust/Order/OrderDetail' specifies that we wish to see data for the OrderDetail element level (Figure 3.16).

```
DECLARE @iNum INT
SET @iNum = 1
SELECT *
FROM OPENXML(@iNum,'/cust/Order/OrderDetail')
```

Results | Messages

	id	parentid	nodetype	localname	prefix	namespaceuri	datatype	prev	text
1	7	4	1	OrderDetail	NULL	NULL	NULL	NULL	NULL
2	8	7	2	ProductID	NULL	NULL	NULL	NULL	NULL
3	10	8	3	#text	NULL	NULL	NULL	NULL	72
4	9	7	2	Quantity	NULL	NULL	NULL	NULL	NULL
5	11	9	3	#text	NULL	NULL	NULL	NULL	4

Query executed successfully. | RENO (11.0 RTM) | Reno\Student (51) | JProCo | 00:00:00 | 5 rows

Figure 3.16 The OPENXML function works with the XML document we stored in memory. Compare this data with our XML document shown in Figure 3.11.

Since XML can have root tags, top-level tags, and many levels of child tags, *rowpatterns* are needed to figure out which level represents your row data. A *rowpattern* is an XPath pattern telling your query where to look for the data that you want to see in your result.

In our current example, the *rowpattern* hint ('/cust/Order/OrderDetail') narrows our query to the attributes found at the OrderDetail element level (Figure 3.16). While the surrounding data isn't immediately interpretable, we can see the text for the ProductID attribute shows a 72, and the text for the Quantity attribute shows a 4.

Shredding from the Rowpattern Level

We want to pull at least one of these columns with the OPENXML function. You might remember that all of our data is at many levels in our XML and the Rowpattern specified the data is at the /cust/Order/OrderDetail level. That level will get our ProductID and Quantity fields as seen in the XML stream below:

```
<cust CustomerID="2" CustomerType="Consumer">
 <Order InvoiceID="943" OrderDate="2008-02-07">
 <OrderDetail ProductID="72" Quantity="4" />
 </Order>
</cust>
```

Adding the WITH clause to our existing query allows us to pick just the values we wish to see. Our query specifies that we are still interested in data from the OrderDetail element level (Figure 3.17). Our WITH clause lists the field names we want (ProductID, Quantity) from this element level and that these values should be expressed as integer data. In other words, ProductID and Quantity are both integers.

```
DECLARE @iNum INT
SET @iNum = 1
SELECT *
FROM OPENXML(@iNum,'/cust/Order/OrderDetail')
WITH (ProductID INT, Quantity INT)
```

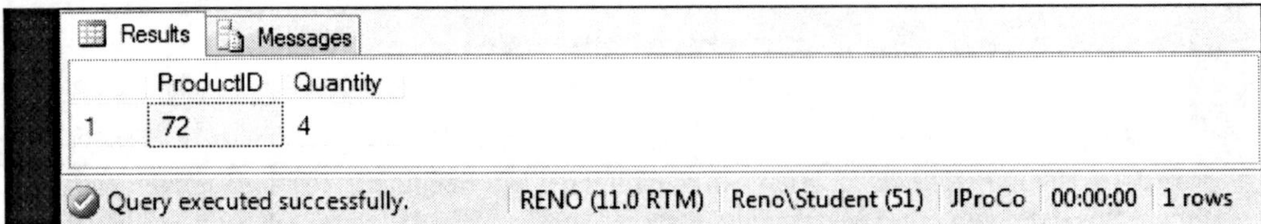

Figure 3.17 The WITH clause allows us to shred data at a single element level.

Basic Shredding Recap

Let's perform an additional start-to-finish example of shredding a single level of XML. We will prepare the XML document, choose a row pattern, and shred some fields from the XML Stream shown below (Figure 3.18). For this example, you will need the Lab3.2Olympics.sql file found in the Resource Files folder located in the companion files located on ***www.Joes2Pros.com***.

```
Lab3.2Olympics.sql...(Reno\Student (51))
'<Olympics>
  <Olympics Mode="Summer">
  <Olympics Name="1984 LA"/>
  <Olympics Name="1988 Seoul"/>
  <Olympics Name="1992 Barcelona"/>
  </Olympics>
  <Olympics Mode="Winter">
  <Olympics Name="1984 Sarajevo"/>
  <Olympics Name="1988 Calgary"/>
  <Olympics Name="1992 France"/>
  </Olympics>
</Olympics>'
```

Figure 3.18 Locate and open the Lab3.2Olympics.sql file.

Add the variable declaration and SET statement, then run the statement to confirm your XML completes without errors (Figure 3.19).

```
Lab3.2Olympics.sql...(Reno\Student (51))*
DECLARE @Doc XML

SET @Doc =
'<Olympics>
  <Olympics Mode="Summer">
  <Olympics Name="1984 LA"/>
  <Olympics Name="1988 Seoul"/>
  <Olympics Name="1992 Barcelona"/>
  </Olympics>
  <Olympics Mode="Winter">
  <Olympics Name="1984 Sarajevo"/>
  <Olympics Name="1988 Calgary"/>
  <Olympics Name="1992 France"/>
  </Olympics>
</Olympics>'
```

Figure 3.19 Add the code shown here and execute to confirm that it runs successfully.

Add the code to store the XML document, declare the document handle variable, execute sp_XML_PrepareDocument, and receive the "claim ticket" handle value for our stored document (Figure 3.20).

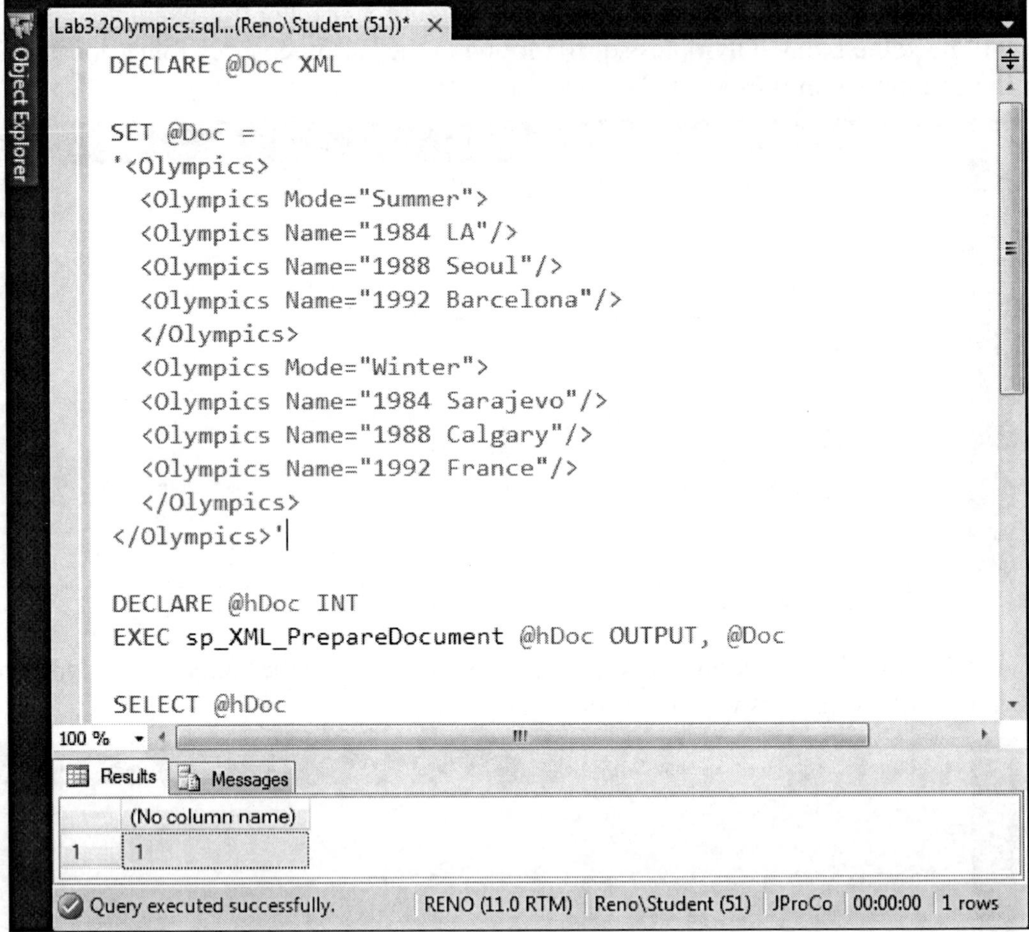

Figure 3.20 Run all of this code and make note of the "claim ticket" for our XML document.

READERNOTE: *The document handle returned by sp_XML_PrepareDocument is 1 the first time the sproc is executed in a Query Editor Window. If you run the sproc again within the same session, each subsequent run will return another handle incremented by (i.e., 3, 5, 7, 9, etc.).*

We want to pull out all the <Olympics> names (e.g., "1984 LA") so we need to identify the needed level. The level we need is two levels below the root. In other words, our data is at the /Olympics/Olympics/Olympics level. As you can see, it's possible to have lower levels use the same name as parent levels.

```
DECLARE @iDoc INT
SET @iDoc = 1
SELECT * FROM
OPENXML (@iDoc,'/Olympics/Olympics/Olympics')
```

	id	parentid	nodetype	localname	prefix	namespaceuri	datatype	prev	text
1	4	2	1	Olympics	NULL	NULL	NULL	NULL	NULL
2	5	4	2	Name	NULL	NULL	NULL	NULL	NULL
3	18	5	3	#text	NULL	NULL	NULL	NULL	198...
4	6	2	1	Olympics	NULL	NULL	NULL	4	NULL
5	7	6	2	Name	NULL	NULL	NULL	NULL	NULL
6	19	7	3	#text	NULL	NULL	NULL	NULL	198...

Query executed successfully. | RENO (11.0 RTM) | Reno\Student (51) | JProCo | 00:00:00 | 18 rows

Figure 3.21 Query the OPENXML function for the third element level details.

Again, we can use a SELECT statement to query the OPENXML function. The first argument in Figure 3.21-Figure 3.22 is the handle and is needed by the OPENXML. The second argument is the *rowpattern* hint for the data we wish to see.

```
DECLARE @iDoc INT
SET @iDoc = 1
SELECT * FROM
OPENXML (@iDoc,'/Olympics/Olympics/Olympics')
WITH([Name] VARCHAR(MAX))
```

	Name
1	1984 LA
2	1988 Seoul
3	1992 Barcelona
4	1984 Sarajevo
5	1988 Calgary
6	1992 France

Query executed successfully. | RENO (11.0 RTM) | Reno\Student (51) | JProCo | 00:00:00 | 6 rows

Figure 3.22 Add a WITH clause to pull just the data belonging to the Name attribute.

We've successfully pulled the data we wanted. As a final step, we want to alias the column as GameName. To accomplish this, we will use the code below (Figure 3.23). As you can see, we simply replace the column name with our intended alias, GameName. Since the name of our XML source field @Name does not match what we want to display, we need to specify how they map. The addition of the columnpattern '@Name' specifies that the data should come from the Name attribute of our XML document. We have chosen to label this column GameName in our tabular (shredded) result.

```
DECLARE @iDoc INT
SET @iDoc = 1
SELECT * FROM
OPENXML (@iDoc,'/Olympics/Olympics/Olympics')
WITH(GameName VARCHAR(MAX) '@Name')
```

	GameName
1	1984 LA
2	1988 Seoul
3	1992 Barcelona
4	1984 Sarajevo
5	1988 Calgary
6	1992 France

Query executed successfully. | RENO (11.0 RTM) | Reno\Student (51) | JProCo | 00:00:00 | 6 rows

Figure 3.23 Add code to replace the column name with "GameName."

Lab 3.2: Preparing XML

Lab Prep: Each lab has one or more Skill Checks. Start with Skill Check 1 and proceed until reaching the Points to Ponder section.

Before beginning this lab, verify that SQL Server 2012 is properly installed and operating. Before running the lab setup script for resetting the database (SQLQueries2012Vol5Chapter1.0-4.2Setup.sql), please make sure to close all query windows within SSMS. An open query window pointing to a database context can lock that database preventing it from updating when the script is executing. A simple way to assure all query windows are closed, is to exit out of SSMS, then open a new instance of SSMS, and lastly run the setup script.

Skill Check 1: Create the XML you see here. Take this XML and prepare it using the correct row pattern to shred just the two fields you see in Figure 3.24.

```
DECLARE @hDoc INT
DECLARE @doc XML
SET @doc =
'<Tournament>
 <Game ID = "1" Title = "Yucks vs. Rotts">
  <Half Home="23" Away = "33"/>
  <Final Home="61" Away = "65"/>
 </Game>
  Game ID = "2" Title = "Fluffs vs. Softies">
  <Half Home="41" Away = "40"/>
  <Final Home="72" Away = "68"/>
 </Game>
</Tournament>'

EXEC sp_XML_PrepareDocument @hDoc OUTPUT, @Doc
--Prepare the XML here
```

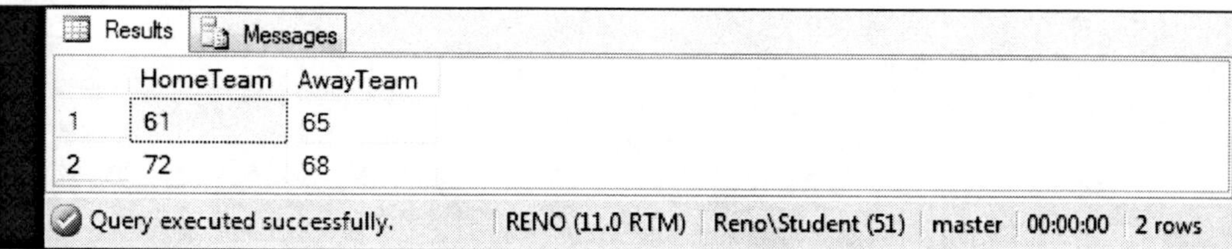

Results | Messages

	HomeTeam	AwayTeam
1	61	65
2	72	68

Query executed successfully. | RENO (11.0 RTM) | Reno\Student (51) | master | 00:00:00 | 2 rows

Figure 3.24 Skill Check 2 produces two fields (HomeTeam, AwayTeam).

Skill Check 2: Create the XML you see below and shred it into the result set at the bottom of Figure 3.25.

```
DECLARE @hDoc INT
DECLARE @doc XML
SET @doc =
'<BigFoods>
     <Store ID = "1" TotalSales = "145000"/>
     <Store ID = "2" TotalSales = "177000"/>
</BigFoods>'

EXEC Sp_XML_PrepareDocument @hDoc OUTPUT, @Doc
--Prepare the XML here
```

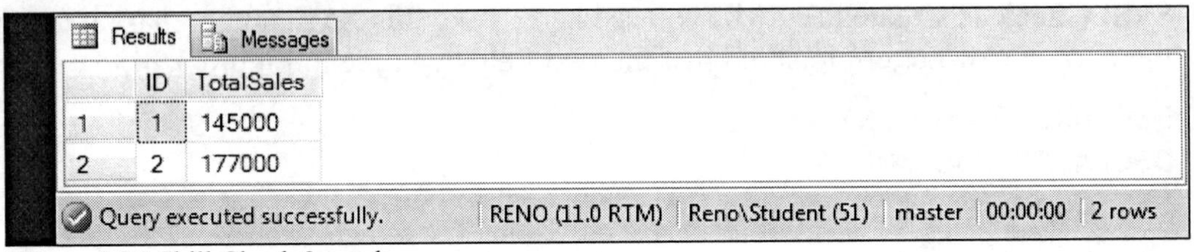

Results | Messages

	ID	TotalSales
1	1	145000
2	2	177000

Query executed successfully. | RENO (11.0 RTM) | Reno\Student (51) | master | 00:00:00 | 2 rows

Figure 3.25 Skill Check 3 result.

Answer Code: The T-SQL code to this lab can be found in the downloadable files in a file named Lab3.2_PreparingXML.sql

Points to Ponder - Shredding XML

1. Before you can process an XML document with T-SQL, you must parse the XML into a tree representation of the various nodes and store it within SQL Server's internal cache using the sp_XML_PrepareDocument stored procedure.
2. The sp_XML_PrepareDocument system stored procedure has two required parameters:
    - handle - an integer handle representing the XML document in memory. Think of this as a label on, or pointer to, the XML data in memory.
    - XML - the XML doc to be processed.
3. After you have parsed XML using sp_XML_PrepareDocument, SELECT from the OPENXML function result to retrieve a rowset from the parsed tree.
4. The OPENXML function has two required input parameters:
    - iDoc - an integer representing a pointer to the XML document in memory.
    - Rowpattern - an XPath pattern identifying the nodes in the XML to be processed as a rowset.
5. The SELECT statement's WITH clause is used to format the rowset and provide any required mapping information (e.g., mapping a field alias to an attribute).
6. The complete process of transforming XML data into a rowset is called shredding.
7. Each time sp_XML_PrepareDocument is executed within the same Query Editor Window session the document handle is returned as an integer that increments by 2 (i.e., 1, 3, 5, 7, 9, etc.).

OPENXML Options

The last section introduced us to the OPENXML function. We learned the two required parameters for this function are the handle (which must be in the form of an integer) and the rowpattern.

The OPENXML function offers some helpful options for querying. This section will explore the two main syntaxes for rowpattern recursion (searching lower levels) and column pattern options (searching one level higher).

Rowpattern Recursion

Suppose you are a manager at a company. You work for a supervisor and likely also have people who report to you. Even at the largest company, every person who works there is an employee, from the CEO on down to managers and individual contributors at all levels. Our recursion example will include an XML document having many element levels named "Emp."

It's common to see elements inside of elements with the same name. Sometimes the name of the element is more important than its exact level. In other words, you could see one employee level nested beneath another employee level, and so forth. In our example, we will see how level recursion can help us locate the data we need within XML tags having the same name.

Let's create a simple XML document showing a small organization having one boss, Tom. Tom will have two employees, Dick and Harry.

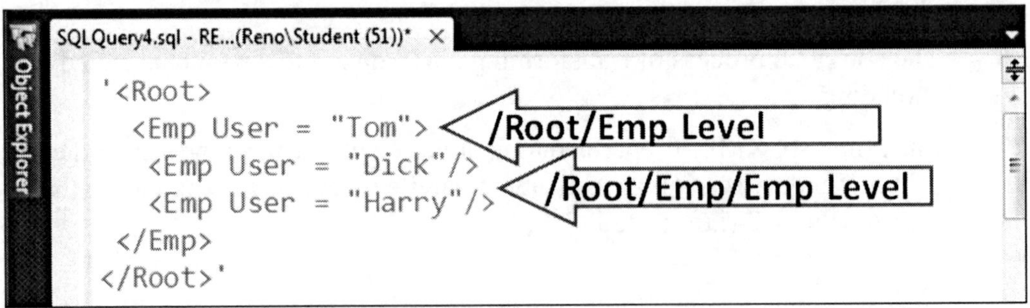

SQLQuery4.sql - RE...(Reno\Student (51))*

```
'<Root>
  <Emp User = "Tom">      /Root/Emp Level
   <Emp User = "Dick"/>
   <Emp User = "Harry"/>  /Root/Emp/Emp Level
 </Emp>
</Root>'
```

Figure 3.26 In a new query window, create this XML document, and enclose it in single quotes.

Add the code to declare the two variables (the integer to give us the document handle and the XML variable to store our XML document), store the XML document into the variable @Doc, prepare the document, and display the handle.

```
DECLARE @hDoc INT
DECLARE @Doc XML

SET @Doc =
'<Root>
 <Emp User = "Tom">
  <Emp User = "Dick"/>
  <Emp User = "Harry"/>
</Emp>
</Root>'

EXEC Sp_XML_PrepareDocument @hDoc OUTPUT, @Doc

SELECT @hDoc
```

Results | Messages

	(No column name)
1	1

Query executed successfully. | RENO (11.0 RTM) | Reno\Student (51) | JProCo | 00:00:00 | 1 rows

Figure 3.27 Our document handle is 1.

Declare the variable to access our XML document and set it equal to our document handle (which is our “claim ticket” number, 1). Then add the SELECT statement to query the result set of the OPENXML function. Our rowpattern parameter (‘/Root/Emp’) specifies that we want only the top-level element.

```
DECLARE @iDoc INT
SET @iDoc=1
SELECT *
FROM OPENXML(@iDoc,'/Root/Emp')
WITH (EmployeeName VARCHAR(MAX) '@User')
```

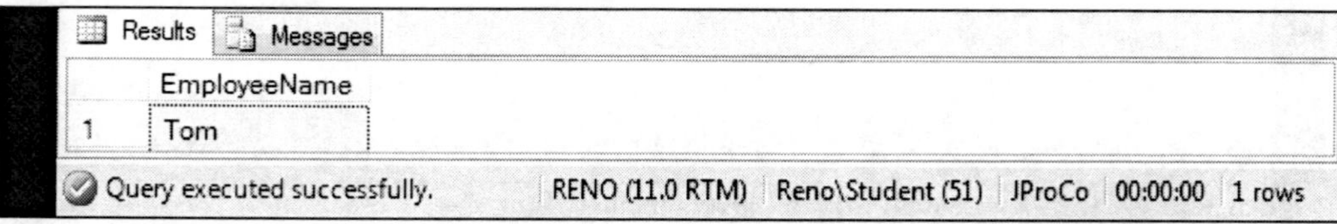

Figure 3.28 We only want to see the highest employee level, which is the boss (Tom).

Now let’s modify our code to see the next level down. The child-level element (rowpattern ‘/Root/Emp/Emp’) contains Dick and Harry (Figure 3.29).

```
DECLARE @iDoc INT
SET @iDoc=1
SELECT *
FROM OPENXML(@iDoc,'/Root/Emp/Emp')
WITH (EmployeeName VARCHAR(MAX) '@User')
```

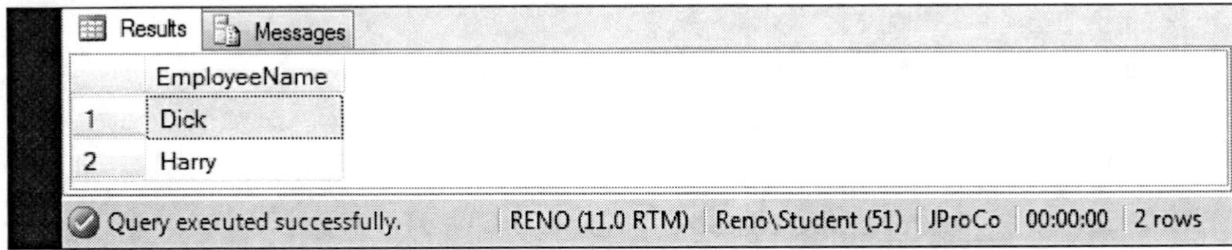

	EmployeeName
1	Dick
2	Harry

Query executed successfully. | RENO (11.0 RTM) | Reno\Student (51) | JProCo | 00:00:00 | 2 rows

Figure 3.29 We want to see the next employee level, which contains Dick and Harry.

A slight modification to our rowpattern parameter specifies that we want to pull data from every level, at or beneath the <Root>, and having an XML tag named <Emp> (Figure 3.30). This is an example of using rowpattern's *relative* navigation capability. Thus far our row level specifications have been absolute - our OPENXML queries have explicitly named each level and instructed SQL Server to pull data from that level. In our next section, we will see some of the tools SQL Server makes available for *relative* navigation of our XML data.

```
DECLARE @iDoc INT
SET @iDoc=1
SELECT *
FROM OPENXML(@iDoc,'/Root//Emp')
WITH (EmployeeName VARCHAR(MAX) '@User')
```

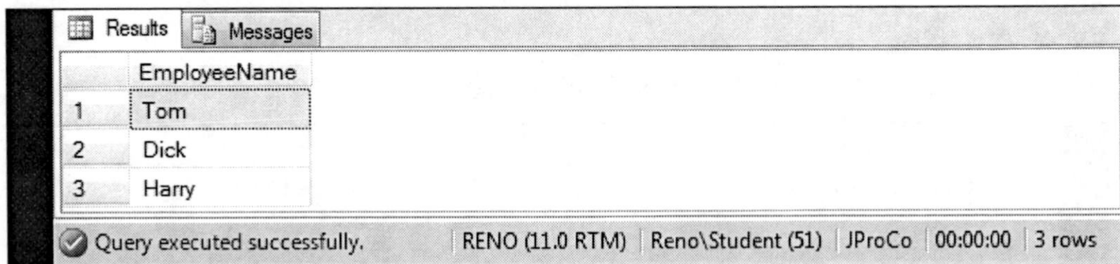

	EmployeeName
1	Tom
2	Dick
3	Harry

Query executed successfully. | RENO (11.0 RTM) | Reno\Student (51) | JProCo | 00:00:00 | 3 rows

Figure 3.30 We want to see data from all levels named "Emp."

Relative Level

We are already familiar with the concept of defining entities or positions in a relative way - that is, as they relate to other entities or positions rather than explicitly calling them by their unique names or fixed positions. In conversation, my dad often refers to his "two younger sons," rather than explicitly using the names "Jeff" and "Rick." At work I sometimes get visitors who come to my door when they are actually looking for the fellow who occupied my office up until a month ago. Rather than giving them his new office number, it is easier to direct them to take the elevator up to the next floor and then to look for the first door on the right. I've found when I told them, "He's moved to room 401", I've always needed to give them the friendly directions anyway. So after the first day, I just skipped the **explicit name** 401 and gave them the **relative location**.

Throughout the Joes 2 Pros series, we have seen the importance of variables to make our T-SQL code more flexible and reusable instead of explicitly hardcoding each value. The OPENXML function similarly offers us the option of pulling data in a relative fashion. In other words, instead of explicitly naming the element levels where we want SQL Server to navigate and pull data, our code can provide rowpattern or column pattern instructions relative to a specified context.

In our next example, the rowpattern option will help us pull data from another level relative to our current position. Recall our example of a large organization with many employee levels. You can use the rowpattern's ability to query relatively and find the managers who are two levels above a certain manager. Perhaps you've been asked to compile a list of all the employees who are three levels beneath your manager.

We now will modify our current code (refer back to Figure 3.30) to include a column specifying each employee's boss. Our goal (shown in Figure 3.31) is to see the boss' name listed alongside each employee (original XML document appears in Figure 3.27). Note that the name of Tom's boss will appear as NULL, since Tom is the highest level boss in the organization.

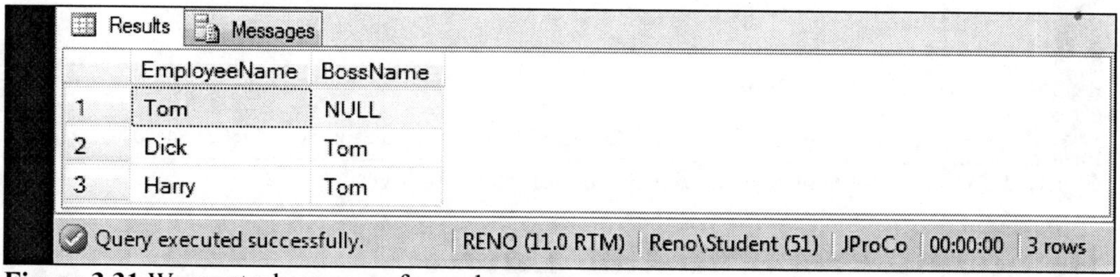

Results | Messages

	EmployeeName	BossName
1	Tom	NULL
2	Dick	Tom
3	Harry	Tom

Query executed successfully. | RENO (11.0 RTM) | Reno\Student (51) | JProCo | 00:00:00 | 3 rows

Figure 3.31 We want a boss name for each person.

Recall in Lab 3.2 we added a column to our OPENXML query by simply defining it inside our WITH clause. The new trick here will be to add '…/' to the front of the column pattern (ColPattern) parameter, e.g. '../@User' (Figure 3.32), which tells SQL Server to search the level above. In other words, we want SQL Server to go up one level from the current context and retrieve the User attribute from that level. The syntax '../../@User' would tell SQL Server to go up two levels and retrieve the User attribute.

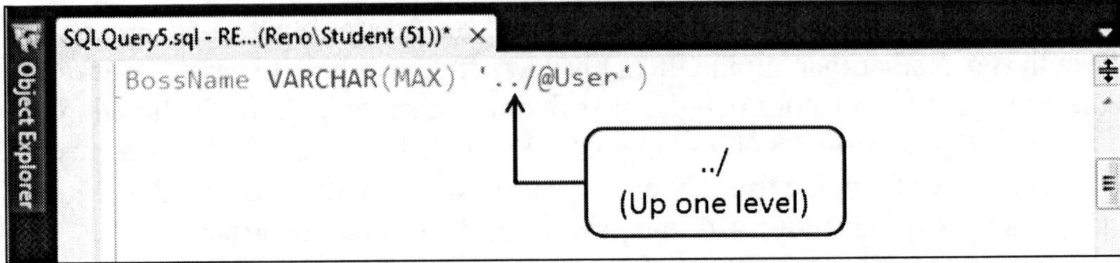

Figure 3.32 This code tells SQL Server to go up one level from the current rowpattern level.

Since our rowpattern itself '/Root//Emp' is relative, it will search for data at the root level and every child-level below. If the '/Root//Emp' rowpattern finds an employee at the fifth level, then the '../@User' colpattern specifier will go up one level (i.e., up to the fourth level) to search for corresponding data. For example, when the rowpattern instruction '/Root//Emp' locates an Emp level, the colpattern '@User' will find the first User attribute (Dick) at the Emp level. The colpattern '../@User' instructs SQL Server to retrieve the User attribute (Tom) from the level above Dick's level (Figure 3.33).

```
DECLARE @iDoc INT
SET @iDoc=1
SELECT *
FROM OPENXML(@iDoc,'/Root//Emp')
WITH (EmployeeName VARCHAR(MAX) '@User',
BossName VARCHAR(MAX) '../@User')
```

Results | Messages

	EmployeeName	BossName
1	Tom	NULL
2	Dick	Tom
3	Harry	Tom

Query executed successfully. | RENO (11.0 RTM) | Reno\Student (51) | JProCo | 00:00:00 | 3 rows

Figure 3.33 Our result shows us the BossName for each employee.

Removing Prepared XML Data

The sproc sp_XML_RemoveDocument will remove an XML document and its handle from memory. If you accidentally create an additional handle during your session or wish to back track and repeate a step, this code will accomplish that for you (Figure 3.34). In older versions of SQL Server, you needed to perform this step to remove your XML document from the internal cache. However, beginning in SQL Server 2005, this is automatically done for you once the session is closed.

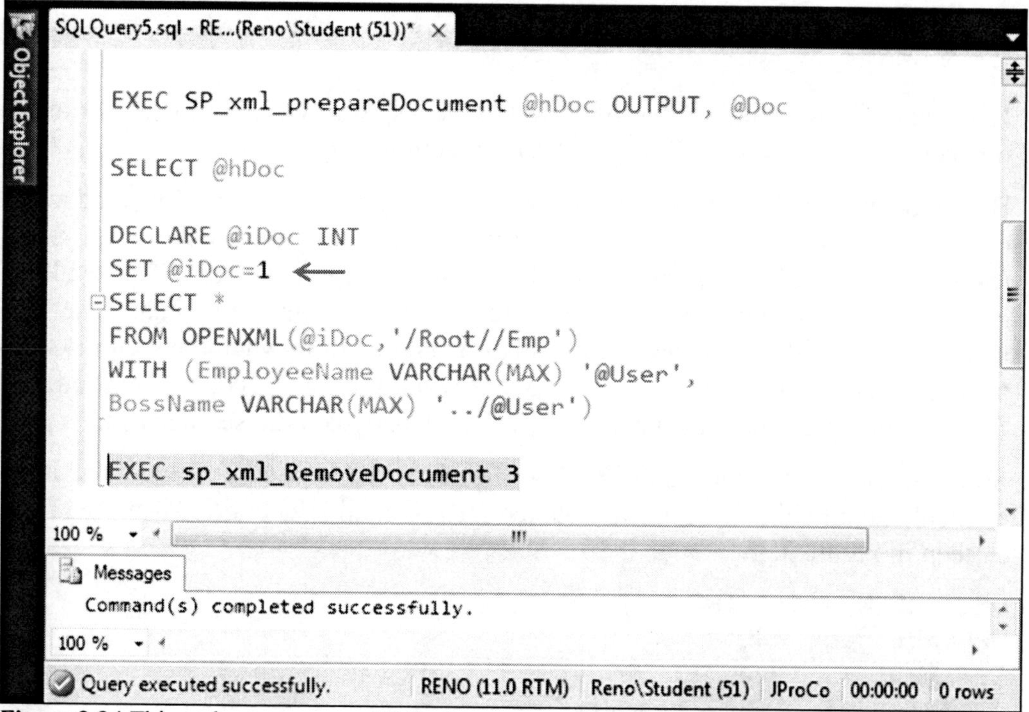

Figure 3.34 This code removes our XML document and its handle from the memory cache.

Lab 3.3: OPENXML Options

Lab Prep: Each lab has one or more Skill Checks. Start with Skill Check 1 and proceed until reaching the Points to Ponder section.

Before beginning this lab, verify that SQL Server 2012 is properly installed and operating. Before running the lab setup script for resetting the database (SQLQueries2012Vol5Chapter1.0-4.2Setup.sql), please make sure to close all query windows within SSMS. An open query window pointing to a database context can lock that database preventing it from updating when the script is executing. A simple way to assure all query windows are closed, is to exit out of SSMS, then open a new instance of SSMS, and lastly run the setup script.

Skill Check 1: Open the Lab3.3SK1.sql file from the Resources folder. The root element and all child elements are named URI. Get all URI entities from the Doc as seen in Figure 3.35.

```
DECLARE @Handle INT
DECLARE @Doc XML
SET @Doc =
 '<URI Name="Joes2Pros.com">
  <URI Name="Books.Joes2Pros.com">
   <URI Name="T-SQL.Books.Joes2Pros.com"/>
   <URI Name="Queries.Books.Joes2Pros.com"/>
   <URI Name="Dev.Books.Joes2Pros.com"/>
  </URI>
  <URI Name="Classes.Joes2Pros.com">
   <URI Name="Seattle.Classes.Joes2Pros.com"/>
   <URI Name="Portland.Classes.Joes2Pros.com"/>
   <URI Name="Spokane.Classes.Joes2Pros.com"/>
  </URI>
 </URI>'
--Prepare the XML here
```

	URI
1	Joes2Pros.com
2	Books.Joes2Pros.com
3	T-SQL.Books.Joes2Pros.com
4	Queries.Books.Joes2Pros.com
5	Dev.Books.Joes2Pros.com
6	Classes.Joes2Pros.com
7	Seattle.Classes.Joes2Pros.com
8	Portland.Classes.Joes2Pros.com
9	Spokane.Classes.Joes2Pros.com

Figure 3.35 The XML document and result for Skill Check 1.

Skill Check 2: Open the Lab3.3SK2.sql file from the Resources folder. Get all URI entities from the Doc as seen in Figure 3.36.

```
DECLARE @Handle INT
DECLARE @Doc XML
SET @Doc =
 '<URI Name="Joes2Pros.com">
  <URI Name="Books.Joes2Pros.com">
   <URI Name="T-SQL.Books.Joes2Pros.com"/>
   <URI Name="Queries.Books.Joes2Pros.com"/>
   <URI Name="Dev.Books.Joes2Pros.com"/>
  </URI>
  <URI Name="Classes.Joes2Pros.com">
   <URI Name="Seattle.Classes.Joes2Pros.com"/>
   <URI Name="Portland.Classes.Joes2Pros.com"/>
   <URI Name="Spokane.Classes.Joes2Pros.com"/>
  </URI>
 </URI>'

--Prepare the XML here
```

Results | Messages

	URI	ParentDomain
1	Joes2Pros.com	NULL
2	Books.Joes2P...	Joes2Pros.c...
3	T-SQL.Books....	Books.Joes...
4	Queries.Book...	Books.Joes...
5	Dev.Books.Jo...	Books.Joes...
6	Classes.Joes...	Joes2Pros.c...
7	Seattle.Classe...	Classes.Joe...
8	Portland.Clas...	Classes.Joe...
9	Spokane.Clas...	Classes.Joe...

Query executed successfully. | RENO (11.0 RTM) | Reno\Student (51) | master | 00:00:00 | 9 rows

Figure 3.36 The XML document and result for Skill Check 2.

Skill Check 3: Remove the document handle from memory that you used to parse this XML from Skill Check 2. You screen should say “Command(s) completed successfully” when complete.

Skill Check 4: Open the Lab3.3SK4.sql file from the Resources folder. Get all Unit entities from the XML document as seen in Figure 3.36

```
DECLARE @hDoc INT
DECLARE @Doc XML

SET @Doc =
'<Unit Item = "Port Authority">
 <Unit Item = "Todd Shipyard">
  <Unit Item = "Keu Maru"/>
  <Unit Item = "Brave Waters"/>
  <Unit Item = "Miss C"/>
 </Unit>
 <Unit Item = "Commencement Bay">
  <Unit Item = "Big Sultan"/>
  <Unit Item = "Amaknak"/>
  <Unit Item = "Pacific Progress"/>
 </Unit>
</Unit>';
```

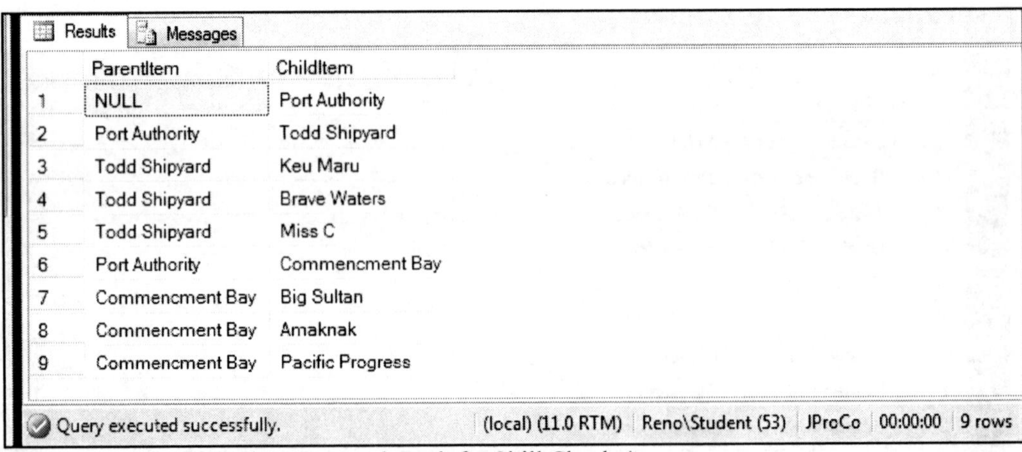

	ParentItem	ChildItem
1	NULL	Port Authority
2	Port Authority	Todd Shipyard
3	Todd Shipyard	Keu Maru
4	Todd Shipyard	Brave Waters
5	Todd Shipyard	Miss C
6	Port Authority	Commencment Bay
7	Commencment Bay	Big Sultan
8	Commencment Bay	Amaknak
9	Commencment Bay	Pacific Progress

Figure 3.37 The XML document and result for Skill Check 4.

Answer Code: The T-SQL code to this lab can be found in the downloadable files in a file named Lab3.3_OPENXMLOptions.sql

Points to Ponder - OPENXML Options

1. If you have several levels of elements with the same name, you can specify all of the levels in your rowpattern by using a double forward slash before the element name:
    - /Root/Employee - Gets only the top-level Employee elements
    - /Root//Employee - Gets the Employee elements at all levels
2. If you want to get data one level above the current level then you specify two dots and a forward slash. The XPath syntax to go up 1 level is '../' before the ColPattern (column pattern).
3. You can have multiple XML trees inside the SQL cache at the same time.
4. Once an XML tree is no longer needed, use sp_XML_RemoveDocument to remove it from the internal cache.
5. In SQL Server 2005, once your query window is closed and your session is done, the internal cache will be cleared. In such cases, you will not need to use the sp_XML_RemoveDocument procedure.
6. Even though you aren't required to use sp_XML_RemoveDocument, it is recommended that you include a remove document step inside stored procedures because the connection to SQL Server is maintained for a longer time where a web service or website makes the connection to SQL Server.
7. Because @hDoc is a local variable, the sp_XML_RemoveDocument must be in the same query session as the sp_XML_RemoveDocument.
8. In SQL Server 2000, the memory used by the internal cache was not cleared by closing your session. You had to use the sp_XML_RemoveDocument procedure or face serious memory leaks.

Chapter Glossary

Column pattern: Sometimes shortened to "ColPattern"; used in conjunction with the OPENXML function; the ColPattern option helps you pull data from another column relative to your current position.

OPENXML: A function used to pull data in a relative fashion; in other words, instead of explicitly naming (i.e., hardcoding) the element levels where we want SQL Server to navigate and pull data, our code can provide rowpattern or column pattern instructions relative to a specified context.

Preparing XML (for SQL): This process includes storing the XML in memory and processing the XML so that all the data and metadata is ready and available for your access via a SQL query.

Rowpattern: Used in conjunction with the OPENXML function; the rowpattern option helps you pull data from another level relative to your current position.

Shredding XML: The complete process of transforming XML data into a rowset.

sp_XML_PrepareDocument: A system stored procedure which parses an XML document into a tree representation of the various nodes and stores it within SQL Server's internal cache; the two required parameters are the handle (an integer handle representing the XML document in memory) and the XML document (i.e., the XML document which you wish to process).

sp_XML_RemoveDocument: A system stored procedure which removes an XML document and its handle from memory.

Review Quiz - Chapter Three

1.) What process will transform XML data to a rowset?

O a. Shredding

O b. Retrieving

2.) Where does sp_XML_PrepareDocument prepare its data?

O a. In the MDF file

O b. In the LDF file

O c. In the internal cache

O d. In the messages window

3.) The sp_XML_PrepareDocument stored procedure requires a parameter that is an XML data type. What is the output parameter for?

O a. The handle as an INT

O b. The handle as an XML

O c. The handle as a VARCHAR

4.) What function is used to take your prepared XML data into a tabular shredded format?

O a. OPENXML

O b. GetXML

O c. RetrieveXML

O d. ShredXML

5.) Which clause is used to specify the fields you want to use from the OPENXML function?

O a. FROM

O b. WITH

O c. HAVING

O d. FOR

O e. WHEN

O f. LET

O g. ORDER BY

6.) You have the following XML depicting the employee hierarchy of the two employees working for Tom:

```
'<Root>
 <Emp User = "Tom">
 <Emp User = "Dick"/>
 <Emp User = "Harry"/>
 </Emp>
<Root>'
```

You want to query the employees in the XML using the OPENXML function. The results will show the User Name of all Employees in the hierarchy. You have already declared an XML handle named @iDoc. Which query would you use?

O a.
```
DECLARE @iDoc INT
SET @iDoc=1
SELECT *
FROM OPENXML(@iDoc,'/Root/Emp/Emp')
WITH (EmployeeName VARCHAR(max) '@User')
```

O b.
```
DECLARE @iDoc INT
SET @iDoc=1
SELECT *
FROM OPENXML(@iDoc,'/Root/Emp')
WITH (EmployeeName VARCHAR(max) '@Emp')
```

O c.
```
DECLARE @iDoc INT
SET @iDoc=1
SELECT *
FROM OPENXML(@iDoc,'/Root//Emp')
WITH (EmployeeName VARCHAR(max) '@User')
```

O d.
```
DECLARE @iDoc INT
SET @iDoc=1
SELECT *
FROM OPENXML(@iDoc,'/Root//Emp')
WITH (EmployeeName VARCHAR(max) '@Emp')
```

7.) You want your rowpattern to only grab the data from the top-level Employee element. Which rowpattern will do this?

O a. /Root/Employee

O b. /Root//Employee

O c. //Root//Employee

8.) You have an application which is calling on T-SQL code which in turn is preparing XML documents and turning the data into a tabular stream. The code is creating new prepared XML without flushing the old XML from the SQL Server memory. You need to run a system stored procedure which will flush the prepared XML from the system's memory. Which T-SQL statement do you use?

O a. sp_XML_RemoveDocument

O b. sp_XML_PrepareDocument

O c. sp_XML_FlushDocument

O d. sp_XML_FlushNamespace

Answer Key

1.) The process of converting XML data to a row set is called shredding, so (a) is the correct answer.

2.) An MDF file is the primary data file and is not used by the system stored procedure to prepare its data, so (a) is incorrect. The LDF file holds the database transaction log used in backup recovery, so (b) is incorrect. The system stored procedure does not prepare data in view in the Message window, so (d) is incorrect. The sp_XML_PrepareDocument prepares its data in the internal cache, so (c) is the correct answer.

3.) The sp_XML_PrepareDocument stored procedure uses a handle to label the output as an integer, so (a) is the correct answer.

4.) GetXML returns XML as a string, so (b) is incorrect. RetreveXML and ShredXML are not actual methods, so (c) and (d) are incorrect. OPENXML returns a rowset or tabular view of XML, so (a) is correct.

5.) When using the OPENXML function the WITH clause is used to specify the fields you want to use, so (b) is the correct answer.

6.) Answer (a) will only query data from the /root/emp/emp level, so (a) is incorrect. Answer (b) is incorrect because the field specifier is referencing @emp which is the element name not attribute data and is looking at only the /root/emp level. Answer (d) is incorrect because the field specifier is referencing @emp. The correct answer is (c) because it is using relative level navigation to find all <emp> level users.

7.) Answer (b) is incorrect because the /Root//Employee relative path will find the Employee elements at any level. //Root//Employee is incorrect syntax, so (c) is incorrect. Answer (a) is correct since it is looking only at the first Employee level after the <root>.(/Root/Employee)

8.) The result of the sp_XML_PrepareDocument stored procedure is what we want to remove so answer (b) is incorrect. sp_XML_FlushDocument and sp_XML_FlushNamespace are not actual system stored procedures so answers (c) and (d) are incorrect. The sp_XML_RemoveDocument system stored procedure is used to free internal memory from sp_XML_PrepareDocument, so (a) is correct.

Bug Catcher Game

To play the Bug Catcher game run the SQLQueries2012Vol5BugCatcher3.pps from the BugCatcher folder of the companion files found at www.Joes2Pros.com.

Chapter 4. Shredding Attributes,Elements & Levels

As SQL Server professionals, we are tasked with bringing data into SQL Server databases so that it can become useful information we can aggregate and then output in the form of reporting or a stream of data made available to another program. XML is one of the many types of inputs and outputs available for use in combination with databases.

From the first three chapters, we understand that XML is an important vehicle for transmitting data between programs and datasources. The near ubiquitousness of XML in IT means we will encounter it on the job and we need to be prepared to handle XML files in our database work. As solution providers, we also need to be familiar with how XML works so we know when to utilize it in accomplishing a development goal.

The last chapter explained and helped us master the steps necessary to prepare our XML document for SQL Server's consumption. We understand the basic flow of shredding XML and are now ready to increase our knowledge by delving into more complex shredding examples. In order to harvest data from XML and bring it into our homebase (i.e., a SQL Server database), we must increase our fluency with XML's methods for storing and organizing data so that we can easily navigate and retrieve our needed data from all levels and types.

As noted in Chapter 1, XML is case-sensitive. In order for your examples and exercises to run properly in Chapters 1 through 7, be sure that your XML fragments precisely match the figures with respect to uppercase and lowercase.

READERNOTE:*Please run the script SQLQueries2012Vol5Chapter1.0-4.2Setup.sqlin order to follow along with the examples in the first section of Chapter 4. You only need to run this script once for all examples in Chapters 1 through 4. All scripts mentioned in this chapter may be found at* ***www.Joes2Pros.com****.*

OPENXML Column Patterns

We learned in the last chapter that a **rowpattern** is useful for targeting the level where you want to get your data. But what if seven out of eight of the values are at one element level and one important value is at another level? Whenever your levels or names don't match, you need a way to specify how that field will get its data. The use of a **column pattern** allows you to expand beyond the level specified by the rowpattern.

While a rowpattern only lets you pick one level, a column pattern (sometimes called **colpattern**) allows you to specify a level for each column in your data.

Open the starter script Lab4.1Starter.sql in a new query window (It will contain the data you see below in Figure 4.1). Choose any database context you wish except the Master db (I've chosen dbBasics). Notice that the data we want is located across three different levels: cust, Order, and OrderDetail.

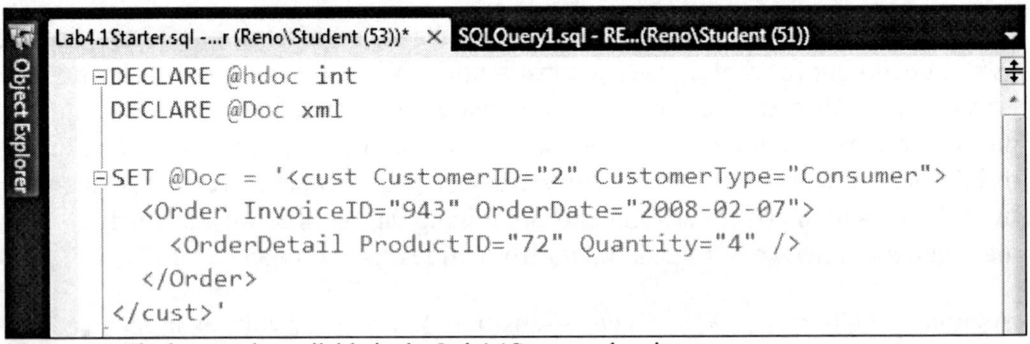

Lab4.1Starter.sql -...r (Reno\Student (53))* × SQLQuery1.sql - RE...(Reno\Student (51))

Object Explorer

```
DECLARE @hdoc int
DECLARE @Doc xml

SET @Doc = '<cust CustomerID="2" CustomerType="Consumer">
  <Order InvoiceID="943" OrderDate="2008-02-07">
    <OrderDetail ProductID="72" Quantity="4" />
  </Order>
</cust>'
```

Figure 4.1 The base code available in the Lab4.1Starter.sql script.

Our next step will be to execute **SP_XML_PrepareDocument** in order to pass in our XML document and receive back the document handle (Figure 4.2).

```
DECLARE @hDoc INT
DECLARE @Doc XML

SET @Doc = '<cust CustomerID="2" CustomerType="Consumer">
 <Order InvoiceID="943" OrderDate="2008-02-07">
  <OrderDetail ProductID="72" Quantity="4" />
 </Order>
</cust>'

EXEC Sp_XML_PrepareDocument @hDoc OUTPUT, @Doc
SELECT @hDoc
```

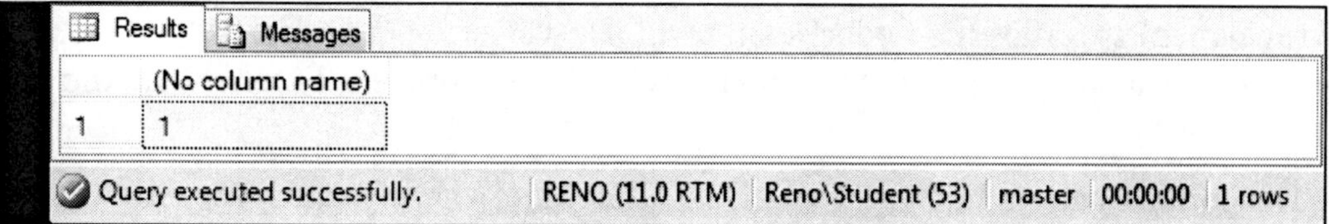

Figure 4.2 Run all of this code together to store & prepare the XML document as @Doc.

Our handle of 1 (our "claim ticket" result received in Figure 4.2) is used in the following code which pulls the data from the OPENXML function using a SELECT statement. Our rowpattern specifies we want data from the OrderDetail level.

(Please note that the code shown in Figures 4.2-4.6 has been run from within one window. In order to conserve space, the Figure 4.3 through Figure 4.6 results are shown with just the code which pulled the data from the OPENXML function.)

```
DECLARE @iDoc INT
SET @iDoc = 1

SELECT *
FROM OPENXML (@iDoc, '/cust/Order/OrderDetail')
```

	id	parentid	nodetype	localname	prefix	namespaceuri	datatype	prev	text
1	7	4	1	OrderDetail	NULL	NULL	NULL	NULL	NULL
2	8	7	2	ProductID	NULL	NULL	NULL	NULL	NULL
3	10	8	3	#text	NULL	NULL	NULL	NULL	72
4	9	7	2	Quantity	NULL	NULL	NULL	NULL	NULL
5	11	9	3	#text	NULL	NULL	NULL	NULL	4

Query executed successfully. | RENO (11.0 RTM) | Reno\Student (53) | master | 00:00:00 | 5 rows

Figure 4.3 Our initial OPENXML query pulls from just one level, /cust/Order/OrderDetail.

Going Up One Level

Suppose we want to see InvoiceID in our result set, but that data is not at our current rowpattern level (/cust/Order/OrderDetail). This data is one level above our rowpattern at the /cust/Order level.

We can add a colpattern hint (../) to specify that we want data pulled from a parent level of our current rowpattern. To go up one level, use the XPath syntax *../@AttributeSpecification* in the column pattern.

Now we will narrow down our result by specifying the three columns OrderDate, ProductID, and Quantity. In Figure 4.3, we can see the latter two values are already being retrieved by our query (ProductID 72 and Quantity 4) because the rowpattern specifies the OrderDetail level. However to get OrderDate, we need our query to also pull from the Order level, which is one level higher than our other data.

The column pattern hints (@OrderDate, @ProductID, @Quantity) specify that we want the values of the attributes (denoted by the @ symbol) pulled from each of these three columns. The additional ../ hint used with @OrderDate ('../@OrderDate') instructs SQL Server to retrieve the data from one level higher than the rowpattern (Figure 4.4).

```
DECLARE @iDoc INT
SET @iDoc = 1

SELECT *
FROM OPENXML (@iDoc, '/cust/Order/OrderDetail')
WITH (OrderDate DATETIME '../@OrderDate',
 ProductID INT '@ProductID', Quantity INT '@Quantity')
```

Results | Messages

	OrderDate	ProductID	Quantity
1	2008-02-07 00:00:00.000	72	4

Query executed successfully. | RENO (11.0 RTM) | Reno\Student (53) | master | 00:00:00 | 1 rows

Figure 4.4 The colpattern ('../@OrderDate') retrieves data from one level higher than the rowpattern.

Renaming a Field

The WITH clause allows you to customize the field headers in your result. Specify your preferred naming, as shown in Figure 4.5 with ProdID and Qty.

```
DECLARE @iDoc INT
SET @iDoc = 1

SELECT *
FROM OPENXML (@iDoc, '/cust/Order/OrderDetail')
WITH (OrderDate DATETIME '../@OrderDate',
 ProdID INT '@ProductID', Qty INT '@Quantity')
```

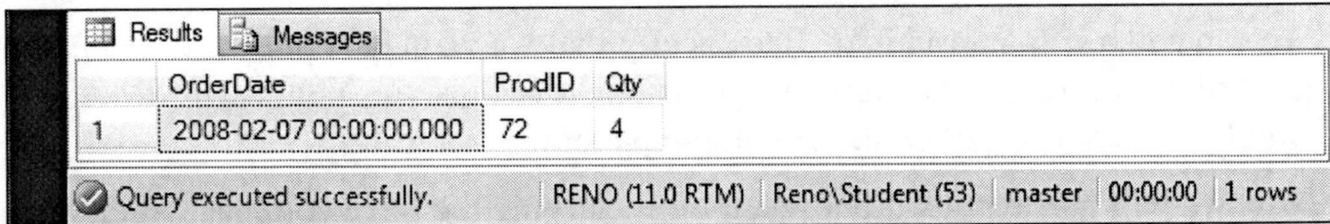

Results | Messages

	OrderDate	ProdID	Qty
1	2008-02-07 00:00:00.000	72	4

Query executed successfully. | RENO (11.0 RTM) | Reno\Student (53) | master | 00:00:00 | 1 rows

Figure 4.5 The WITH clause allows you to customize and alias your field headers.

Attributes versus Elements

When pulling data which is contained in attributes, prefix the field name with the @ sign and enclose it in single quotation marks (e.g., '@Quantity' as shown in Figures 4.4 through 4.6).

To pull the values for data which is contained in elements, simply list the field name in your WITH clause and enclose the name in single quotes.

If the <Quantity> data were contained in elements instead of in attributes, the field reference would have appeared in our WITH clause as 'Quantity', instead of '@Quantity'. This is illustrated in the following comparison:

```
--'@Quantity' in the Column Pattern: Quantity is an attribute

'<cust CustomerID="2" CustomerType="Consumer">
 <Order InvoiceID="943" OrderDate="2008-02-07">
  <OrderDetail ProductID="72" Quantity="4" />
 </Order>
</cust>'

--'Quantity' in the Column Pattern: Quantity is element text

'<cust CustomerID="2" CustomerType="Consumer">
 <Order InvoiceID="943" OrderDate="2008-02-07">
  <OrderDetail ProductID="72">
   <Quantity>
    4<Quantity>
 </OrderDetail>
 </Order>
</cust>'
```

READERNOTE: In both cases, Quantity is a child of <OrderDetail>. In the first example, Quantity is an attribute child, and in the second example it's an element child.

Going Up Multiple Levels

We know the hint ../ instructs SQL Server to search for data one level above the current rowpattern. To specify multiple levels higher than the rowpattern, add another instance of the parent hint (../) to your rowpattern. *Examples:*

The code ../ in your ColPattern will search one level above the rowpattern.
The code ../../ in your ColPattern will search two levels above the rowpattern. The code ../../../ will search three levels above the rowpattern, and so forth.

Using these ColPattern hints allows us to pull all the values from every level of our current XML document (Figure 4.6 results based on the original XML document shown in Figure 4.1). Observe that the InvoiceID and OrderDate column patterns are going up one level, while the Customer and CustomerType column patterns are going up two levels.

```
DECLARE @iDoc INT
SET @iDoc = 1

SELECT *
FROM OPENXML (@iDoc, '/cust/Order/OrderDetail')
WITH (
OrderID INT '../@InvoiceID',
CustID INT '../../@CustomerID',
[Type] VARCHAR (MAX) '../../@CustomerType',
OrderDate DATETIME '../@OrderDate',
ProdID INT '@ProductID',
Qty INT '@Quantity')
```

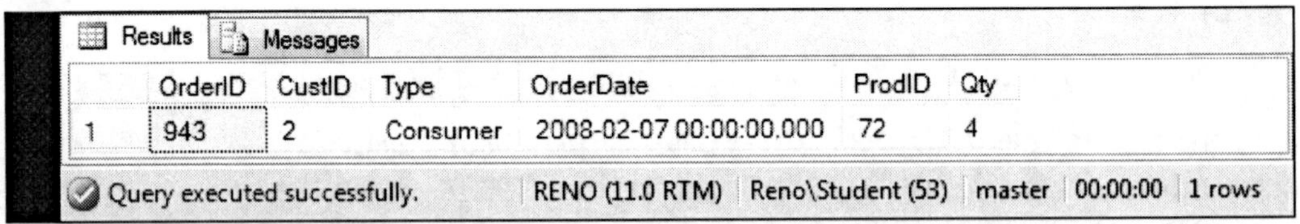

Results | Messages

	OrderID	CustID	Type	OrderDate	ProdID	Qty
1	943	2	Consumer	2008-02-07 00:00:00.000	72	4

Query executed successfully. | RENO (11.0 RTM) | Reno\Student (53) | master | 00:00:00 | 1 rows

Figure 4.6 We have specified column patterns which search for columnar data at one and two levels (Order level and cust level, respectively) above the rowpattern (the OrderDetail level).

Lab 4.1: OPENXML Column Patterns

Lab Prep: Each lab has one or more Skill Checks. Start with Skill Check 1 and proceed until reaching the Points to Ponder section.

Before beginning this lab, verify that SQL Server 2012 is properly installed and operating. Before running the lab setup script for resetting the database (SQLQueries2012Vol5Chapter1.0-4.2Setup.sql), please make sure to close all query windows within SSMS. An open query window pointing to a database context can lock that database preventing it from updating when the script is executing. A simple way to assure all query windows are closed, is to exit out of SSMS, then open a new instance of SSMS, and lastly run the setup script.

Skill Check 1: Open the resource file Lab4.1SK1.sql to retrieve the code you see here:

```
DECLARE @hDoc INT
DECLARE @doc XML

SET @doc =
'<BigFoods>
 <Store ID = "1"><TotalSales>145000</TotalSales>
 </Store>
 <Store ID = "2"><TotalSales>177000</TotalSales>
 </Store>
</BigFoods>'
```

Once you have opened Lab4.1SK1.sql write a query that shreds the XML into tabular form. When done your result will resemble Figure 4.7.

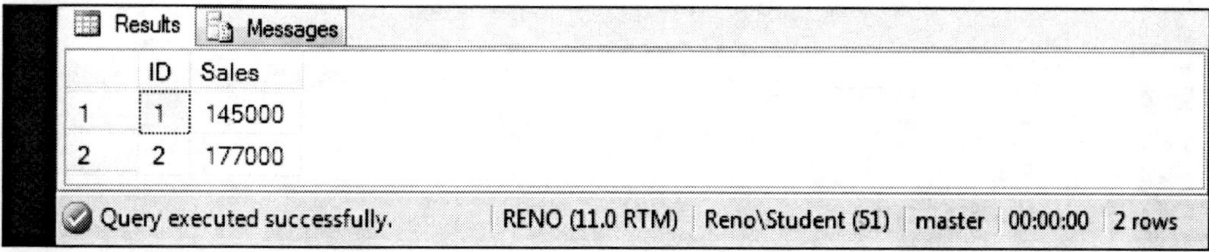

	ID	Sales
1	1	145000
2	2	177000

Figure 4.7 The result of Skill Check 1.

Skill Check 2: Open the resource file Lab4.1SK2.sql to retrieve the code you see here:

```
DECLARE @hDoc INT
DECLARE @Doc XML

SET @Doc =
'<Company Name="JProCo">
 <Structure Name="Building 1">
  <Room Name="Kitchen"> <Status>Open</Status></Room>
  <Room Name="Library"> <Status>Open</Status></Room>
  <Room Name="Rainier Boardroom"> <Status>Closed</Status>
  </Room>
 </Structure>
 <Structure Name="Building 2">
  <Room Name="Pool"> <Status>Open</Status></Room>
  <Room Name="Smoothie Bar"> <Status>Open</Status> </Room>
  <Room Name="Andes Boardroom"> <Status>Open</Status>
  </Room>
 </Structure>
</Company>'

EXEC Sp_XML_PrepareDocument @hDoc OUTPUT, @Doc
```

Once you have opened Lab4.1SK2.sql write a query that shreds the XML into tabular form. When done the result set should have all values from all levels as fields (Figure 4.8).

Results | Messages

	Company	Structure	RoomName	RoomStatus
1	JProCo	Building 1	Kitchen	Open
2	JProCo	Building 1	Library	Open
3	JProCo	Building 1	Rainier Boardroom	Closed
4	JProCo	Building 2	Pool	Open
5	JProCo	Building 2	Smoothie Bar	Open
6	JProCo	Building 2	Andes Boardroom	Open

Query executed successfully. | RENO (11.0 RTM) | Reno\Student (51) | master | 00:00:00 | 6 rows

Figure 4.8 The result of Skill Check 2.

Points to Ponder - OPENXML Column Patterns

1. The OPENXML function takes an integer handle parameter which represents your XML and a rowpattern to specify at what level you want to extract your data.
2. The WITH clause contains column patterns which combine the OPENXML function's rowpattern with the XPath instructions for each field.
3. If you are retrieving attribute data at the same level as the rowpattern specified in the OPENXML function, and the field headers are named the same as the fields, then you can omit the XPath for that field.

READERNOTE: The script Lab4.2Starter.sql contains the XML document shown in this section's examples and is available at ***www.Joes2Pros.com***.

OPENXML Parameters

We are now familiar with the two required parameters of the OPENXML table-valued function: 1) the document handle which identifies the in-memory location of the XML document, and 2) the rowpattern. There is one more optional parameter which can make your life easier when your data is stored in a mixture of attributes and elements.

OPENXML Flag (Optional)

The third parameter of the OPENXML function is the flag. The flag is optional - if you do not specify a flag, your query will search only for values mapped as attributes. Key values for this flag are 1, 2, or 3:

1 = searches for attributes (if no flag specified, your query will bring in the values which are mapped as attributes)

2 = searches for elements

3 = searches for attributes and elements

Begin by opening the starter script Lab4.2Starter.sql in a new query window (It will contain the data you see below in Figure 4.9). Choose any database context you wish except the Master db (Here we have chosen TSQLTestDB).

Lab4.2Starter.sql -...r (Reno\Student (51))*

```
DECLARE @Doc xml
SET @Doc =
'<SalesInvoice InvoiceID="1000" CustomerID="123" OrderDate="2004-03-07">
  <Items>
    <Item ProductCode="12" Quantity="2" UnitPrice="12.99"><ProductName>Bike</ProductName></Item>
    <Item ProductCode="41" Quantity="1" UnitPrice="17.45"><ProductName>Helmet</ProductName></Item>
    <Item ProductCode="2" Quantity="1" UnitPrice="2.99"><ProductName>Water Bottle</ProductName></Item>
  </Items>
</SalesInvoice>'
```

Figure 4.9 The base code available in the Lab4.2Starter.sql script.

Our next step will be to execute SP_XML_PrepareDocument in order to pass our XML document into the memory cache and receive back the document handle of 1 (Our "claim ticket" shown in Figure 4.10).

```
DECLARE @Doc xml
SET @Doc =
'<SalesInvoice InvoiceID="1000" CustomerID="123"
OrderDate="2004-03-07">
 <Items>
  <Item ProductCode="12" Quantity="2"
   UnitPrice="12.99"><ProductName>Bike</ProductName>
  </Item>
  <Item ProductCode="41" Quantity="1" UnitPrice="17.45">
   <ProductName>Helmet</ProductName>
  </Item>
  <Item ProductCode="2" Quantity="1" UnitPrice="2.99">
   <ProductName>Water Bottle</ProductName>
  </Item>
 </Items>
</SalesInvoice>'

DECLARE @HandleDoc INT

EXEC sp_XML_PrepareDocument @HandleDoc OUTPUT, @Doc
SELECT @HandleDoc AS HandleDoc
```

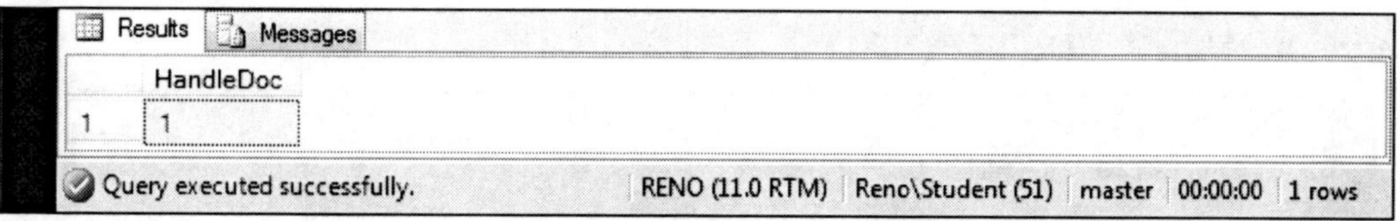

Figure 4.10 Run all of this code to store & prepare the XML document at @Doc.

No flag parameter included in the code below indicates that we only want to see attribute data. Values are present for all fields except the element (<ProductName>), which shows all null values in our tabular result (Figure 4.11).

```
DECLARE @iNum INT
SET @iNum = 1

SELECT * FROM
OPENXML (@iNum, 'SalesInvoice/Items/Item')
WITH
(ProductCode INT,
Quantity INT,
UnitPrice MONEY,
ProductName VARCHAR(50))
```

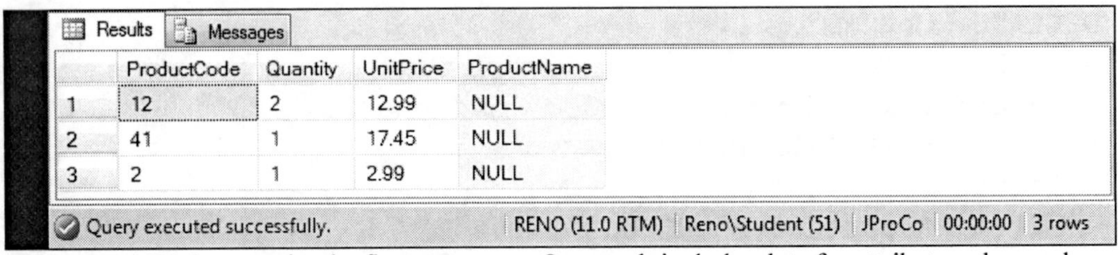

	ProductCode	Quantity	UnitPrice	ProductName
1	12	2	12.99	NULL
2	41	1	17.45	NULL
3	2	1	2.99	NULL

Query executed successfully. | RENO (11.0 RTM) | Reno\Student (51) | JProCo | 00:00:00 | 3 rows

Figure 4.11 We have omitted a flag parameter. Our result includes data for attribute values only.

This is because when you use OPENXML and you're matching on an exact field name, SQL Server looks for *attributes* by default. ProductName is the precise field name to search for this element. However, our code isn't searching for an element - it's searching for attribute data only (Figure 4.12).

```
DECLARE @iNum INT
SET @iNum = 1

SELECT * FROM
OPENXML (@iNum, 'SalesInvoice/Items/Item', 1)
WITH
(ProductCode INT,
Quantity INT,
UnitPrice MONEY,
ProductName VARCHAR(50))
```

	ProductCode	Quantity	UnitPrice	ProductName
1	12	2	12.99	NULL
2	41	1	17.45	NULL
3	2	1	2.99	NULL

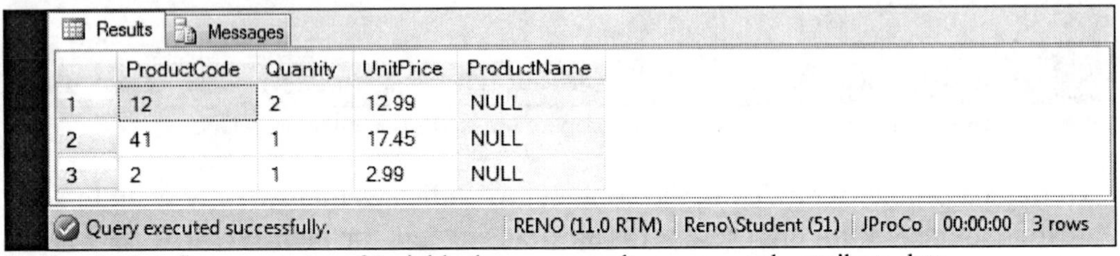

Query executed successfully. | RENO (11.0 RTM) | Reno\Student (51) | JProCo | 00:00:00 | 3 rows

Figure 4.12 A flag parameter of 1 yields the same result - we see only attribute data.

Now we see element data because our flag is set to 2 (Figure 4.13). Notice it found a <ProductName> as a child element of the rowpattern. There are no values for ProductCode, Quantity, or UnitPrice, as those are all attributes (Figure 4.10).

```
DECLARE @iNum INT
SET @iNum = 1

SELECT * FROM
OPENXML (@iNum, 'SalesInvoice/Items/Item', 2)
WITH (ProductCode INT, Quantity INT, UnitPrice MONEY,
 ProductName VARCHAR(50))
```

Results | Messages

	ProductCode	Quantity	UnitPrice	ProductName
1	NULL	NULL	NULL	Bike
2	NULL	NULL	NULL	Helmet
3	NULL	NULL	NULL	Water Bottle

Query executed successfully. | RENO (11.0 RTM) | Reno\Student (51) | JProCo | 00:00:00 | 3 rows

Figure 4.13 A flag parameter value of 2 searches for element data only.

With our flag set to 3, we finally get all of the data points we want to see. The parameter value of 3 instructs our code to look for both attribute and element data (Figure 4.14).

```
DECLARE @iNum INT
SET @iNum = 1

SELECT * FROM
OPENXML (@iNum, 'SalesInvoice/Items/Item', 3)
WITH
(ProductCode INT,
Quantity INT,
UnitPrice MONEY,
ProductName VARCHAR(50))
```

Results | Messages

	ProductCode	Quantity	UnitPrice	ProductName
1	12	2	12.99	Bike
2	41	1	17.45	Helmet
3	2	1	2.99	Water Bottle

Query executed successfully. | RENO (11.0 RTM) | Reno\Student (51) | JProCo | 00:00:00 | 3 rows

Figure 4.14 A flag parameter value of 3 searches for data from both attributes and elements.

This optional flag is very handy for bringing in all of the attribute and element data we want. Notice that we are able to accomplish this without needing to specify any custom column patterns in any of our examples (Figure 4.11- Figure 4.14). Again, this is due to the fact that our code specifies field names which match the field names as they appear in the XML document.

For any fields which are aliased (i.e., whose names do not match the field names in the XML document), we would need to specify a column pattern in order for our attribute and/or element values to appear in our tabular result (Figure 4.15).

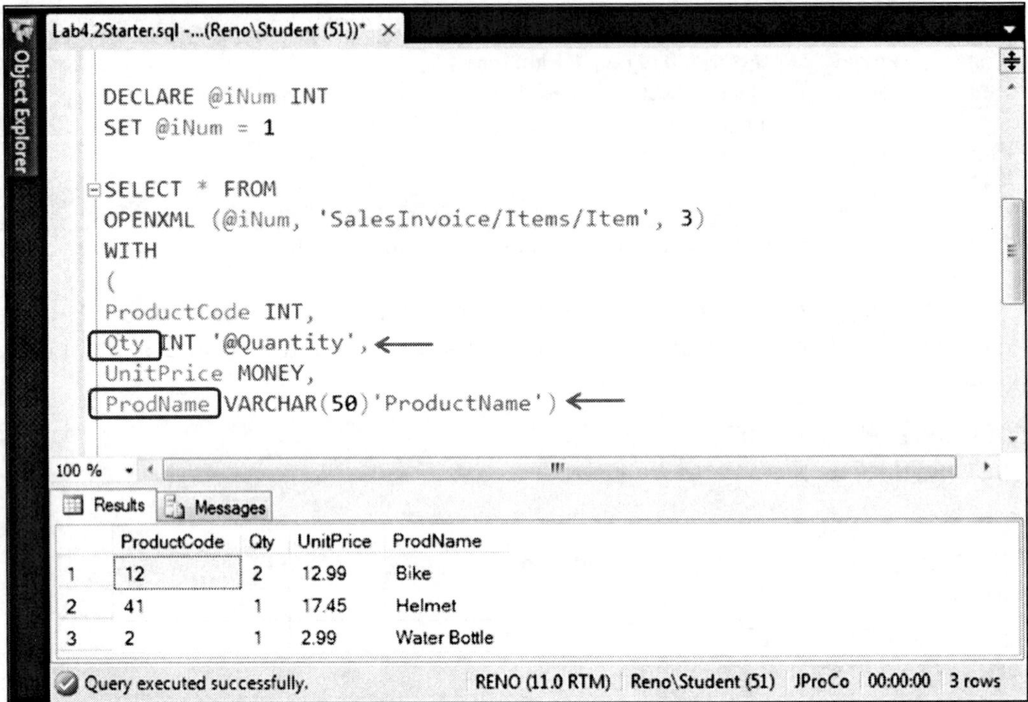

Figure 4.15 Attribute and/or element fields whose names do not match their field names in the XML document must include column patterns.

(Please note that the code shown in Figures 4.9-4.15 has been run from within the same window. In order to conserve space, the Figure 4.10 through Figure 4.15 results are shown with just the code which pulled the data from the OPENXML function.)

Lab 4.2: OPENXML Parameters

Lab Prep: Each lab has one or more Skill Checks. Start with Skill Check 1 and proceed until reaching the Points to Ponder section.

Before beginning this lab, verify that SQL Server 2012 is properly installed and operating. Before running the lab setup script for resetting the database (SQLQueries2012Vol5Chapter1.0-4.2Setup.sql), please make sure to close all query windows within SSMS. An open query window pointing to a database context can lock that database preventing it from updating when the script is executing. A simple way to assure all query windows are closed, is to exit out of SSMS, then open a new instance of SSMS, and lastly run the setup script.

Skill Check 1: Open the Lab4.2SK1.sql file to retrieve the code you see here:

```
DECLARE @hDoc INT
DECLARE @doc XML
SET @doc =
'<BigFoods>
 <Store ID = "1"><TotalSales>145000</TotalSales>
 </Store>
 <Store ID = "2"><TotalSales>177000</TotalSales>
 </Store>
</BigFoods>'
```

Write a query with the correct flag parameter value in your OPENXML function to grab the ID and Total Sales from the /BigFoods/Store row pattern. You should not be using any custom ColPattern to get this result. When done your result should resemble the figure you here.

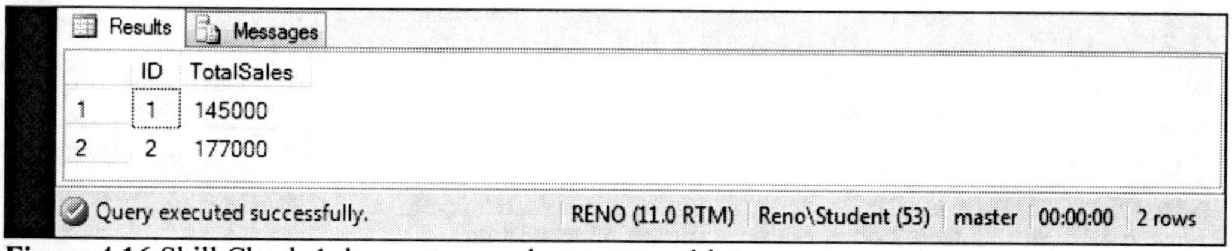

Results | Messages

	ID	TotalSales
1	1	145000
2	2	177000

Query executed successfully. | RENO (11.0 RTM) | Reno\Student (53) | master | 00:00:00 | 2 rows

Figure 4.16 Skill Check 1 does not use column pattern hints.

Skill Check 2: Open the Lab4.2SK2.sql file to retrieve the code you see here:

```
DECLARE @hDoc INT
DECLARE @Doc XML

SET @Doc =
'<Company Name="JProCo">
  <Structure Name="Building 1">
   <Room Name="Kitchen"> <Status>Open</Status></Room>
   <Room Name="Library"> <Status>Open</Status></Room>
   <Room Name="Rainier Boardroom">
<Status>Closed</Status></Room>
  </Structure>
  <Structure Name="Building 2">
   <Room Name="Pool"> <Status>Open</Status></Room>
   <Room Name="Smoothie Bar"> <Status>Open</Status> </Room>
   <Room Name="Andes Boardroom"> <Status>Open</Status>
</Room>
  </Structure>
</Company>'
```

Write a query uses the correct flag parameter value in your OPENXML function to grab the [Name] and [Status] from the /Company/Structure/Room rowpattern. You should not be using any custom ColPattern to get this result. When done your result should resemble Figure 4.17.

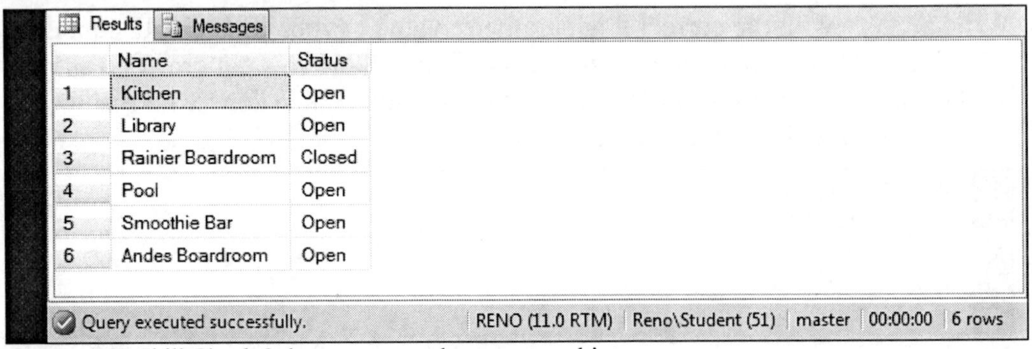

Results | Messages

	Name	Status
1	Kitchen	Open
2	Library	Open
3	Rainier Boardroom	Closed
4	Pool	Open
5	Smoothie Bar	Open
6	Andes Boardroom	Open

Query executed successfully. | RENO (11.0 RTM) | Reno\Student (51) | master | 00:00:00 | 6 rows

Figure 4.17 Skill Check 2 does not use column pattern hints.

Answer Code: The T-SQL code to this lab can be found in the downloadable files in a file named Lab4.2_OPENXMLParameters.sql

Points to Ponder - OPENXML Parameters

1. The first parameter of the OPENXML function is the document handle (a.k.a., your "claim ticket"). This parameter is required.
2. The second parameter of the OPENXML function is the rowpattern. This parameter is required.
3. The third parameter of the OPENXML function is the flag. This parameter is optional.
4. The OPENXML Flags determine attribute or element centricity:
    - use mapping (attributes)
    - use attribute values
    - use element values
    - retrieve both element and attribute values

Chapter Glossary

Column pattern: Sometimes shortened to "ColPattern"; used in conjunction with the OPENXML function; the ColPattern option helps you pull data from another column relative to your current position.

Document handle: An integer used to identify the in-memory location of the XML document. The document handle (a.k.a., your "claim ticket") is the first parameter of the OPENXML function. This parameter is required. Typically written as HDoc.

OPENXML: A function used to pull data in a relative fashion; in other words, instead of explicitly naming (i.e., hardcoding) the element levels where we want SQL Server to navigate and pull data, our code can provide rowpattern or column pattern instructions relative to a specified context.

OPENXML flags: These instruct the OPENXML function whether to use attribute and/or element centricity. The flag is the optional third parameter of the OPENXML function. Possible values are 0, 1, 2, or 3.

Preparing XML (for SQL): This process includes storing the XML in memory and processing the XML so that all the data and metadata is ready and available for your access via a SQL query.

Rowpattern: Used in conjunction with the OPENXML function; the rowpattern option helps you pull data from another level relative to your current position.

Shredding XML: The complete process of transforming XML data into a rowset.

sp_XML_PrepareDocument: A system stored procedure which parses an XML document into a tree representation of the various nodes and stores it within SQL Server's internal cache; the two required parameters are the handle (an integer handle representing the XML document in memory) and the XML document (i.e., the XML document which you wish to process).

sp_XML_RemoveDocument: A system stored procedure which removes an XML document and its handle from memory.

WITH clause: When used with the OPENXML function, allows you to customize and alias your field headers.

Review Quiz - Chapter Four

1.) You want your column pattern to capture the value of the <Color> element. You are not allowed to change any of the OPENXML parameters. The rowpattern is set to the correct level but you are getting no data. Your WITH statement looks like this:

```
WITH (MyColor VARCHAR(15) '@Color')
```

What should your column pattern say to get the value?

O a. `'MyColor'`

O b. `'Color'`

O c. `'/Color@'`

O d. `' /Color'`

O e. `' //Color'`

2.) You want your column pattern to capture the value of the <Color> element. You are not allowed to change any of the OPENXML parameters. The rowpattern is set one row below the <Color> element. Your WITH statement looks like this:

```
WITH (MyColor VARCHAR(15) '@Color')
```

What should your column pattern say to get the value?

O a. `'MyColor'`

O b. `'Color@'`

O c. `'Color'`

O d. `'../Color'`

O e. `'.//Color'`

3.) All your data is in child elements below the /Root/Data level. Some of your data is in elements and some is in attributes. You want to capture all the fields based on their default names. Which OPENXML flag value do you use?

O a. `OPENXML (@HandleDoc, 'Root/Data', 0)`

O b. `OPENXML (@HandleDoc, 'Root/Data', 1)`

O c. `OPENXML (@HandleDoc, 'Root/Data', 2)`

O d. `OPENXML (@HandleDoc, 'Root/Data', 3)`

Answer Key

1.) The answer ‘MyColor does not match the xml, so (a) is incorrect. Answer (c) uses incorrect syntax and is incorrect. Answer (d) is searching up one level and is incorrect. Answer uses ..// which is incorrect syntax and the answer is incorrect. Answer (b) is correct and will capture the value of the <Color> element

2.) The answer ‘MyColor’ does not match the xml, so (a) is incorrect. Answer (b) will capture the value of the <Color> element only at the specified level. Answer (c) uses incorrect syntax and is incorrect. Answer (d) is searching up one level, so (d) is the correct answer.

3.) The third optional input parameter in the OPENXML statement of 0 defaults to attribute centric mapping, so (a) is incorrect. An input parameter of 1 is also attribute centric, so (b) is incorrect. An input parameter of 2 is element centric mapping, so (c) is incorrect. The input parameter of 3 is both element and attribute centric so the correct answer is (d).

Bug Catcher Game

To play the Bug Catcher game run the SQLQueries2012Vol5BugCatcher4.pps from the BugCatcher folder of the companion files found at www.Joes2Pros.com.

Chapter 5. XML Queries

In Chapter 2, we used T-SQL code to stream tabular data and queries from SQL Server into an XML output. Since we took a SQL Server data source and viewed it in XML format, you may think we have already run some XML queries. We later took an XML data source, sent it into SQL Server, and saw the data in a tabular format.

Despite these steps we've taken to become familiar with XML, we still haven't performed any substantial XML querying. We haven't yet taken an XML data source and queried it for just a fragment of the information we want. XML queries get the data you want from an XML source and display the results as XML.

Since this chapter leads us into XQuery, we first need to discuss the XML data type. XQuery works only with the XML data type and its methods.

As noted in Chapter 1, XML is case-sensitive. In order for your examples and exercises to run properly in Chapters 1 through 7, be sure that your XML fragments precisely match the figures with respect to uppercase and lowercase.

READERNOTE:*Please run the script SQLQueries2012Vol5Chapter5.0Setup.sql in order to follow along with the examples in the first section of Chapter 5. All scripts mentioned in this chapter may be found at* ***www.Joes2Pros.com****.*

XML Data Type

Integers hold numbers with no decimal points, VARCHARs hold strings of varying length, and the Geography data type holds a position on the earth. Introduced in SQL Server 2005, the XML data type holds and understands valid XML strings.

If an XML document is essentially one long character string, then why should there be a separate XML data type? Like the Geography data type, XML has some built-in functions and methods to help with searching and querying the data inside. For example, the XML data type can detect the difference between valid XML strings (either a valid XML fragment or a well-formed XML document) versus strings which aren't valid XML.

XML as a Field

You can declare a field as an XML data type at the time you create a table in SQL Server, or you can add an XML field later. This would potentially give each record in your table its own well-formed XML data.

How might this capability be a benefit? Suppose you need to store credit history data for each customer. Some customers have one credit reference, some have many, and a few have none at all. These one-to-many relationships could be defined with a new table called dbo.CreditHistory, since a single field does not implement multiple relationships very well. However, XML would allow for this through a series of related tags and without the need to create a separate table.

Our first example will add an XML field to an existing table. The CurrentProducts table (JProCo.dbo.CurrentProducts) has 7 fields and 485 records (Figure 5.1).

Results | Messages

	ProductID	ProductName	RetailPrice	Origination...	ToBe...	Category	SupplierID
1	1	Underwater Tou...	61.483	2006-08-11...	0	No-Stay	0
2	2	Underwater Tou...	110.6694	2007-10-03...	0	Overnight-Stay	0
3	3	Underwater Tou...	184.449	2009-05-09...	0	Medium-Stay	0
4	4	Underwater Tou...	245.932	2006-03-04...	0	Medium-Stay	0
5	5	Underwater Tou...	307.415	2001-07-18...	0	LongTerm-Stay	0
6	6	Underwater Tou...	553.347	2008-06-30...	1	LongTerm-Stay	0

Query executed successfully. | RENO (11.0 RTM) | Reno\Student (51) | JProCo | 00:00:00 | 485 rows

Figure 5.1 The CurrentProducts table has 7 fields and 485 records.

This ALTER TABLE statement code adds a nullable XML field named CategoryCodes to the CurrentProducts table (Figure 5.2).

```
ALTER TABLE CurrentProducts
ADD CategoryCodes XML NULL
GO
```

Messages
Command(s) completed successfully.
0 rows

Figure 5.2 This code adds an XML field, CategoryCodes, to the CurrentProducts table.

If we re-run our SELECT statement, we can see the new field showing in the table.

```
SELECT * FROM CurrentProducts
```

	ProductID	ProductName	RetailPrice	Origination...	ToB...	Category	Sup...	CategoryCodes
1	1	Underwater Tour ...	61.483	2006-08-1...	0	No-Stay	0	NULL
2	2	Underwater Tour ...	110.6694	2007-10-0...	0	Overnight-Stay	0	NULL
3	3	Underwater Tour ...	184.449	2009-05-0...	0	Medium-Stay	0	NULL
4	4	Underwater Tour ...	245.932	2006-03-0...	0	Medium-Stay	0	NULL
5	5	Underwater Tour ...	307.415	2001-07-1...	0	LongTerm-Stay	0	NULL
6	6	Underwater Tour ...	553.347	2008-06-3...	1	LongTerm-Stay	0	NULL

Query executed successfully. | RENO (11.0 RTM) | Reno\Student (51) | JProCo | 00:00:00 | 485 rows

Figure 5.3 The CategoryCodes field now shows in the table.

We want to add some data to the new column. Run this code to populate the CategoryCodes field for ProductID 1 with a well-formed XML (Figure 5.4).

```
UPDATE CurrentProducts
SET CategoryCodes =
'<Root>
 <Category ID = "1"/>
 <Category ID = "4"/>
</Root>'
WHERE ProductID = 1
```

Messages
(1 row(s) affected)
0 rows

Figure 5.4 This code populates the ProductID 1 CategoryCodes field with this well-formed XML.

By again running the SELECT statement, we see the newly populated record in the CategoryCodes field. An XML hyperlink shows for Product 1 (Figure 5.5).

```
SELECT * FROM CurrentProducts
```

Results | Messages

	ProductID	ProductName	RetailPrice	Origina...	ToB...	Category	Sup...	CategoryCodes
1	1	Underwater Tour ...	61.483	2006-...	0	No-Stay	0	<Root><Category ID="1" /><Category ID="4" /></Ro...
2	2	Underwater Tour ...	110.6694	2007-...	0	Overni...	0	NULL
3	3	Underwater Tour ...	184.449	2009-...	0	Mediu...	0	NULL
4	4	Underwater Tour ...	245.932	2006-...	0	Mediu...	0	NULL
5	5	Underwater Tour ...	307.415	2001-...	0	LongT...	0	NULL
6	6	Underwater Tour ...	553.347	2008-...	1	LongT...	0	NULL

Query executed successfully. | RENO (11.0 RTM) | Reno\Student (51) | JProCo | 00:00:00 | 485 rows

Figure 5.5 An XML hyperlink shows for Product 1's CategoryCodes field.

If we click the XML hyperlink in Figure 5.5, we see the table entity contains this XML result (Figure 5.6).

Object Explorer | CategoryCodes1.xml × | SQLQuery2.sql - RE...(Reno\Student (51))*

```
<Root>
  <Category ID="1" />
  <Category ID="4" />
</Root>
```

Figure 5.6 This XML document is contained in one table entity of the CurrentProducts table.

Recall the situation we described earlier where a credit history could be stored as one field within a customer's record. Our results here in Figures 5.5 and 5.6 show how this data could appear and how adding an XML field to an existing table would save us from having to create a separate table to contain each customer's credit history data.

XML Variables

SQL Server can declare variables of the XML data type just as easily as it can declare XML fields.

In our next example, we will set an XML variable @Item equal to another well-formed XML (Figure 5.7 through Figure 5.11).

This code will declare our variable @Item as an XML data type. We then will set this variable equal to our well-formed XML document (Figure 5.7). This XML document is short, and we can easily see that it is well-formed. It has a <root> tag, a top-level element containing attributes, and each beginning tag has a corresponding ending tag.

```
DECLARE @Item XML
SET @Item =
'<Root>
 <Category ID = "1"/>
 <Category ID = "3"/>
</Root>'
```

```
Messages
Command(s) completed successfully.
                                                         0 rows
```

Figure 5.7 Running this code sets the variable @Item equal to this well-formed XML.

The XML data type detects whether an XML is valid (i.e., either a valid XML fragment or a well-formed XML document). Thus, when our code ran successfully (Figure 5.7), it provided additional confirmation that our XML document is well-formed. For illustrative purposes, we will momentarily remove a necessary character. Notice the forward slash in the ending tag of the first <Category> element has been removed. Since the document is no longer well-formed, the code will not run (Figure 5.8).

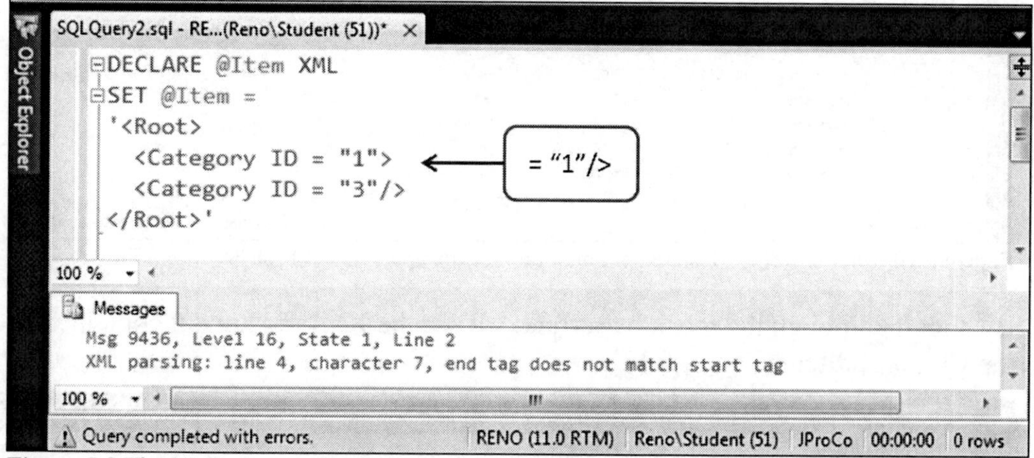

Figure 5.8 The XML data type will not accept this XML because it is not well-formed.

Of course, we want to add back the missing character so that our XML once again is well-formed.

Our next step will be to set an entity in CurrentProducts equal to our variable @Item. We don't want every value in the CategoryCodes column to be affected, just Product 2. Be sure to run all of the code shown here (Figure 5.9) together. The scope of the variable @Item makes it available only during runtime. Therefore, in order for your UPDATE statement to use the variable @Item, the code declaring this variable must be included in the same transaction.

```
DECLARE @Item XML
SET @Item =
'<Root>
 <Category ID = "1"/>
 <Category ID = "3"/>
</Root>'

UPDATE CurrentProducts
SET CategoryCodes = @Item
WHERE ProductID = 2
```

Messages
(1 row(s) affected)
0 rows

Figure 5.9 This value of the XML variable will populate the second CategoryCodes record.

Our SELECT statement shows us the newly updated CategoryCodes value for Product 2 (Figure 5.10).

```
SELECT * FROM CurrentProducts
```

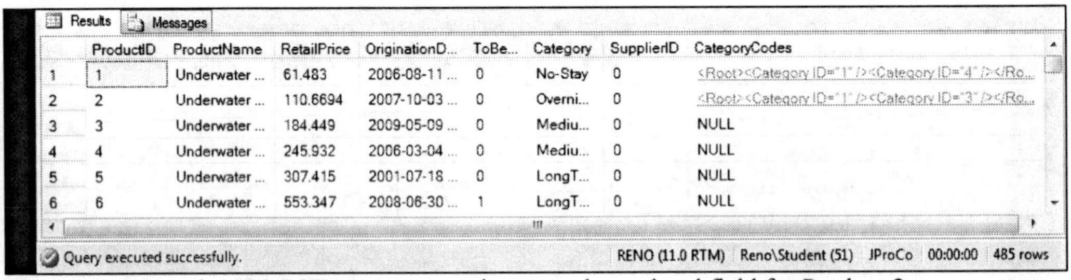

Results | Messages

	ProductID	ProductName	RetailPrice	OriginationD...	ToBe...	Category	SupplierID	CategoryCodes
1	1	Underwater ...	61.483	2006-08-11 ...	0	No-Stay	0	<Root><Category ID="1" /><Category ID="4" /></Ro...
2	2	Underwater ...	110.6694	2007-10-03 ...	0	Overni...	0	<Root><Category ID="1" /><Category ID="3" /></Ro...
3	3	Underwater ...	184.449	2009-05-09 ...	0	Mediu...	0	NULL
4	4	Underwater ...	245.932	2006-03-04 ...	0	Mediu...	0	NULL
5	5	Underwater ...	307.415	2001-07-18 ...	0	LongT...	0	NULL
6	6	Underwater ...	553.347	2008-06-30 ...	1	LongT...	0	NULL

Query executed successfully. | RENO (11.0 RTM) | Reno\Student (51) | JProCo | 00:00:00 | 485 rows

Figure 5.10 Run the SELECT statement again to see the updated field for Product 2.

By clicking through the result hyperlink, we see the XML document contained in the variable @Item (Figure 5.11).

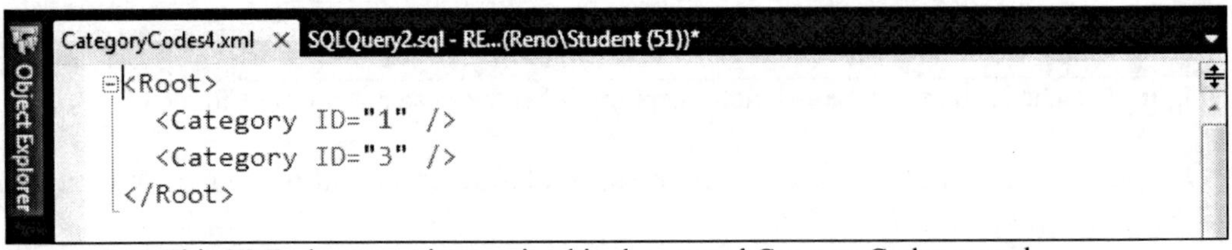

CategoryCodes4.xml × SQLQuery2.sql - RE...(Reno\Student (51))*

Object Explorer

```
<Root>
  <Category ID="1" />
  <Category ID="3" />
</Root>
```

Figure 5.11 This XML document is contained in the second CategoryCodes record.

Implicit Casting

If you have a VARCHAR which is full of tags and happens to be designed just like a valid XML, then are those essentially the same thing? Yes, they are. If you tell SQL Server to treat this VARCHAR as an XML, you will gain the ability to query this data for fragments which you need to pull from it. In fact, it's so easy that if the VARCHAR is well-formed, you can feed it directly into an XML without even any type of conversion. Just a simple equal sign does the trick.

SET @MyXML = @MyVarchar

This is no different than taking a small int and assigning it to an integer.

SET @ MyInt = @MySmallInt

Any time you are allowed to assign values from one data type to another without needing to use CONVERT or CAST, is called **implicit casting.**

Now let's repeat this process and observe what is special about the XML data type (i.e., versus a VARCHAR).

Begin by declaring a VARCHAR(max) variable called @sItem and setting it equal to the string of characters shown in Figure 5.12 (*Be sure to type the characters precisely as you see them in Figure 5.12).* While the XML data type is able to check and confirm that your XML is valid, the VARCHAR data type does not have this capability. For example, if you omit an element tag or incorrectly punctuate an attribute, the variable will accept and load whatever you include between the two single quote marks.)

```
DECLARE @sItem VARCHAR(MAX)
SET @sItem =
'<Root>
<Category ID = "1"/>
<Category ID = "5"/>
</Root>'
```

Messages
Command(s) completed successfully.
0 rows

Figure 5.12 This code declares a VARCHAR(max) variable and sets it equal to a string.

Our next step will be to insert this variable into the XML field (CategoryCodes) of the CurrentProducts table (Figure 5.13). The code appears to have run successfully and updated one record.

```
DECLARE @sItem VARCHAR(MAX)
SET @sItem =
'<Root>
<Category ID = "1"/>
<Category ID = "5"/>
</Root>'

UPDATE CurrentProducts
SET CategoryCodes = @sItem
WHERE ProductID = 3
```

Messages
(1 row(s) affected)
0 rows

Figure 5.13 This code sends our **VARCHAR**(max) value into the XML field, CategoryCodes.

```
SELECT * FROM CurrentProducts
```

Results | Messages

	Pr...	ProductName	RetailPrice	Origin...	ToB...	Category	S...	CategoryCodes
1	1	Underwater...	61.483	2006...	0	No-Stay	0	<Root><Category ID="1" /><Category ID="4" /></Ro...
2	2	Underwater...	110.6694	2007...	0	Overnig...	0	<Root><Category ID="1" /><Category ID="3" /></Ro...
3	3	Underwater...	184.449	2009...	0	Mediu...	0	<Root><Category ID="1" /><Category ID="5" /></Ro...
4	4	Underwater...	245.932	2006...	0	Mediu...	0	NULL
5	5	Underwater...	307.415	2001...	0	LongTe...	0	NULL
6	6	Underwater...	553.347	2008...	1	LongTe...	0	NULL

Query executed successfully. | RENO (11.0 RTM) | Reno\Student (51) | JProCo | 00:00:00 | 485 rows

Figure 5.14 The CategoryCodes value for Product 3 appears to be an XML hyperlink.

By again running our SELECT statement, we see an XML hyperlink appearing for Product 3's CategoryCodes (Figure 5.14). And when we click the hyperlink, we see the data we loaded into it from the VARCHAR variable (Figure 5.15).

CategoryCodes5.xml | SQLQuery2.sql - RE...(Reno\Student (51))*

Object Explorer

```
<Root>
  <Category ID="1" />
  <Category ID="5" />
</Root>
```

Figure 5.15 By clicking Product 3's hyperlink, we see the XML data from our VARCHAR variable.

Implicit casting allowed us to populate an XML field with data from a VARCHAR variable in this case because our VARCHAR data happened to fulfill the requirements of valid XML. Thus far our examples have included well-formed XML documents. We also know that valid XML fragments will work equally well, as we will see later.

Lab 5.1: XML Data Type

Lab Prep: Each lab has one or more Skill Checks. Start with Skill Check 1 and proceed until reaching the Points to Ponder section.

Before beginning this lab, verify that SQL Server 2012 is properly installed and operating. Before running the lab setup script for resetting the database (SQLQueries2012Vol5Chapter5.1Setup.sql), please make sure to close all query windows within SSMS. An open query window pointing to a database context can lock that database preventing it from updating when the script is executing. A simple way to assure all query windows are closed, is to exit out of SSMS, then open a new instance of SSMS, and lastly run the setup script.

Skill Check 1: Declare a variable named @item as an XML Data type and populate it with Category 2, 4 and 10. Feed the following XML into the CategoryCodes field for ProductID 5.

```
<Root>
 <Category ID = "2"/>
 <Category ID = "4"/>
 <Category ID = "10"/>
</Root>
```

When done your result should resemble

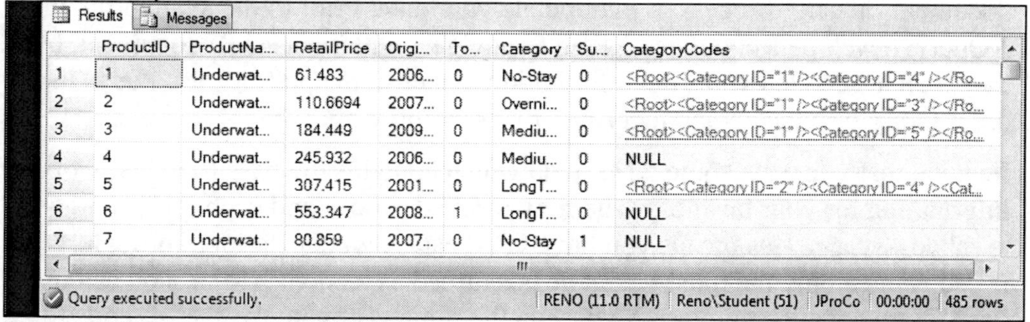

Results | Messages

	ProductID	ProductNa...	RetailPrice	Origi...	To...	Category	Su...	CategoryCodes
1	1	Underwat...	61.483	2006...	0	No-Stay	0	<Root><Category ID="1" /><Category ID="4" /></Ro...
2	2	Underwat...	110.6694	2007...	0	Overni...	0	<Root><Category ID="1" /><Category ID="3" /></Ro...
3	3	Underwat...	184.449	2009...	0	Mediu...	0	<Root><Category ID="1" /><Category ID="5" /></Ro...
4	4	Underwat...	245.932	2006...	0	Mediu...	0	NULL
5	5	Underwat...	307.415	2001...	0	LongT...	0	<Root><Category ID="2" /><Category ID="4" /><Cat...
6	6	Underwat...	553.347	2008...	1	LongT...	0	NULL
7	7	Underwat...	80.859	2007...	0	No-Stay	1	NULL

Query executed successfully. | RENO (11.0 RTM) | Reno\Student (51) | JProCo | 00:00:00 | 485 rows

Figure 5.16 The result for Skill Check 1.

Answer Code: The T-SQL code to this lab can be found in the downloadable files in a file named Lab5.1_XML_DataType.sql.

Points to Ponder - XML Data Type

1. SQL Server 2005 and newer versions offer a new data type called XML.
2. The XML data type can be cast from any character data type as long as the character data represents a valid XML fragment or well-formed XML document.
3. When SQL Server implicitly casts XML from character data it might make some alignment modifications to the data (e.g., truncating leading or trailing spaces) but the data and tags remain the same.
4. The XML data type is a LOB (large object type) and may contain up to 2 GB.

XQuery

XQuery is the shorthand term for the **XML Query Language**, the programming language used to handle and query XML data. SQL Server supports most features available in XQuery. XML is layered with elements inside of elements much like your computer's hard drive contains folders inside of folders. XPath is a subset of XQuery, but XPath has no processing capabilities. Like a navigator with a map, XPath can only help point you to the desired level or place within an XML document - it can't process or manipulate your data. Prior to the availability of XQuery, developers could use XPath to navigate within an XML document, but they then needed to export the information to a custom app (e.g., a C# app) in order to perform the actual querying or processing work.

Imagine that you have some XML data which contains the past 10 years' worth of information for your business. The root is called <root> and each top-level node is called <year>. This means you have 10 <year> elements to look through. What if you wanted only the most recent year returned as its own XML? You can use the XQuery languge to query XML data the same way you use T-SQL code to retrieve just the records you need from tabular data.

The XML data type has a built-in method called query() which allows you to query the XML for the parts you need. The basics of XQuery are really as simple as specifying the level (like /root/year/) that you want and then optionally picking the value from the level that you want.

XQuery Levels

How deep into the XML is the data which you want to extract? The level (or Path) which your XQuery uses is called the XPath expression. To get the first listed year from the top level, your XPath might be expressed as the /root/year[1] XPath. To get the second year listed, you would write the /root/year[2] XPath. Let's explore some XPath examples using our music data to get a feel for how this works.

Let's look at the MusicHistory table in the JProCo database. This table has one field (MusicDetails) which is an XML data type (Figure 5.17).

```
SELECT *
FROM MusicHistory
```

Results | Messages

	MusicTypeID	MusicTypeName	MusicDetails
1	1	Country	NULL
2	2	Soul	NULL
3	3	Rock	<Music><Song TitleID="13159"><WriterName>Neil Dia...

Query executed successfully. | RENO (11.0 RTM) | Reno\Student (51) | JProCo | 00:00:00 | 3 rows

Figure 5.17 You should see the MusicHistory table in your instance of the JProCo database.

We will itemize our SELECT list to include just the MusicDetails field. We will further narrow our query so we can take a closer look at the XML value in the third record (Figure 5.18).

```
SELECT *
FROM MusicHistory
WHERE MusicTypeID =3
```

Results | Messages

	MusicTypeID	MusicTypeName	MusicDetails
1	3	Rock	<Music><Song TitleID="13159"><WriterName>Neil Dia...

Query executed successfully. | RENO (11.0 RTM) | Reno\Student (51) | JProCo | 00:00:00 | 1 rows

Figure 5.18 We've narrowed down our query to focus on the XML field in Record 3.

When we click through the XML hyperlink we see the contents of the field. The root element is Music. However, we are interested in Song level. We want to pull out just the XML fragment containing all of the data at or below the Song level (Figure 5.19).

MusicDetails1.xml × SQLQuery8.sql - RE...(Reno\Student (51))*

```xml
<Music>
  <Song TitleID="13159">
    <WriterName>Neil Diamond</WriterName>
    <Title>Red Red Wine</Title>
    <Singer OrderID="1">
      <BandName>Neil Diamond</BandName>
    </Singer>
    <Singer OrderID="2">
      <BandName>UB40</BandName>
    </Singer>
  </Song>
  <Song TitleID="13160">
    <WriterName>Prince</WriterName>
    <Title>Manic Monday</Title>
    <Singer OrderID="1">
      <BandName>The Bangles</BandName>
    </Singer>
  </Song>
</Music>
```

Figure 5.19 The XML contained in Record 3 of the MusicHistory table.

We will use the *query() method* to specify that we want to go beyond the Music level to the Song level (Figure 5.20). Note that the XQuery syntax requires methods and functions to be lowercase - if you attempt to run this code with a capital Q, you will get an error message.

```sql
SELECT MusicDetails.query('/Music/Song')
FROM MusicHistory
WHERE MusicTypeID =3
```

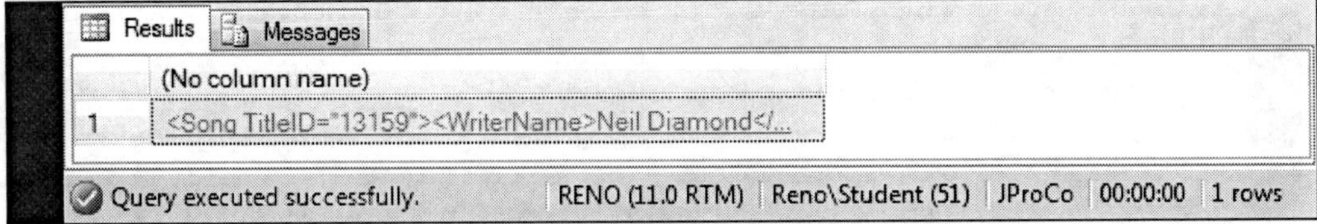

Figure 5.20 query() allows us to specify the element level we want.

When we click through the hyperlink produced by our query (Figure 5.20), we see this XML result (Figure 5.21).We see the two songs appearing at the top-level <Song> element. We do not see the <Music> element.

xmlresult20.xml × SQLQuery8.sql - RE...(Reno\Student (51))*

```
<Song TitleID="13159">
  <WriterName>Neil Diamond</WriterName>
  <Title>Red Red Wine</Title>
  <Singer OrderID="1">
    <BandName>Neil Diamond</BandName>
  </Singer>
  <Singer OrderID="2">
    <BandName>UB40</BandName>
  </Singer>
</Song>
<Song TitleID="13160">
  <WriterName>Prince</WriterName>
  <Title>Manic Monday</Title>
  <Singer OrderID="1">
    <BandName>The Bangles</BandName>
  </Singer>
</Song>
```

Figure 5.21 Our query produces this XML result and shows the two songs from the <Song> level.

Relative Element Path

Our next goal will be to modify our existing code in order to retrieve just the second song (Song TitleID 13160). Our current code returns all data from the Song level. Adding a [2] to the XPath will return just the second song.

```
SELECT MusicDetails.query('/Music/Song[2]')
FROM MusicHistory
WHERE MusicTypeID =3
```

Figure 5.22 Our code now specifies that we want just the second song.

Our code was successful. The XML result now contains just the second song (TitleID 13160, Manic Monday) (Figure 5.23).

```
xmlresult21.xml  ×  SQLQuery8.sql - RE...(Reno\Student (51))*
<Song TitleID="13160">
  <WriterName>Prince</WriterName>
  <Title>Manic Monday</Title>
  <Singer OrderID="1">
    <BandName>The Bangles</BandName>
  </Singer>
</Song>
```

Figure 5.23 We now see just the second song.

This [2] we added to our code forms what's known as a **relative element path** (Later we will see a related concept known as an **absolute element path**).

While our code achieved the desired result, a more properly formatted way would have been to put parentheses around the level before specifying the item.

```
SELECT MusicDetails.query('(/Music/Song)[2]')
FROM MusicHistory
WHERE MusicTypeID =3
```

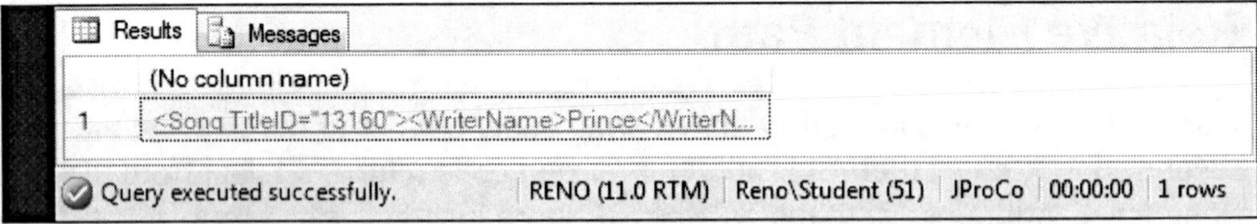

Figure 5.24 The preferred syntax includes parentheses around the element level.

We next will modify our query to return just the first song (Song TitleID 13159). Given the previous example, we would expect this code (Figure 5.25) to pull out the first song.

```
SELECT MusicDetails.query('(/Music/Song)[1]')
FROM MusicHistory
WHERE MusicTypeID =3
```

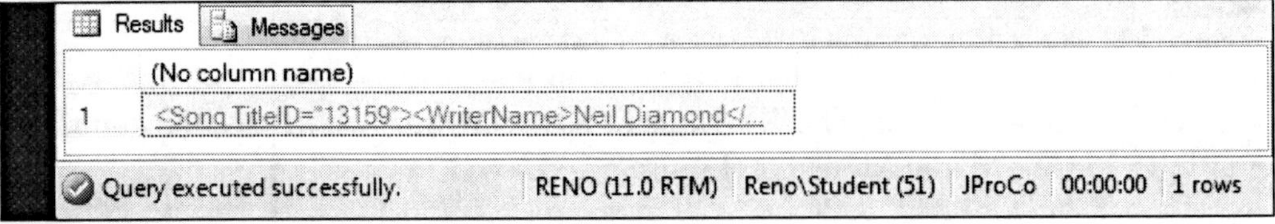

Figure 5.25 We've modified our code to return just the first song.

```
<Song TitleID="13159">
  <WriterName>Neil Diamond</WriterName>
  <Title>Red Red Wine</Title>
  <Singer OrderID="1">
    <BandName>Neil Diamond</BandName>
  </Singer>
  <Singer OrderID="2">
    <BandName>UB40</BandName>
  </Singer>
</Song>
```

Figure 5.26 The first song has two singers and was written by Neil Diamond.

Now let's adjust our code to return just the XML fragment showing the name of the song writer, Neil Diamond.

```
<Song TitleID="13159">
  <WriterName>Neil Diamond</WriterName>
  <Title>Red Red Wine</Title>
  <Singer OrderID="1">
    <BandName>Neil Diamond</BandName>
  </Singer>
  <Singer OrderID="2">
    <BandName>UB40</BandName>
  </Singer>
</Song>
```

"Neil Diamond" is at the /Music/Song/WriterName XML path level

Figure 5.27 Our next goal is to return just the XML fragment highlighted here.

To accomplish our goal, we need to add /WriterName to the XPath specified by our existing code. We previously were at the /Music/Song level. We want to go one level deeper to the <WriterName> element.

```
SELECT MusicDetails.query('(/Music/Song[1]/WriterName)')
FROM MusicHistory
WHERE MusicTypeID =3
```

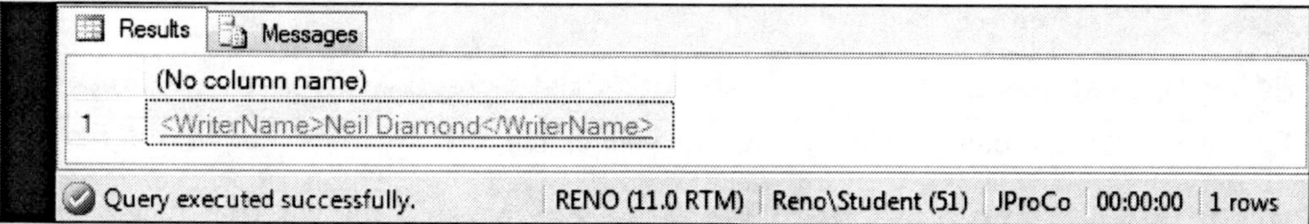

Figure 5.28 Our code now specifies the WriterName level.

By clicking through the XML hyperlink, we see our code successfully pulled out an XML fragment containing just the data we asked for (Figure 5.29).

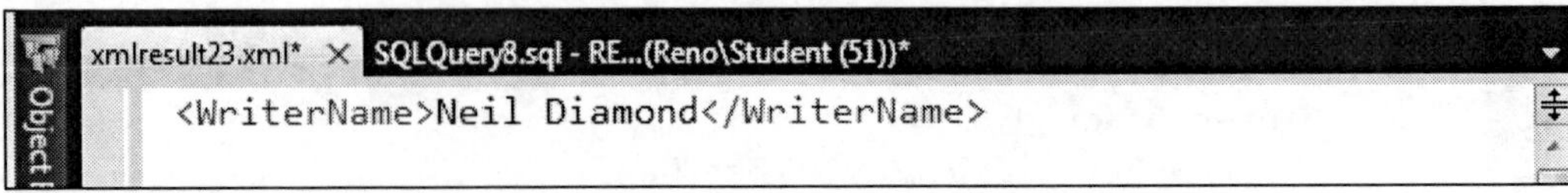

Figure 5.29 Our code successfully retrieved just the data we specified.

The text() Function

The text() function is one of XQuery's data accessor functions.

Next we want to pull out just the writer's name (Neil Diamond). The <WriterName> element consists of a beginning tag, an ending tag, and the text between the tags. The portion we wish to isolate is known as the *element text.* The *text()* function retrieves element text without the element tags.

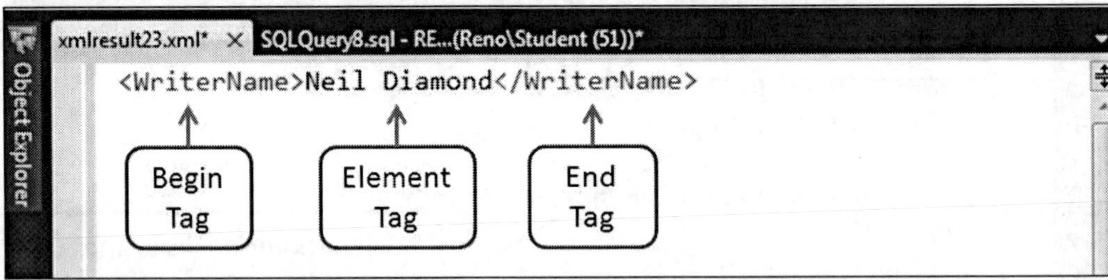

Figure 5.30 Next we want to pull out the element text, Neil Diamond.

To accomplish this, we simply need to add the text function to our current code (Figure 5.31). Again, observe that the function must be in lowercase letters - it will error if you attempt this code with a capital T (/Text()').

```
SELECT
MusicDetails.query('(/Music/Song[1]/WriterName)/text()')
FROM MusicHistory
WHERE MusicTypeID =3
```

Figure 5.31 We are adding the text() function to our current code.

By clicking the XML hyperlink, we see our code successfully pulled out an XML fragment containing just the text between the element tags (Figure 5.32).

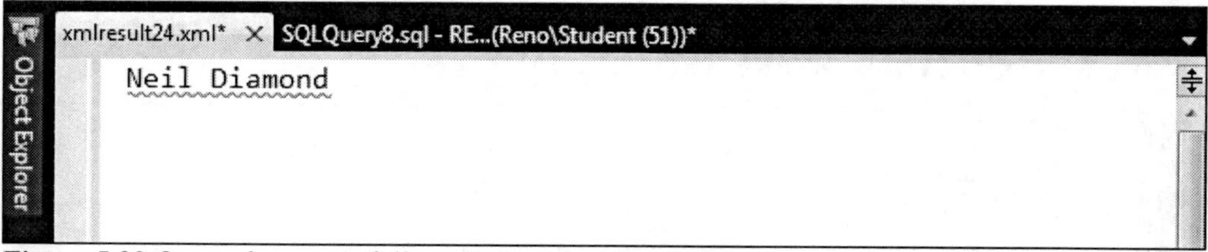

Figure 5.32 Our code successfully pulled out just the element text, Neil Diamond.

Next we will switch gears and revert back to the code we used earlier (Figure 5.25). For our next example, we need to pull data from a higher level.

```
SELECT MusicDetails.query('/Music/Song [1]')
FROM MusicHistory
WHERE MusicTypeID =3
```

Results | Messages

	(No column name)
1	<Song TitleID="13159"><WriterName>Neil Diamond</...

Query executed successfully. | RENO (11.0 RTM) | Reno\Student (51) | JProCo | 00:00:00 | 1 rows

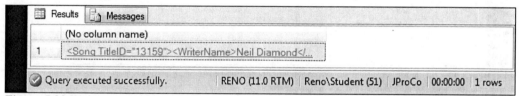

Figure 5.33 We've reverted back to our previous code which returns just the first song.

Our XML hyperlink is the same as we saw previously (in Figure 5.26). We see all the data for just the first song. Notice that this song has two singers, Neil Diamond and UB40 (Figure 5.34). Our next example will pull out the more recent singer, UB40.

xmlresult22.xml | SQLQuery8.sql - RE...(Reno\Student (51))*

```
<Song TitleID="13159">
  <WriterName>Neil Diamond</WriterName>
  <Title>Red Red Wine</Title>
  <Singer OrderID="1">
    <BandName>Neil Diamond</BandName>
  </Singer>
  <Singer OrderID="2">
    <BandName>UB40</BandName>
  </Singer>
</Song>
```

Figure 5.34 The first song has two singers. We will pull out data for UB40.

We've modified our code to show us only the second singer, UB40 (Figure 5.35).

```
SELECT MusicDetails.query('(/Music/Song[1]/Singer)[2]')
FROM MusicHistory WHERE MusicTypeID =3
```

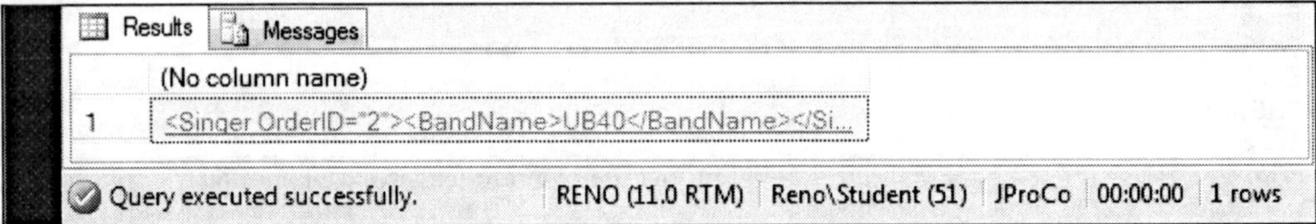

Figure 5.35 Our code now retrieves only the second singer (UB40).

As expected, the XML hyperlink shows us data for just the second singer, UB40 (Figure 5.36).

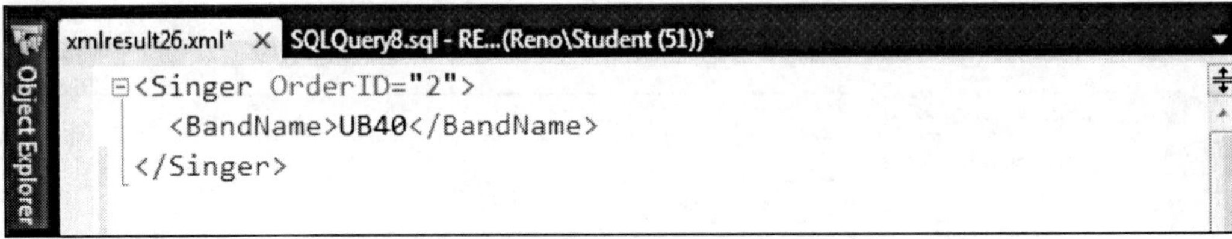

Figure 5.36 Our XML result also shows just the second singer (UB40).

Next we will modify our code to retrieve an XML fragment containing only the <BandName> element (Figure 5.37 and Figure 5.38).

```
SELECT
MusicDetails.query('/Music/Song[1]/Singer[2]/BandName')
FROM MusicHistory WHERE MusicTypeID =3
```

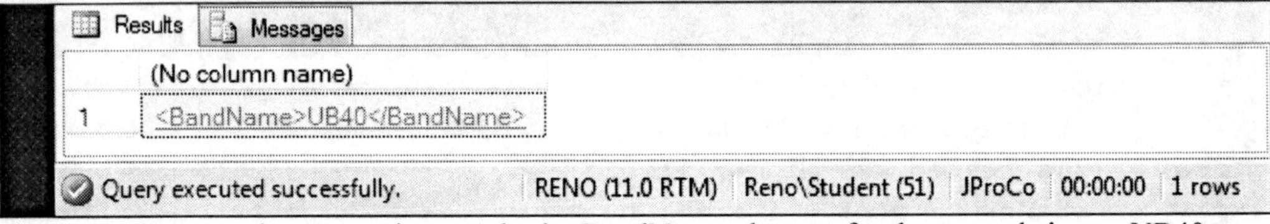

Figure 5.37 Our code now retrieves only the BandName element for the second singer, UB40.

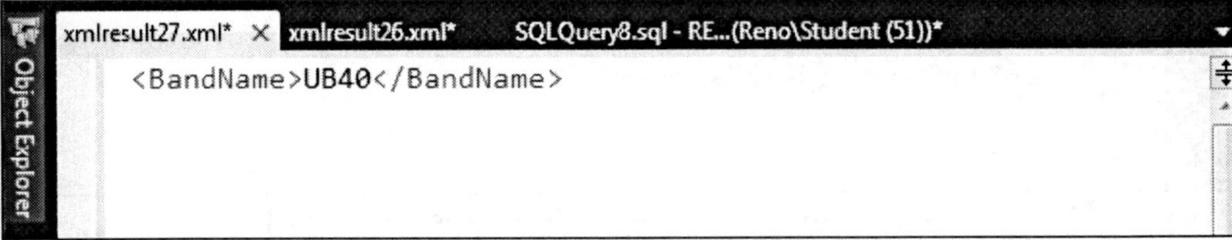

Figure 5.38 Our XML result also shows just the BandName element.

And finally, we'll use the text() function to pull out just the band name, which is the text between the element tags:

```
SELECT MusicDetails.query
 ('/Music/Song[1]/Singer[2]/BandName/text()')
FROM MusicHistory WHERE MusicTypeID =3
```

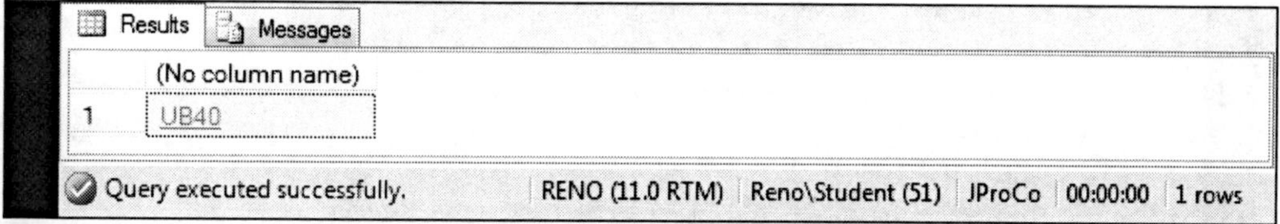

Figure 5.39 Our code now retrieves only the BandName text element.

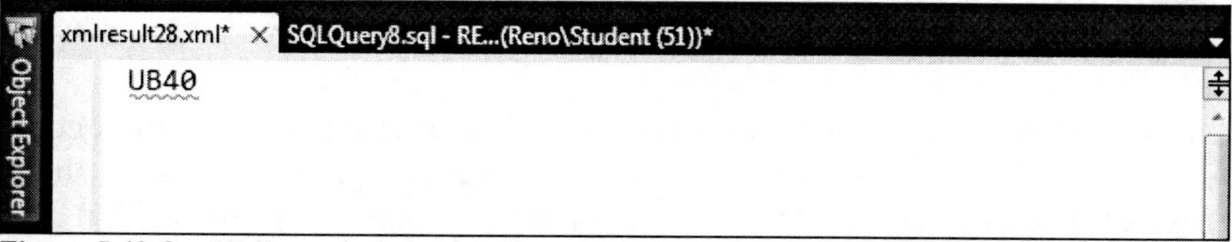

Figure 5.40 Our XML result shows just the text element for the BandName, UB40.

The Absolute Element Path

For our final examples, let's again revert back to our previous code which pulls out just the first top-level son (as shown in Figure 5.25 and Figure 5.33).

```
SELECT MusicDetails.query('/Music/Song[1]')
FROM MusicHistory WHERE MusicTypeID = 3
```

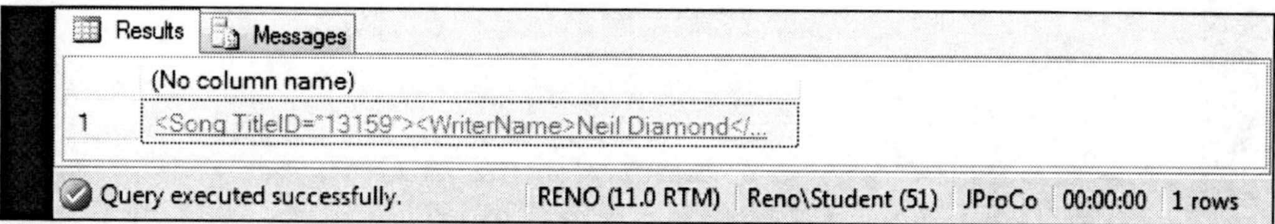

Figure 5.41 We've reverted back to our previous code which returns just the first song.

Our XML hyperlink shows the same data we saw previously (See Figure 5.26 and Figure 5.34). We see all the data for just the first song, TitleID 13159.

```
<Song TitleID="13159">
  <WriterName>Neil Diamond</WriterName>
  <Title>Red Red Wine</Title>
  <Singer OrderID="1">
    <BandName>Neil Diamond</BandName>
  </Singer>
  <Singer OrderID="2">
    <BandName>UB40</BandName>
  </Singer>
</Song>
```

Figure 5.42 This XML contains all the data for the first song, TitleID 13159.

Notice that our current code uses the *relative element path* in order to pull out this song (TitleID 13159). But suppose a Song 13158 gets added to the catalog. In that case, the current query wouldn't pull your intended song - the path specified by the current query ('/Music/Song[1]') will always pull whichever song appears first in the top-level tag.

We should be prepared for this possibility and learn how to pull out the top-level element by its attribute ID and not simply by its position. This is known as the *absolute element path* (Figure 5.43).

```
SELECT MusicDetails.query('/Music/Song[@TitleID=13159]')
FROM MusicHistory WHERE MusicTypeID = 3
```

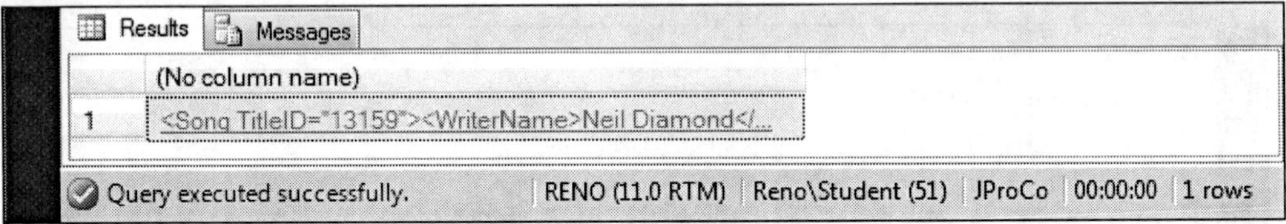

Figure 5.43 This code pulls the data for the song for TitleID 13159.

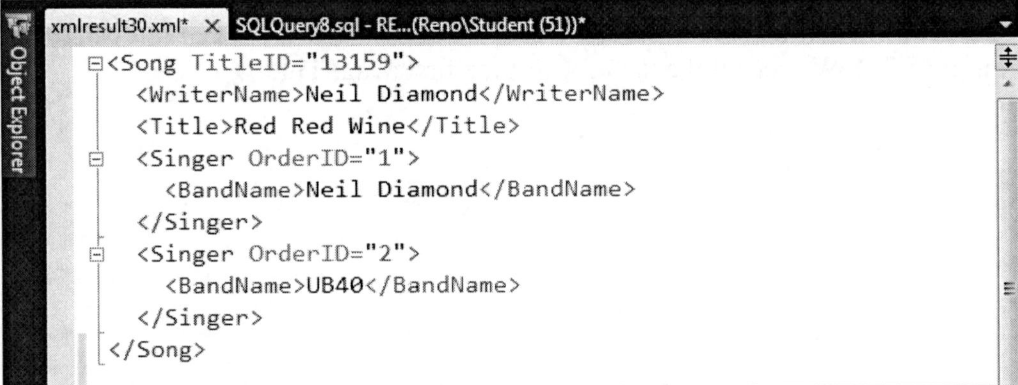

Figure 5.44 This XML contains all the data for the song for TitleID 13159.

Now let's test this technique once again by pulling out the data for song ID 13160 (Figure 5.45).

```
SELECT MusicDetails.query('/Music/Song[@TitleID=13160]')
FROM MusicHistory WHERE MusicTypeID = 3
```

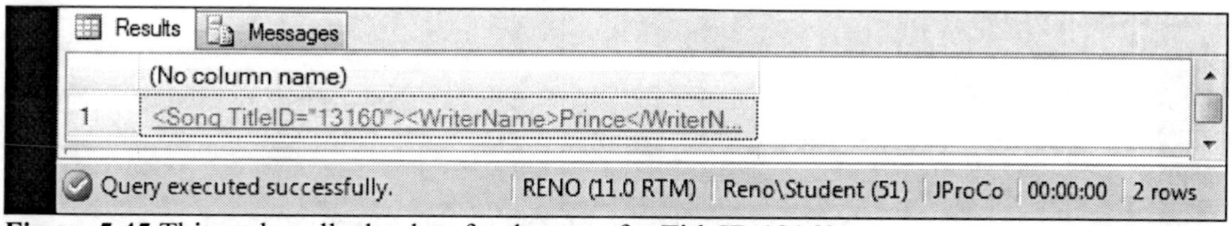

```
Results | Messages
   (No column name)
1  <Song TitleID="13160"><WriterName>Prince</WriterN...
Query executed successfully. | RENO (11.0 RTM) | Reno\Student (51) | JProCo | 00:00:00 | 2 rows
```

Figure 5.45 This code pulls the data for the song for TitleID 13160.

```
xmlresult31.xml*  SQLQuery8.sql - RE...(Reno\Student (51))*
<Song TitleID="13160">
  <WriterName>Prince</WriterName>
  <Title>Manic Monday</Title>
  <Singer OrderID="1">
    <BandName>The Bangles</BandName>
  </Singer>
</Song>
```

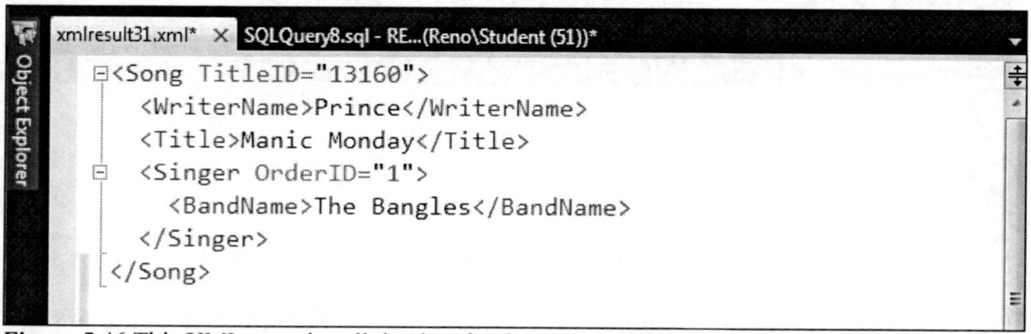

Figure 5.46 This XML contains all the data for the song for TitleID 13160.

The data() Function

Let's look at another example where we will pull specific data out of an XML fragment (Figure 5.47).

```
DECLARE @Book XML
SET @Book =
 '<Format Style="Paperback" Price= "25.00"/>
 <Format Style="Kindle" Price= "7.99"/>'
```

```
Messages
Command(s) completed successfully.
                                        0 rows
```

Figure 5.47 Type this XML fragment precisely as you see it here.

Our ultimate goal will be to search for the Kindle item and pull out just its price.

Run the SELECT statement you see here (Figure 5.48), in order to generate the XML result (Figure 5.49).

```
DECLARE @Book XML
SET @Book =
'<Format Style="Paperback" Price= "25.00"/>
<Format Style="Kindle" Price= "7.99"/>'

SELECT @Book
```

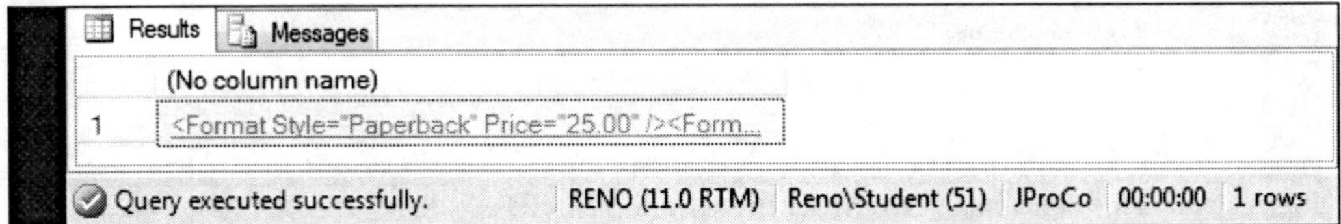

Figure 5.48 Run the statement SELECT @Book in order to generate the XML result.

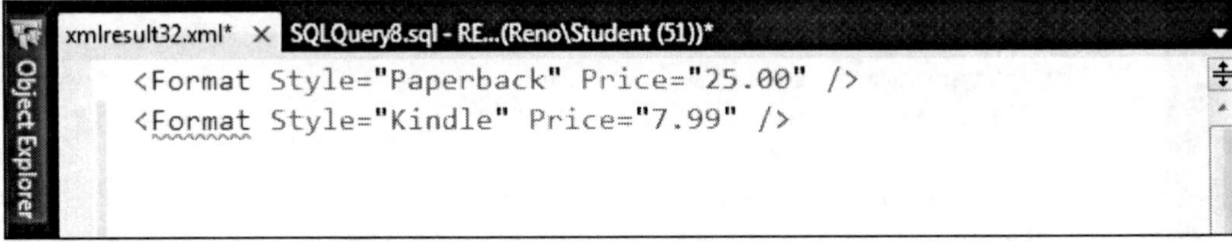

Figure 5.49 The XML fragment resulting from the statement SELECT @Book.

Our next step will be to isolate the information for just the Kindle (Figure 5.50).

```
DECLARE @Book XML
SET @Book =
'<Format Style="Paperback" Price= "25.00"/>
<Format Style="Kindle" Price= "7.99"/>'

SELECT @Book.query('(/Format[@Style="Kindle"])')
```

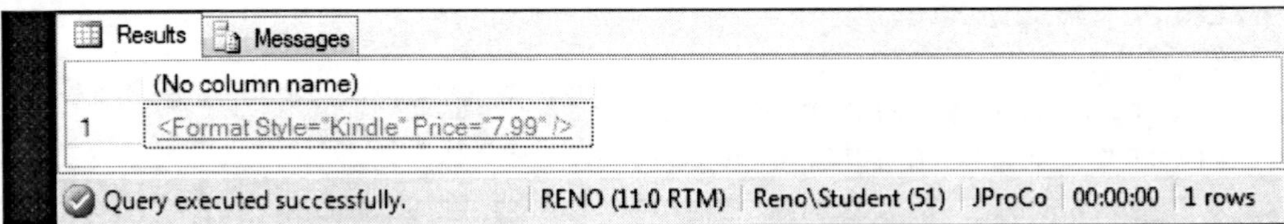

Figure 5.50 This query will isolate just the information where the Style attribute is “Kindle”.

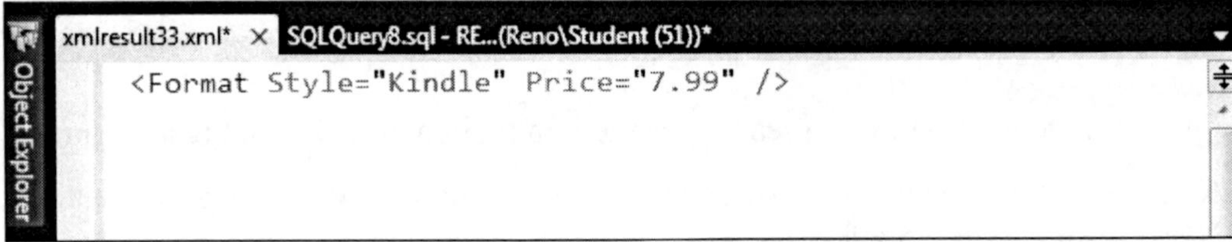

Figure 5.51 The XML fragment contains information only for the Kindle.

We are searching on the attribute "Kindle", but what we actually want to pull out is the corresponding Price data. Notice that if we attempt to add the attribute Price to our query, we get the error *"XQuery [xquery()]: Attribute may not appear outside of an element"* (Figure 5.52).

```
DECLARE @Book XML
SET @Book =
'<Format Style="Paperback" Price= "25.00"/>
<Format Style="Kindle" Price= "7.99"/>'

SELECT @Book.query('(/Format[@Style="Kindle"]/@Price)')
```

```
Messages
Msg 2396, Level 16, State 1, Line 6
XQuery [query()]: Attribute may not appear outside of an element
                                                          0 rows
```

Figure 5.52 Our query isn't yet complete and produces this error message.

Our query needs the **data () function** to be added, and then it returns precisely the result we want. It searches for the Price attribute belonging to the Kindle and returns just its data, namely 7.99 (Figure 5.53).

```
DECLARE @Book XML
SET @Book =
'<Format Style="Paperback" Price= "25.00"/>
<Format Style="Kindle" Price= "7.99"/>'

SELECT @Book.query('data (/Format[@Style="Kindle"]/@Price)')
```

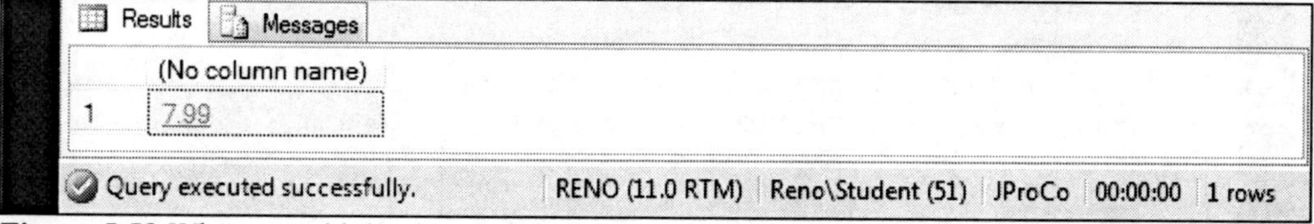

Figure 5.53 When we add the data () function to our query, we get precisely the result we want.

Now let's run another example using the data () function with a table. Run the following code to create the simple table, Books (Figure 5.54).

```
CREATE TABLE Books
(BookName VARCHAR(50),
Pricing XML)
```

```
Messages
Command(s) completed successfully.
                                                          0 rows
```

Figure 5.54 Run this code to create the Books table.

Insert two records into the Books table (Figure 5.55).

```
INSERT INTO Books
VALUES
  ('SQL Queries 2012 Joes 2 Pros Vol1',
  '<Format Style="Paperback" Price= "25.00"/>
  <Format Style="Kindle" Price= "7.99"/>')

INSERT INTO Books
VALUES
  ('SQL Queries 2012 Joes 2 Pros Vol2',
  '<Format Style="Paperback" Price= "39.99"/>
  <Format Style="Kindle" Price= "9.50"/>')
```

Figure 5.55 This code inserts two records into the Books table.

Our first step will be to isolate the information for just the Kindle books.

```
SELECT BookName,
  Pricing.query('(/Format[@Style="Kindle"]')
FROM Books
```

Figure 5.56 Run this code to isolate the information for just the Kindle books.

The result of our query displays the Style and Price attributes for each of our two Kindle books (*SQL Queries 2012 Joes 2 Pros Volume 1*, *SQL Queries 2012 Joes 2 Pros Volume 2*).

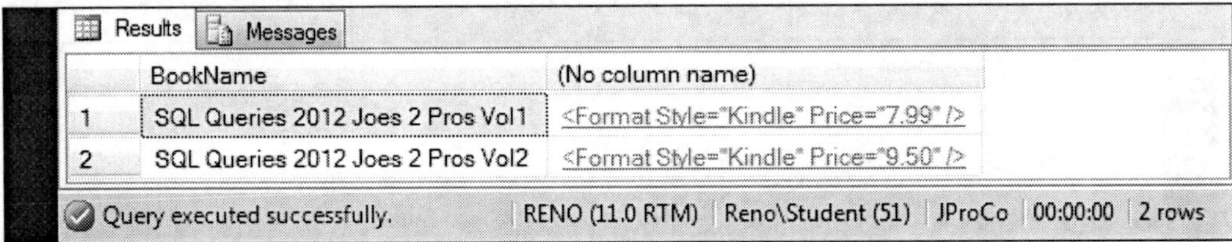

Figure 5.57 The result of our query (the query is shown in Figure 5.56).

Notice that each result link contains an XML fragment for one book.

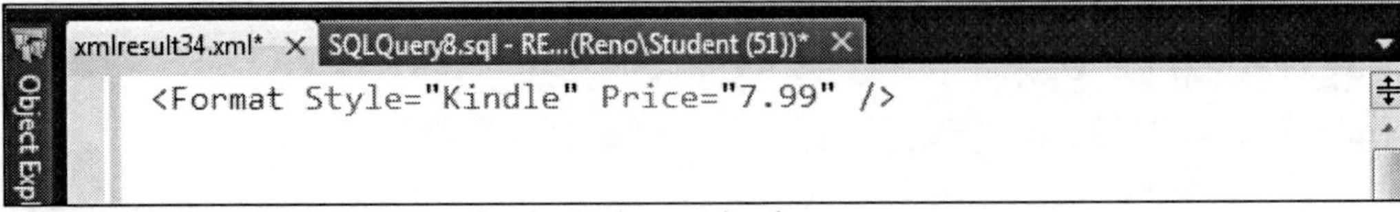

Figure 5.58 The XML fragment for the Volume 1 book.

```
<Format Style="Kindle" Price="9.50" />
```

Figure 5.59 The XML fragment for the Volume 2 book.

Rather than the XML fragment, we want to see only the price for each book. In order to accomplish this, we need to write our query to return the data it finds for the path (/Format[@Style="Kindle"]/@Price).

```
SELECT BookName,
  Pricing.query('data(/Format[@Style="Kindle"]/@Price')
FROM Books
```

Figure 5.60 Our query returns the data for the specified path.

	BookName	(No column name)
1	SQL Queries 2012 Joes 2 Pros Vol1	7.99
2	SQL Queries 2012 Joes 2 Pros Vol2	9.50

Query executed successfully. | RENO (11.0 RTM) | Reno\Student (51) | JProCo | 00:00:00 | 2 rows

Figure 5.61 Our query successfully returns just the price data for each Kindle book.

Lab 5.2: XQuery

Lab Prep: Each lab has one or more Skill Checks. Start with Skill Check 1 and proceed until reaching the Points to Ponder section.

Before beginning this lab, verify that SQL Server 2012 is properly installed and operating. Before running the lab setup script for resetting the database (SQLQueries2012Vol5Chapter5.2Setup.sql), please make sure to close all query windows within SSMS. An open query window pointing to a database context can lock that database preventing it from updating when the script is executing. A simple way to assure all query windows are closed, is to exit out of SSMS, then open a new instance of SSMS, and lastly run the setup script.

Skill Check 1: Pull out TitleID=13159 from the /Music/Song level regardless of the order it appears in the XML field. Pull out the second singer for this song.

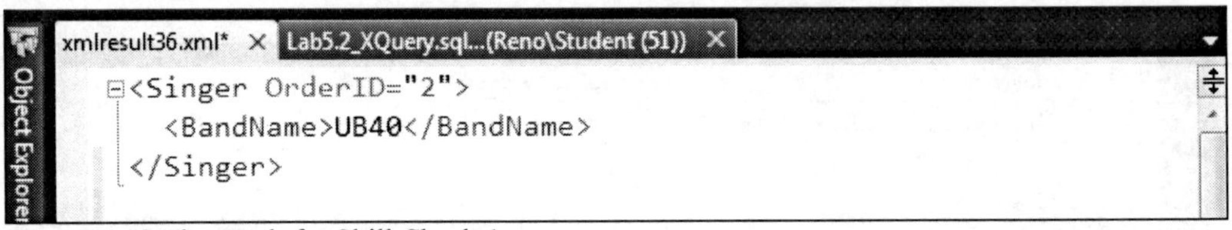

xmlresult36.xml* × Lab5.2_XQuery.sql...(Reno\Student (51)) ×

```
<Singer OrderID="2">
  <BandName>UB40</BandName>
</Singer>
```

Figure 5.62 The result for Skill Check 1.

Skill Check 2: From Olympics table, pull out the XML from the Odetails field where the Olympics ID = 2.

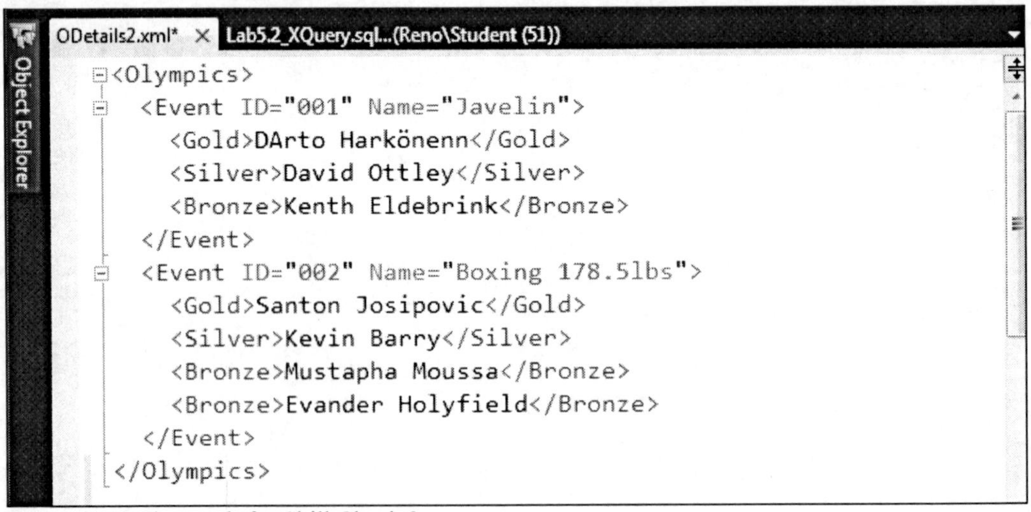

ODetails2.xml* × Lab5.2_XQuery.sql...(Reno\Student (51))

```
<Olympics>
  <Event ID="001" Name="Javelin">
    <Gold>DArto Harkönenn</Gold>
    <Silver>David Ottley</Silver>
    <Bronze>Kenth Eldebrink</Bronze>
  </Event>
  <Event ID="002" Name="Boxing 178.5lbs">
    <Gold>Santon Josipovic</Gold>
    <Silver>Kevin Barry</Silver>
    <Bronze>Mustapha Moussa</Bronze>
    <Bronze>Evander Holyfield</Bronze>
  </Event>
</Olympics>
```

Figure 5.63 The result for Skill Check 2.

Skill Check 3: Pull out the second record from the Olympics table and show the XML from the Odetails field. Show the XML fragment from the first top-level <Event> in the XML data.

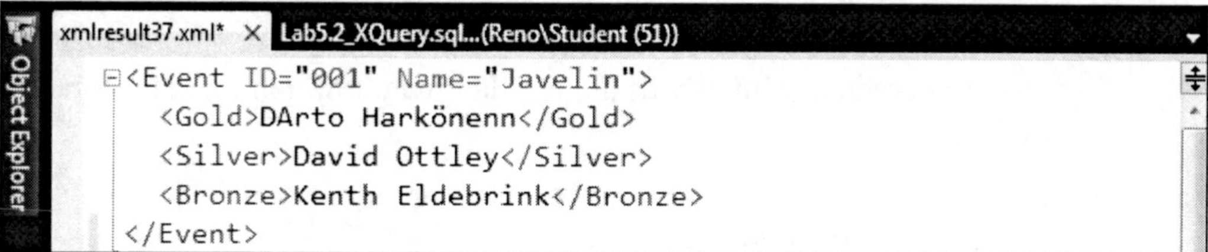

Figure 5.64 The result for Skill Check 3.

Skill Check 4: Pull out the second record from the Olympics table and show the XML from the Odetails field. Show the XML fragment from the <Gold> medal element under the first top-level <Event> in the XML data.

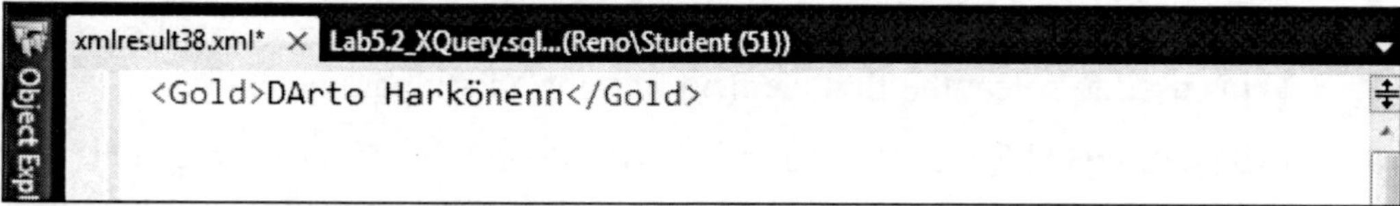

Figure 5.65 The result for Skill Check 4.

Skill Check 5: Use the text() function to pull out just the text from Skill Check 4.

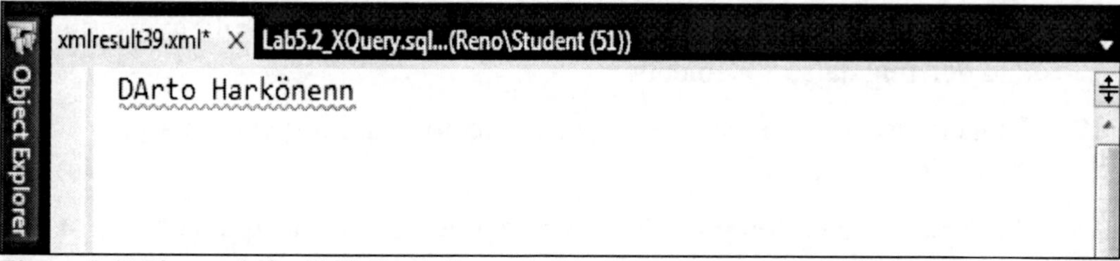

Figure 5.66 The result for Skill Check 5.

Skill Check 6: Pull out the second record from the Olympics table and show the XML from the Odetails field. Show the XML fragment from the <Bronze> medal element under the <Event> with Event ID=002.

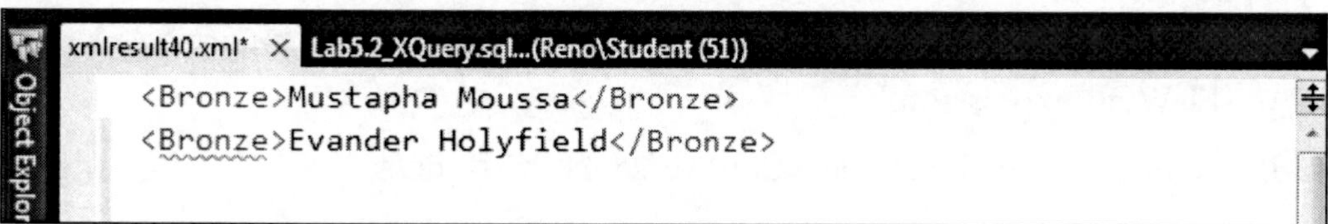

Figure 5.67 The result for Skill Check 6.

Answer Code: The T-SQL code to this lab can be found in the downloadable files in a file named Lab5.2_XQuery.sql

Points to Ponder - XQuery

1. The XML data type has a built-in method called query() which allows you to query for the parts of the XML you need.
2. XQuery was created primarily as a query language for getting data stored in an XML form.
3. XQuery is a query and functional programming language that is designed to query collections of XML data.
4. The main purpose of XQuery is to get information out of XML databases.
5. XQuery uses a valid XPath expression like /Music/Song as a parameter.
6. / slashes are used for traversing element names in a downward direction.
7. [@*name*] is used to extract attributes.
8. [1] is used to select the first element of your XPath parameter.
9. /Music/Song[1]/Singer[@OrderID=1] would get the <Singer> element having an 'OrderID' attribute value of 1, all for the first song.
10. XQuery is a flexible query language which extracts data from an XML stream.
11. XQuery is also capable of manipulating XML data by updating, inserting, and deleting data or elements.
12. XQuery uses the XPath expression syntax to address specific parts of an XML document.
13. An XPath expression provides the path to a level or location based on a tree-structure of the information contained in an XML stream.
14. XPath is a subset of XQuery.
15. XPath is a query language for selecting nodes from an XML stream.
16. An XPath expression is often called "an XPath."
17. XPath offers a "for" expression which is a mini-version of the XQuery FLWOR expression.
18. XQuery is a path language to traverse the XML data.
    - Path XQuery /Emp/Location
    - Value XQuery /Emp/Location[ID="1"]
19. XQuery stands for the XML Querying Language.

Chapter Glossary

Implicit casting: When a program allows you to assign values from one data type to another without the need to use CONVERT or CAST, this is implicit casting.

Flag Parameter: These instruct the OPENXML function whether to use attribute and/or element centricity. The flag is the optional third parameter of the OPENXML function. Possible values are 0, 1, 2, or 3.

query(): A built-in method of the XML data type; allows you to query for just the needed parts of an XML.

text(): One of XQuery's data accessor functions.

XML data type: Holds and understands valid XML strings; introduced in SQL Server 2005.

XQuery: Works only with the XML data type and its methods.

Review Quiz - Chapter Five

1.) What is the name of the root node in the code below?

```
<TV><Show>Bob on the job </Show></TV>
```

O a. TV

O b. Show

O c. Bob on the Job

2.) You have the following XML stream.

```
<TV>
 <Show Name="Bob on the Job">
  <Starring>
   <Actor>Bob</Actor>
   <Actor>Patrick</Actor>
  </Starring>
 </Show>
 <Show Name="Way Kendall">
  <Starring>
   <Actor>Lisa</Actor>
   <Actor>Peter</Actor>
  </Starring>
 </Show>
</TV>
```

You need to enter the query parameter to get All Actors from the first TV show element, as seen here:

```
<Starring>
 <Actor>Bob</Actor>
 <Actor>Patrick</Actor>
</Starring>
```

Which XPath will get you this Fragment?

O a. 'TV/Show[1]/Starring'

O b. 'TV/Show[2]/Starring'

O c. 'TV/Show[1]/Starring/Actor'

O d. 'TV/Show[2]/Starring/Actor'

O e. 'TV/Show[1]

3.) You have the following XML stream.

```
<TV>
 <Show Name="Bob on the Job">
  <Starring>
   <Actor>Bob</Actor>
   <Actor>Patrick</Actor>
  </Starring>
 </Show>
 <Show Name=”Way Kendall”>
  <Starring>
   <Actor>Lisa</Actor>
   <Actor>Peter</Actor>
  </ Starring >
 </Show>
</TV>
```

You need to enter the query parameter to get the second actor from the first TV show element, as seen here:

```
<Actor>Patrick</Actor>
```

What XPath will get you this Fragment?

O a. 'TV/Show[1]/Starring/Actor[1]'

O b. 'TV/Show[1]/Starring/Actor[2]'

O c. 'TV/Show[2]/Starring/Actor[1]'

O d. 'TV/Show[2]/Starring/Actor[2]'

4.) The XML and VARCHAR(max) data types will both store XML data. What are two key differences between these two types?

☐ a. The XML data type does not allow root tags.

☐ b. The VARCHAR(max) does not allow root tags.

☐ c. The XML data type will only accept well-formed XML.

☐ d. The VARCHAR(max) data type will only accept well-formed XML.

☐ e. The XML data type will not truncate leading or trailing spaces.

☐ f. The VARCHAR(max) data type will not truncate leading or trailing spaces.

5.) You have a table named Buildings that has an XML column named StoreHours. The code that created and populated this table is seen in the code below.

```
CREATE TABLE Buildings
(StoreName VARCHAR(25),
StoreHours XML)

INSERT INTO Buildings
VALUES ('Goa',
'<hours dayofWeek="Monday" open="8:00" closed= "18:00"/>
<hours dayofWeek="Tuesday" open="8:00" closed= "18:00"/>
<hours dayofWeek="Wednesday" open="8:00" closed= "18:00"/>
<hours dayofWeek="Saturday" open="9:00" closed= "17:00"/>')

INSERT INTO Buildings
VALUES ('Ahmedabad',
'<hours dayofWeek="Monday" open="9:00" closed= "18:00"/>
<hours dayofWeek="Tuesday" open="9:00" closed= "18:00"/>
<hours dayofWeek="Wednesday" open="11:00" closed= "18:00"/>
<hours dayofWeek="Saturday" open="11:00" closed= "17:00"/>')
```

You need to write a query that returns a list of Buildings and their opening time for Wednesday. Which code segment should you use?

O a.
```
SELECT StoreName, StoreHours.value
 ('/hours[1]/@open', 'time')
FROM Buildings
WHERE StoreHours.value
 ('/hours[1]/@dayofWeek', 'VARCHAR(20)') = @Day
```

O b.
```
SELECT StoreName, StoreHours.value
 ('/hours[1]/@open', 'time')
FROM Buildings
WHERE StoreHours.exist
 ('/hours[@dayofWeek=" Wednesday"]') = 1
```

O c.
```
SELECT StoreName,
StoreHours.query
 ('data/hours[@dayofWeek="Wednesday"]/@open')
FROM Buildings
```

6.) You have the following XML stream.

```
<TV>
 <Show Name="Bob on the Job">
  <Starring>
   <Actor>Bob</Actor>
   <Actor>Patrick</Actor>
  </Starring>
 </Show>
 <Show Name=”Way Kendall”>
  <Starring>
   <Actor>Lisa</Actor>
   <Actor>Peter</Actor>
  </Starring>
 </Show>
</TV>
```

You need to enter the query parameter to get All Actors from the first TV show's Starring element, as seen here:

```
<Actor>Bob</Actor>
<Actor>Patrick</Actor>
```

Which XPath will get you this Fragment?

O a. 'TV/Show[1]/Starring'
O b. 'TV/Show[2]/Starring'
O c. 'TV/Show[1]/Starring/Actor'
O d. 'TV/Show[2]/Starring/Actor'
O e. 'TV/Show[1]'
O f. 'TV/Show[2]'

Answer Key

1.) <Show> is the first level element name, so (b) is incorrect. Bob on the Job is the <Show> element value, so (c) is incorrect. <TV> is the root node, so (a) is the correct answer.

2.) The relative element path in answers (b) and (d) specifies the second <Show>, so (b) and (d) are incorrect. The path in answer (c) specifies one level too deep, so (c) is incorrect. The path in answer (e) is one level up, so (e) is incorrect. The path in answer (a) is looking for the first relative element in the <Starring> element, so (a) is the correct answer.

3.) Answer (a) is looking for the first <Actor> of the first <Show>, so (a) is incorrect. Answer (c) is looking for the first <Actor> of the second <Show>, so (c) is incorrect. Answer (d) is looking for the second <Actor> of the second <Show>, so (d) is incorrect. The correct answer is (b) the first <Show> and second <Actor>.

4.) The XML data type will only accept well-formed XML and the VARCHAR(MAX) data type will not truncate leading or trailing spaces so the correct answers are (c) and (f).

5.) The question asks for a list of Buildings and their opening time for Wednesday. The only code that will pull just data is in answer (c). Since answer (c) uses the Data() function it is the correct answer.

6.) Answers (a) and (b) will return the <Starring > element tag, so (a) and (b) are incorrect. Answer (d) will return the <Actor> elements from the second show, so (d) is incorrect. Answers (e) and (f) will return the <Show> element tag, so (e) and (f) are incorrect. The only answer that returns just the <Actor> elements of the first <Show> is (c) which is the correct answer.

Bug Catcher Game

To play the Bug Catcher game run the SQLQueries2012Vol5BugCatcher5.pps from the BugCatcher folder of the companion files found at www.Joes2Pros.com.

Chapter 6. XQuery Extensions

We know the XML data type was first introduced in SQL Server 2005. This data type continues in SQL Server 2008 and 2102 where expanded XML features are available. Along with the XML data type comes the power of the XQuery language to analyze and query the values contained in your XML instance.

We will continue to build our expertise using XQuery to query, analyze and manipulate our XML data. Our code will leverage XPath expressions to "navigate" to the levels and nodes where we want the XML data type methods to perform their work. The methods we will explore are query, value, exist and modify (All lowercase, since everything in XQuery is case-sensitive). You may occasionally hear developers refer to these as "XQuery methods."

This chapter will demonstrate these built-in methods (also called functions), as well as show you some keyword extensions (FOR, LET, WHERE, ORDER BY, and RETURN).

As noted in Chapter 1, XML is case-sensitive. In order for your examples and exercises to run properly in Chapters 1 through 7, be sure that your XML fragments precisely match the figures with respect to uppercase and lowercase.

READERNOTE:*Please run the SQLQueries2012Vol5Chapter6.0Setup.sql script in order to follow along with the examples in the first section of Chapter 6. All scripts mentioned in this chapter may be found at* ***www.Joes2Pros.com****.*

READERNOTE: A data element is misspelled in Chapter 6 for illustrative purposes (The band name "The Bangles" appears as "Bangles"). The "correction" of this value serves as an example in Lab 6.1, where we explore the methods for updating values using XQuery.

XML Data Type Method Basics

Functions versus Methods. Until this point in each volume of the *Joes 2 Pros* series, we have used the term "functions" to refer to commands which require a set of parentheses in order to perform their work (e.g., MAX(), COUNT()) SQL programmers also call these functions). However, XML and object-oriented programming (OOP) refer to these command items as "methods." Since this book focuses on SQL Server's interaction and interoperability with other programming languages, we will be good guests and speak their language.

In the last chapter, we became proficient at using the most common method of the XML data type. The query() method allowed us to take an entire XML stream and query just a specific piece of it. We passed in an XPath and got back an XML fragment.

All XML data type methods require an XPath expression as one of the (or the only) XQuery parameter(s), but not all of the methods return data. Some of these methods simply analyze the data at that level and return a status to you. The remainder of this section breaks down four of these methods: query(), value(), exist(), and modify().The nodes() method will be covered in Chapter 7

MusicDetails3.xml × SQLQuery10.sql - R...(Reno\Student (51))*

Object Explorer

```
<Music>
  <Song TitleID="13159">
    <WriterName>Neil Diamond</WriterName>
    <Title>Red Red Wine</Title>
    <Singer OrderID="1">
      <BandName>Neil Diamond</BandName>
    </Singer>
    <Singer OrderID="2">
      <BandName>UB40</BandName>
    </Singer>
  </Song>
  <Song TitleID="13160">
    <WriterName>Prince</WriterName>
    <Title>Manic Monday</Title>
    <Singer OrderID="1">
      <BandName>Bangles</BandName>
    </Singer>
  </Song>
  <Song TitleID="13161">
    <WriterName>Roy Orbison</WriterName>
    <Title>Pretty Woman</Title>
    <Singer OrderID="1">
      <BandName>Roy Orbison</BandName>
    </Singer>
    <Singer OrderID="2">
      <BandName>Van Halen</BandName>
    </Singer>
  </Song>
</Music>
```

Figure 6.1 In this chapter, we will expand on the XML document containing the Music dataset.

The query() Method

As we saw in the last chapter, this method basically needs an XPath expression in the XQuery parameter and returns an XML data type.

Here is a recap of the code we used to retrieve an XML fragment containing only the BandName element (Chapter 5 as Figures 5.37 and 5.38).

The XPath expression ('/Music/Song[1]/Singer[2]/BandName') specifies that we want to navigate to the <BandName> element of the second Singer of the first Song (Red Red Wine). The query() method returns the XML fragment containing everything between (and including) the beginning and ending tags of that <BandName> element, which is UB40 (Figure 6.2).

```
SELECT MusicDetails.query
 ('/Music/Song[1]/Singer[2]/BandName')
FROM dbo.MusicHistory WHERE MusicTypeID = 3
```

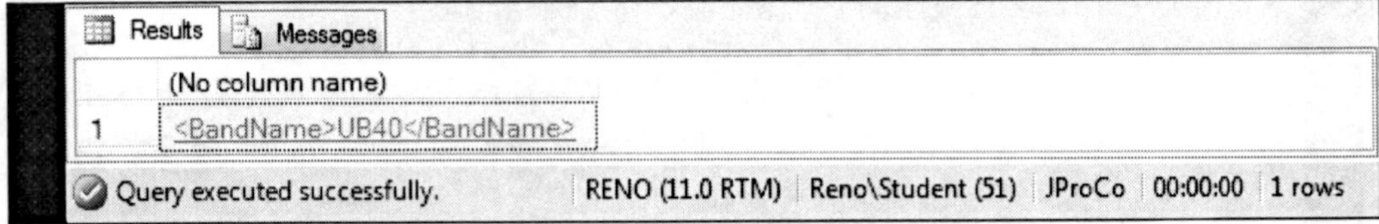

Figure 6.2 query() retrieves the BandName element for the second Singer of the first Song.

When we click through the hyperlink result, it launches an XML query window within SQL Server Management Studio (Figure 6.3).

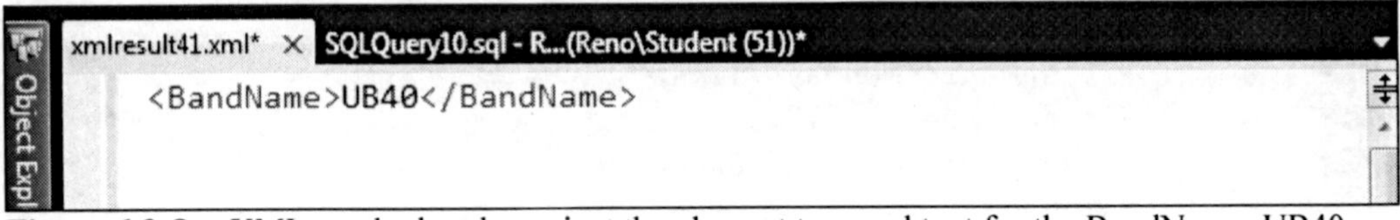

Figure 6.3 Our XML result also shows just the element tags and text for the BandName, UB40.

We also used the text() function in conjunction with query() to return element text (i.e., an XML fragment without element tags). Essentially the query() method only returns XML data -- if you need a single name or value, then you must add text() to the XPath expression in your query() parameter.

Here text() pulls out just the <BandName> value, which is the text between the element tags (Figure 6.4).

```
SELECT MusicDetails.query
 ('/Music/Song[1]/Singer[2]/BandName/text()')
FROM dbo.MusicHistory WHERE MusicTypeID = 3
```

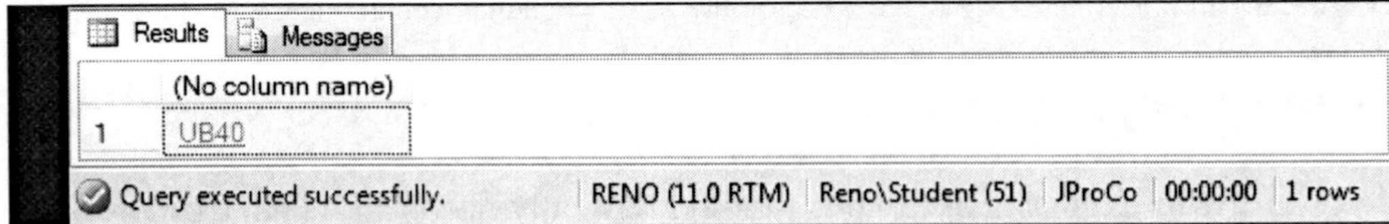

Figure 6.4 We have added text() to our existing code in order to retrieve just the BandName.

When we click through the hyperlink result, we see only the element text, UB40. We have used XQuery to query our XML document and returned to SQL Server just the data we wanted (Figure 6.5).

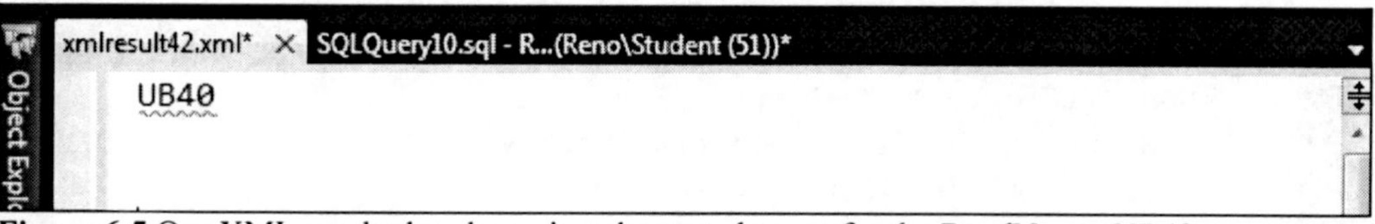

Figure 6.5 Our XML result also shows just the text element for the BandName, UB40.

Let's switch gears and go back up to the <Song> level for our next query() example. This code will return all items found at the <Song> level (Figure 6.6).

```
SELECT MusicDetails.query('/Music/Song')
FROM dbo.MusicHistory WHERE MusicTypeID = 3
```

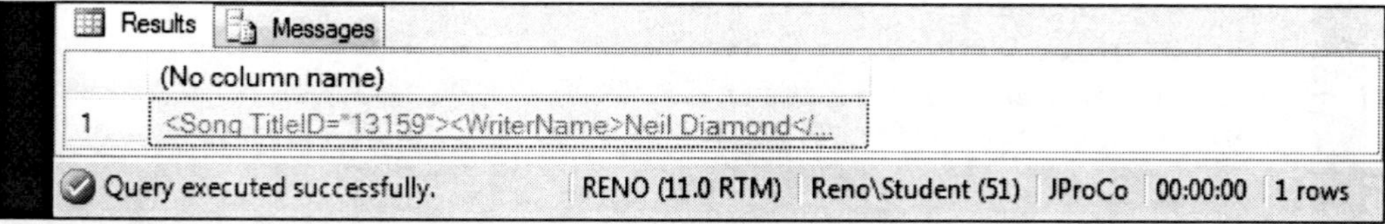

Figure 6.6 The query() method returns all items found at the Song level.

When we click through the result hyperlink, we see the XML fragment for all three songs: Red Red Wine, Manic Monday and Pretty Woman (Figure 6.7).

```
xmlresult43.xml  X  SQLQuery10.sql - R...(Reno\Student (51))*
<Song TitleID="13159">
  <WriterName>Neil Diamond</WriterName>
  <Title>Red Red Wine</Title>
  <Singer OrderID="1">
    <BandName>Neil Diamond</BandName>
  </Singer>
  <Singer OrderID="2">
    <BandName>UB40</BandName>
  </Singer>
</Song>
<Song TitleID="13160">
  <WriterName>Prince</WriterName>
  <Title>Manic Monday</Title>
  <Singer OrderID="1">
    <BandName>Bangles</BandName>
  </Singer>
</Song>
<Song TitleID="13161">
  <WriterName>Roy Orbison</WriterName>
  <Title>Pretty Woman</Title>
  <Singer OrderID="1">
    <BandName>Roy Orbison</BandName>
  </Singer>
  <Singer OrderID="2">
    <BandName>Van Halen</BandName>
  </Singer>
</Song>
```

Figure 6.7 The query() method returns all items found at the Song level.

Next we will specify just the first Song, Red Red Wine (Figure 6.8 and Figure 6.9).

```
SELECT MusicDetails.query('/Music/Song[1]')
FROM dbo.MusicHistory WHERE MusicTypeID = 3
```

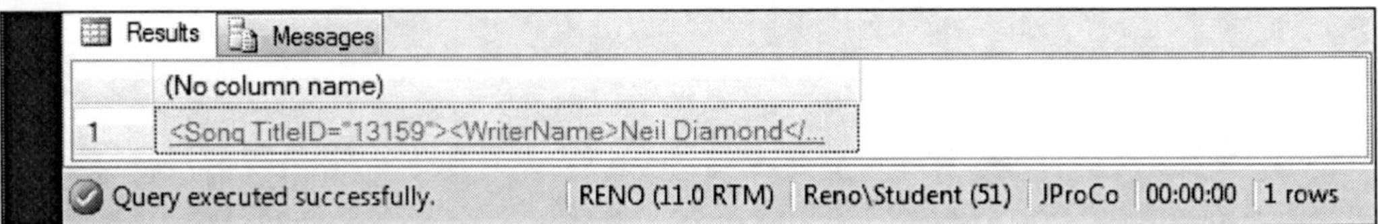

Figure 6.8 We want to see just the first song.

```
xmlresult44.xml* × SQLQuery10.sql - R...(Reno\Student (51))*
<Song TitleID="13159">
  <WriterName>Neil Diamond</WriterName>
  <Title>Red Red Wine</Title>
  <Singer OrderID="1">
    <BandName>Neil Diamond</BandName>
  </Singer>
  <Singer OrderID="2">
    <BandName>UB40</BandName>
  </Singer>
</Song>
```

Figure 6.9 Our result is an XML fragment containing just the first song.

This code specifies that we want data for all <Singer> elements found for the first Song (Figure 6.10 and Figure 6.11).

```
SELECT MusicDetails.query('/Music/Song[1]/Singer')
FROM dbo.MusicHistory WHERE MusicTypeID = 3
```

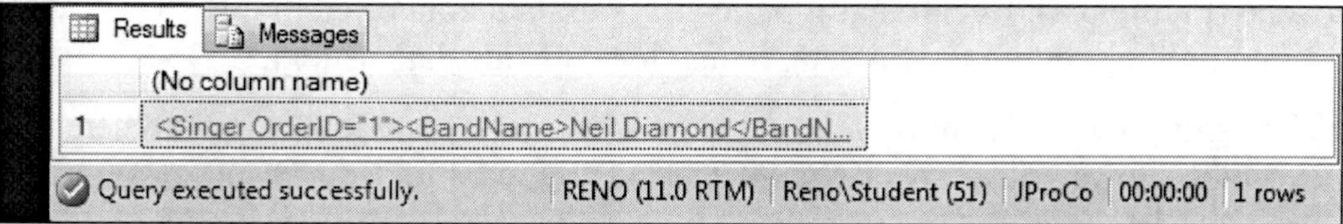

Figure 6.10 Our code now specifies our search should begin at the Singer level.

```
xmlresult45.xml* × SQLQuery10.sql - R...(Reno\Student (51))*
<Singer OrderID="1">
  <BandName>Neil Diamond</BandName>
</Singer>
<Singer OrderID="2">
  <BandName>UB40</BandName>
</Singer>
```

Figure 6.11 Our result is an XML fragment containing all singers of the first song.

This code specifies that we want query() to return data for just the first Singer found for the first Song (Figure 6.12 and Figure 6.13).

```
SELECT MusicDetails.query('(/Music/Song[1]/Singer)[1]')
FROM dbo.MusicHistory WHERE MusicTypeID = 3
```

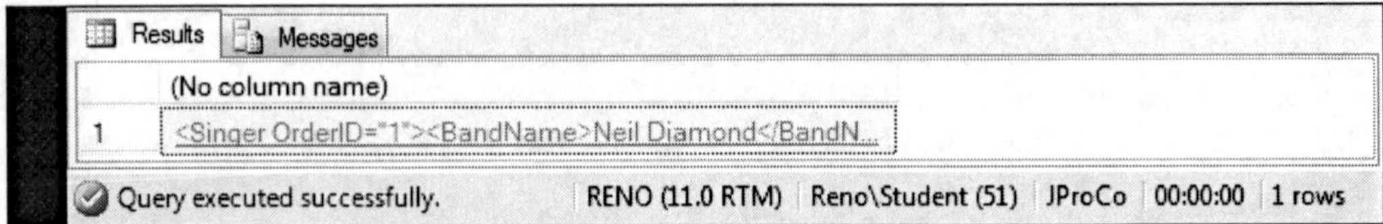

Figure 6.12 This code will return data for just the first Singer of the first Song (Red Red Wine).

xmlresult46.xml* × SQLQuery10.sql - R...(Reno\Student (51))*

```
<Singer OrderID="1">
  <BandName>Neil Diamond</BandName>
</Singer>
```

Figure 6.13 This XML fragment contains data for Neil Diamond, the first Singer of the first Song.

The value() Method

The next method we will explore is value(). Earlier we used the query() method in combination with the text() function to pull out just the element text for a single value (Figure 6.4). Recall that it pulled out our data converted to text (Not XML). When pulling out numerical data, it also formats this data as text.

The value() method achieves the same goal as query() and text() do together, except it allows you to specify the data type you want for your result. It returns just your data (without the metadata - no element tags) and gives you the freedom to specify any data type you would like (i.e., not just XML or text). In other words, if you are pulling from a <Price> element, then you might want the result returned as a Money or a Decimal data type. If you are pulling from the <Singer> element, you might specify that the returning data should be a Varchar.

This method provides an efficient way to retrieve data directly from an XML file and return it to SQL Server.

The query syntax is very similar to our current code (Figure 6.12). We will use value() to return the same data (first Singer of the first Song). Substitute "value" in place of "query" and run the code. The resulting error message prompts us to supply a second parameter (Figure 6.14). ***The value() method requires two argumets (parameters).***

```
SELECT MusicDetails.value('(/Music/Song[1]/Singer)[1]')
FROM dbo.MusicHistory WHERE MusicTypeID = 3
```

```
Messages
Msg 174, Level 15, State 1, Line 2
The value function requires 2 argument(s).
                                                    0 rows
```

Figure 6.14 The value() method requires two parameters, an XPath expression and a data type.

Observe that XQuery gives us the freedom to specify data types which are compatible with character data (e.g., char(20), VARCHAR(max)).

```
SELECT
 MusicDetails.value
  ('(/Music/Song[1]/Singer)[1]','NVARCHAR(100)')
FROM dbo.MusicHistory WHERE MusicTypeID = 3
```

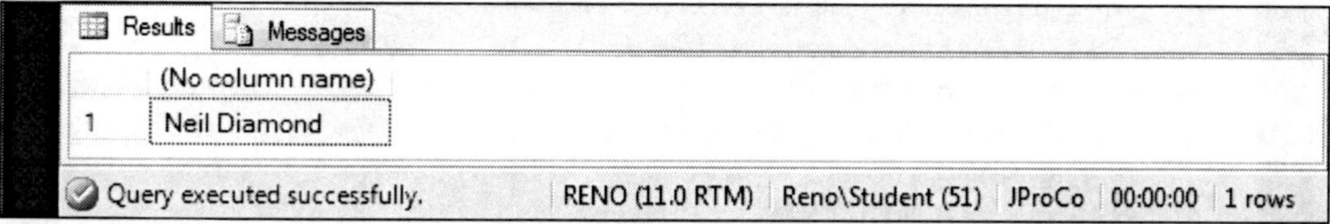

Figure 6.15 When we supply a data type, value() returns just the data we specified.

The exist() Method

In this method you don't want any data returned from the XML stream. You just want to check to know whether it is there. The exist() method will check for the existence and even the value of the XPath expression you specify.

Let's return to our code which shows us all the top-level nodes (as seen in Figures 6.6 and 6.7). When we click through the result hyperlink, we see the XML fragment for all three songs: Red Red Wine, Manic Monday and Pretty Woman.

```
SELECT MusicDetails.query('/Music/Song')
FROM dbo.MusicHistory WHERE MusicTypeID = 3
```

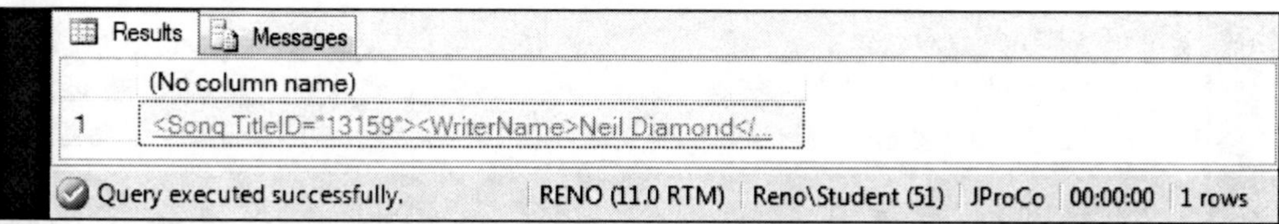

Figure 6.16 For our next example, we are returning to our code showing all three songs.

Now let's drill in and find the fragment which contains data for the Song with TitleID 13161, regardless of whether it is at, or below, the top-level element (<Song>).

```
SELECT MusicDetails.query('/Music/Song[@TitleID=13161]')
FROM dbo.MusicHistory WHERE MusicTypeID = 3
```

Results | Messages

	(No column name)
1	<Song TitleID="13161"><WriterName>Roy Orbison</WriterName><Title>Pretty Woman</Title>...

Query executed successfully. | RENO (11.0 RTM) | Reno\Student (51) | JProCo | 00:00:00 | 1 rows

Figure 6.17 We are searching by attribute for the song whose TitleID is 13161.

xmlresult1.xml × SQLQuery1.sql - RE...(Reno\Student (51))*

Object Explorer

```
<Song TitleID="13161"> ←
  <WriterName>Roy Orbison</WriterName>
  <Title>Pretty Woman</Title>
  <Singer OrderID="1">
    <BandName>Roy Orbison</BandName>
  </Singer>
  <Singer OrderID="2">
    <BandName>Van Halen</BandName>
  </Singer>
</Song>
```

Figure 6.18 Our XML result shows all elements and attributes for Song with TitleID = 13161.

Let's observe what happens when we try to query for a TitleID which doesn't exist. Our XML document contains the TitleIDs 13159, 13160, and 13161 (as we saw earlier in Figure 6.7). Let's modify our code to specify the non-existent TitleID 13162 (Figure 6.19). XQuery doesn't give us an error message - it simply returns an empty string.

```
SELECT MusicDetails.query('/Music/Song[@TitleID=13162]')
FROM dbo.MusicHistory WHERE MusicTypeID = 3
```

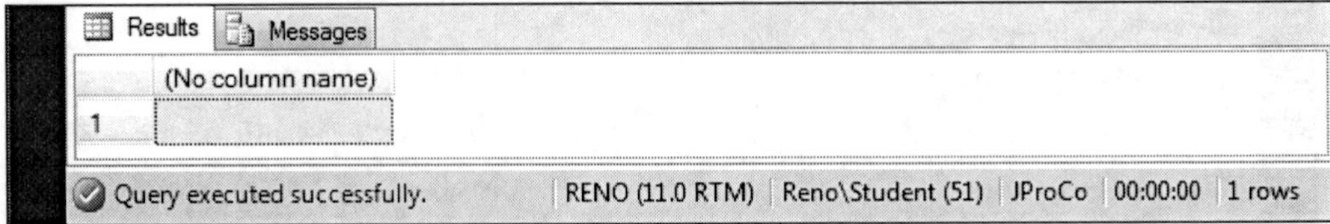

Figure 6.19 TitleID 13162 doesn't exist, so query() returns an empty string.

Next we will modify our current code to include the exist() method. The syntax and functionality is nearly identical to the syntax we used to search for TitleIDs

13161 and 13162, except that the exist() method doesn't return data from your XML document. Instead, it returns a "0" if the data doesn't exist or a "1" if the data does exist.

Now let's simply find out whether 13162 exists. Rather than returning a piece of the XML, it will return a 1 for 'Yes' or a 0 for 'No'.

```
SELECT MusicDetails.exist('/Music/Song[@TitleID=13162]')
FROM dbo.MusicHistory WHERE MusicTypeID = 3
```

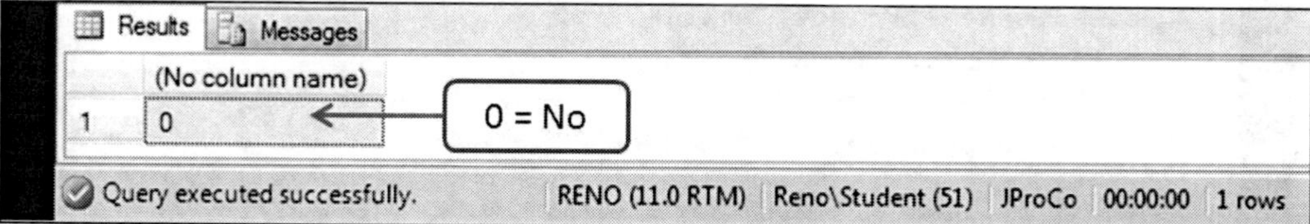

Figure 6.20 This 0 indicates that the TitleID we specified (13162) doesn't exist.

Let's repeat the step for TitleID 13161, an item that we know exists.

```
SELECT MusicDetails.exist('/Music/Song[@TitleID=13161]')
FROM dbo.MusicHistory WHERE MusicTypeID = 3
```

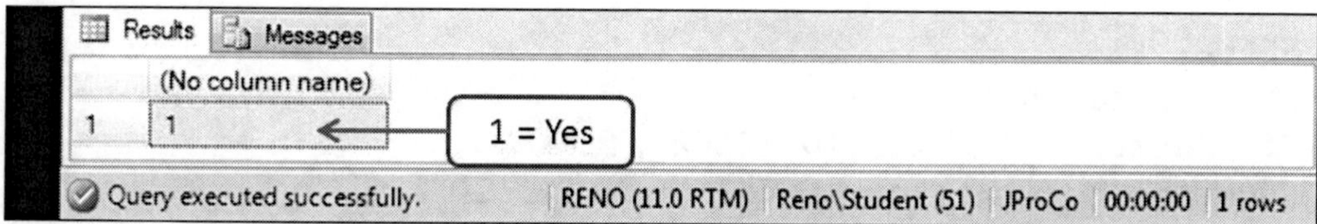

Figure 6.21 This 1 indicates that yes, the TitleID we specified (13161) does exist.

The modify() Method

The modify() method allows you to change values directly in your XML stream. Like all other XML data type methods, it needs an XPath parameter to know which value to change. However, unlike the other methods, modify() works with an UPDATE statement - it won't work with a SELECT statement.

Also, modify() can only work with one data value at a time (a mathematical and programming concept known as a *singleton*).

We will use TitleID 13160 (Manic Monday) to explore the modify() method.

```
SELECT
 MusicDetails.query
 ('/Music/Song[@TitleID=13160]')
FROM dbo.MusicHistory WHERE MusicTypeID = 3
```

Figure 6.22 Our code retrieves all data for the Song with the TitleID of 13160.

```
xmlresult2.xml*  X  SQLQuery1.sql - RE...(Reno\Student (51))*
<Song TitleID="13160">
  <WriterName>Prince</WriterName>
  <Title>Manic Monday</Title>
  <Singer OrderID="1">
    <BandName>Bangles</BandName>
  </Singer>
</Song>
```

Figure 6.23 The XML fragment containing all data for the Song with the TitleID of 13160.

Next, we would like our code to pull out an XML fragment for the <Title> element.

```
SELECT
 MusicDetails.query
 ('/Music/Song[@TitleID=13160]/Title')
FROM dbo.MusicHistory WHERE MusicTypeID = 3
```

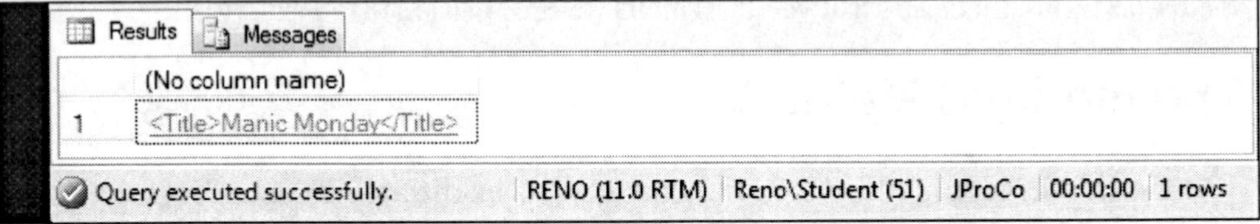

Figure 6.24 We have narrowed our code to retrieve the XML fragment for just the Title element.

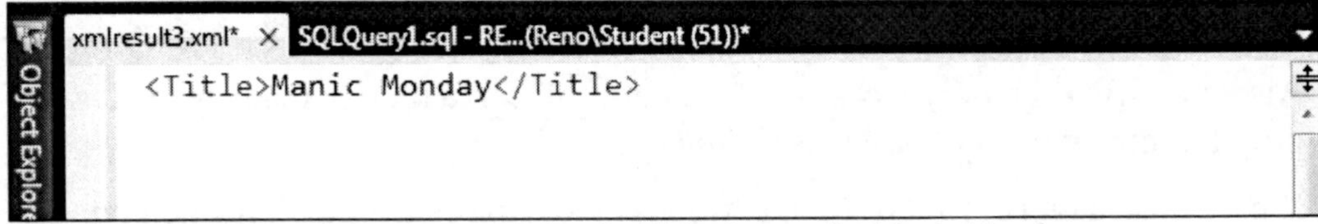

Figure 6.25 The XML fragment containing the Title element for Manic Monday.

Let's modify our code to retrieve only the element text "Manic Monday."

```
SELECT
 MusicDetails.query
 ('/Music/Song[@TitleID=13160]/Title/text()')
FROM dbo.MusicHistory WHERE MusicTypeID = 3
```

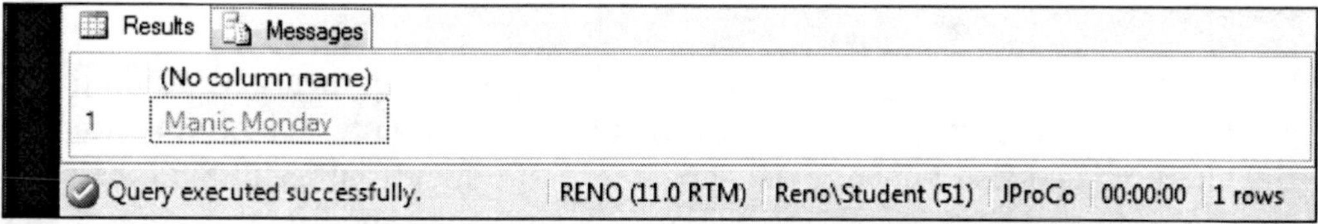

Figure 6.26 Our code uses text() to retrieve only the element text for "Manic Monday."

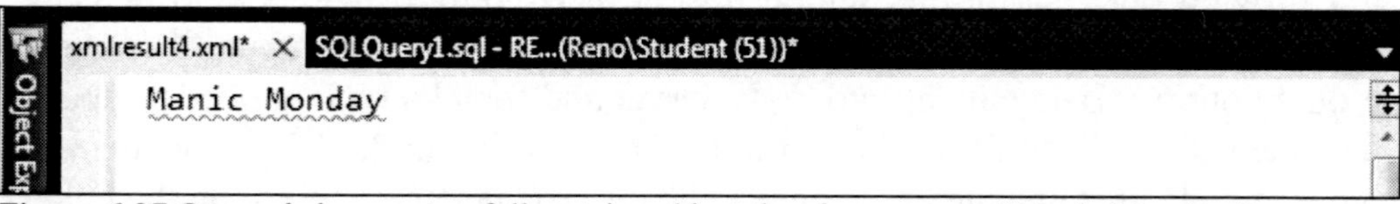

Figure 6.27 Our code has successfully retrieved just the element text, "Manic Monday."

As we've done with each new method in this chapter, we have used our familiar tools query() and text() to scaffold and bring our code to a good juncture for introducing the new method. We need to first add one refinement to our current code before we can bring in the modify() method.

Earlier we mentioned the modify() method will only work with one data value at a time. While it won't alter the result of our current code, we need to add a"[1]" to specify that we only want a single item retrieved (Figure 6.28).

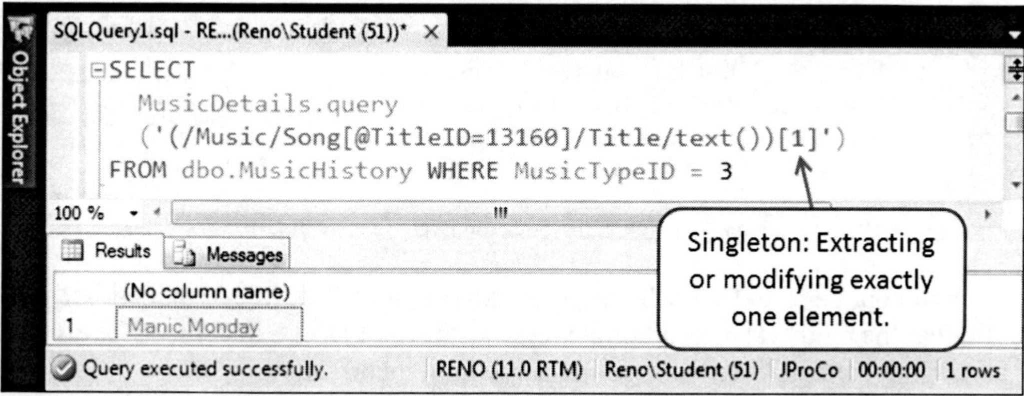

Figure 6.28 Adding the [1] to our code ensures that only one value will be retrieved.

Since there is no limit to the number of elements which can be under another element, any given XPath may have many children. For example, the XPath of /week/day would have three elements below and, therefore, isn't a singleton:

```
<week>
 <day>Monday<day/>
 <day>Tuesday<day/>
 <day>Wednesday<day/>
<week>
```

However, if you changed your XPath to be (/week/day)[1], then you would just get Monday. Again, since each Song can only have one Title, specifying the singelton of [1] doesn't change the appearance of our current result but it helps prepare us for the next method we will explore, which is modify().

Let's review our goal for this demonstration. The modify() method allows us to change a value in our XML file, which is a helpful capability. Suppose we've brought our XML document into SQL Server and found a typo or need to update just one value. We don't need to rerun the step to bring in the XML document in order to make that change - we can use the modify() method and write the change directly to the XML stream contained in our SQL Server instance.

Our scenario is that the title "Manic Monday" needs to be changed to "Walk Like an Egyptian" (Figure 6.29). Since modify() is going to replace the current title, Manic Monday, with the new title, we need to add some code to handle the change. For readability, we will move our existing XPath parameter for Manic Monday **(/Music/Song[@TitleID=13160]/Title/text())[1]** down one line to make room for two additional clauses. The syntax is essentially this:

'replace value of *(XPath expression for current item)[1]* with *"new value"'*

Figure 6.29 We have added code to handle replacing the old value with the new value.

Let's run our code and see whether it works (Figure 6.30). Recall that earlier we said that the modify() method only works with an UPDATE statement. This messaging confirms that we've done something incorrectly.

```
Messages
Msg 8137, Level 16, State 1, Line 1
Incorrect use of the XML data type method 'modify'. A non-mutator method is
expected in this context.
                                                                    0 rows
```

Figure 6.30 SQL Server is telling us that the modify() method is not being used correctly.

This reminds us that XQuery's modify() method belongs in the SET clause of an UPDATE statement. *The modify() method will not work with a SELECT statement.*

We need to add an UPDATE statement and change "SELECT MusicDetails.modify" to "SET MusicDetails.modify" (Figure 6.31).

Perfect - our revised code runs, and we see the confirmation (1 row(s) affected).

```
UPDATE dbo.MusicHistory
SET MusicDetails.modify('replace value of
 (/Music/Song[@TitleID=13160]/Title/text())[1]
 with "Walk Like an Egyptian"')
FROM dbo.MusicHistory
WHERE MusicTypeID = 3
```

```
Messages
(1 row(s) affected)
                                                    0 rows
```

Figure 6.31 Our UPDATE statement appears to run and confirm that 1 row was updated.

Now return to our original query (shown in Figure 6.22) and run a SELECT statement to confirm that the title was updated correctly (Figure 6.32).

```
SELECT MusicDetails.query('/Music/Song[@TitleID=13160]')
FROM dbo.MusicHistory
WHERE MusicTypeID = 3
```

Figure 6.32 We will run a SELECT statement to confirm that TitleID 13160 was properly updated.

```
xmlresult5.xml*   SQLQuery1.sql - RE...(Reno\Student (51))*
<Song TitleID="13160">
  <WriterName>Prince</WriterName>
  <Title>Walk Like an Egyptian</Title>  <----
  <Singer OrderID="1">
    <BandName>Bangles</BandName>
  </Singer>
</Song>
```

Figure 6.33 Our SELECT statement confirms that the Title is now "Walk Like an Egyptian."

Lab 6.1: XML Data Type Methods

Lab Prep: Each lab has one or more Skill Checks. Start with Skill Check 1 and proceed until reaching the Points to Ponder section.

Before beginning this lab, verify that SQL Server 2012 is properly installed and operating. Before running the lab setup script for resetting the database (SQLQueries2012Vol5Chapter6.1Setup.sql), please make sure to close all query windows within SSMS. An open query window pointing to a database context can lock that database preventing it from updating when the script is executing. A simple way to assure all query windows are closed, is to exit out of SSMS, then open a new instance of SSMS, and lastly run the setup script.

Skill Check 1: Prince did not write "Walk Like an Egyptian." Using what you've learned, change the WriterName to "Liam Sternberg" for Song 13160.

```
SELECT * FROM dbo.MusicHistory
WHERE MusicTypeID = 3
```

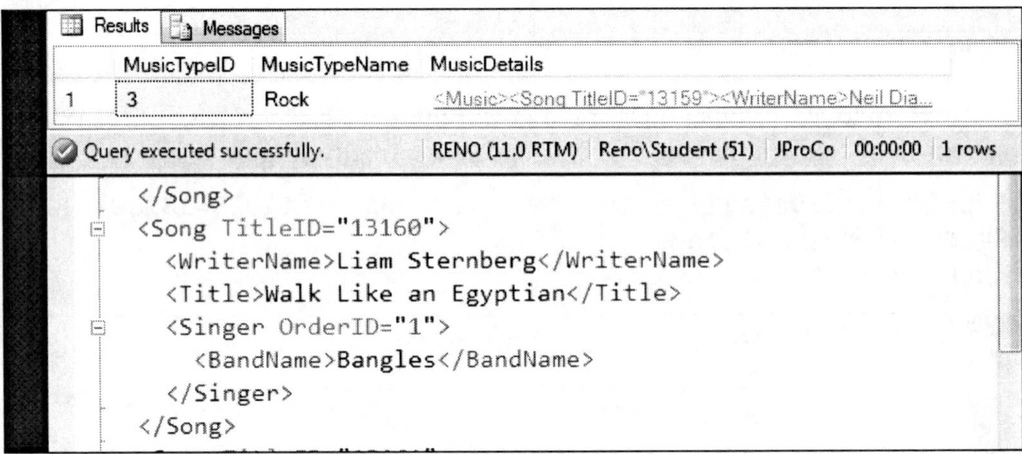

Figure 6.34 The result for Skill Check 1.

Skill Check 2: A <BandName> was misspelled. It should be "The Bangles" instead of just "Bangles". Make this change to correct the name.

```
SELECT * FROM dbo.MusicHistory
WHERE MusicTypeID = 3
```

	MusicTypeID	MusicTypeName	MusicDetails
1	3	Rock	<Music><Song TitleID="13159"><WriterName>Neil Diamond<...

Query executed successfully. | RENO (11.0 RTM) | Reno\Student (51) | JProCo | 00:00:00 | 1 rows

```
<Song TitleID="13160">
  <WriterName>Liam Sternberg</WriterName>
  <Title>Walk Like an Egyptian</Title>
  <Singer OrderID="1">
    <BandName>The Bangles</BandName>
  </Singer>
</Song>
```

Figure 6.35 The result for Skill Check 2.

Skill Check 3: Use the exist() method on the Olympics table to see if there is an event named "Boxing 178.5 lbs.".

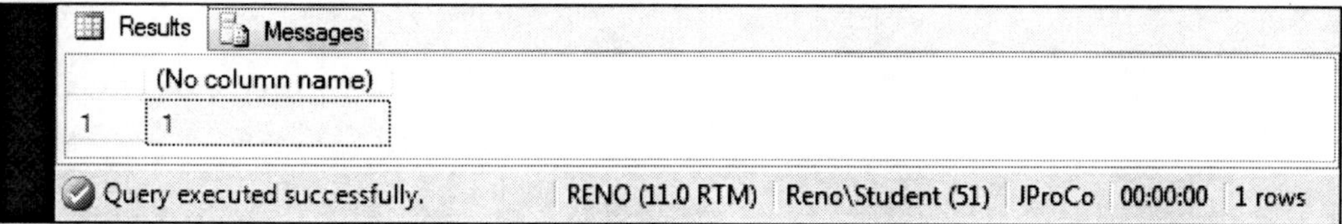

Figure 6.36 Skill Check 3 uses the exist() method.

Skill Check 4: Using what you've learned, change the name of TitleID=13159 to add a hyphen to make the Title element text "Red-Red Wine".

```
<Song TitleID="13159">
  <WriterName>Neil Diamond</WriterName>
  <Title>Red-Red Wine</Title>
  <Singer OrderID="1">
    <BandName>Neil Diamond</BandName>
  </Singer>
  <Singer OrderID="2">
    <BandName>UB40</BandName>
  </Singer>
</Song>
```

Figure 6.37 The result for Skill Check 4.

Answer Code: The T-SQL code to this lab can be found in the downloadable files in a file named Lab6.1_XQueryMethods.sql

XML Data Type Methods - Points to Ponder

1. Since SQL Server 2005, the XML data type provides five methods.
    - query() - used to extract XML fragments from an XML data type.
    - value() - used to extract a single value from an XML document.
    - exist() - used to determine if a specified node exists. Returns 1 if it does exist, returns 0 if it doesn't exist.
    - modify() - updates XML data in an XML data type.
    - nodes() - shreds XML data into multiple rows ***(this method will be covered in Chapter 7).***
2. The value() method requires two parameters, one for the XQuery and the other for the data type you wish to capture.
3. The modify() method works only with an UPDATE clause in the SET block.

XQuery FLWOR Expressions

Most developers I've encountered whose work includes XML generally consider the FLWOR expressions to be the real power of XQuery. While I tend to agree with them, unfortunately the real power of these expressions is best showcased in larger scale, data-intensive environments, or in data warehousing scenarios requiring frequent iterations and complex queries against massive stores of XML data.

For those planning to work extensively with XML, I highly recommend additional study of the many resources available in this area. As this book's focus is XML's interoperability with SQL Server, you won't become an expert on a topic as vast as FLWOR from this chapter alone. Due to the success and rapid adoption of Microsoft SQL Server in the Enterprise and BI markets, it is increasingly important for SQL developers and DBAs to be familiar with other programming languages (e.g., C#, .NET CLR, XQuery) which interoperate with SQL Server. The aim of this book is to expose SQL developers, analysts and DBAs to these other languages they will encounter in their SQL-centric work and to be somewhat of a "survival guide" in this area.

With that said, there is still plenty we can do to understand the mechanics of the XQuery FLWOR expressions and observe their application in smaller-scale demonstrations. These keywords are part of the XQuery standard, which was formulated by an international consortium (the World Wide Web Consortium or W3C) and not invented by Microsoft. In fact, SQL Server 2005 supported only some of the FLWOR statements. With SQL Server 2008, all of the FLWOR statements are now supported.

Overview

We have seen that it's possible (although rare) for one Olympic event to result in a tie (e.g., two Silver or two Bronze medal winners). However, it's not uncommon for a song to be re-recorded and sung by more than one singer. We have encountered this in our Music dataset (contained in JProCo.dbo.MusicHistory).

One way to find these one-to-many relationship instances is to search for cases where an element, such as <Title>, has two child elements of exactly the same name, such as <Singer> or <Bandname>. A quick glance at the <Music> XML document (Figure 6.39) shows us two Titles with multiple singers (Red-Red Wine and Pretty Woman).

Now suppose that our MusicHistory table contains millions of Titles. You could search manually for the <Title> or <Song> elements having multiple <Singer>

elements, but that would not be a fun or efficient use of time. Instead, it would be preferable to have a robust query run through our giant XML file and give us options to specify our desired criteria.

We know that SQL Server uses criteria with words like WHERE, HAVING, NOT and IN (among others). XQuery also has its own set of words to use. These XQuery expressions are the focus of this section.

MusicDetails1.xml × SQLQuery2.sql - RE...(Reno\Student (53))*

```
<Music>
  <Song TitleID="13159">
    <WriterName>Neil Diamond</WriterName>
    <Title>Red-Red Wine</Title>
    <Singer OrderID="1">
      <BandName>Neil Diamond</BandName>
    </Singer>
    <Singer OrderID="2">
      <BandName>UB40</BandName>
    </Singer>
  </Song>
  <Song TitleID="13160">
    <WriterName>Liam Sternberg</WriterName>
    <Title>Walk Like an Egyptian</Title>
    <Singer OrderID="1">
      <BandName>The Bangles</BandName>
    </Singer>
  </Song>
  <Song TitleID="13161">
    <WriterName>Roy Orbison</WriterName>
    <Title>Pretty Woman</Title>
    <Singer OrderID="1">
      <BandName>Roy Orbison</BandName>
    </Singer>
    <Singer OrderID="2">
      <BandName>Van Halen</BandName>
    </Singer>
  </Song>
</Music>
```

Figure 6.38 The Music dataset contained in the JProCo.dbo.MusicHistory table.

First we will explore piece-by-piece how to accomplish the goal of finding all elements at the <Song> level with two or more Singers below them.

To explore how we might tackle this, let's first look at one of those Songs which we know was performed by multiple Singers (Figure 6.40).

```
SELECT MusicDetails.query ('/Music/Song [3]')
FROM dbo.MusicHistory
Where MusicTypeID = 3
```

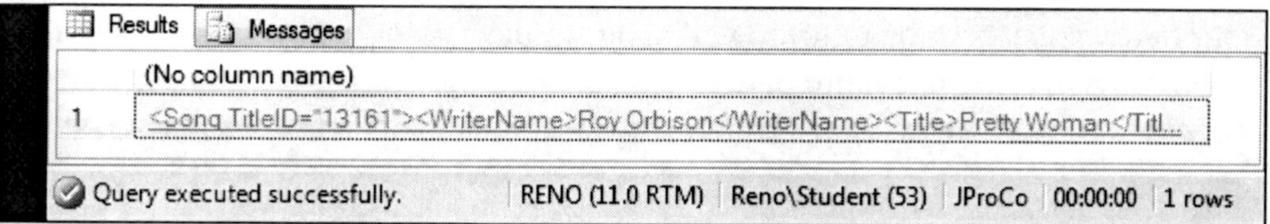

Figure 6.39 We'll begin by looking at the third song, which was performed by multiple singers.

The first Singer of "Pretty Woman" was Roy Orbison. The second Singer was Van Halen (Figure 6.40).

xmlresult1.xml* × SQLQuery2.sql - RE...(Reno\Student (53))*

```
<Song TitleID="13161">
  <WriterName>Roy Orbison</WriterName>
  <Title>Pretty Woman</Title>
  <Singer OrderID="1">
    <BandName>Roy Orbison</BandName>
  </Singer>
  <Singer OrderID="2">
    <BandName>Van Halen</BandName>
  </Singer>
</Song>
```

Figure 6.40 This song was sung by two Singers (Roy Orbison and Van Halen).

XPath Alias

Let's revise our code, beginning by removing the level 3 indicator, because we want to query all the songs (i.e., not just the third one).

Instead we'll use this code (Figure 6.41). Observe that our code is aliasing the level **/Music/Song** as **$ManyHits**. Therefore returning **$ManyHits** is the same as returning **/Music/Song** (Figure 6.41).

```
SELECT MusicDetails.query
 ('for $ManyHits in /Music/Song return $ManyHits')
FROM dbo.MusicHistory
Where MusicTypeID = 3
```

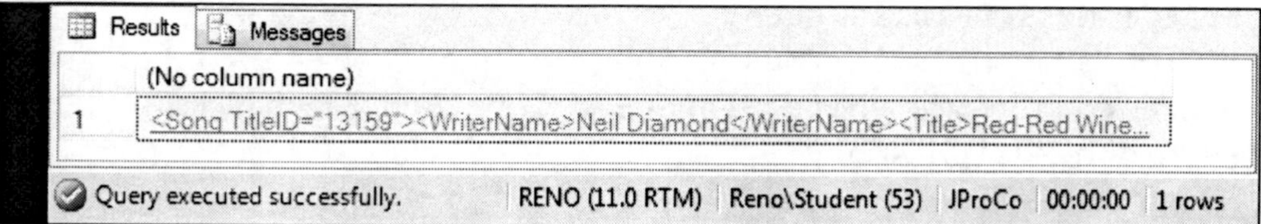

Figure 6.41 Our code aliases the level /Music/Song as $ManyHits and essentially returns all songs in the catalog.

Our query appears to be returning all songs in the catalog because we haven't yet specified any criteria (Figure 6.42).

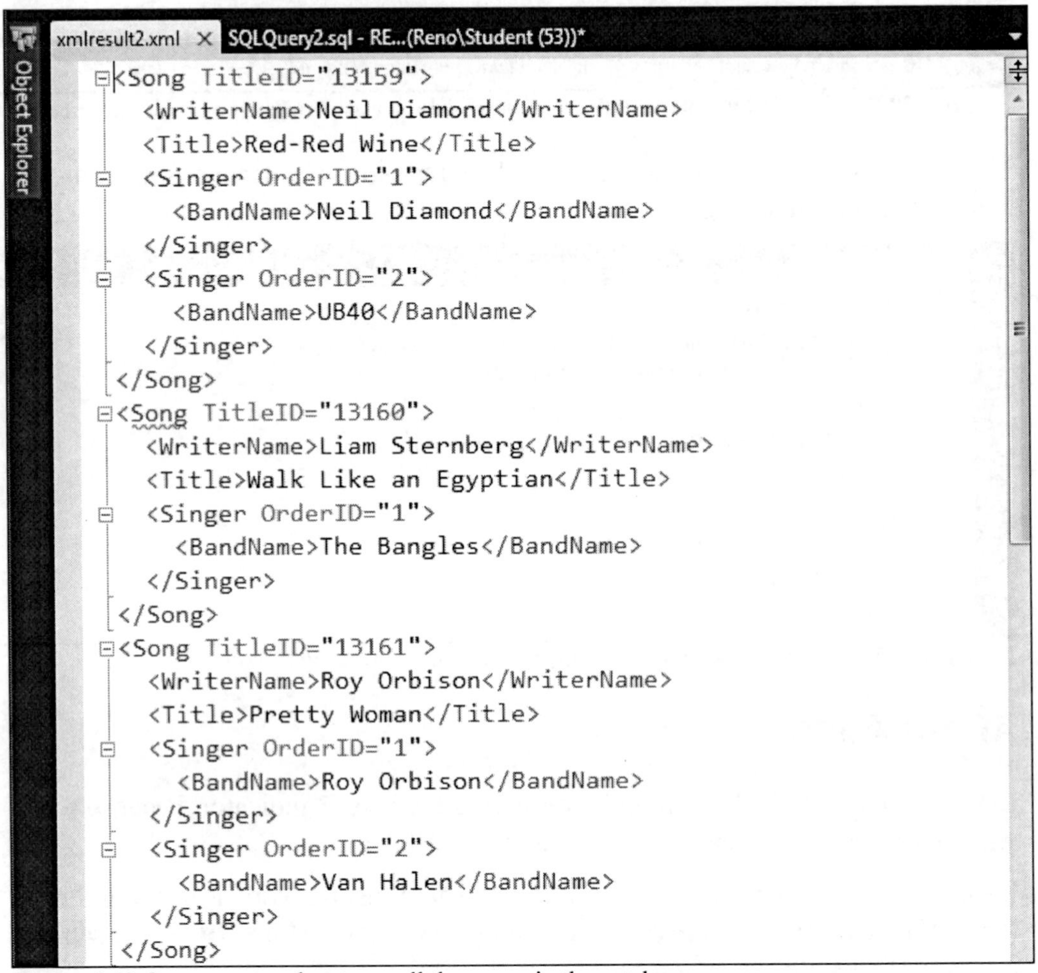

Object Explorer

xmlresult2.xml × SQLQuery2.sql - RE...(Reno\Student (53))*

```
<Song TitleID="13159">
  <WriterName>Neil Diamond</WriterName>
  <Title>Red-Red Wine</Title>
  <Singer OrderID="1">
    <BandName>Neil Diamond</BandName>
  </Singer>
  <Singer OrderID="2">
    <BandName>UB40</BandName>
  </Singer>
</Song>
<Song TitleID="13160">
  <WriterName>Liam Sternberg</WriterName>
  <Title>Walk Like an Egyptian</Title>
  <Singer OrderID="1">
    <BandName>The Bangles</BandName>
  </Singer>
</Song>
<Song TitleID="13161">
  <WriterName>Roy Orbison</WriterName>
  <Title>Pretty Woman</Title>
  <Singer OrderID="1">
    <BandName>Roy Orbison</BandName>
  </Singer>
  <Singer OrderID="2">
    <BandName>Van Halen</BandName>
  </Singer>
</Song>
```

Figure 6.42 Our current code returns all the songs in the catalog.

When we add some filtering criteria, our code will get us closer to the desired result. The criteria we've added here specifies: "Where the count of <Singer> levels under each $ManyHits level is greater than 1" (Figure 6.43).

```
SELECT MusicDetails.query
 ('for $ManyHits in /Music/Song
where count ($ManyHits/Singer) > 1 return $ManyHits')
FROM dbo.MusicHistory
Where MusicTypeID = 3
```

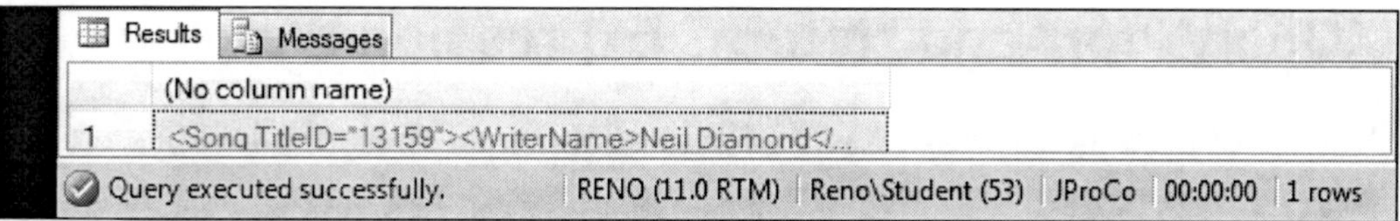

Figure 6.43 Our criteria specifies: "Where the count of Singer levels under each $ManyHits level is greater than 1".

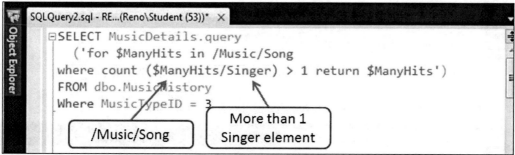

SQLQuery2.sql - RE...(Reno\Student (53))*

```
SELECT MusicDetails.query
  ('for $ManyHits in /Music/Song
where count ($ManyHits/Singer) > 1 return $ManyHits')
FROM dbo.MusicHistory
Where MusicTypeID = 3
```

/Music/Song

More than 1 Singer element

Figure 6.44 At **/Music/Song** level we will count how many Singer elements are present.

Our result is precisely what we wanted to see: each song returned has more than one singer (Figure 6.45).

xmlresult3.xml* SQLQuery2.sql - RE...(Reno\Student (53))*

```
<Song TitleID="13159">
  <WriterName>Neil Diamond</WriterName>
  <Title>Red-Red Wine</Title>
  <Singer OrderID="1">
    <BandName>Neil Diamond</BandName>
  </Singer>
  <Singer OrderID="2">
    <BandName>UB40</BandName>
  </Singer>
</Song>
<Song TitleID="13161">
  <WriterName>Roy Orbison</WriterName>
  <Title>Pretty Woman</Title>
  <Singer OrderID="1">
    <BandName>Roy Orbison</BandName>
  </Singer>
  <Singer OrderID="2">
    <BandName>Van Halen</BandName>
  </Singer>
</Song>
```

Figure 6.45 Each song returned has more than one singer. Notice that The Bangles' song doesn't appear in this XML fragment.

XQuery "for" and "return" Expression Words

Notice we used the expression word **for** to establish an alias for a level.

```
SQLQuery2.sql - RE...(Reno\Student (53))*
SELECT MusicDetails.query
   ('for $ManyHits in /Music/Song
where count ($ManyHits/Singer) > 1 return $ManyHits')
FROM dbo.MusicHistory
Where MusicTypeID = 3
```

Figure 6.46 The **for** expression helped us to establish an alias for the /Music/Song level.

We used **return** to show us the results found by our code.

```
SQLQuery2.sql - RE...(Reno\Student (53))*
SELECT MusicDetails.query
   ('for $ManyHits in /Music/Song
where count ($ManyHits/Singer) > 1 return $ManyHits')
FROM dbo.MusicHistory
Where MusicTypeID = 3
```

Figure 6.47 The **return** expression showed us the results found by our code.

XQuery "where"

The **where** expression in XQuery is somewhat similar to our use of the WHERE clause in T-SQL.

We used **where** to find the criteria we needed:

```
SQLQuery2.sql - RE...(Reno\Student (53))*
SELECT MusicDetails.query
   ('for $ManyHits in /Music/Song
where count ($ManyHits/Singer) > 1 return $ManyHits')
FROM dbo.MusicHistory
Where MusicTypeID = 3
```

Figure 6.48 Criteria: *"**where** the count of Singer levels under each $ManyHits level is greater than 1".*

We used three of the five XQuery statements known by the acronym F-L-W-O-R which is pronounced "flower". While you will always see FLWOR in caps, you must use lowercase lettering in order for your code to run.

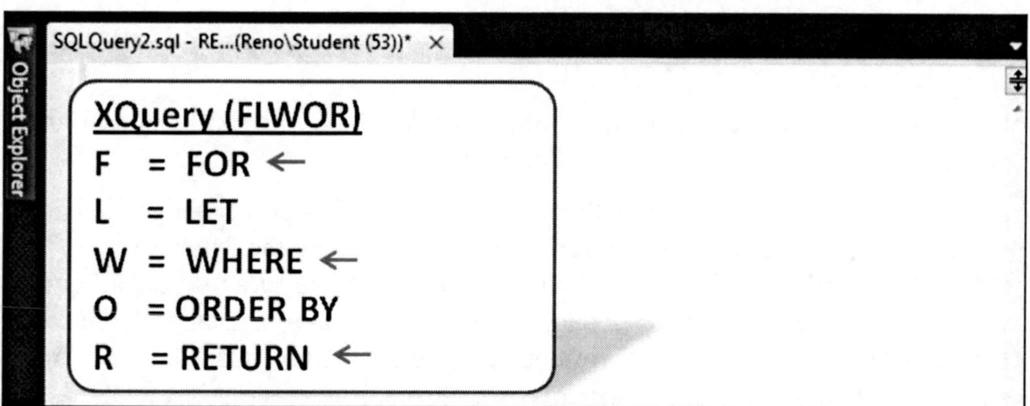

Figure 6.49 Our example utilized three of the five XPath extensions.

Lab 6.2: XQuery FLWOR Expressions

Lab Prep: Each lab has one or more Skill Checks. Start with Skill Check 1 and proceed until reaching the Points to Ponder section.

Before beginning this lab, verify that SQL Server 2012 is properly installed and operating. Before running the lab setup script for resetting the database (SQLQueries2012Vol5Chapter6.2Setup.sql), please make sure to close all query windows within SSMS. An open query window pointing to a database context can lock that database preventing it from updating when the script is executing. A simple way to assure all query windows are closed, is to exit out of SSMS, then open a new instance of SSMS, and lastly run the setup script.

Skill Check 1: Using the dbo.Olympics table, find all the events from the Odetails field that have multiple Bronze medal winners. If an event has multiple <Bronze> elements, then show that entire event.

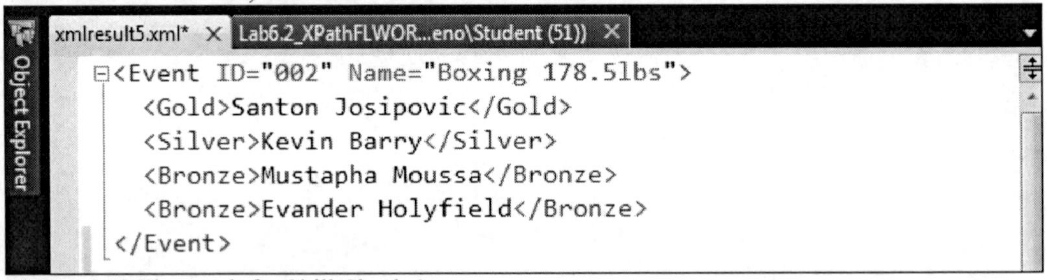

```
<Event ID="002" Name="Boxing 178.5lbs">
  <Gold>Santon Josipovic</Gold>
  <Silver>Kevin Barry</Silver>
  <Bronze>Mustapha Moussa</Bronze>
  <Bronze>Evander Holyfield</Bronze>
</Event>
```

Figure 6.50 The result for Skill Check 1.

Answer Code: The T-SQL code to this lab can be found in the downloadable files in a file named Lab6.2_XQueryFLWORExpressions.sql

XQuery FLWOR Expressions - Points to Ponder

1. The query() method uses XPath expression syntax to address specific parts of an XML document. It assists with a SQL-like "FLWOR expression" for performing joins.
2. A FLWOR expression is made of one or more of the five clauses after which it is named: **F**OR, **L**ET, **W**HERE, **O**RDER BY, **R**ETURN.
3. XQuery defines the FLWOR iteration syntax. FLWOR is the acronym based on the following keywords: for, let, where, order by, and return.
4. SQL Server 2005 supported most of the FLWOR iteration syntax while SQL Server 2008 and 2012 supports all of them.
5. LET was not supported in SQL Server 2005 but has been supported since the 2008 version of SQL Server.

Shredding XML Nodes

Before starting this section the Lab6.3Starter.sql file needs to be opened into a new query window. It can be found in the Resources folder of the Vol5 Companion files, which should have been downloaded to the Joes2JPros folder on the C:\ drive.

Even a large XML stream with millions of nodes only has one root node. The deeper the rowpattern in your XPath the more node iterations you have. Let's look at a subset of our XML for the rock songs as seen here from the Lab6.3Starter.sql file:

```
SET @Doc=
'<Music>
 <Song TitleID="13159"><Title>Red-Red Wine</Title>
  <Singer OrderID="1" BandName="Neil Diamond"/>
  <Singer OrderID="2" BandName="UB40"/>
 </Song>
 <Song TitleID="13160"><Title>Manic Monday</Title>
  <Singer OrderID="1" BandName="The Bangles"/>
 </Song>
 <Song TitleID="13161"><Title>Pretty Woman</Title>
  <Singer OrderID="1" BandName="Roy Orbison"/>
  <Singer OrderID="2" BandName="Van Halen"/>
   <BandName>Van Halen</BandName>
 </Song>
</Music>'
```

READERNOTE: For the XML stream above please note that we have moved a few nodes in line with each other in this XML so it appears together on the written page.

In our MusicHistory.MusicDetails XML stream (for the rock songs) it breaks down this way:

- /Music XPath = 1 Node (the root)
- /Music/Song XPath = 3 Nodes (13159, 13160, and 13161)
- /Music/Song/Singer XPath = 5 Nodes (Neil Diamond, UB40, The Bangles, Roy Orbison, and Van Halen)

Picking the right XPath returns the records we want. We used this knowledge for our rowpattern when shredding XML back in Chapter 3. The rowpattern allowed us to choose the nodes that make up our records. That, combined with the ColPattern for each field allow us to get the collection of fields. Using the number handle was a formality as the real work was in the patterns getting the right values from the right nodes. In this section we will shred XML with an XPath into nodes without needing to use OPENXML or keep track of numbered handles. This is possible with the nodes() method of the XML data type.

The nodes() Method

Take a look at the following code. It should look very familiar with three song records in XML stored in an XML data type variable called @Doc. If we run the code and SELECT it we will see the link in Figure 6.51.

```
DECLARE @Doc XML

SET @Doc='<Music>
 <Song TitleID="13159">
  <WriterName>Neil Diamond</WriterName>
  <Title>Red-Red Wine</Title>
  <Singer OrderID="1">
   <BandName>Neil Diamond</BandName>
  </Singer>
  <Singer OrderID="2">
   <BandName>UB40</BandName>
  </Singer>
 </Song>
 <Song TitleID="13160">
  <WriterName>Prince</WriterName>
  <Title>Manic Monday</Title>
  <Singer OrderID="1">
   <BandName>The Bangles</BandName>
  </Singer>
 </Song>
 <Song TitleID="13161">
  <WriterName>Roy Orbison</WriterName>
  <Title>Pretty Woman</Title>
  <Singer OrderID="1" BandName="Roy Orbison">
   <BandName>Roy Orbison</BandName>
  </Singer>
  <Singer OrderID="2">
```

```
   <BandName>Van Halen</BandName>
  </Singer>
 </Song>
</Music>'

SELECT @Doc
```

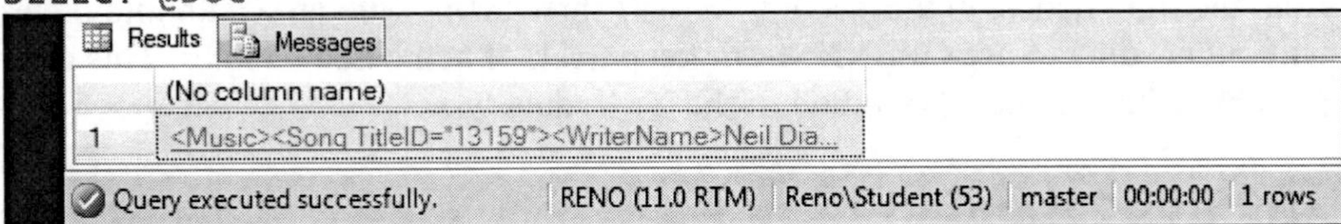

Figure 6.51 Using SELECT @Doc returns this link.

If we open the link in Figure 6.51 and collapse the top-level nodes notice we have three songs or three nodes at the /Music/Song level (Figure 6.52).

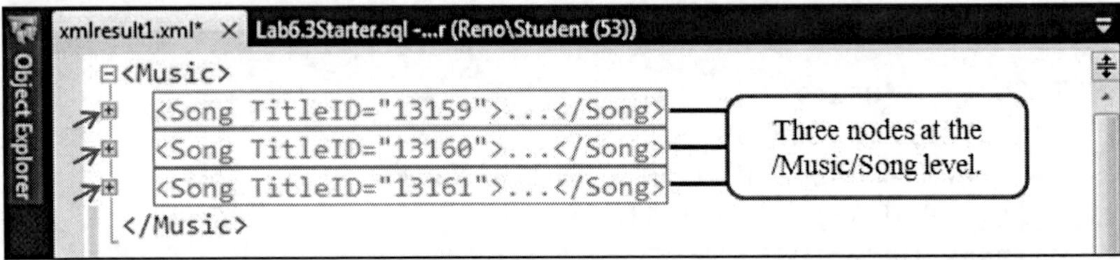

Figure 6.52 This has the top nodes collapsed and shows the three nodes at the /Music/Song level.

Right now it looks like the three nodes in Figure 6.52 are one record in our result set (Figure 6.51). How do we turn this into three records of XML fragments as opposed to one complete well-formed XML? The three /Music/Song level nodes in Figure 6.52 will represent our three records. The nodes() method will produce the result needed.

The following basic SELECT statement is our staring point:

```
SELECT @Doc
```

Instead of selecting the @Doc directly lets SELECT FROM @DOC with the nodes() method. This code is a learning step and will not work since the nodes() method needs an XPath.

```
SELECT
FROM @Doc.nodes()
```

The next step gets us closer to having our code run without error, but keep following along until we get to the next figure. The nodes() method will need to know the XPath. We want to see all three songs. Since each song is at the /Music/Song level we will use the following XPath:

```
SELECT
FROM @Doc.nodes('/Music/Song')
```

The FROM clause normally expects a named table to produce a tabular result. Because the nodes() method in this example is in the FROM clause it needs to represent and look like a table. To do this we will simply alias the method. In this example we will alias this AS a table named Songs.

```
SELECT
FROM @Doc.nodes('/Music/Song') AS Songs
```

Sometimes tables have no records but they always have fields. Like any table it has at least one field. Most tables have many fields. So a table is likely to contain a collection of records but sometimes a table may have no records at all. A table must have at least one field. That means a table is guaranteed to be a collection of at least one field. In other words a table will have a collection of columns even if it has no records.

Currently our Songs table does not have any defined way to refer to the collection of fields that make up this table alias. If we look back at the original XML there are several field options from the different elements and attributes such as TitleID, WriterName, BandName, etc. We need to specify to our Songs table that all these possible fields are inside a collection which we will call SongRow:

```
SELECT
FROM @Doc.nodes('/Music/Song') AS Songs(SongRow)
```

SongRow is like a suitcase that holds all of our field names for the table Songs. The first value we want to pull out is going to be the Title. From the Songs table, SELECT the SongRow collection and query the ('Title') element:

```
SELECT SongRow.query('Title')
FROM @Doc.nodes('/Music/Song') AS Songs(SongRow)
```

Upon running this code we see the results of Figure 6.53.

```
Lab6.3Starter.sql -...r (Reno\Student (53))*   SQLQuery3.sql - RE...(Reno\Student (51))

--Lab 6.3 Starter
DECLARE @Doc XML

SET @Doc=
'<Music>
  <Song TitleID="13159">
~~~~~~~~~~~~~~~~~~~~~~~~~~~~~~~~~~~~~~~~~~~~~~~~~~~~~~~~~~~~
    <Title>Pretty Woman</Title>
    <Singer OrderID="1" BandName="Roy Orbison">
      <BandName>Roy Orbison</BandName>
    </Singer>
    <Singer OrderID="2">
      <BandName>Van Halen</BandName>
    </Singer>
  </Song>
</Music>'

SELECT SongRow.query('Title')
FROM @Doc.nodes('/Music/Song') AS Songs(SongRow)
```

	(No column name)
1	<Title>Red-Red Wine</Title>
2	<Title>Manic Monday</Title>
3	<Title>Pretty Woman</Title>

Figure 6.53 This shows the three Title elements as three records in our result set.

To recap the nodes() method, alias the *tablename* with the rows stored within the column collection (or field collection) in parentheses. In the SELECT statement specify the column(s) as seen in Figure 6.54.

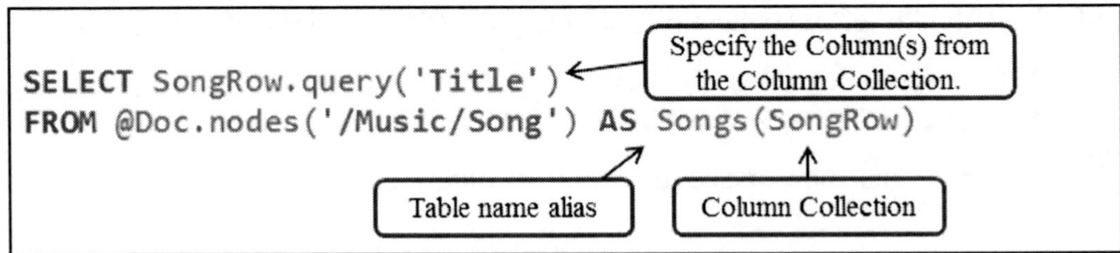

Figure 6.54 This illustrates the basic nodes() method.

Combining value() and nodes() methods

The nodes() method can shred an XML data type into a tabular stream while allowing us to identify the rowpattern that make up each node. Let's start this section where we left off.

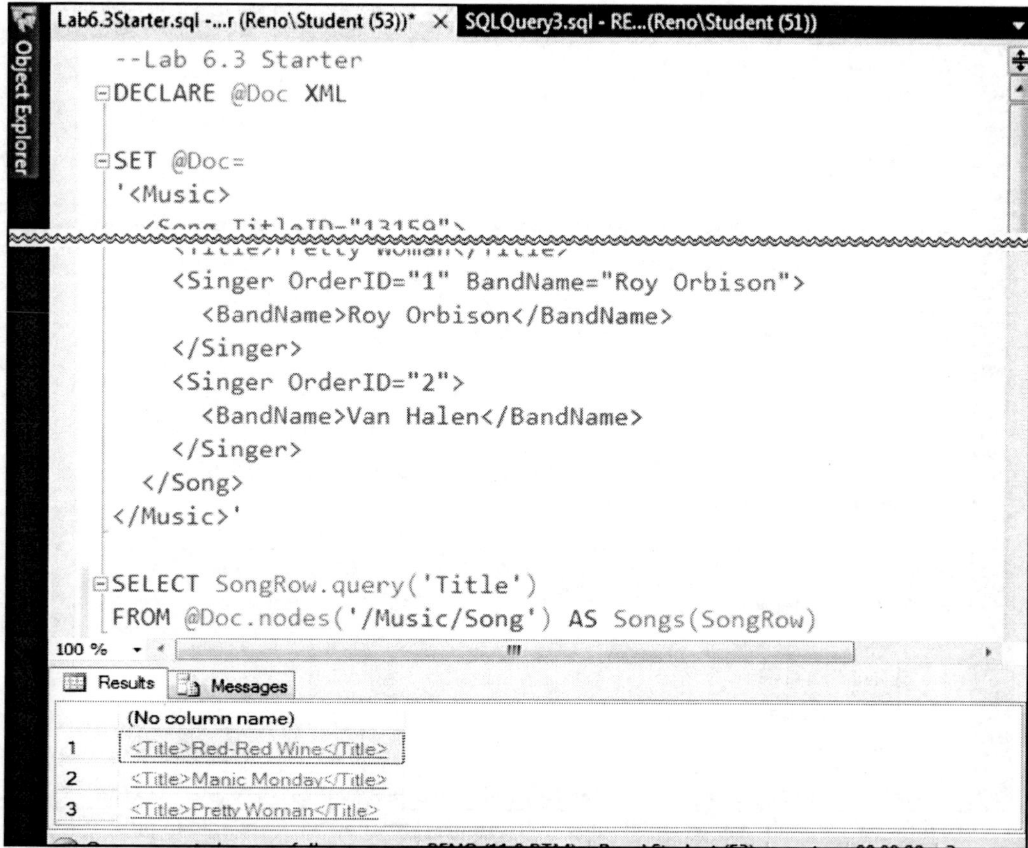

Figure 6.55 This shows using the nodes() method three records were returned.

By specifying that our node is at the /Music/Song level we returned three XML fragments (Figure 6.55). The first record is <Title>Red-Red Wine</Title> which is a very small XML fragment showing us that song title in an XML element. What if we wanted Red-Red Wine as VARCHAR data without XML? In other words we don't need the data with tags showing as XML fragments. We really want parsed values not XML fragments to make up our three rows. This is a simple change in the query. Change the SELECT list to use the value() method instead of query() and add a second argument that specifies the data type. The value() method needs a singleton [1] so add that to the Title in the first parameter as seen in the following code:

```
SELECT SongRow.value('Title[1]', 'VARCHAR(100)')
FROM @Doc.nodes('/Music/Song') AS Songs(SongRow)
```

Upon running this code we see the results of Figure 6.56.

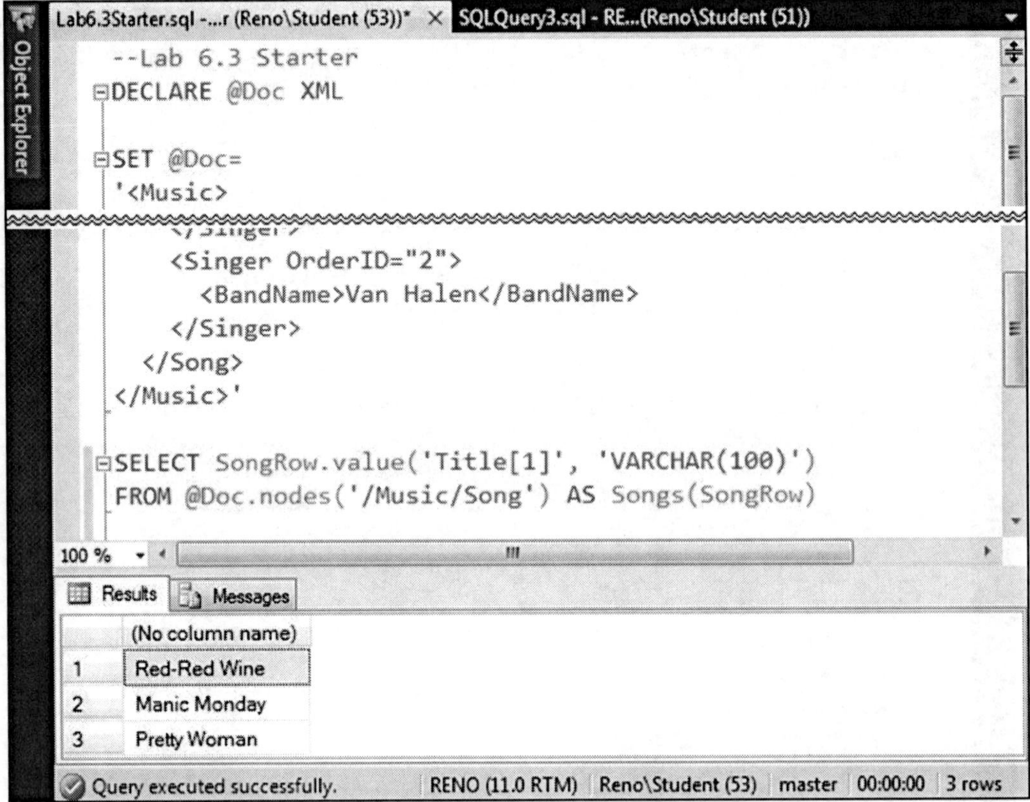

Figure 6.56 By using the value() method with the nodes() method we were able to pull VARCHAR data out of the XML stream.

By using the value() method with the nodes() method we were able to pull VARCHAR data from the XML stream (Figure 6.56). We want to pull out another field from the SongRow column collection. The <Title> element worked and is a child of <Song>. The <TitleID> is also a child of <Song> as an attribute. The nice thing about an attribute is they are guaranteed to be singletons.

It makes sense for ID to be the first field listed in a query so we can drop the Title down to the second line of our SELECT list and create another field. Let's make TitleID our first field by placing it in front of Title in the SELECT list. TitleID is an INT and we will alias it as TitleID and Title AS Title:

```
SELECT SongRow.value('@TitleID', 'INT') AS TitleID,
 SongRow.value('Title[1]','VARCHAR(100)') AS Title
FROM @Doc.nodes('/Music/Song') AS Songs(SongRow)
```

Since attributes are guaranteed to be singletons it is not necessary to specify [1] in the query. This code now pulls out two fields from the SongRow collection (Figure 6.57) since we used two different value() methods (one for each field).

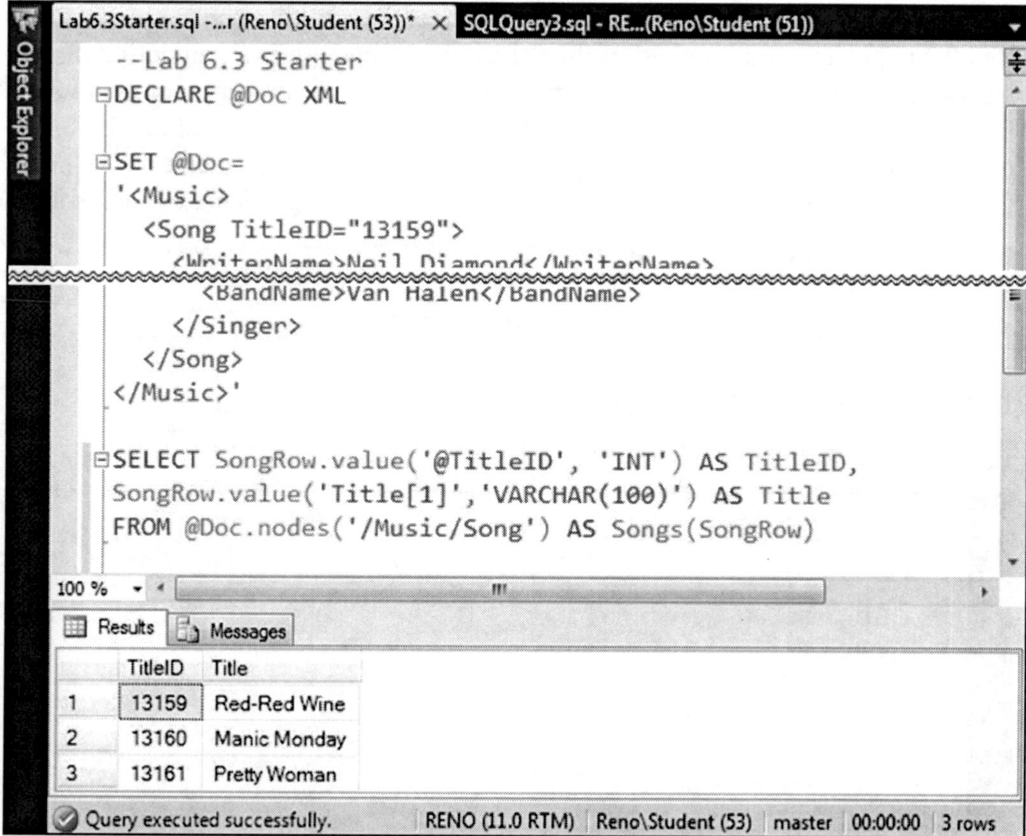
Lab6.3Starter.sql -...r (Reno\Student (53))*
SQLQuery3.sql - RE...(Reno\Student (51))
Object Explorer
--Lab 6.3 Starter
DECLARE @Doc XML
SET @Doc=
'<Music>
<Song TitleID="13159">
<BandName>Van Halen</BandName>
</Singer>
</Song>
</Music>'
SELECT SongRow.value('@TitleID', 'INT') AS TitleID,
SongRow.value('Title[1]','VARCHAR(100)') AS Title
FROM @Doc.nodes('/Music/Song') AS Songs(SongRow)
100 %
Results
Messages
TitleID Title
1 13159 Red-Red Wine
2 13160 Manic Monday
3 13161 Pretty Woman
Query executed successfully.
RENO (11.0 RTM)
Reno\Student (53)
master
00:00:00
3 rows
Figure 6.57 This shows the TitleID as an INT and Title as a VARCHAR(100) in the result set.

We were able to pull out the TitleID as well as the Title using the value() method and nodes() methods together (Figure 6.57). Let's take a moment and look at the XML we are working from.

```
'<Music>
  <Song TitleID="13159">
    <WriterName>Neil Diamond</WriterName>
    <Title>Red-Red Wine</Title>
    <Singer OrderID="1">
      <BandName>Neil Diamond</BandName>
    </Singer>
    <Singer OrderID="2">
      <BandName>UB40</BandName>
    </Singer>
  </Song>
```

<Singer> is a child of <Song>

<BandName> is a child of <Singer>

Figure 6.58 This illustrates the hierarchy of the BandName level node.

Let's use what we know and pull out the first BandName for each singer. BandName is not a direct child of the /Music/Song node, it is a grandchild. Since the specified node level is /Music/Song how do we reach down two more levels for BandName? In the value() method we can specify the additional levels needed. In this case it is Singer[1]/BandName[1]. These are elements so we need to specify the singleton to pull the first Singer and first BandName of each song:

```
SELECT SongRow.value('@TitleID', 'INT') AS TitleID,
 SongRow.value('Title[1]','VARCHAR(100)') AS Title,
 SongRow.value('Singer[1]/BandName[1]', 'VARCHAR(100)')
  AS BandName
FROM @Doc.nodes('/Music/Song') AS Songs(SongRow)
```

Let's add this to the rest of the code and run it.

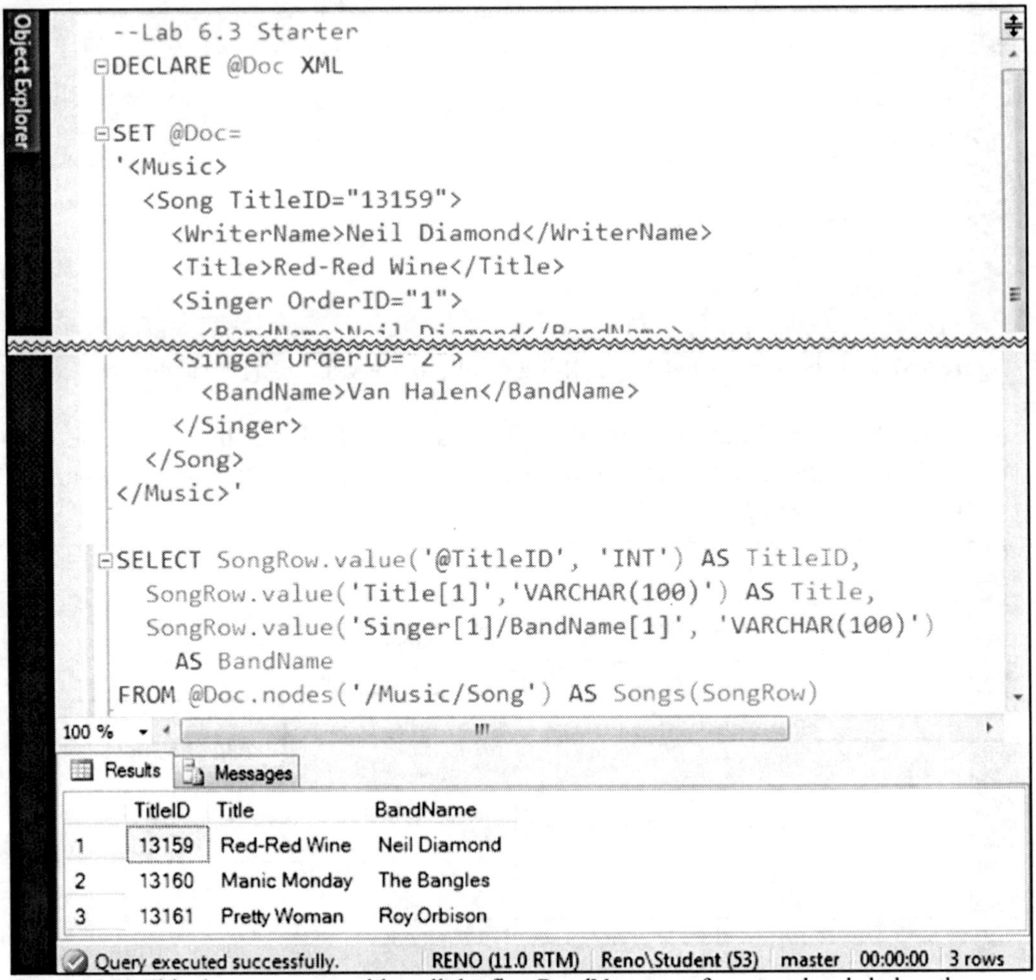

```
--Lab 6.3 Starter
DECLARE @Doc XML

SET @Doc=
'<Music>
  <Song TitleID="13159">
    <WriterName>Neil Diamond</WriterName>
    <Title>Red-Red Wine</Title>
    <Singer OrderID="1">
      <BandName>Neil Diamond</BandName>
    <Singer OrderID="2">
      <BandName>Van Halen</BandName>
    </Singer>
  </Song>
</Music>'

SELECT SongRow.value('@TitleID', 'INT') AS TitleID,
  SongRow.value('Title[1]','VARCHAR(100)') AS Title,
  SongRow.value('Singer[1]/BandName[1]', 'VARCHAR(100)')
    AS BandName
FROM @Doc.nodes('/Music/Song') AS Songs(SongRow)
```

Results | Messages

	TitleID	Title	BandName
1	13159	Red-Red Wine	Neil Diamond
2	13160	Manic Monday	The Bangles
3	13161	Pretty Woman	Roy Orbison

Query executed successfully. | RENO (11.0 RTM) | Reno\Student (53) | master | 00:00:00 | 3 rows

Figure 6.59 This shows we were able pull the first BandName out from two levels below the specified level of /Music/Song using the value() method with nodes().

Using the value() method along with the nodes() method we have been able to shred our XML without using OPENXML or handles.

Lab 6.3: Shredding XML Nodes

Lab Prep: Each lab has one or more Skill Checks. Start with Skill Check 1 and proceed until reaching the Points to Ponder section.

Before beginning this lab, verify that SQL Server 2012 is properly installed and operating. Before running the lab setup script for resetting the database (SQLQueries2012Vol5Chapter6.3Setup.sql), please make sure to close all query windows within SSMS. An open query window pointing to a database context can lock that database preventing it from updating when the script is executing. A simple way to assure all query windows are closed, is to exit out of SSMS, then open a new instance of SSMS, and lastly run the setup script.

Skill Check 1: Using the Book5Presidents.sql file from the Resources folder, show all the first and last names from the /PresidentList/Presidents node level. Use the nodes() and value() methods together to get the result. You should have 42 records as seen in Figure 6.60.

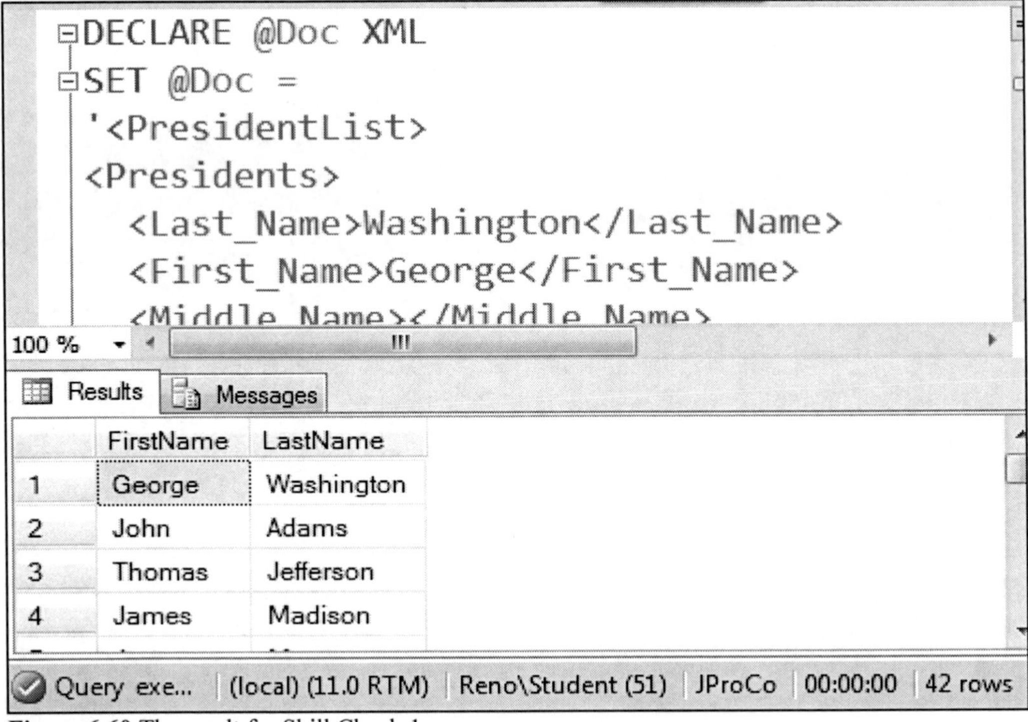

Figure 6.60 The result for Skill Check 1.

Answer Code: The T-SQL code to this lab can be found in the downloadable files in a file named Lab6.3_Shredding_XML_Nodes.sql

Points to Ponder - Shredding XML Nodes

1. The nodes() method can shred an XML data type into a tabular stream while allowing you to identify the rowpattern that makes up each node.

2. A single instance from the nodes() method is a row that has one or more columns.

3. The nodes() method returns a rowset that contains tabular data based on the original XML data.

4. The nodes() method is used to create records from your XML and the value() method pulls out the fields from your rows.

5. After the nodes() method, you alias the table name with the rows stored in the column collection in parentheses like this: *TableName*(*ColumnCollection*)

6. The nodes() method supports query(), value(), and exist() methods.

Chapter Glossary

exist(): A built-in method of the XML data type; used to determine if a specified node exists. Returns 1 if it does exist, returns 0 if it doesn't exist.

FLWOR: The XPath expressions For, Let, Where, Order By, Return. Often referred to as the "flower statements." The Let clause is new to SQL Server 2008; the other clauses were also available in SQL Server 2005.

modify(): A built-in method of the XML data type; updates XML data in an XML data type. This method works only with an UPDATE clause in the SET block.

nodes(): A built-in method of the XML data type; shreds XML data into multiple rows (This method will be covered in Chapter 7).

query(): A built-in method of the XML data type; allows you to query for just the needed parts of an XML.

value(): A built-in method of the XML data type; used to extract a single value from an XML document. This method requires two parameters, one for the XQuery and the other for the data type you wish to capture.

Review Quiz - Chapter Six

1.) What is another name for a Method?

O a. Operator
O b. Function
O c. System

2.) Which XML data type method requires more than one parameter?

O a. query()
O b. value()
O c. exist()
O d. modify()
O e. All of them
O f. Only query() and value()

3.) Which method requires an XPath expression as the first parameter?

O a. query()
O b. value()
O c. exist()
O d. modify()
O e. All of them
O f. Only XQuery() and Value()

4.) Which method returns an XML fragment from the source XML?

O a. query()
O b. value()
O c. exist()
O d. modify()
O e. All of them
O f. Only query() and value()

5.) Which XML data type method returns a "1" if found and "0" if the specified XPath is not found in the source XML?

O a. query()
O b. value()
O c. exist()
O d. modify()
O e. All of them
O f. Only query() and value()

6.) Which XML data type method allows you to pick the data type of the value that is returned from the source XML?

O a. query()
O b. value()
O c. exist()
O d. modify()
O e. All of them
O f. Only query() and value()

7.) Which method will not work with a SQL SELECT statement?

O a. query()
O b. value()
O c. exist()
O d. modify()
O e. All of them
O f. Only query() and value()

8.) Which of the following is not a FLWOR statement?

O a. For
O b. Let
O c. Where
O d. Or
O e. Return

9.) Which statement will alias the /Olympics/Summer path as $AllSummer?

O a. $AllSummer as /Olympics/Summer

O b. /Olympics/Summer as $AllSummer

O c. for $AllSummer in /Olympics/Summer

O d. for /Olympics/Summer in $AllSummer

Answer Key

1.) An operator is a symbol that performs an action on an expression, so (a) is incorrect. A system is the assemblage of all the parts that make up your SQL Server, so (c) is incorrect. Both function and method are a set of code blocks or statements that transact a logical operation, so (b) is the correct answer.

2.) The query(), exist(), and modify() data type methods all require one argument, so (a), (c), (d), (e), and (f) are all incorrect. The value data type method requires two arguments, so (b) is the correct answer.

3.) The query(), value(), exist(), and modify() data type methods all require an XPath expression as the first parameter, so (e) is the correct answer.

4.) value() returns just the data specified, so (b) is incorrect. The exist() method returns either a 1for yes or 0 for no, so (c) is incorrect. The modify() data type method works with an UPDATE statement to change values directly in the XML stream. Since modify() does not work with a SELECT statement (d) is incorrect. Both (e) and (f) are also incorrect. The query() method returns an XML fragment, so (a) is the correct answer.

5.) The exist() method returns a 0 for no and a 1 for yes, so (c) is the correct answer.

6.) The value() method requires two parameters, one for the XQuery and the other for the data type you wish to capture, so (b) is the correct answer.

7.) The modify() data type method will not work with SELECT but will work with UPDATE, so (d) is the correct answer.

8.) FLWOR stands for **F**OR, **L**ET, **W**HERE, **O**RDER BY, **R**ETURN. OR is not part of FLWOR, so (d) is the correct answer.

9.) The correct syntax for aliasing an XPath is FOR *alias* IN */Path/Path, so (c)* is the correct answer.

Bug Catcher Game

To play the Bug Catcher game run the SQLQueries2012Vol5BugCatcher6.pps from the BugCatcher folder of the companion files found at www.Joes2Pros.com.

Chapter 7. XML Data Binding

An action we frequently perform is joining two or more related tables into a single tabular result set which essentially looks like a new table that contains more fields. SQL Server allows us to perform these logical joins dynamically at query execution time. In Volume 2 (*SQL Queries 2012 Joes 2 Pros Volume 2*) we even saw how a table could be joined to a function to produce a new tabular result set.

The robust capabilities of the XML data type allow us to *bind* (another term for joining) a SQL Server table to an XML document and make a new tabular result set. Similarly, we can bind related SQL Server data and XML data to create an expanded XML data source.

In this chapter, we will learn how to bind XML to SQL Server data and *vice versa.* We also will see the nodes method, which is the one remaining XML data type method we haven't yet utilized.

As noted in Chapter 1, XML is case-sensitive. In order for your examples and exercises to run properly in Chapters 1 through 7, be sure that your XML fragments precisely match the figures with respect to uppercase and lowercase.

READERNOTE:*Please run the SQLQueries2012Vol5Chapter7.0Setup.sql script in order to follow along with the examples in the first section of Chapter 7. All scripts mentioned in this chapter may be found at* ***www.Joes2Pros.com****.*

Binding XML Data to SQL Server Data

A SQL Server table and an XML document may contain many records of related data which you need to combine into one report. Perhaps you need to send this report to a data partner as a new, more elaborate XML stream. Or perhaps you need to store the result set as a new table in SQL Server for an ADO (**A**ctiveX **D**ata **O**bject) to render a report.

If your final output for the combined data will be a tabular result set, then you need to bind the XML data to your SQL Server data. This section of the chapter details that process.

CROSS APPLY

If you studied *SQL Queries 2012 Joes 2 Pros Volume 2*, you may remember we use CROSS APPLY to match each row in a table to a value from a function. The data from the table and the function are combined to give you more fields. For example, if you have a table called Customer and a function called fn_GetCustomerOrders(), you could have a result set showing all customers and how many orders they have accumulated, even though orders are not contained in the Customer table. By binding the function to the table with a CROSS APPLY, you get an enhanced result set with the corresponding records from both sources.

We will use a similar process with CROSS APPLY in this chapter. In this case we will CROSS APPLY an XQuery statement to the table, which will bind the XML data to our table.

Let's begin by looking at the MusicHistory table. If you successfully ran the first reset script for this chapter (SQLQueries2012Vol5Chapter7.0Setup.sql), then you should see all fields of the three records populated, including each record of the XML data type field (MusicDetails) now containing an XML file (Figure 7.1).

```
SELECT *
FROM MusicHistory
```

Results | Messages

	MusicTypeID	MusicTypeName	MusicDetails
1	1	Country	<Music><Song TitleID="11109"><WriterName>The Cha...
2	2	Soul	<Music><Song TitleID="12151"><WriterName>Bob We...
3	3	Rock	<Music><Song TitleID="13159"><WriterName>Neil Dia...

Query executed successfully. | RENO (11.0 RTM) | Reno\Student (51) | JProCo | 00:00:00 | 3 rows

Figure 7.1 The current Music catalog contained in the MusicHistory table.

By clicking through the first result hyperlink, we see two Country songs below (Figure 7.2). If we click through all the hyperlinks, we will see the catalog now contains six songs: two Country songs (TitleIDs 11109 and 11110), one Soul song (TitleID 12151), and the three Rock songs we worked with in Chapter 6 (TitleIDs 13159, 13160, 13161).

MusicDetails2.xml × SQLQuery3.sql - RE...(Reno\Student (51))*

Object Explorer

```
<Music>
  <Song TitleID="11109">
    <WriterName>The Charlie Daniels Band</WriterName>
    <Title>The Devil Went Down to Georgia</Title>
    <Singer OrderID="1">
      <BandName>The Charlie Daniels Band</BandName>
    </Singer>
    <Singer OrderID="2">
      <BandName>Travis Tritt</BandName>
    </Singer>
  </Song>
  <Song TitleID="11110">
    <WriterName>Dewayne Blackwell, Earl Bud Lee</WriterName>
    <Title>Friends in Low Places</Title>
    <Singer OrderID="1">
      <BandName>Garth Brooks</BandName>
    </Singer>
  </Song>
</Music>
```

Two Country Songs

Figure 7.2 The Music catalog now contains six songs, including two Country songs.

Let's look ahead to our goal, which will be to pull out multiple nodes (a.k.a., elements) from the XML data in the MusicDetails field and see those appear alongside the data from the MusicHistory table in a SQL Server query.

Results | Messages

MusicTypeID	MusicTypeName	MusicDetails	TitleID	WriterName
1	Country	<Music><Song TitleID="11109"><WriterName>The Charlie...	11109	The Charlie Daniels Band
1	Country	<Music><Song TitleID="11109"><WriterName>The Charlie...	11110	Dewayne Blackwell, Earl Bud Lee
2	Soul	<Music><Song TitleID="12151"><WriterName>Bob West, ...	12151	Bob West, Berry Gordy, Willie Hutch, Hal Davis
3	Rock	<Music><Song TitleID="13159"><WriterName>Neil Diamo...	13159	Neil Diamond
3	Rock	<Music><Song TitleID="13159"><WriterName>Neil Diamo...	13160	Liam Sternberg
3	Rock	<Music><Song TitleID="13159"><WriterName>Neil Diamo...	13161	Roy Orbison

Figure 7.3 Our goal will be to see nodes from the XML data appear as fields in our SQL query.

Let's begin the process of building our query by filtering in just Music Type 3, the Rock music record (Figure 7.4). This doesn't impact our main query, but it will narrow the dataset we see during most of our demo to the same Rock data we've studied during the last two chapters.

```
SELECT *
FROM MusicHistory
WHERE MusicTypeID = 3
```

Results | Messages

	MusicTypeID	MusicTypeName	MusicDetails
1	3	Rock	<Music><Song TitleID="13159"><WriterName>Neil Dia...

Query executed successfully. | RENO (11.0 RTM) | Reno\Student (51) | JProCo | 00:00:00 | 1 rows

Figure 7.4 Narrow the query to just Music Type 3.

There are three songs contained in the XML document for Music Type 3 (Rock). We know that TitleID is of one of the nodes we want to be able to query as if it were a field in the MusicHistory table (Figure 7.5).

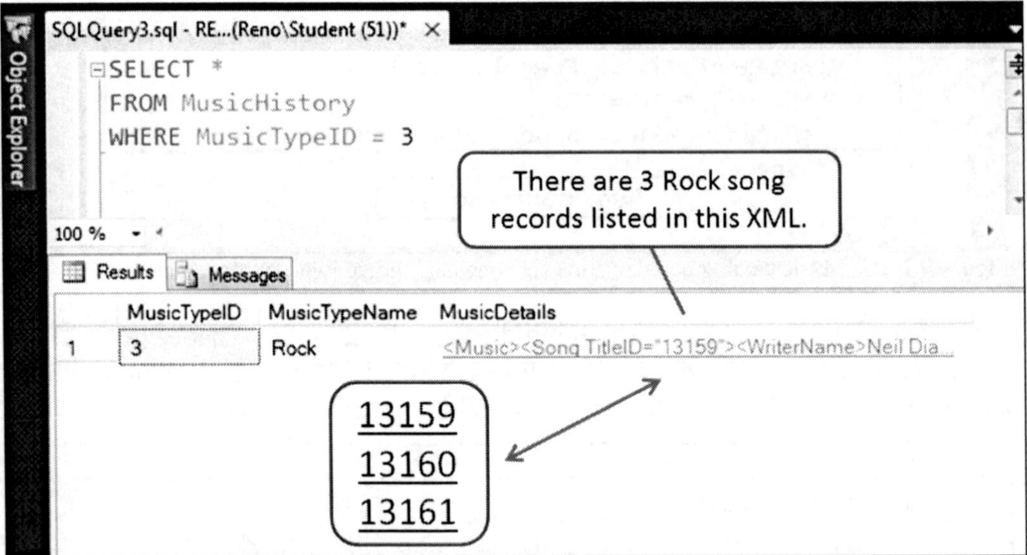

Figure 7.5 There are three Rock songs contained in this XML document, each having a TitleID.

Before we add CROSS APPLY to our code, we need to review the *nodes* and *value* methods of the XML data type.

The nodes() Method

As mentioned in an earlier chapter, the *nodes()* method can be used to shred XML into a tabular result set. The *nodes()* method accepts an XPath parameter and binds XML data to your table as though it were a join.

Just like binding a table-valued function to a SQL table, there can be many values contained in one XPath level (e.g., /Music/Song has TitleID and WriterName) but CROSS APPLY only lets you choose one name to represent the XML fragment containing the nodes which will become the applied records (In our example, we will call the column **SongTbl(SongDetails)**). SongDetails is the materialized collection of fields which will contain the many values we want.

How can we isolate just the value we want? This is why we must use the value() method in combination with the nodes() method. Think of the nodes() method the way you would think of a rowpattern. It picks the level and gets you rows. From there you get to pick the column. That is where the value() method comes in. Think of the value() method the way you think of a colpattern. You specify the column that you want from the row.

The value() Method

The value() method works with the rows returned by the nodes() method and pulls out the field value you need. If you want many values pulled from the node, use the value() method many times in your field SELECT list (as we will see later in Figures 7.12 and 7.13). Each expression can be aliased and is separated by a comma, as with any field SELECT list pulling from a regular table.

Combining SQL and XML Fields in a Tabular Result

Now we are ready to write the rest of the code needed to accomplish our goal of binding our XML data to the MusicHistory table and querying both in a tabular result. Our next step appears in Figure 7.6.

We know CROSS APPLY will bind the XML data in the MusicDetails field to the MusicHistory table. After the FROM clause, we will add CROSS APPLY MusicDetails. We know the nodes() method is needed to shred the XML data in the MusicDetails field.

The nodes() method requires an XPath expression as a parameter. The <Song> level (/Music/Song) contains the TitleID, which is one datapoint we know our result will contain.

The next piece of our code is the alias **SongTbl(SongDetails)** for the fragment shred at the /Music/Song level. We must alias the rowset returned by the nodes() method, and the name must be in a *Table(Column)* format. SongTbl(SongDetails) will essentially act as a table whose fields we can combine with the MusicHistory table. Recall that CROSS APPLY only allows us to choose a single name to represent the XML fragment containing the nodes which will become our applied fields (Figure 7.6).

```
SELECT *
FROM MusicHistory
CROSS APPLY MusicDetails.nodes('/Music/Song')  AS SongTbl(SongDetails)
WHERE MusicTypeID = 3
```

Table.Column   Table(Column)

Figure 7.6 Add the CROSS APPLY clause with the nodes() method and alias the rowset.

Let's take a moment to review what the new column implies. If we were to run the query in the left panel, the result would be the well-formed XML document with the root <Music> and containing the three Rock songs (Figure 7.7). Earlier we saw that this query produces one record (refer to Figure 7.4).

Figure 7.7 The right panel is the result produced by the query in the left panel.

By contrast, notice that when we modify the code and add the query() method pulling from the /Music/Song level, a different result is produced. This XQuery statement produces three distinct XML fragments, each representing a song (13159, 13160, and 13161) and each supplying a record to the calling code. Each <song> record will have the columns TitleID, <WriterName>, <Title>, and <Singer>, since these are the direct child-level elements of the /Music/Song level.

Figure 7.8 This XQuery statement produces three distinct XML fragments.

Our CROSS APPLY statement works similarly (Figure 7.9). The XPath parameter (i.e., the /Music/Song level) gets applied to **SongTbl(SongDetails)**, which means that this level supplies three records to **SongTbl(SongDetails)**.

Later we will see that with **SongTbl(SongDetails)**, we are able to pull data from any of the four "fields" (TitleID, WriterName, Title, Singer) (Since only three of these fields contain data, we will focus on those). Only the value() method will retrieve one field at a time for our SELECT list (we will see this in our final steps, Figures 7.11 through 7.13).

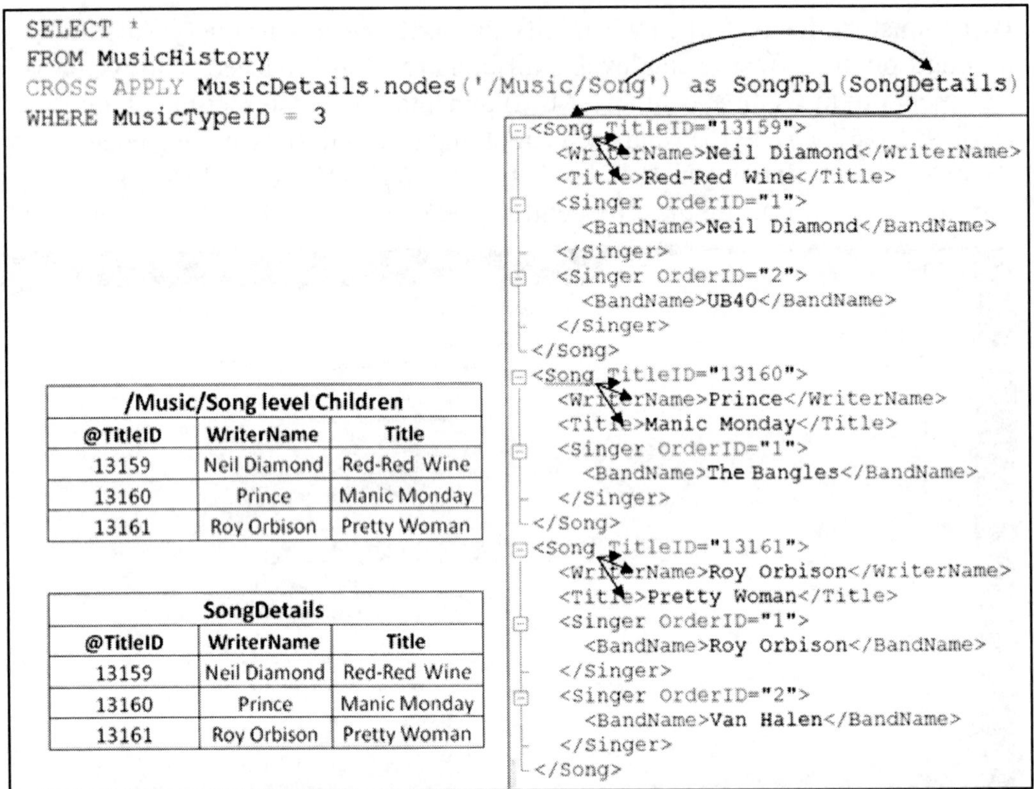
```
SELECT *
FROM MusicHistory
CROSS APPLY MusicDetails.nodes('/Music/Song') as SongTbl(SongDetails)
WHERE MusicTypeID = 3
```

/Music/Song level Children		
@TitleID	WriterName	Title
13159	Neil Diamond	Red-Red Wine
13160	Prince	Manic Monday
13161	Roy Orbison	Pretty Woman

SongDetails		
@TitleID	WriterName	Title
13159	Neil Diamond	Red-Red Wine
13160	Prince	Manic Monday
13161	Roy Orbison	Pretty Woman

```
<Song TitleID="13159">
  <WriterName>Neil Diamond</WriterName>
  <Title>Red-Red Wine</Title>
  <Singer OrderID="1">
    <BandName>Neil Diamond</BandName>
  </Singer>
  <Singer OrderID="2">
    <BandName>UB40</BandName>
  </Singer>
</Song>
<Song TitleID="13160">
  <WriterName>Prince</WriterName>
  <Title>Manic Monday</Title>
  <Singer OrderID="1">
    <BandName>The Bangles</BandName>
  </Singer>
</Song>
<Song TitleID="13161">
  <WriterName>Roy Orbison</WriterName>
  <Title>Pretty Woman</Title>
  <Singer OrderID="1">
    <BandName>Roy Orbison</BandName>
  </Singer>
  <Singer OrderID="2">
    <BandName>Van Halen</BandName>
  </Singer>
</Song>
```

Figure 7.9 This XQuery statement provides 3 Rock records with 4 fields to the CROSS APPLY.

If we attempt to run this code now, we will get an error message that reminds us that we cannot directly use the column returned by the nodes() method (Figure 7.10) - we will need to use the value() method to pull out the values we want from the SongDetails column.

```
SELECT *
FROM MusicHistory
CROSS APPLY MusicDetails.nodes('/Music/Song')
AS SongTbl(SongDetails)
WHERE MusicTypeID = 3
```

```
Messages
Msg 493, Level 16, State 1, Line 1
The column 'SongDetails' that was returned from the nodes() method cannot be
used directly. It can only be used with one of the four XML data type methods,
exist(), nodes(), query(), and value(), or in IS NULL and IS NOT NULL checks.
                                                                      0 rows
```

Figure 7.10 This error message reminds us that the nodes() method can't be used directly.

Next we will use the value() method to pull out the TitleID attribute. We will have TitleID returned as an integer data type (Figure 7.11).

```
SELECT SongDetails.value('@TitleID', 'INT')
FROM MusicHistory
CROSS APPLY MusicDetails.nodes('/Music/Song')
AS SongTbl(SongDetails)
WHERE MusicTypeID = 3
```

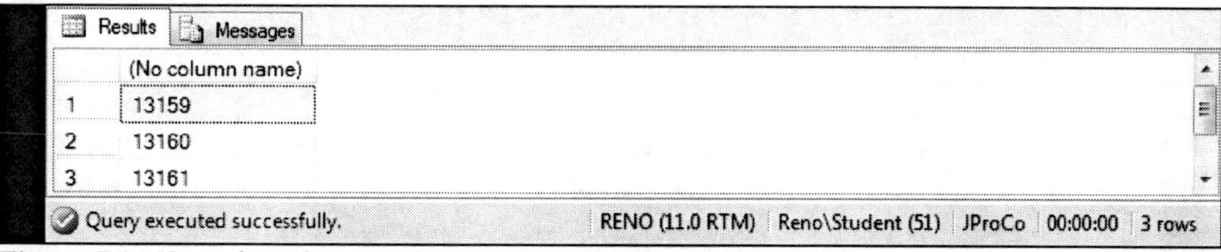

Figure 7.11 Have the value() method pull out TitleID and return it as an integer.

We will add the MusicTypeID field, and we'll also pull out the first WriterName as a VARCHAR. Notice that our column header is empty ("No column name"), since it hasn't been aliased (Figure 7.11).

```
SELECT SongDetails.value('@TitleID', 'INT'),
SongDetails.value('WriterName[1]', 'VARCHAR(MAX)')
FROM MusicHistory
CROSS APPLY MusicDetails.nodes('/Music/Song')
AS SongTbl(SongDetails)
WHERE MusicTypeID = 3
```

Results | Messages

	(No column name)	(No column name)
1	13159	Neil Diamond
2	13160	Prince
3	13161	Roy Orbison

Query executed successfully. | RENO (11.0 RTM) | Reno\Student (51) | JProCo | 00:00:00 | 3 rows

Figure 7.12 Pull out the first WriterName for each song.

As a best practice, we will alias both fields coming from our XML data, so that we don't have any empty column names (Figure 7.12). Finally, we will remove the WHERE clause, so that our result contains data from all three Music Types (Country, Soul, and Rock) (Figure 7.13).

Our final result achieves our goal. It contains data from the SQL Server table (MusicHistory) and the cross-applied XML data (Figure 7.13).

```
SELECT MusicTypeID, SongDetails.value
 ('@TitleID', 'INT') AS TitleID,
 SongDetails.value
 ('WriterName[1]', 'VARCHAR(MAX)') AS WriterName
FROM MusicHistory CROSS APPLY MusicDetails.nodes
 ('/Music/Song') AS SongTbl(SongDetails)
```

	MusicTypeID	TitleID	WriterName
1	1	11109	The Charlie Daniels Band
2	1	11110	Dewayne Blackwell, Earl Bud Lee
3	2	12151	Bob West, Berry Gordy, Willie Hutch, Hal Davis
4	3	13159	Neil Diamond
5	3	13160	Prince
6	3	13161	Roy Orbison

Query executed successfully. | RENO (11.0 RTM) | Reno\Student (51) | JProCo | 00:00:00 | 6 rows

Figure 7.13 Our final result contains data from the SQL Server table and the XML stream contained in the MusicDetails field of each of record.

Let's take a closer look at how CROSS APPLY is accomplishing our goal. We know that CROSS APPLY allows us to combine two dissimilar data streams into a single result.

```
SELECT MusicTypeID, SongDetails.value
  ('@TitleID','INT') AS TitleID,
  SongDetails.value
  ('WriterName[1]','VARCHAR(MAX)') AS WriterName
FROM MusicHistory CROSS APPLY MusicDetails.nodes
  ('/Music/Song') AS SongTbl(SongDetails)
```

CROSS APPLY allows a table to be joined to another type of data stream.

Figure 7.14 CROSS APPLY allows you to join a table to another type of data stream.

In our previous work with the CROSS APPLY operator, we saw it combine a table with a table-valued function and behave similarly to an inner join. In this sample from Volume 2 we see CROSS APPLY matching each CustomerID from the Customer table with each CustomerID represented by the function dbo.fn_GetCustomerOrders (Figure 7.15).

```
SELECT * FROM Customer AS cu
CROSS APPLY dbo.fn_GetCustomerOrders (cu.CustomerID)
```

Results | Messages

	CustomerID	CustomerType	FirstName	LastName	CompanyName	InvoiceID	CustomerID
1	597	Consumer	Thomas	Anderson	NULL	9	597
2	736	Consumer	William	Carter	NULL	10	736
3	47	Consumer	Sarah	Campbell	NULL	15	47
4	251	Consumer	Deborah	Moore	NULL	19	251
5	529	Consumer	Carol	Smith	NULL	20	529
6	151	Consumer	Carol	Young	NULL	22	151

Query executed successfully. | RENO (11.0 RTM) | Reno\Student (51) | JProCo | 00:00:00 | 6959 rows

Figure 7.15 A previous CROSS APPLY example from Book 2 *(SQL Queries 2012 Joes 2 Pros Volume 2.*

You may be wondering how CROSS APPLY is working in our current example, since there is no ON clause or single field serving to correlate our SQL Server table (MusicHistory) with our XML data contained in the MusicDetails field.

Each record in the XML field (MusicDetails) is acting like its own table. The nodes() method returns each song as a separate record to the new rowset SongTbl(SongDetails), as we saw earlier in Figure 7.9. It also keeps track of each XML field's original rowset in the parent table (MusicHistory) and knows that the two songs 11109 and 11110 are related to MusicTypeID 1 and MusicTypeName Country (Figure 7.16).

```
SELECT *
FROM MusicHistory
```

Results | Messages

	MusicTypeID	MusicTypeName	MusicDetails
1	2 Songs for Country		<Music><Song TitleID="11109"><WriterName>The Cha...
2	2	Soul	<Music><Song TitleID="12151"><WriterName>Bob We...
3	3 Songs for Rock		<Music><Song TitleID="13159"><WriterName>Neil Dia...

Query executed successfully. | RENO (11.0 RTM) | Reno\Student (51) | JProCo | 00:00:00 | 3 rows

Figure 7.16 Each of the three MusicDetails records is acting like a table.

In other words, the XML data was turned into a tabular result set (Figure 7.17).

```
SELECT MusicTypeID, SongDetails.value
 ('@TitleID', 'INT') AS TitleID,
 SongDetails.value
 ('WriterName[1]','VARCHAR(MAX)') AS WriterName
FROM MusicHistory CROSS APPLY MusicDetails.nodes
 ('/Music/Song') AS SongTbl(SongDetails)
```

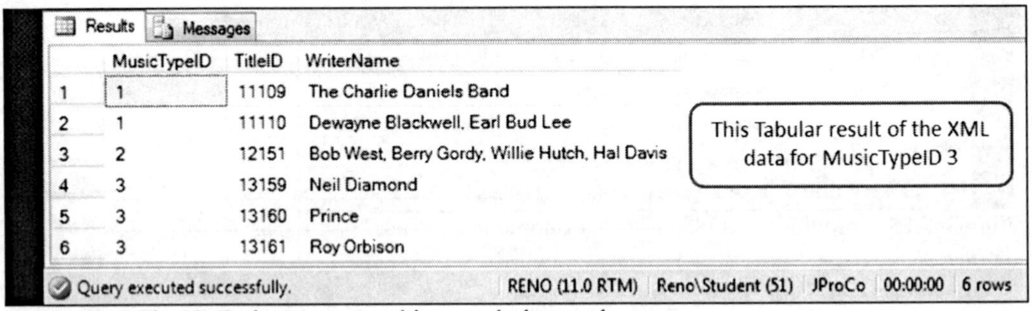

Results | Messages

	MusicTypeID	TitleID	WriterName
1	1	11109	The Charlie Daniels Band
2	1	11110	Dewayne Blackwell, Earl Bud Lee
3	2	12151	Bob West, Berry Gordy, Willie Hutch, Hal Davis
4	3	13159	Neil Diamond
5	3	13160	Prince
6	3	13161	Roy Orbison

This Tabular result of the XML data for MusicTypeID 3

Query executed successfully. | RENO (11.0 RTM) | Reno\Student (51) | JProCo | 00:00:00 | 6 rows

Figure 7.17 The XML data was turned into a tabular result set.

Lab 7.1: Binding XML to SQL

Lab Prep: Each lab has one or more Skill Checks. Start with Skill Check 1 and proceed until reaching the Points to Ponder section.

Before beginning this lab, verify that SQL Server 2012 is properly installed and operating. Before running the lab setup script for resetting the database (SQLQueries2012Vol5Chapter7.1Setup.sql), please make sure to close all query windows within SSMS. An open query window pointing to a database context can lock that database preventing it from updating when the script is executing. A simple way to assure all query windows are closed, is to exit out of SSMS, then open a new instance of SSMS, and lastly run the setup script.

Skill Check 1: Continue building on your code from the last section and expand it to pull in the Title field. Make sure all fields are aliased as you see below (Figure 7.18).

	MusicTypeID	TitleID	WriterName	Title
1	1	11109	The Charlie Daniels Band	The Devil Went Down to Georgia
2	1	11110	Dewayne Blackwell, Earl Bud Lee	Friends in Low Places
3	2	12151	Bob West, Berry Gordy, Willie Hutch, Hal Davis	I'll Be There
4	3	13159	Neil Diamond	Red-Red Wine
5	3	13160	Prince	Manic Monday
6	3	13161	Roy Orbison	Pretty Woman

Query executed successfully. RENO (11.0 RTM) Reno\Student (51) JProCo 00:00:00 6 rows

Figure 7.18 Skill Check 1 result.

Answer Code: The T-SQL code to this lab can be found in the downloadable files in a file named Lab7.1_BindingXMLtoSQL.sql

Points to Ponder - Binding XML to SQL

1. SQL Server (since SQL 2005) provides Microsoft specific extensions that enhance XQuery and allow you to reference relational columns or variables.
2. Referencing relational columns in your XML field is known as "binding" the relational column.
3. Use CROSS APPLY with the nodes() and value() methods to bind your XML to rows in a table.
4. Binding data is a concept similar to joining data.
5. We can bind related SQL Server data and XML data to create an expanded XML data source.
6. CROSS APPLY allows us to combine two dissimilar data streams into a single result.
7. In our previous work with the CROSS APPLY operator, we saw it combine a table with a table-valued function and behave similarly to an INNER JOIN.
8. Use CROSS APPLY with an XQuery statement to bind the XML data to a table.
9. The nodes() method accepts an XPath parameter and binds XML data to your table as though it were a join.
10. CROSS APPLY lets you choose only one name to represent the XML fragment containing the nodes which will become the applied fields.
11. To isolate just the value we want from an XML fragment, we use the value() method.
12. Think of the nodes() method the way you would think of a rowpattern. It picks the level and gets you rows. From there, you get to pick the column.

Binding SQL to XML

In the last section we stepped through an example of binding XML data to a SQL Server table. In this section, we will do the reverse. Our main focus will be an XML file, and we will bring data from a SQL Server table into our XML file.

Let's look at a new JProCo table which contains XML data, the DeliverySchedule table. Currently it shows two delivery drivers, Sally (Driver 1) and Johnny (Driver 2) (Figure 7.19).

```
SELECT *
FROM DeliverySchedule
```

Results | Messages

	ScheduleID	ScheduleDate	DeliveryRoute	DeliveryDriver	DeliveryList
1	1	2012-10-27 ...	3	Silly Sally	<DeliveryList><Delivery SalesOrderID="4365
2	2	2012-10-27 ...	7	Big Johnny	<DeliveryList><Delivery SalesOrderID="4366

Query executed successfully. | RENO (11.0 RTM) | Reno\Student (51) | JProCo | 00:00:00 | 2 rows

Figure 7.19 The DeliverySchedule table.

We will narrow our query to show just DeliveryList, which is an XML field containing the drivers' delivery routes (Figure 7.20).

```
SELECT DeliveryList
FROM DeliverySchedule
```

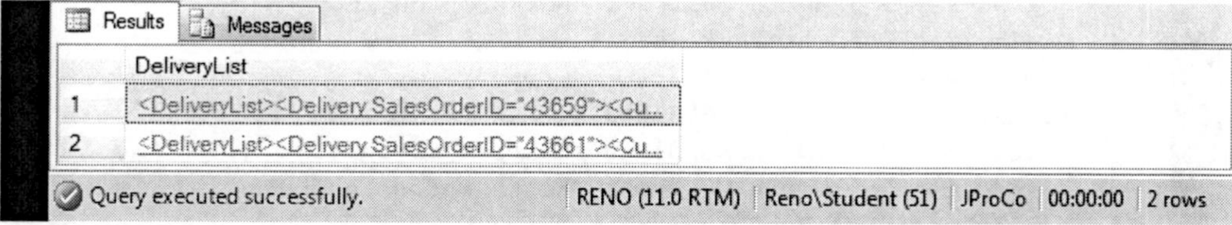

Results | Messages

	DeliveryList
1	<DeliveryList><Delivery SalesOrderID="43659"><Cu...
2	<DeliveryList><Delivery SalesOrderID="43661"><Cu...

Query executed successfully. | RENO (11.0 RTM) | Reno\Student (51) | JProCo | 00:00:00 | 2 rows

Figure 7.20 Itemize the query to show just the DeliveryList field, which contains XML data.

Click through the result hyperlink and see that Sally's delivery schedule includes the addresses for the two deliveries she will be making (Figure 7.21).

```
<DeliveryList>
  <Delivery SalesOrderID="43659">
    <CustomerName>Steve Schmidt</CustomerName>
    <Address>6126 North Sixth Street, Rockhampton</Address>
    <PrePaid>Credit</PrePaid>
  </Delivery>
  <Delivery SalesOrderID="43660">
    <CustomerName>Tony Lopez</CustomerName>
    <Address>6445 Cashew Street, Rockhampton</Address>
    <PrePaid>Credit</PrePaid>
  </Delivery>
</DeliveryList>
```

Figure 7.21 Sally's delivery schedule (from result link shown in Figure 7.20).

Johnny's delivery schedule includes the addresses for the three stops he will be making (Figure 7.22).

```
<DeliveryList>
  <Delivery SalesOrderID="43661">
    <CustomerName>Lenny Lewis</CustomerName>
    <Address>444 North N Street, Rockhampton</Address>
    <PrePaid>Credit</PrePaid>
  </Delivery>
  <Delivery SalesOrderID="43662">
    <CustomerName>Mandy Meyers</CustomerName>
    <Address>555 North M Street, Rockhampton</Address>
    <PrePaid>Credit</PrePaid>
  </Delivery>
  <Delivery SalesOrderID="43663">
    <CustomerName>Nick Nordlund</CustomerName>
    <Address>665 North N street, Rockhampton</Address>
    <PrePaid>COD</PrePaid>
  </Delivery>
</DeliveryList>
```

Figure 7.22 Johnny's delivery schedule (from result link shown in Figure 7.20).

XPath and FLWOR Recap

We will again need to combine our knowledge of XPath with the power of the FLWOR statements from the last chapter. Let's begin with a quick recap.

XPath

Let's use an XQuery statement to pull the data from the <Delivery> level ('/DeliveryList/Delivery') out of the DeliveryList (Figure 7.23). Specifying our XPath at this level, we get each Delivery listed for each of our drivers.

```
SELECT DeliveryList.query('/DeliveryList/Delivery')
FROM DeliverySchedule
```

Results | Messages

	(No column name)
1	<Delivery SalesOrderID="43659"><CustomerName>Stev...
2	<Delivery SalesOrderID="43661"><CustomerName>Len...

Query executed successfully. | RENO (11.0 RTM) | Reno\Student (51) | JProCo | 00:00:00 | 2 rows

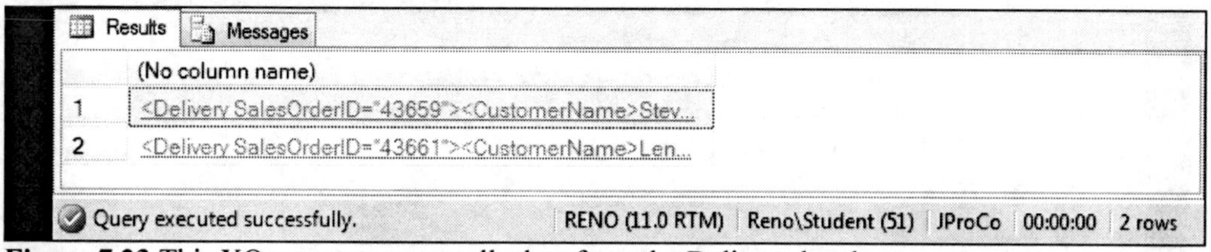

Figure 7.23 This XQuery statement pulls data from the Delivery level.

xmlresult6.xml* × SQLQuery4.sql - RE...(Reno\Student (51))*

Object Explorer

```
<Delivery SalesOrderID="43659">
  <CustomerName>Steve Schmidt</CustomerName>
  <Address>6126 North Sixth Street, Rockhampton</Address>
  <PrePaid>Credit</PrePaid>
</Delivery>
<Delivery SalesOrderID="43660">
  <CustomerName>Tony Lopez</CustomerName>
  <Address>6445 Cashew Street, Rockhampton</Address>
  <PrePaid>Credit</PrePaid>
</Delivery>
```

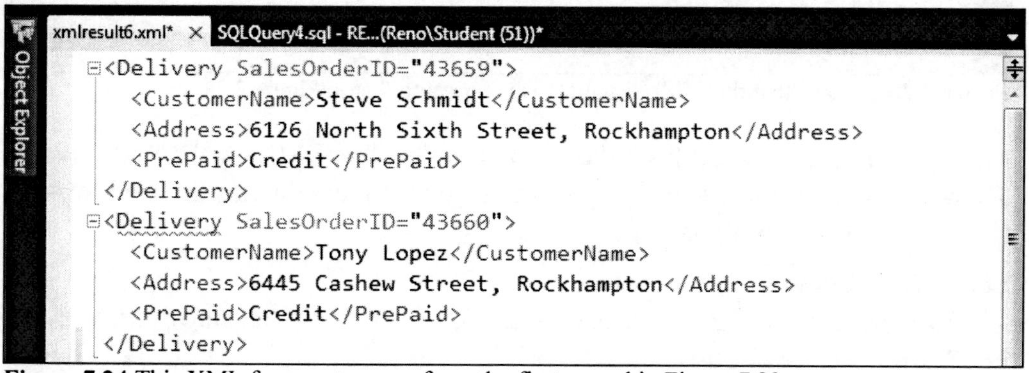

Figure 7.24 This XML fragment comes from the first record in Figure 7.23.

FLWOR

In the last chapter, we learned about the XQuery expressions known by the FLWOR acronym ("for", "let", "where", "order by", "return").

We will use **for** and **return** expressions to alias the <Delivery> level (/DeliveryList/Delivery). Observe that the query in Figure 7.25 returns the same result as the query in Figure 7.23 (Results shown in Figure 7.26 and Figure 7.24).

```
SELECT DeliveryList.query
('for $d in /DeliveryList/Delivery return $d')
FROM DeliverySchedule
```

Results | Messages

	(No column name)
1	<Delivery SalesOrderID="43659"><CustomerName>Stev...
2	<Delivery SalesOrderID="43661"><CustomerName>Len...

Query executed successfully. | RENO (11.0 RTM) | Reno\Student (51) | JProCo | 00:00:00 | 2 rows

Figure 7.25 This query aliases the <Delivery> level (/DeliveryList/Delivery) as $d.

xmlresult7.xml × SQLQuery4.sql - RE...(Reno\Student (51))*

```
<Delivery SalesOrderID="43659">
  <CustomerName>Steve Schmidt</CustomerName>
  <Address>6126 North Sixth Street, Rockhampton</Address>
  <PrePaid>Credit</PrePaid>
</Delivery>
<Delivery SalesOrderID="43660">
  <CustomerName>Tony Lopez</CustomerName>
  <Address>6445 Cashew Street, Rockhampton</Address>
  <PrePaid>Credit</PrePaid>
</Delivery>
```

Figure 7.26 Observe that this XML fragment is identical to that in Figure 7.24.

Modify your query to pull from the Address level. The XML for the first driver contains two addresses. The XML for the second driver contains three addresses (Figure 7.27 through Figure 7.29).

```
SELECT DeliveryList.query
 ('for $d in /DeliveryList/Delivery return $d/Address')
FROM DeliverySchedule
```

Figure 7.27 Our XQuery statement now pulls from the Address level.

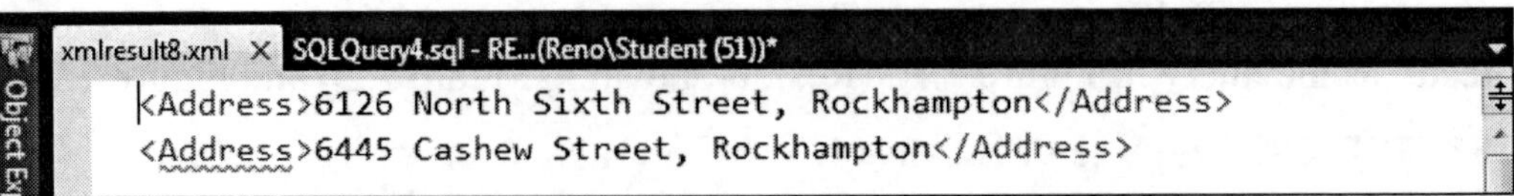

Figure 7.28 The XML fragment containing the two addresses on Sally's delivery route.

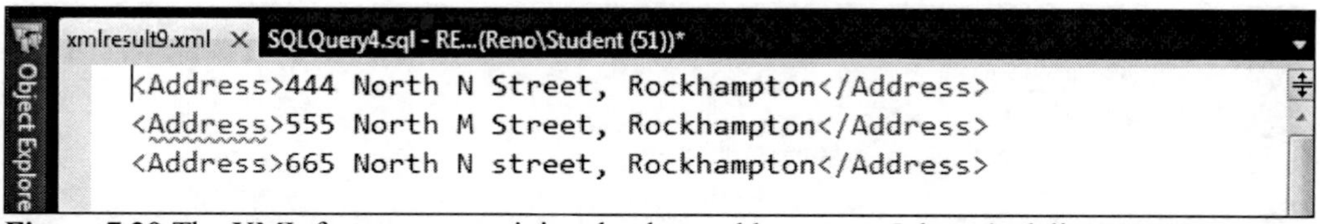

```
<Address>444 North N Street, Rockhampton</Address>
<Address>555 North M Street, Rockhampton</Address>
<Address>665 North N street, Rockhampton</Address>
```

Figure 7.29 The XML fragment containing the three addresses on Johnny's delivery route.

At this deep of a level, we no longer have well-formed XML. Most of the examples we've seen in this section have been fragments with a number of nodes sitting side by side and no <root>. In the next topic discussion, we will see that we can impose our own level in order to make this well-formed XML.

Adding XML Tags

You can use any or all of the XML tags from your XML data. What if you wanted to add a new tag of your own that does not exist in your table or XML data? You can add your own custom tags as part of your XPath statement.

Use {} {for $d in /DeliveryList/Delivery return $d/Address}

Change the parentheses enclosing your current XQuery statement to curly braces. Instead of (), these will become {}.

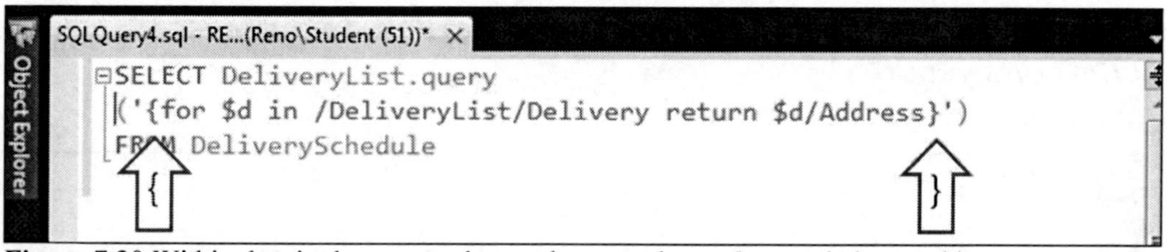

```
SELECT DeliveryList.query
('{for $d in /DeliveryList/Delivery return $d/Address}')
FROM DeliverySchedule
```

Figure 7.30 Within the single quotes, change the parentheses () to curly braces { }.

Within the single quotes, add a beginning tag <DeliveryRoute> and an ending tag </DeliveryRoute> before and after our existing XQuery statement (i.e., which we enclosed in curly braces {}).

Run this code and notice that we have added our own <DeliveryRoute> level (Figure 7.31and Figure 7.32).

```
SELECT DeliveryList.query ('<DeliveryRoute>
 {for $d in /DeliveryList/Delivery return $d/Address}
 </DeliveryRoute>')
FROM DeliverySchedule
```

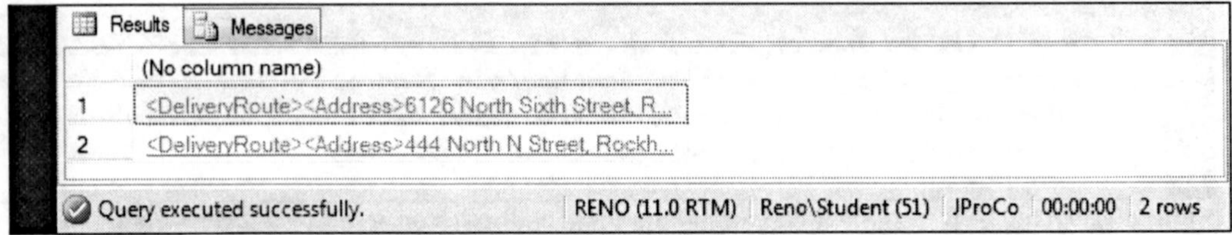

Figure 7.31 This code imposes our own level <DeliveryRoute>.

We have added the root tag <DeliveryRoute>, which wasn't contained in the original XML document.

```
<DeliveryRoute>
  <Address>6126 North Sixth Street, Rockhampton</Address>
  <Address>6445 Cashew Street, Rockhampton</Address>
</DeliveryRoute>
```

Figure 7.32 We have added a root tag that wasn't contained in the original XML file.

Add a top-level tag indicating which driver is responsible for each route. First use a placeholder "me" in place of the driver's name.

```
SELECT DeliveryList.query ('<DeliveryRoute>
<DriverName>me</DriverName>
{for $d in /DeliveryList/Delivery return $d/Address}
</DeliveryRoute>')
FROM DeliverySchedule
```

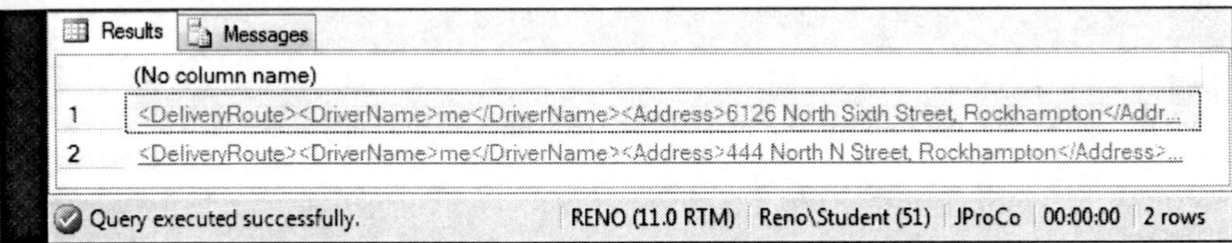

Figure 7.33 Add a top-level tag <DriverName> with the element tag "Me" as a placeholder.

Despite the placeholder "Me" temporarily serving as the element value for <DriverName>, we know this is actually Sally's and Johnny's route data (Figure 7.34 and Figure 7.35, respectively).

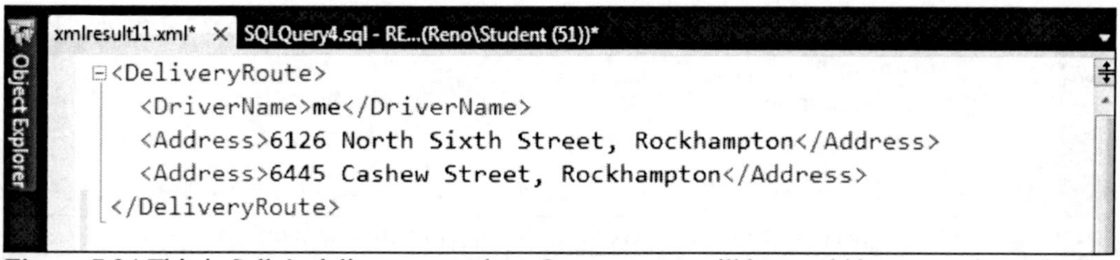

```
xmlresult11.xml*  ×  SQLQuery4.sql - RE...(Reno\Student (51))*
Object Explorer
<DeliveryRoute>
  <DriverName>me</DriverName>
  <Address>6126 North Sixth Street, Rockhampton</Address>
  <Address>6445 Cashew Street, Rockhampton</Address>
</DeliveryRoute>
```

Figure 7.34 This is Sally's delivery route data. Our next step will be to add her name dynamically.

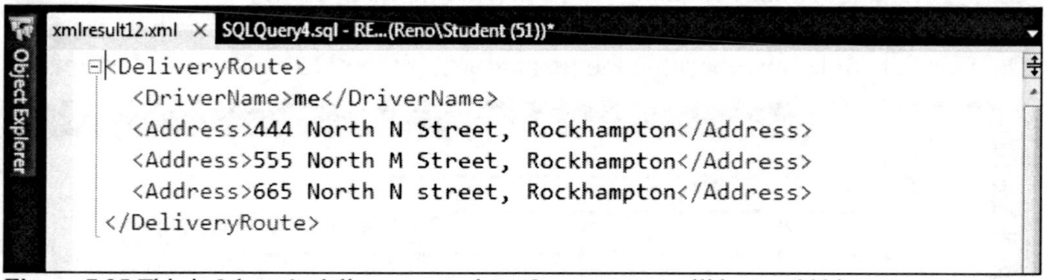

```
xmlresult12.xml  ×  SQLQuery4.sql - RE...(Reno\Student (51))*
Object Explorer
<DeliveryRoute>
  <DriverName>me</DriverName>
  <Address>444 North N Street, Rockhampton</Address>
  <Address>555 North M Street, Rockhampton</Address>
  <Address>665 North N street, Rockhampton</Address>
</DeliveryRoute>
```

Figure 7.35 This is Johnny's delivery route data. Our next step will be to add his name.

The sql:column() Function

This is one of XQuery's SQL Server extension functions. To get values from a column in a SQL Server table, you use the **sql:column** function.

In our current query (last shown in Figure 7.33), replace the word "Me" with the following expression:

{sql:column("DeliveryDriver")}

```
SQLQuery4.sql - RE...(Reno\Student (51))*  ×
Object Explorer
SELECT DeliveryList.query ('<DeliveryRoute>
<DriverName>{sql:column("DeliveryDriver")}</DriverName>
 {for $d in /DeliveryList/Delivery return $d/Address}
</DeliveryRoute>')
FROM DeliverySchedule
```

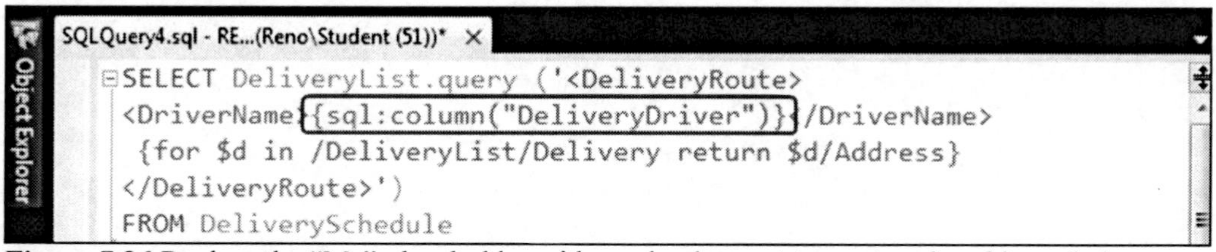

Figure 7.36 Replace the "Me" placeholder with a sql:column statement enclosed in curly braces.

Our XQuery statement will dynamically pull the driver name from the DeliveryDriver field of the DeliverySchedule table. In this way, we are binding the SQL Server table to the XML data (Figure 7.37).

```
SELECT DeliveryList.query ('<DeliveryRoute>
<DriverName>{sql:column("DeliveryDriver")}</DriverName>
{for $d in /DeliveryList/Delivery return $d/Address}
</DeliveryRoute>')
FROM DeliverySchedule
```

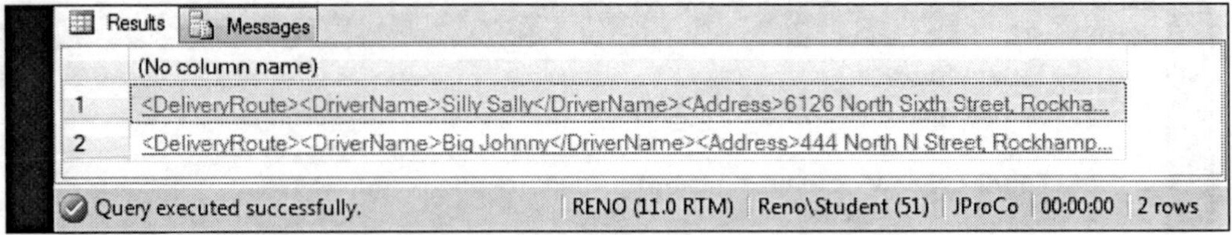

Figure 7.37 Our XQuery statement now contains the sql:column function.

Our XML result stream contains data from the XML document and from the SQL Server table (JProCo.dbo.DeliverySchedule). The <DriverName> values from the DeliverySchedule table became the text values of the <DriverName> elements.

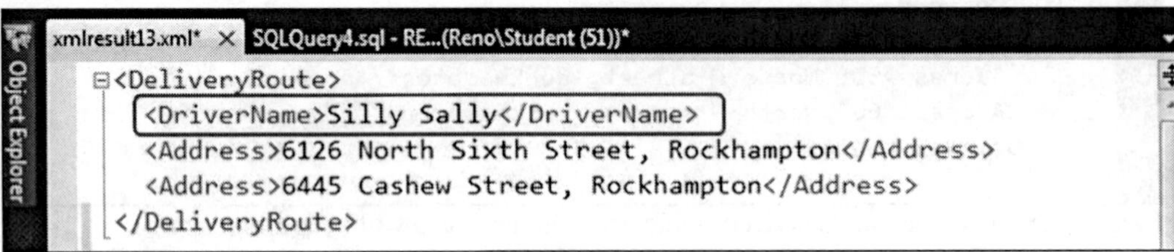

Figure 7.38 Our final XML result stream contains data from the XML document and from the SQL Server table, DeliverySchedule.

Lab 7.2: Binding SQL to XML

Lab Prep: Each lab has one or more Skill Checks. Start with Skill Check 1 and proceed until reaching the Points to Ponder section.

Before beginning this lab, verify that SQL Server 2012 is properly installed and operating. Before running the lab setup script for resetting the database (SQLQueries2012Vol5Chapter7.2Setup.sql), please make sure to close all query windows within SSMS. An open query window pointing to a database context can lock that database preventing it from updating when the script is executing. A simple way to assure all query windows are closed, is to exit out of SSMS, then open a new instance of SSMS, and lastly run the setup script.

Skill Check 1: Add the DeliveryRoute field from the DeliverySchedule table as the first top element named <RouteNo>. When you click on the first record, your XML should resemble the figure you see here.

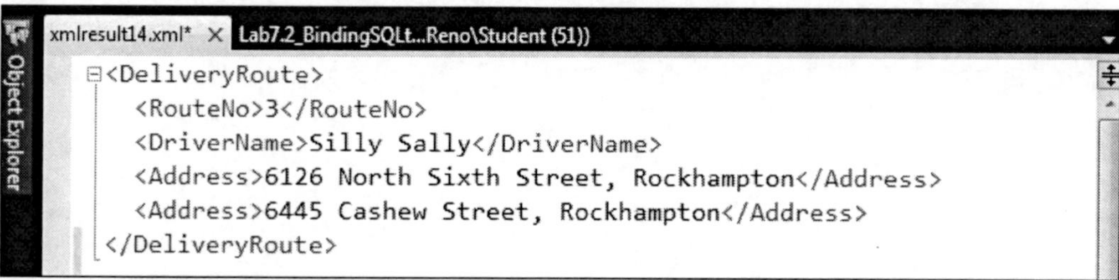

Figure 7.39 Skill Check 1 result.

Skill Check 2: Query the MusicHistory table at the /Music/Song/Title path and add the <genre> root tag with a Name attribute. Populate the attribute with the sql:column value from the MusicTypeName field.

```
xmlresult18.xml*  X  Lab7.2_BindingSQLt...Reno\Student (51))
<genre Name="Rock">
  <Title>Red-Red Wine</Title>
  <Title>Manic Monday</Title>
  <Title>Pretty Woman</Title>
</genre>
```

Figure 7.40 Skill Check 2 result.

Answer Code: The T-SQL code to this lab can be found in the downloadable files in a file named Lab7.2_BindingSQLtoXML.sql

Points to Ponder - Binding SQL to XML

1. You can combine SQL to an XML data stream to produce an XML result set. This is essentially adding dat from your table to the XML stream generated from the query() method.
2. You can use any or all of the XML tags from your XML data and add in new tags and data from the SQL Server table.
3. The sql:column function is one of XQuery's SQL Server extension functions.
4. To get values from a column in a SQL Server table, you use the sql:column function from within the query() method.

Chapter Glossary

Binding SQL to XML: Referencing relational columns in your XML field is known as "binding" the relational column.

Binding XML to SQL: Combining SQL to an XML data stream in order to produce an XML result set. This is essentially adding data from a table to the XML stream generated from the query() method.

CROSS APPLY: An operator which enables the combining of two dissimilar data streams. In this chapter, we use it in conjunction with the nodes() and values() methods to bind XML to rows in a table.

nodes(): An XQuery expression which behaves somewhat like a rowpattern; it picks the level and gets you rows. From there, you get to pick the column.

query(): A built-in method of the XML data type; allows you to query for just the needed parts of an XML.

value(): An XQuery expression which allows you to isolate just the value you want from an XML fragment.

Review Quiz - Chapter Seven

1.) You want to combine the results of a SQL Server table and XML into a single tabular result. What technique will allow you to bind these two sources of data?

O a. CROSS APPLY

O b. INNER APPLY

O c. INNER JOIN

O d. CROSS JOIN

2.) You are writing a query which returns data from a table in SQL Server. Some of the data is stored as relational data and some is stored in XML data type columns. Your query needs to return a relational result set that contains data from relational fields and attribute values from XML data type columns. Which two functions must you use to return all of them in a result set?

□ a. The value() method

□ b. The exist() method

□ c. The query() method

□ d. The nodes() method

3.) You can bind table data with XML data but can only display fields from one or the other in your field SELECT list.

O a. True

O b. False

4.) You have the following code.

```
SELECT SongInfo.value('@TitleID', 'int')
FROM MusicHistory
CROSS APPLY MusicDetails.nodes('/Music/Song') AS
WHERE MusicTypeID = 3
```

Complete the code after the AS to produce a result set.

O a. AS SongTbl(SongInfo)

O b. AS SongInfo(SongTbl)

O c. AS SongTbl(SongInfo).value()

O d. AS SongInfo (SongTbl).value()

5.) Look at this XQuery following statement:

```
query('<DeliveryRoute>for $d in /DeliveryList/Delivery return
$d/Address </DeliveryRoute>')
```

What is wrong with this code?

O a. The root tag is missing.

O b. Slashes are facing the wrong way.

O c. Need curly braces before and after the <DeliveryRoute> element.

O d. Need curly braces inside the custom tags (around the XPath expression).

6.) Your Customer table has a Location field, which stores an XML fragment that contains details of one or more Locations, as shown here:

```
<Location City="Sydney" Address="..." PhoneNumber="..." />
<Location City="Chicago" Address="..." PhoneNumber="..." />
<Location City="London" Address="..." PhoneNumber="..." />
```

You need to write a query that returns a row for each of the customer's Locations. Include the customer name, city and the entire XML starting at the root. Which query should you use?

O a.
```
SELECT
CustomerName,
Location.query('for $i in /Location return data
($i/@City)'),
Location.query('for $i in /Location return $i')
FROM Customer
```

O b.
```
SELECT
CustomerName,
Location.query('data (/Location/@City)'),
Location.query('/Location')
FROM Customer
```

O c.
```
SELECT CustomerName, loc.value('@City', 'VARCHAR(100)'),
loc.query('.')
FROM Customer
CROSS APPLY Customer.Location.nodes('/Location') Locs(loc)
```

7.) Look at this XQuery following statement:

```
('<root><DriverScore>{ }</DriverScore>
{for $d in /root/Driver return $d/Total}</root>')
```

You want the DriverScore tag element value to pull from the Rating field of the dbo.CompanyDriver table. What code should you put in the curly braces, between the DriverScore element tags?

O a. sql:column("DeliveryDriver")
O b. column:sql("DeliveryDriver")
O c. sql:column("dbo.CompanyDriver")
O d. column:sql("dbo.CompanyDriver")
O e. sql:column("Rating")
O f. column:sql("Rating")

Answer Key

1.) INNER APPLY does not exist, so (b) is incorrect. INNER JOIN joins two tables on a common field, so (c) is incorrect. CROSS JOIN joins two tables with every combination, so (d) is incorrect. CROSS APPLY binds an XQuery statement to a table, so (a) is correct.

2.) The value() method works with the row returned by the nodes() method and pulls out the field value, so answers (a) and (d) are correct.

3.) You can bind table data with XML data and display fields from both in your field SELECT list so the answer is false, (b).

4.) The value method belongs in the SELECT list and not the CROSS APPLY, making (c) and (d) wrong. The SELECT list determines the file collection name so SongInfo must be in the parentheses, making (b) wrong. Answer (a) is the correct answer.

5.) This query needs curly braces inside the custom tags and around the XPath expression, so (d) is the correct answer.

6.) To pull multiple rows from a corresponding XML instance you need to use CROSS APPLY, making (c) correct.

7.) The correct syntax to pull out a column from SQL into an XML instance is {sql:column}, so (b), (d) and (f) are wrong. The name of the field we want to pull out is “Rating”, so (e) is correct.

Bug Catcher Game

To play the Bug Catcher game run the SQLQueries2012Vol5BugCatcher7.pps from the BugCatcher folder of the companion files found at www.Joes2Pros.com.

Chapter 8. Importing & Exporting XML

At most large wedding receptions there is often a wide selection of very tasty foods on hand for all the guests to enjoy. Yet at most wedding halls they usually don't have a full chef kitchen to make such fancy food on site. Thanks to the catering services, food that was created across town can be brought on site and presented in a finished form at the needed event.

If we have XML data in your SQL server, how do you think it got there? You can be sure that most XML is not typed by hand into SQL Server. Odds are the XML was imported from an external source and brought into SQL server. Once in SQL server, you can easily do all the parsing and shredding operations to get your work done. This Chapter will focus on some of the simpler ways to import and export XML to SQL server.

READERNOTE: *Please run the SQLQueries2012Vol5Chapter8.0Setup.sql script in order to follow along with the examples in the first section of Chapter 8. All scripts mentioned in this chapter may be found at* ***www.Joes2Pros.com****.*

XML Importing & Exporting Tools

We can create XML data from a query in SQL server and then export it to an XML file. We can also take an XML file and import that into an XML stream into SQL server and then shred it. This section will show the importing and exporting process between SQL and an external XML file.

XML Parsing Revisited

We have parsed data from a table into XML many times. Our next goal will be similar, but with a new facet. Instead of taking the data from the MgmtTraining table and turning it into an XML stream displayed on screen, we will create an XML file. This file will be called mTrain.xml. Take a look at the MgmtTraining table in Figure 8.1.

```
SELECT *
FROM MgmtTraining
```

	ClassID	ClassName	ClassDurationHours	ApprovedDate
1	1	Embracing Diversity	12	2007-01-01 00:00:00.000
2	2	Interviewing	6	2007-01-15 00:00:00.000
3	3	Difficult Negotiations	30	2008-02-12 00:00:00.000
4	4	Empowering Others	18	2012-10-16 20:56:33.193

Query executed successfully. | RENO (11.0 RTM) | Reno\Student (51) | JProCo | 00:00:00 | 4 rows

Figure 8.1 This shows the MgmtTraining table.

Currently this data is shown in a tabular format (aka a table result set) and not as XML yet. Once the mTrain.xml file is created the data of all records will be laid out in attributes in an XML stream and will resemble Figure 8.3.

The data in Figure 8.1 can be saved as XML in many ways, such as all attributes, all elements, a mixture of attributes and elements, or nested elements. Because there are many choices it makes sense to do a quick recap of parsing XML. Let's take the data from the MgmtTraining table and turn it into well-formed XML RAW using the code in Figure 8.2.

```
SELECT *
FROM MgmtTraining
FOR XML RAW, ROOT
```

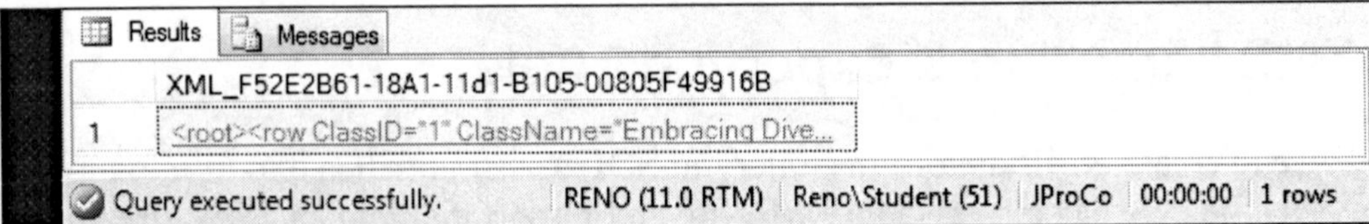

Figure 8.2 This shows the link for the well-formed XML RAW.

When the link from Figure 8.2 is expanded we see all of our data in attributes as seen in Figure 8.3.

SQLQuery5.sql - RE...(Reno\Student (51))* XML_F52E2B61-18A...00805F49916B3.xml

```
<root>
  <row ClassID="1" ClassName="Embracing Diversity" ClassDurat
  <row ClassID="2" ClassName="Interviewing" ClassDurationHour
  <row ClassID="3" ClassName="Difficult Negotiations" ClassDu
  <row ClassID="4" ClassName="Empowering Others" ClassDuratic
</root>
```

Figure 8.3 This shows the well-formed XML from clicking the link seen in Figure 8.2.

Figure 8.3 resembles what we want the resulting XML to look like. We will keep the XML simple as one level of all attributes. The main focus is on the process of saving the XML file rather than the complexity of the XML stream itself.

Exporting XML

All the examples in this section will be saved to the C:\Joes2Pros folder. The Joes2Pros folder on your computer may have files from previous practice labs. For the figures in this chapter to be clear, the Joes2Pros folder has been emptied as seen in Figure 8.4 below.

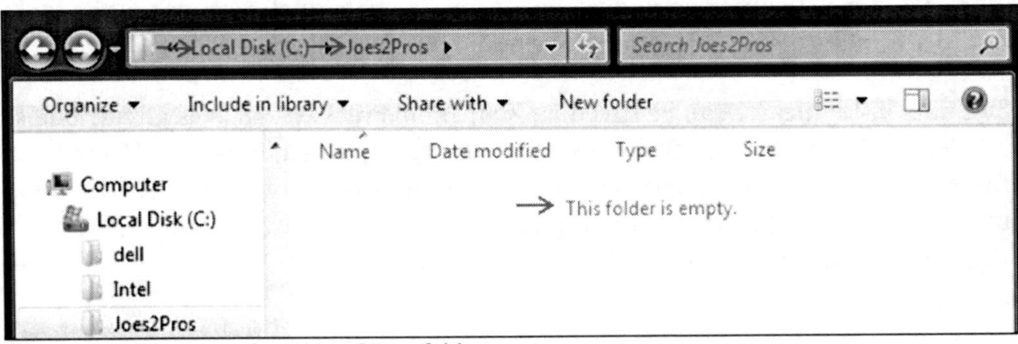

Figure 8.4 This shows the C:\Joes2Pros folder empty.

Exporting XML data to a file is very similar to how we export tabular data to a file. Before learning to export XML, Let's recap how we exported tabular data from a table by using BCP. Start by opening a Command Prompt (Figure 8.5).

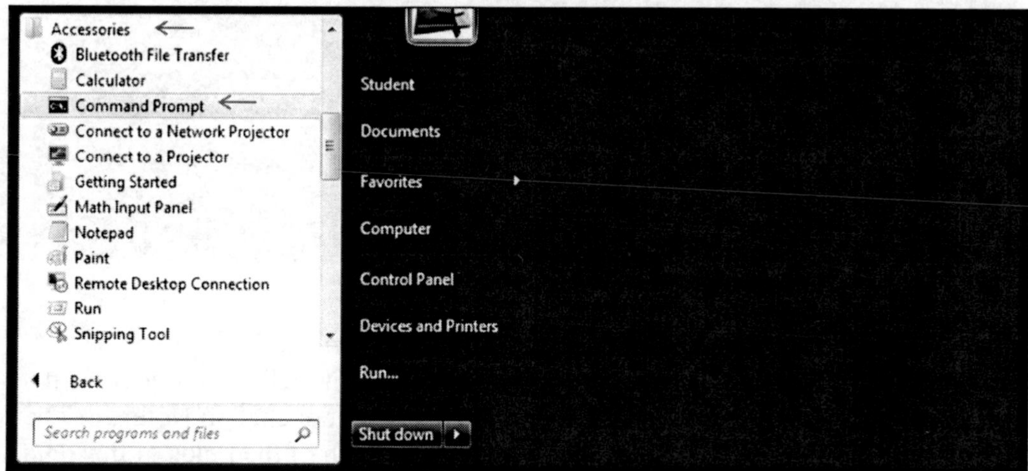

Figure 8.5 This shows a Command Prompt located under **All Programs** > **Accessories**.

Once the Command Prompt is open use the change directory command (cd Joes2Pros) to set the Command Prompt to the Joes2Pros folder (Figure 8.6).

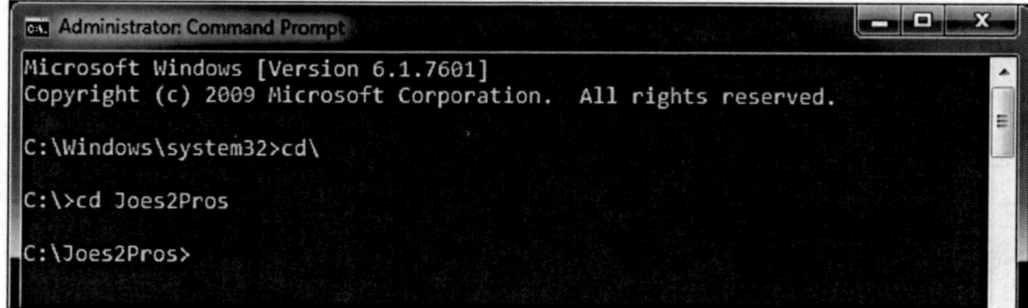

Figure 8.6 This shows the Command Prompt set to the Joes2Pros folder.

To export the MgmtTraining table using BCP type the following code into the Command Prompt as seen in Figure 8.7:

```
BCP JProCo.dbo.MgmtTraining out C:\Joes2Pros\mTrainTable.txt -c -T
```

```
Administrator: Command Prompt
Microsoft Windows [Version 6.1.7601]
Copyright (c) 2009 Microsoft Corporation.  All rights reserved.

C:\Windows\system32>cd\Joes2Pros

C:\Joes2Pros>BCP JProCo.dbo.MgmtTraining out C:\Joes2Pros\mTrainTable.txt -c -T

Starting copy...

4 rows copied.
Network packet size (bytes): 4096
Clock Time (ms.) Total     : 1      Average : (4000.00 rows per sec.)

C:\Joes2Pros>
```

Figure 8.7 This shows the BCP has copied 4 rows into the mTrainTable.txt file.

Once the BCP has been executed successfully the command Prompt will say "4 rows copied." (Figure 8.7) In Figure 8.8 we see the mTrainTable.txt document saved at the destination C:\Joes2Pros and the document opened in Notepad. The Open mTrainTable.txt file shows the four records. Each of the fields of this data is separated by tabs.

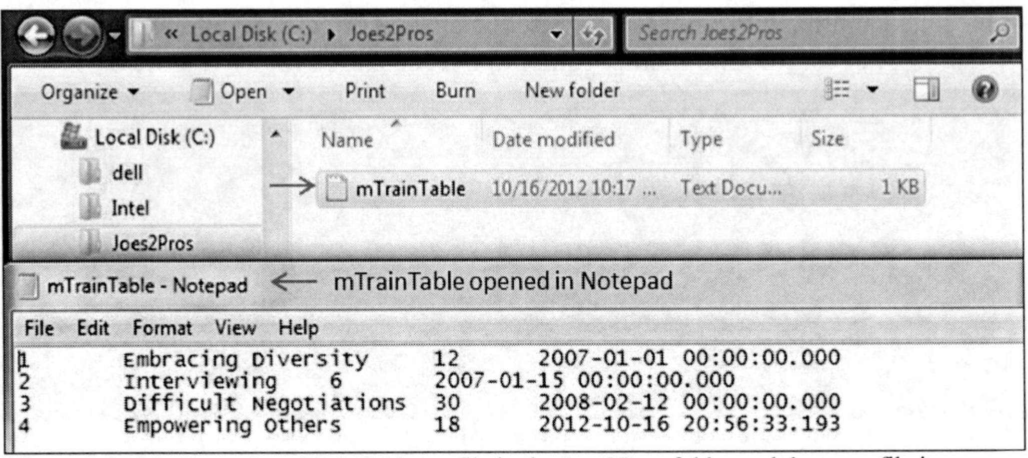

Figure 8.8 This shows the mTrainTable.txt file in the Joes2Pros folder and the open file in Notepad.

In Figure 8.7 we used BCP to save the entire table. BCP can also be used to save part of a table. The "out" option was used by BCP to save the data to a file. Take a look at the following query in Figure 8.9.

```
SELECT *
FROM MgmtTraining
WHERE ClassID > 1
```

	ClassID	ClassName	ClassDurationHours	ApprovedDate
1	2	Interviewing	6	2007-01-15 00:00:00.000
2	3	Difficult Negotiations	30	2008-02-12 00:00:00.000
3	4	Empowering Others	18	2012-10-16 20:56:33.193

Query executed successfully. | RENO (11.0 RTM) | Reno\Student (51) | JProCo | 00:00:00 | 3 rows

Figure 8.9 This shows the MgmtTraining table WHERE ClassID > 1.

The WHERE clause limits our results from four records to three. Instead of using BCP to put out the entire table let's use the "queryout" option to put out only those records in the query from Figure 8.9.

Open a Command Prompt and set it to C:\Joes2Pros then instead of entering the table location we will use a query that references the table. Substitute the "out" option with "queryout" and set the save path to C:\Joes2Pros\mTrainQuery.txt. Keep it set as character data and as a trusted connection as shown in Figure 8.10.

```
BCP "SELECT * FROM JProCo.dbo.MgmtTraining WHERE ClassID > 1"
queryout C:\Joes2Pros\mTrainQuery.txt -c -T
```

```
Administrator: Command Prompt
Microsoft Windows [Version 6.1.7601]
Copyright (c) 2009 Microsoft Corporation.  All rights reserved.

C:\Windows\system32>cd\Joes2Pros

C:\Joes2Pros>BCP "SELECT * FROM JProCo.dbo.MgmtTraining WHERE ClassID > 1" query
out C:\Joes2Pros\mTrainQuery.txt -c -T

Starting copy...

3 rows copied.
Network packet size (bytes): 4096
Clock Time (ms.) Total     : 1      Average : (3000.00 rows per sec.)

C:\Joes2Pros>
```

Figure 8.10 This shows BCP copied 3 rows using the "queryout" command.

The query returned 3 rows (Figure 8.9) and our BCP copied three rows (Figure 1.10). Figure 8.11 shows the mTrainQuery.txt file in Windows Explorer and the file opened in Notepad. The records are tab delimited from the query of the MgmtTraining table.

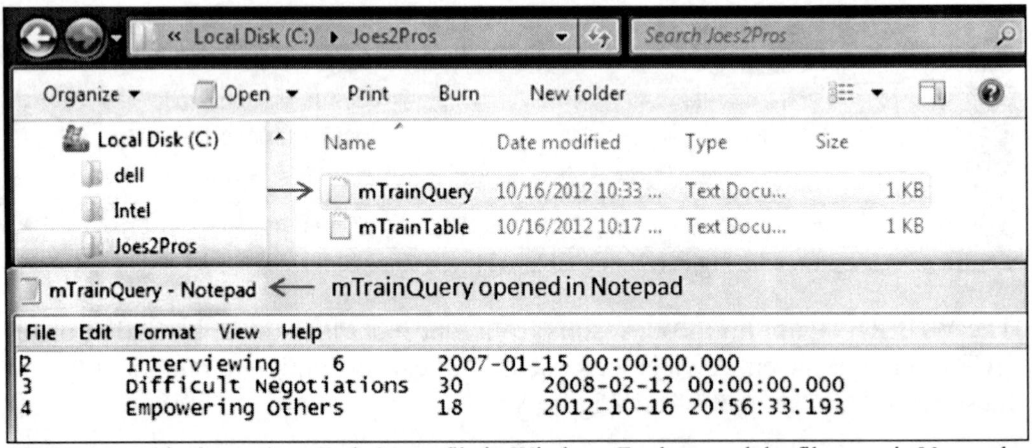

Figure 8.11 This shows the mTrainQuery file in Windows Explorer and the file open in Notepad.

BCP can do more than export tabular data to a file. BCP can also export data as XML to a file. Earlier in this chapter we wrote the following query to convert the MgmtTraining table into well-formed XML:

```
SELECT *
FROM MgmtTraining
FOR XML RAW, ROOT
```

For BCP to export the MgmtTraining table as XML you just need to add the FOR XML RAW to the query earlier from Figure 8.10. It would also make sense to call the file mTrain.xml instead of mTrain.txt. With this change to the command line, execute the BCP statement seen in Figure 1.12.

BCP "SELECT * FROM JProCo.dbo.MgmtTraining FOR XML RAW, ROOT" queryout "C:\Joes2Pros\mTrain.xml" -c -T

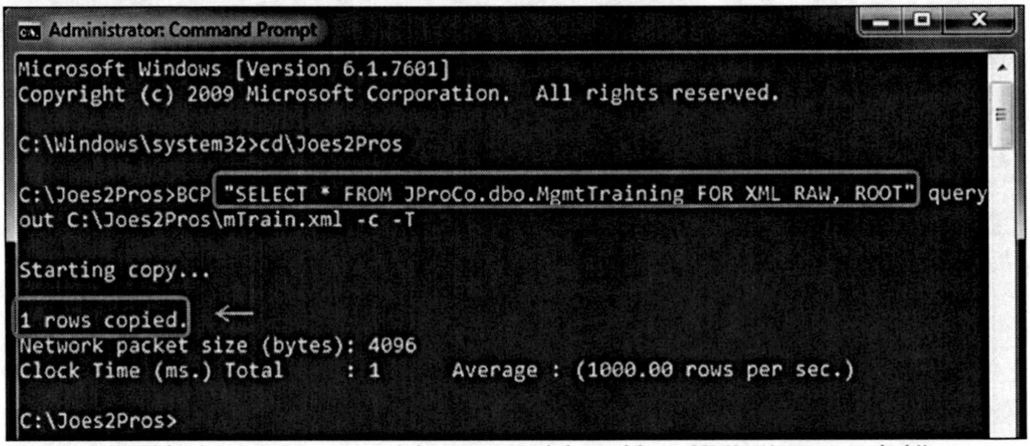

Figure 8.12 This shows BCP exported the MgmtTraining table as XML "1 rows copied.".

We know there are four locations in the Location table. Why does Figure 8.12 only show one row was copied? The XML <root> acts like a single row. BCP exported the entire table as one "row" of XML with four top-level elements. Look in Windows Explorer and we can see the mTrain.xml document. Open it to find the exact same content as the XML stream we ran from the query (Figure 8.13).

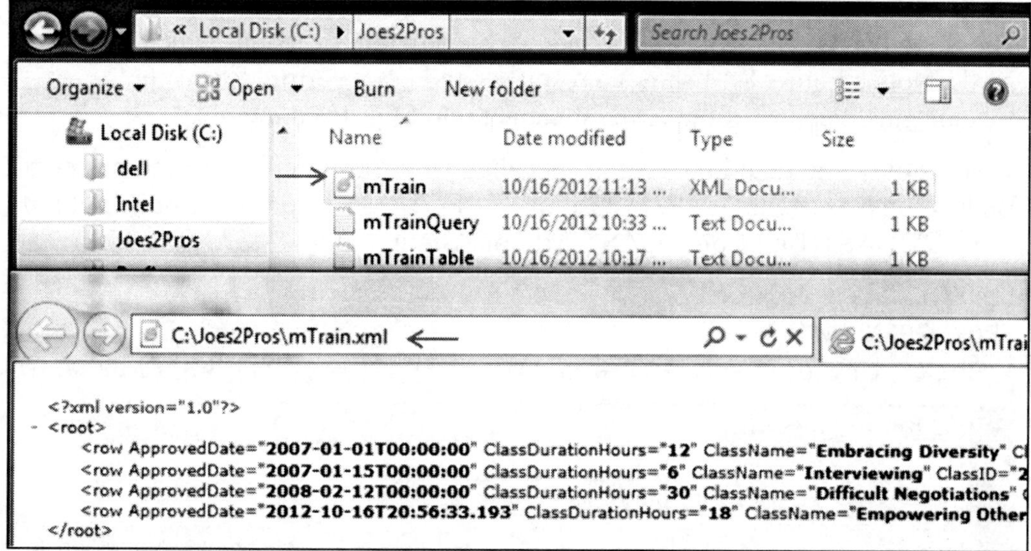

Figure 8.13 This shows the mTrain document in Windows Explorer and its XML contents.

Importing XML

We know how to write a query against XML that already resides in a table. What if the XML is not in SQL server yet? Often times your XML sits in a file. Is it possible to query XML directly from a file? What about the mTrain.xml file that is saved in the C:\Joes2Pros folder from the previous section (Figure 8.13).

The OPENROWSET() function has a bulk option which can load the data from a single file on the file system in SQL Server. We will start our query using SELECT * FROM but we will not be selecting from a table. We will SELECT * FROM OPENROWSET() instead (Figure 8.14).

```
SELECT *
FROM OPENROWSET
 (BULK 'C:\Joes2Pros\mTrain.xml', SINGLE_BLOB) AS XmlTrain
```

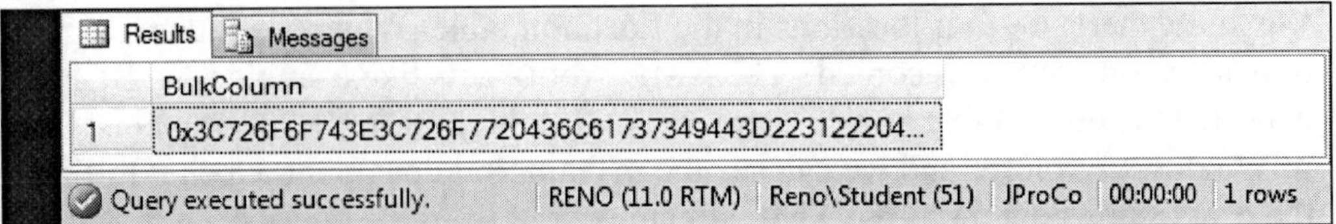

Figure 8.14 This shows the results of OPENROWSET() before we do any casting.

The SINGLE_BLOB works for Windows encoding conversions which include XML. Notice Figure 8.14 shows a result set and not an error. This is the Hexadecimal version of the XML streamed into SQL from the file.

There is only one field in the result set called BulkColumn. We want to pull in the BulkColumn as actual XML. Instead of SELECT * let's itemize this one field to SELECT CAST(BulkColumn AS XML) as seen in Figure 8.15.

```
SELECT CAST(BulkColumn AS XML)
FROM OPENROWSET
 (BULK 'C:\Joes2Pros\mTrain.xml', SINGLE_BLOB) AS XmlTrain
```

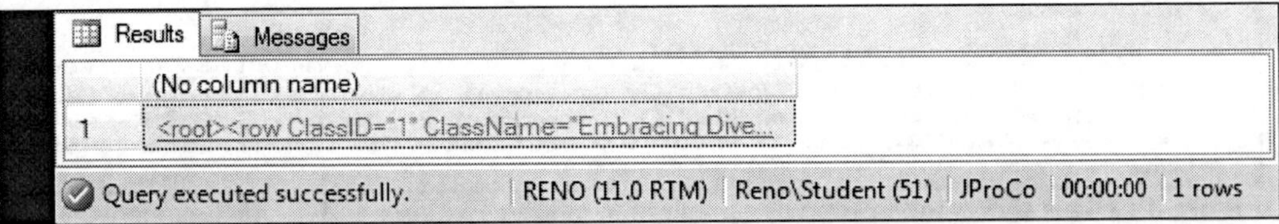

Figure 8.15 This shows CAST() returns the result formatted as an XML data type.

```
xmlresult1.xml  X  SQLQuery6.sql - RE...(Reno\Student (51))*
<root>
  <row ClassID="1" ClassName="Embracing Diversity" ClassDurat
  <row ClassID="2" ClassName="Interviewing" ClassDurationHour
  <row ClassID="3" ClassName="Difficult Negotiations" ClassDu
  <row ClassID="4" ClassName="Empowering Others" ClassDuratic
</root>
```

Figure 8.16 This shows the XML code from the link in Figure 8.15.

Figure 8.16 shows the four records that we queried directly from the mTrain.XML file.

There are many times that we need to capture XML into a table or a variable for later processing. To do this, DECLARE a variable called @XmlDoc as an XML data type and then SELECT the variable to be equal to the BulkColumn. To verify our code, SELECT the variable to see it as a result set as shown in Figure 8.17.

```
DECLARE @XmlDoc XML
SELECT @XmlDoc = BulkColumn
FROM OPENROWSET(BULK 'C:\Joes2Pros\mTrain.xml', SINGLE_BLOB)
 AS XmlTrain

SELECT @XmlDoc
```

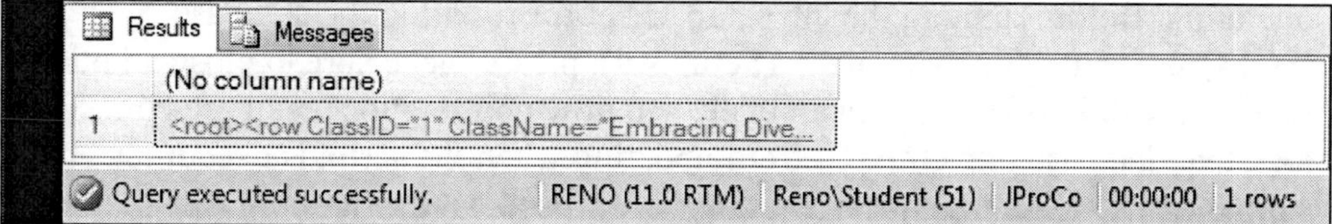

Figure 8.17 This shows the result has been successfully captured to the variable (Figure 8.18).

Once the result set is up, click the hyperlink to see the XML in its own query pane (Figure 8.18).

Figure 8.18 This shows the result from the link in Figure 8.17.

Lab 8.1: XML Importing & Exporting Tools

Lab Prep: Each lab has one or more Skill Checks. Start with Skill Check 1 and proceed until reaching the Points to Ponder section.

Before beginning this lab, verify that SQL Server 2012 is properly installed and operating. Before running the lab setup script for resetting the database (SQLQueries2012Vol5Chapter8.1Setup.sql), please make sure to close all query windows within SSMS. An open query window pointing to a database context can lock that database preventing it from updating when the script is executing. A simple way to assure all query windows are closed, is to exit out of SSMS, then open a new instance of SSMS, and lastly run the setup script.

Skill Check 1: Using Bulk Copy Program and the Windows Command Prompt export all the records of the Location table to the C:\Joes2Pros\Location.txt. When done your result should resemble Figure 8.19.

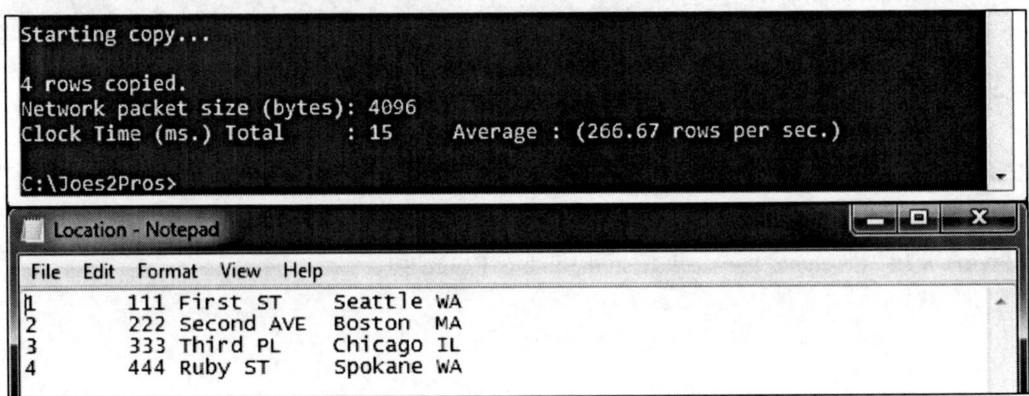

Figure 8.19 This shows the Command Prompt and the Location.xml file result from Skill Check 1.

Skill Check 2: Copy the Lab8.1SK2.xml file from the Resources folder to the C:\Joes2Pros folder. Write a query to import the C:\Joes2Pros\Lab8.1SK2.xml file into a variable named @XmlDoc. When done the result will resemble Figure 8.20.

```
SELECT @XmlDoc
```

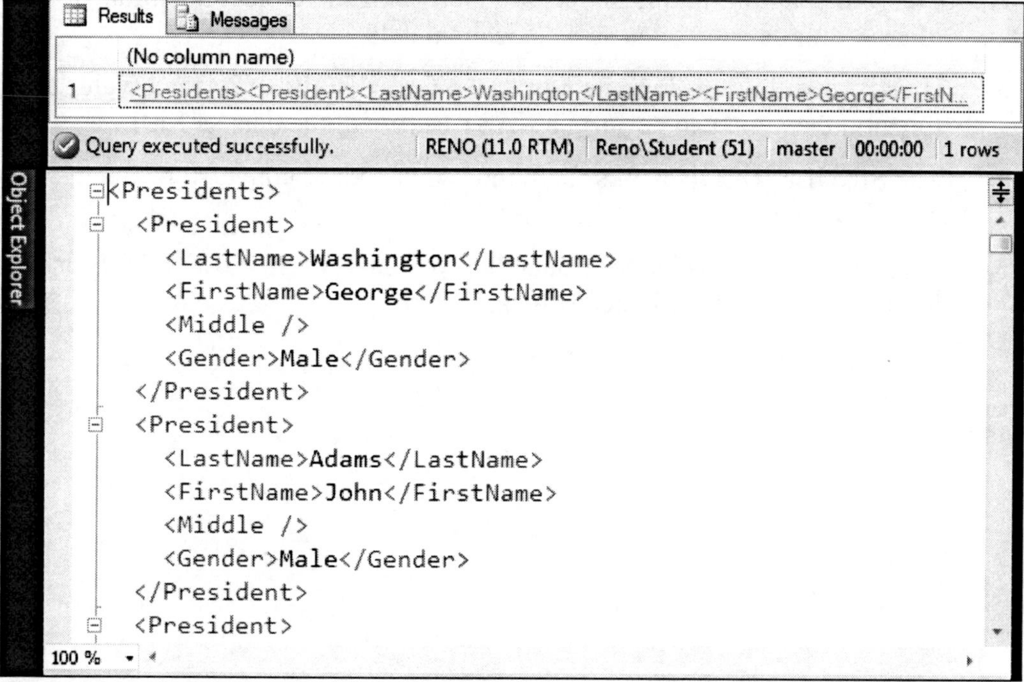

Figure 8.20 This shows the result of Skill Check 2.

Answer Code: The T-SQL code to this lab can be found in the downloadable files in a file named Lab8.1_Importing&ExportingXML.sql

Points to Ponder - Importing & Exporting XML

1. The OPENROWSET function has a BULK option which loads data from a single file in the file system in SQL server.
2. The BulkColumn field from the OPENROWSET() table-valued function returns your data encoded as hexadecimal data.
3. If you are pulling in XML data from the OPENROWSET() table-valued function then you can perform a CAST to stream the data as XML.
4. The SINGLE_BLOB works for Windows encoding conversion which include XML.
5. If you wanted to do character data then you can use SINGLE_CLOB or SINGLE_NCLOB for Unicode data.

Shredding Imported XML

In the first section of this chapter, we took the MgmtTraining table, streamed it as XML and saved that XML as a file called mTrain.xml in the Joes2Pros folder (Figure 8.21). That means you currently have the mTrain.xml file in your Joes2Pros folder. If you are starting with this section and want to go straight to the lab, you can find the mTrain.xml file located in the Resources folder. Copy this file to the Joes2Pros folder on the C:\ drive to begin.

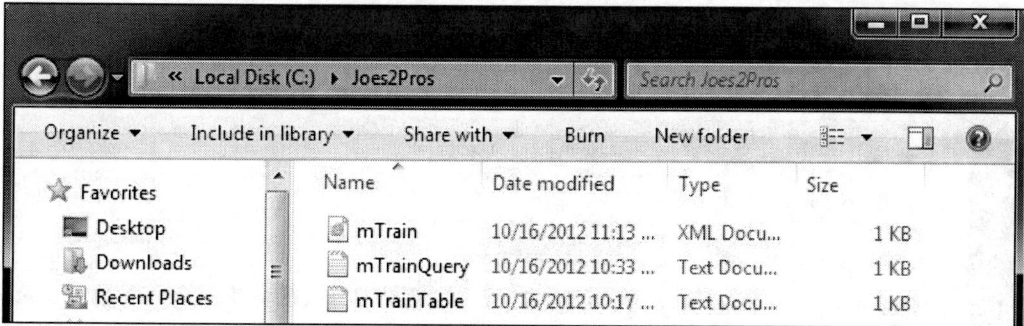

Figure 8.21 The files saved in C:\Joes2Pros from the previous section.

OPENROWSET

Let's look at what's inside the mTrainXML file, by running the OPENROWSET() function using the query from the previous section:

```
SELECT *
FROM OPENROWSET
 (BULK 'C:\Joes2Pros\mTrain.xml', SINGLE_BLOB) AS XmlTrain
```

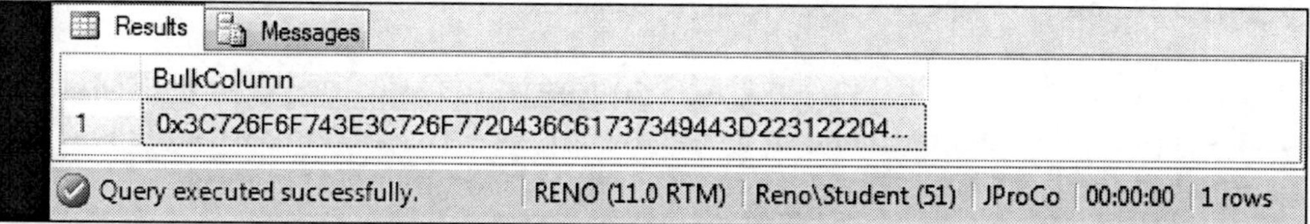

Figure 8.22 This shows the query returned the XML encoded as a binary.

Remember, the OPENROWSET() function has a BULK option which loads data from a single file in the file system to the server you're trying to pull it from. In this case the BULK option is pulling the mTrain.xml file from C:\Joes2Pros. The query is only pulling in one field. We used SELECT * and found the field. When casting, it is better to get the field by its name in the SELECT statement:

```
SELECT BulkColumn
FROM OPENROWSET
 (BULK 'C:\Joes2Pros\mTrain.xml', SINGLE_BLOB) AS XmlTrain
```

The BulkColumn field from the OPENROWSET() table-valued function returns data and codes it as hexadecimal. If the data being pulled from the OPENROWSET() table-valued function is XML, then a CAST can be used to format the streamed data as XML. The result of running the CAST is seen in Figure 8.23 and Figure 8.24.

```
SELECT CAST(BulkColumn AS XML)
FROM OPENROWSET
 (BULK 'C:\Joes2Pros\mTrain.xml', SINGLE_BLOB) AS XmlTrain
```

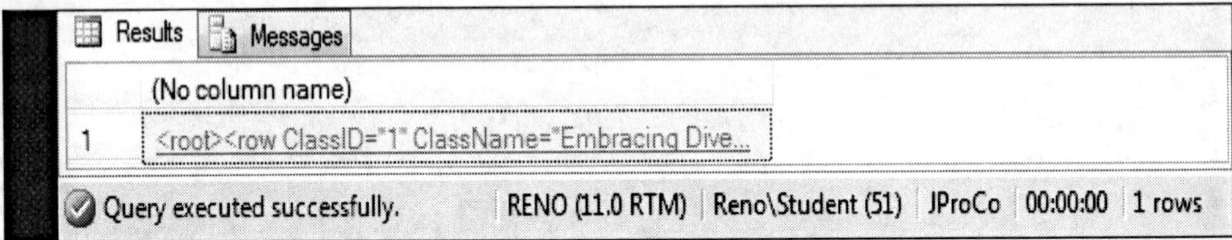

Figure 8.23 This shows CAST was used to stream the data as XML.

```
xmlresult1.xml  X  SQLQuery1.sql - RE...(Reno\Student (51))*
<root>
  <row ClassID="1" ClassName="Embracing Diversity" ClassDurat
  <row ClassID="2" ClassName="Interviewing" ClassDurationHour
  <row ClassID="3" ClassName="Difficult Negotiations" ClassDu
  <row ClassID="4" ClassName="Empowering Others" ClassDuratic
</root>
```

Figure 8.24 This shows the link from Figure 8.23 opened.

Figure 8.23 and Figure 8.24 used CAST to format the streamed data as XML. Let's capture the stream inside of a variable. If we DELARE the variable and set it equal to the CAST it will return the message: "Command(s) completed successfully." At this point we have only placed the data into temporary memory.

```
DECLARE @XmlDoc XML
SELECT @XmlDoc = CAST(BulkColumn AS XML)
FROM OPENROWSET
 (BULK 'C:\Joes2Pros\mTrain.xml', SINGLE_BLOB) AS XmlTrain
```

We want to see what our XML looks like so we add one more line to our code. To see what this variable has for its XML value we add a SELECT statement that calls on the @XmlDoc variable (Figure 8.25).

```
DECLARE @XmlDoc XML
SELECT @XmlDoc = CAST(BulkColumn AS XML)
FROM OPENROWSET
 (BULK 'C:\Joes2Pros\mTrain.xml', SINGLE_BLOB) AS XmlTrain

SELECT @XmlDoc
```

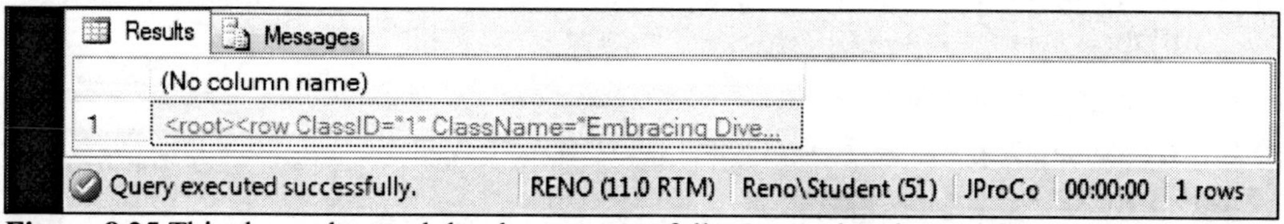

Figure 8.25 This shows the result has been successfully captured to the variable

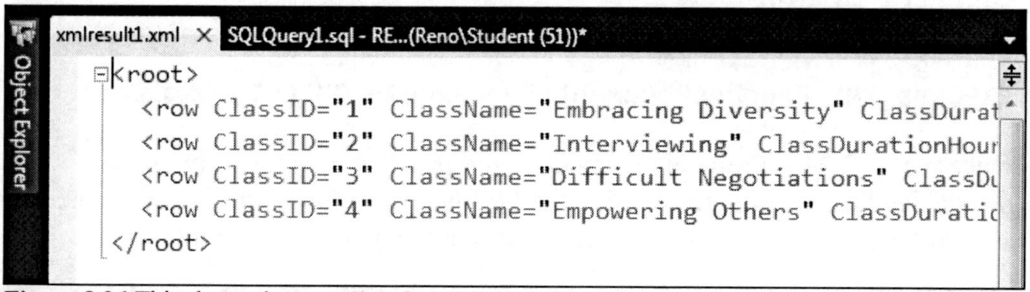

Figure 8.26 This shows the open link from Figure 8.25.

The XML stream has been captured inside of a variable and is now ready for shredding.

XML Shredding Revisited

The following OPENROWSET() function did a good job producing an XML stream in our SQL Server that came from an XML file:

```
DECLARE @XmlDoc XML
SELECT @XmlDoc = CAST(BulkColumn AS XML)
FROM OPENROWSET
 (BULK 'C:\Joes2Pros\mTrain.xml', SINGLE_BLOB) AS XmlTrain

SELECT @XmlDoc
```

Once we have an XML stream, we can perform shredding operations using the sp_XML_PrepareDocument stored procedure along with the OPENXML() row set function.

We want to see our data in a tabular stream instead of an XML stream. To do this, our focus is on shredding the XML so comment out the SELECT @XmlDoc statement. The tabular result should be the only result we see in the result pane when we finish. The next step is to DECLARE an @docHandle as an INT data type. When XML is prepared, two things happen during the exchange. We give the stored procedure the XML data and it gives us back a handle which we can use in the OPENXML query. With the @DocHandle declared we can call on the stored procedure. The stored procedure gives us a handle in the output saved to the @DocHandle variable and in exchange we give it the XML stream from the @XmlDoc variable.

```
DECLARE @XmlDoc XML
SELECT @XmlDoc = BulkColumn
FROM OPENROWSET
 (BULK 'C:\Joes2Pros\mTrain.xml', SINGLE_BLOB) AS XmlTrain
--SELECT @XmlDoc

DECLARE @DocHandle INT
EXEC sp_XML_PrepareDocument @DocHandle OUTPUT, @XmlDoc;
```

Once the sp_XML_PrepareDocument stored procedure hands us back the @DocHandle, we can open it using the OPENXML() function. Take a moment to look at the XML data which has all the data associated with attributes.

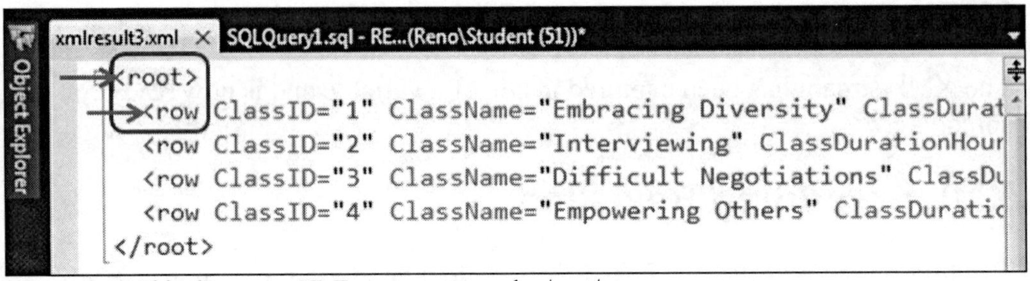

```
xmlresult3.xml  X  SQLQuery1.sql - RE...(Reno\Student (51))*
<root>
  <row ClassID="1" ClassName="Embracing Diversity" ClassDurat
  <row ClassID="2" ClassName="Interviewing" ClassDurationHour
  <row ClassID="3" ClassName="Difficult Negotiations" ClassDu
  <row ClassID="4" ClassName="Empowering Others" ClassDuratic
</root>
```

Figure 8.27 This shows our XML row pattern to be /root/row.

We don't have any data at the <root> level. All of our data is at the /root/row level. To get all four records out we need to specify the row pattern. Figure 8.27 shows our row pattern needs to match the XML data and be set to /root/row.

```
DECLARE @XmlDoc XML
SELECT @XmlDoc = BulkColumn
FROM OPENROWSET
 (BULK 'C:\Joes2Pros\mTrain.xml', SINGLE_BLOB) AS XmlTrain
--SELECT @XmlDoc

DECLARE @DocHandle INT
EXEC sp_XML_PrepareDocument @DocHandle OUTPUT, @XmlDoc;

SELECT * FROM OPENXML(@DocHandle, '/root/row')
```

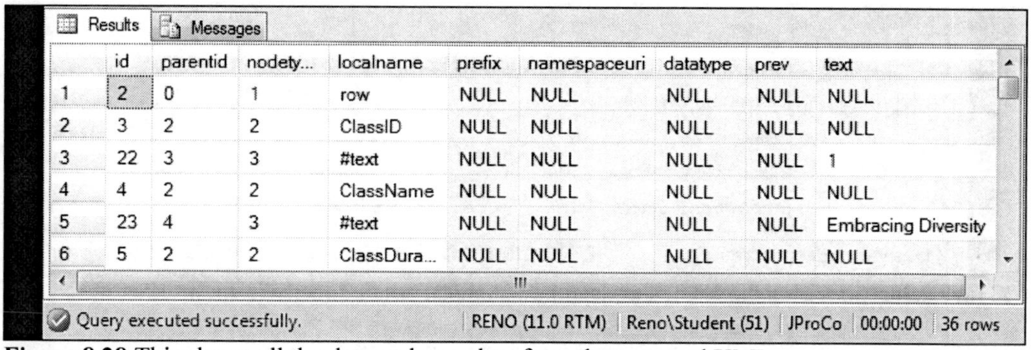

Results | Messages

	id	parentid	nodety...	localname	prefix	namespaceuri	datatype	prev	text
1	2	0	1	row	NULL	NULL	NULL	NULL	NULL
2	3	2	2	ClassID	NULL	NULL	NULL	NULL	NULL
3	22	3	3	#text	NULL	NULL	NULL	NULL	1
4	4	2	2	ClassName	NULL	NULL	NULL	NULL	NULL
5	23	4	3	#text	NULL	NULL	NULL	NULL	Embracing Diversity
6	5	2	2	ClassDura...	NULL	NULL	NULL	NULL	NULL

Query executed successfully. | RENO (11.0 RTM) | Reno\Student (51) | JProCo | 00:00:00 | 36 rows

Figure 8.28 This shows all the data and metadata from the prepared XML.

Figure 8.28 shows all of the data and metadata that describes what the sp_XML_PrepareDocument stored procedure just prepared. Now it is time to specify the row patterns (Figure 8.29).

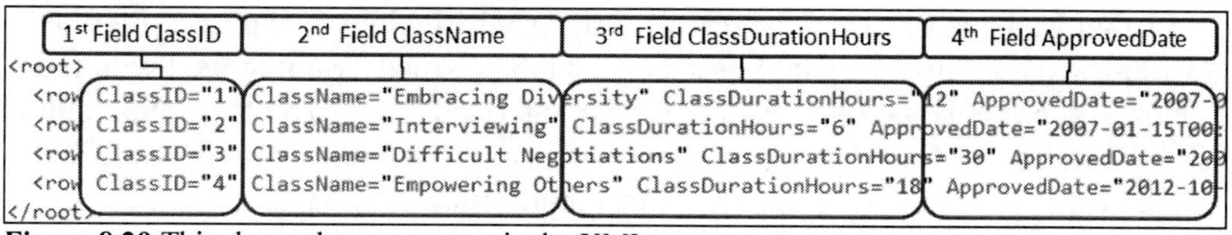

1st Field ClassID | 2nd Field ClassName | 3rd Field ClassDurationHours | 4th Field ApprovedDate

```
<root>
  <row ClassID="1" ClassName="Embracing Diversity" ClassDurationHours="12" ApprovedDate="2007-0
  <row ClassID="2" ClassName="Interviewing" ClassDurationHours="6" ApprovedDate="2007-01-15T00:
  <row ClassID="3" ClassName="Difficult Negotiations" ClassDurationHours="30" ApprovedDate="200
  <row ClassID="4" ClassName="Empowering Others" ClassDurationHours="18" ApprovedDate="2012-10-
</root>
```

Figure 8.29 This shows the row pattern in the XML.

To specify a pattern, add a WITH clause to the SELECT statement and in parentheses specify ClassID as an INT from the attribute @ClassID. The ClassName field is a VARCHAR(50) from the attribute @ClassName. The ClassDurationHours is an INT from the attribute @ClassDurationHours. The ApprovedDate is a DATETIME from the attribute @ApprovedDate.

```
DECLARE @XmlDoc XML
SELECT @XmlDoc = BulkColumn
FROM OPENROWSET
 (BULK 'C:\Joes2Pros\mTrain.xml', SINGLE_BLOB) AS XmlTrain
--SELECT @XmlDoc

DECLARE @DocHandle INT
EXEC sp_XML_PrepareDocument @DocHandle OUTPUT, @XmlDoc;

SELECT * FROM OPENXML(@DocHandle, '/root/row')
WITH (ClassID INT '@ClassID',
 ClassName VARCHAR(50) '@ClassName',
 ClassDurationHours INT '@ClassDurationHours',
 ApprovedDate DATETIME '@ApprovedDate')
```

	ClassID	ClassName	ClassDurationHours	ApprovedDate
1	1	Embracing Diversity	12	2007-01-01 00:00:00.000
2	2	Interviewing	6	2007-01-15 00:00:00.000
3	3	Difficult Negotiations	30	2008-02-12 00:00:00.000
4	4	Empowering Others	18	2012-10-16 20:56:33.193

Query executed successfully. | RENO (11.0 RTM) | Reno\Student (51) | JProCo | 00:00:00 | 4 rows

Figure 8.30 This shows the XML shredded into a tabular result directly from the XML file.

We have successfully shredded the XML file directly into a tabular result (Figure 8.30).

Inserting Shredded XML Data into a Table

Now that we have successfully shredded the XML file into a tabular result, the last task will be fairly simple. Let's create a table named TrainingFeed with four fields to capture the tabular result from our shredded XML. The table should have four fields named ClassID, ClassName, ClassDurationHours and ApprovedDate. Each of these fields will need to have the appropriate data type.

```
CREATE TABLE TrainingFeed
 (ClassID INT NOT NULL,
 ClassName VARCHAR(50) NOT NULL,
 ClassDurationHours INT NULL,
 ApprovedDate DATETIME NULL)
GO
```

Messages
Command(s) completed successfully.
0 rows

Figure 8.31 This shows the TrainingFeed table was created successfully.

In Figure 8.31 we see the "Command(s) completed successfully." message from our CREATE TABLE statement. Now we need to take the SELECT statement that produces the tabular result from Figure 8.30 and place it inside an insert statement which will insert the tabular data into the TrainingFeed Table we created in Figure 8.31.

```
DECLARE @XmlDoc XML
SELECT @XmlDoc = BulkColumn
FROM OPENROWSET
 (BULK 'C:\Joes2Pros\mTrain.xml', SINGLE_BLOB) AS XmlTrain
--SELECT @XmlDoc

DECLARE @DocHandle INT
EXEC sp_XML_PrepareDocument @DocHandle OUTPUT, @XmlDoc;

INSERT INTO TrainingFeed
SELECT * FROM OPENXML(@DocHandle, '/root/row')
WITH (ClassID INT '@ClassID',
 ClassName VARCHAR(50) '@ClassName',
 ClassDurationHours INT '@ClassDurationHours',
 ApprovedDate DATETIME '@ApprovedDate')
```

Messages
(4 row(s) affected)
0 rows

Figure 8.32 The tabular result was successfully inserted into the TrainingFeed table.

In Figure 8.32 we see that four records were inserted into the TrainingFeed table. A quick query from that table will show the result set you see in Figure 8.33.

```
SELECT * FROM TrainingFeed
```

Results | Messages

	ClassID	ClassName	ClassDurationHours	ApprovedDate
1	1	Embracing Diversity	12	2007-01-01 00:00:00.000
2	2	Interviewing	6	2007-01-15 00:00:00.000
3	3	Difficult Negotiations	30	2008-02-12 00:00:00.000
4	4	Empowering Others	18	2012-10-16 20:56:33.193

Query executed successfully. | RENO (11.0 RTM) | Reno\Student (51) | JProCo | 00:00:00 | 4 rows

Figure 8.33 This shows the TrainingFeed table with the XML data inserted from the XML file.

Congratulations! With persistence we have captured our shredded XML into a table directly from a file.

Lab 8.2: Shredding Imported XML

Lab Prep: Each lab has one or more Skill Checks. Start with Skill Check 1 and proceed until reaching the Points to Ponder section.

Before beginning this lab, verify that SQL Server 2012 is properly installed and operating. Before running the lab setup script for resetting the database (SQLQueries2012Vol5Chapter8.2Setup.sql), please make sure to close all query windows within SSMS. An open query window pointing to a database context can lock that database preventing it from updating when the script is executing. A simple way to assure all query windows are closed, is to exit out of SSMS, then open a new instance of SSMS, and lastly run the setup script.

Skill Check 1: Copy the Lab8.2SK1.XML file from the Resources folder to the C:\Joes2Pros folder. Select all fields and all records from the C:\Joes2Pros\Resources\Lab8.2SK1.XML. When done the result should resemble Figure 8.34.

Results | Messages

	LastName	FirstName	Middle	Gender
1	Washington	George		Male
2	Adams	John		Male
3	Jefferson	Thomas		Male
4	Madison	James		Male
5	Monroe	James		Male
6	Adams	John	Quincy	Male

Query executed successfully. | RENO (11.0 RTM) | Reno\Student (51) | JProCo | 00:00:00 | 42 rows

Figure 8.34 This shows the result of Skill Check 1.

Answer Code: The T-SQL code to this lab can be found in the downloadable files in a file named Lab8.2_ShreddingImportedXML.sql.

Points to Ponder - Shredding Imported XML

1. Once you have an XML stream, you can perform your shredding operations using the sp_XML_PrepareDocument stored procedure and the OPENXML rowset function.
2. You can insert shredded XML directly into a table by placing your INSERT INTO *TableName* statement directly above the rowset created by the OPENXML function.

Glossary

OPENROWSET: A connection to remote data from an external data source.

QUERYOUT: An option of BCP that sends the results of a query to a persisted file.

SINGLE_BLOB: Helps the XML parser in SQL Server import data encoded as the XML set in the XML stream declaration.

Tabular Stream: A result set of rows and columns that look like a table. A typical query from SQL is displayed as a tabular result.

XML Stream: Data that is saved as either well-formed XML or a valid XML fragment.

Review Quiz - Chapter Eight

1.) The OPENROWSET() table-valued function returns a result set of just one field. What is the name of that field?

O a. BulkColumn

O b. OPENXML

O c. DataColumn

O d. OPENROWSET

2.) You have the following code:

```
DECLARE @XmlDoc XML
SELECT @XmlDoc = BulkColumn
FROM --Keyword here
 (BULK 'C:\Joes2Pros\mTrain.xml', SINGLE_BLOB) AS XmlTrain
SELECT @XmlDoc
```

You want to open the XML file into an XML stream in your result set. What keyword do you use after the FROM keyword?

O a. OPENXML

O b. BulkColumn

O c. OPENROWSET

3.) You want all the records of your Employee table to be saved into a file named Employee.xml in the C:\Joes2Pros folder. Which BCP option can save data to a file as XML?

O a. IN

O b. OUT

O c. QUERYOUT

O d. XMLOUT

Answer Key

1.) The OPENROWSET() Function returns a field (not a keyword), making (b) and (d) incorrect. The name of the field it returns is BulkColumn, making (a) the correct answer.

2.) We need a keyword after the word FROM, so (b) is wrong. OPENXML is used against a handle and not a file, so (a) is wrong. To get XML from a file you can use OPENROWSET, so (c) is correct.

3.) The IN keyword sends data into SQL from a file. We want to export from SQL to a file, so (a) is incorrect. Both OUT and QUERYOUT send data to a file but OUT only does this from a table using a tabular result, so (b) is incorrect. There is no option called XMLOUT, so (d) is incorrect. QUERYOUT allows you to append your query with FOR XML to send an XML stream to a file, making (c) correct.

Bug Catcher

To play the Bug Catcher game run the SQLQueries2012Vol5BugCatcher8.pps from the BugCatcher folder of the companion files found at www.Joes2Pros.com.

Chapter 9. XML Namespaces

Living in the USA I often send and receive mail to other places in the USA and Canada. When sending within my own country I don't need to add a fourth line in the postal address for country. There is an Ontario USA and an Ontario Canada. If I just put Ontario without specifying a country then it means Ontario USA. When I send mail to Canada then that fourth line is needed. The simple name of Ontario can be used without having to qualify which one it is.

In this example you can say Canada and the USA are two different namespaces. By calling on the namespace you want to use there can be duplicate simple names (like Ontario) in different namespaces (like the USA and Canada). This chapter will show how to use XML namespaces which act like element families within your XML stream.

READERNOTE:*Please run the SQLQueries2012Vol5Chapter9.0Setup.sql script in order to follow along with the examples in the first section of Chapter 9. All scripts mentioned in this chapter may be found at* ***www.Joes2Pros.com****.*

Using XML Namespaces

In a stream of data that might contain employee names, customer names and vendor names it might not be enough to have an element called <name> to convey what you mean. Also, making all elements have compound names like <CustomerCompanyName> might make the XML naming conventions longer than you want them to be. To make the best of both worlds we can explore the use of XML Namespaces.

Levels Naming with a Single Element

Take a look at the following query. Notice the XML for the @XmlDoc variable. It is well-formed with a root and name level that contains "Lee Osako".

```
DECLARE @XmlDoc XML =
'<root>
<Name>Lee Osako</Name>
</root>'
SELECT @XmlDoc
```

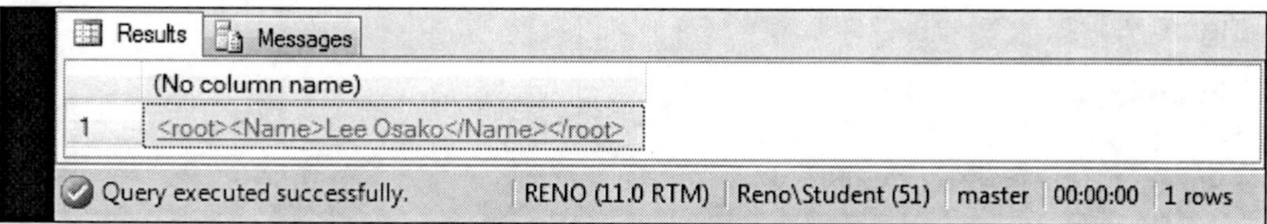

Figure 9.1 This shows the @XmlDoc variable contains the entire XML.

The DECLARE statement sets the variable equal to the entire XML. When we called on the @XmlDoc variable with the SELECT statement it is not a surprise we returned the entire well-formed XML stream (Figure 9.1). Click on the link in the previous figure and you will see the XML from the query:

```
<root>
 <Name>Lee Osako</Name>
</root>
```

What if only the data in the XML is needed? We require just the name "Lee Osako". To do this we must run an XQuery. In the SELECT statement following the variable add ".query()" and in the parentheses put the XPath starting with the /root level and down to the /root/Name level (Figure 9.2).

READERNOTE: *the XPath is case sensitive and must be an exact match to what is in the XML.*

```
DECLARE @XmlDoc XML =
'<root>
<Name>Lee Osako</Name>
</root>'
SELECT @XmlDoc.query('/root/Name')
```

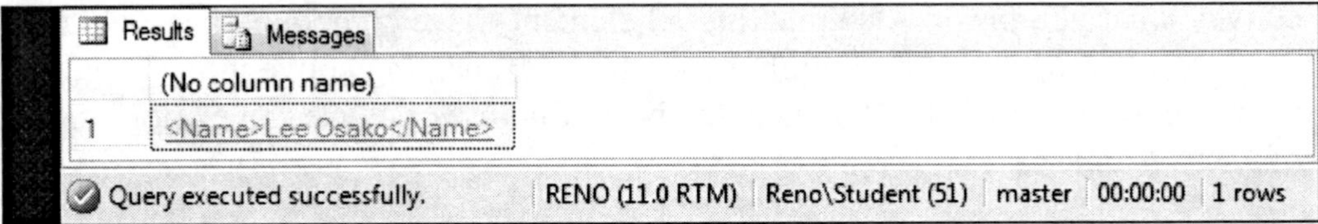

Figure 9.2 This shows the XQuery pulled out just the name element.

Click the link in the result of Figure 9.2 and notice only the name element with the text "Lee Osako" was queried:

```
<Name>Lee Osako</Name>
```

XQuery is great at using XPath to specify the location of the needed data. What if only the name itself is needed and not the XML element? Let's use the text() function to return just the name "Lee Osako" and not the <Name> </Name> nodes. At the end of the XPath in the SELECT statement add /text() as shown in Figure 9.3.

```
DECLARE @XmlDoc XML =
'<root>
<Name>Lee Osako</Name>
</root>'
SELECT @XmlDoc.query('/root/Name/text()')
```

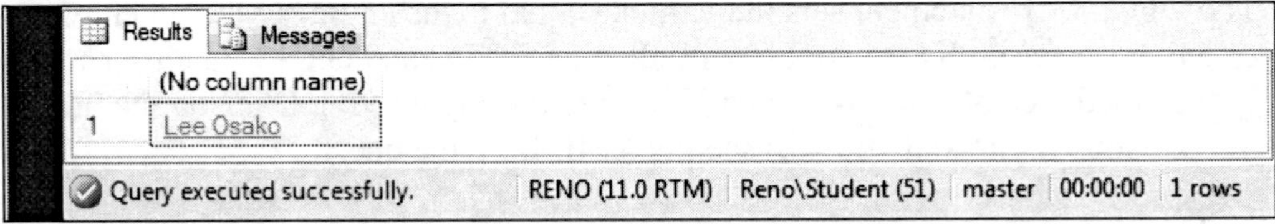

Figure 9.3 The text() method returned just "Lee Osako" without the XML element.

Using the text() method in the XQuery just gets "Lee Osako" and no element tags around the name (Figure 9.3). Let's add more data to our XML stream. We have the <Name> element "Lee Osako" but what if we add the name of the customer account that Lee is in charge of. To do this, add another set of <Name></Name> tags at the same level in the XML. Between the tags put "Joes 2 Pros Inc." which is the customer account that "Lee Osako" is in charge of.

Given that we are specifying the /root/Name level in the XQuery, will it pull in the first <Name> element "Lee Osako", or the second <Name> element, "Joes 2 Pros Inc."?

```
DECLARE @XmlDoc XML =
'<root>
<Name>Lee Osako</Name>
<Name>Joes 2 Pros Inc.</Name>
</root>'
SELECT @XmlDoc.query('/root/Name/text()')
```

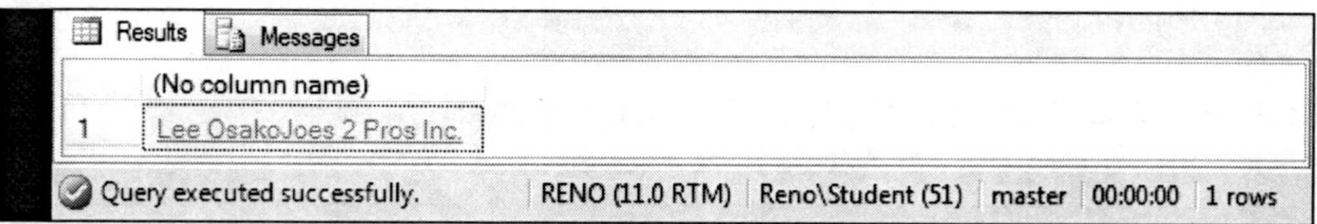

Figure 9.4 This shows XQuery pulled all data from the specified level when the path is ambiguous.

When XQuery encounters an ambiguous path it pulls out all of the data that it encounters at that level. The XPath was looking for the element <Name>. Since "Lee Osako" and Joes 2 Pros are both at the /root/Name level the XQuery returned both in the result set (Figure 9.4). These are two different names that represent two different things. "Lee Osako" is the employee and Joes2Pros Inc. is the customer account "Lee Osako" manages. The two names need to be differentiated. The first <Name> element should be <EmployeeName> and the second <Name> element should be <CustomerName>. Make sure to match both the beginning and ending tags to maintain the well-formed XML:

```
DECLARE @XmlDoc XML =
'<root>
<EmployeeName>Lee Osako</EmployeeName>
<CustomerName>Joes 2 Pros Inc.</CustomerName>
</root>'
SELECT @XmlDoc.query('/root/EmployeeName/text()')
```

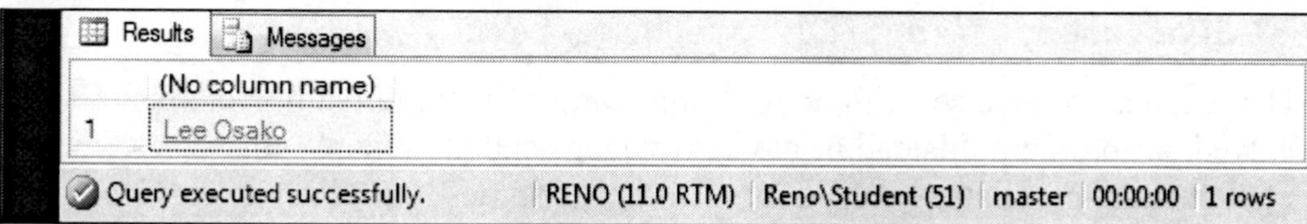

Figure 9.5 This shows XQuery pulled out "Lee Osako" from the EmployeeName level.

To pull out only "Lee Osako", make sure the XPath specifies the root/EmployeeName level (Figure 9.5).

One way to solve ambiguous XPath names is to differentiate all element attributes by using more distinct element names. We have pulled out the <EmployeeName> "Lee Osako", but what if we want the <CustomerName> element as well? To add the <CustomerName> element to our result follow the first XQuery with a comma and insert a second XQuery with the <CustomerName> level specified in the XPath (Figure 9.6).

```
DECLARE @XmlDoc XML =
'<root>
<EmployeeName>Lee Osako</EmployeeName>
<CustomerName>Joes 2 Pros Inc.</CustomerName>
</root>'
SELECT @XmlDoc.query('/root/EmployeeName/text()'),
@XmlDoc.query('/root/CustomerName/text()')
```

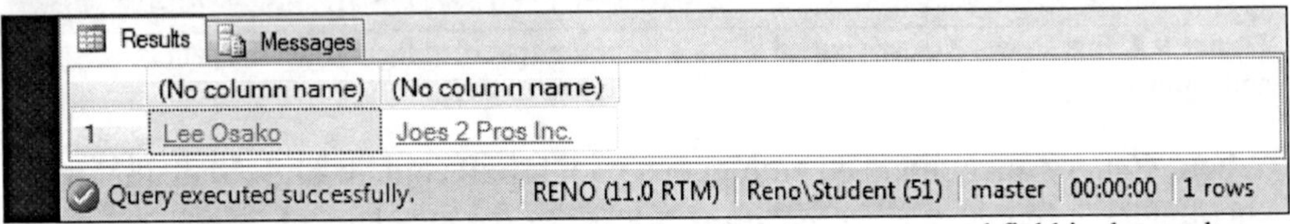

	(No column name)	(No column name)
1	Lee Osako	Joes 2 Pros Inc.

Query executed successfully. | RENO (11.0 RTM) | Reno\Student (51) | master | 00:00:00 | 1 rows

Figure 9.6 This shows the second XQuery added Joes2Pros Inc. to a second field in the result.

The first XQuery pulled out "Lee Osako" in the first field and the second XQuery pulled out Joes2Pros Inc. in the second field of the result (Figure 9.6).

Declaring XML Namespaces

Take a look at the following code from the previous section:

```
DECLARE @XmlDoc XML =
'<root>
<EmployeeName>Lee Osako</EmployeeName>
<CustomerName>Joes 2 Pros Inc.</CustomerName>
</root>'
SELECT @XmlDoc.query('/root/EmployeeName/text()'),
@XmlDoc.query('/root/CustomerName/text()')
```

Using the more precise <EmployeeName> and <CustomerName> elements solved our problem. Instead of having two tags called <Name> that our XQuery could not differentiate, we used more complex names like <EmployeeName> and <CustomerName>.

What if company requirements specify that Name should be the element for both "Lee Osako" and "Joes 2 Pros Inc."? We find ourselves right back where we started. <Name>Lee Osako</Name> and <Name>Joes2Pros Inc.</Name> are in two different families. In XML we call different families as namespaces. The question now becomes how can we differentiate the <Name> element of the Employee family and the <Name> element of the Customer family? We need to create namespaces. Prefix the <Name> element with Employee by adding a colon between Employee and Name in the opening and closing tags of the XML element. Doing this denotes that "Lee Osako" is in the <Name> element of the Employee Namespace. Next make sure the XPath matches in both cases. This looks good but gives us an error.

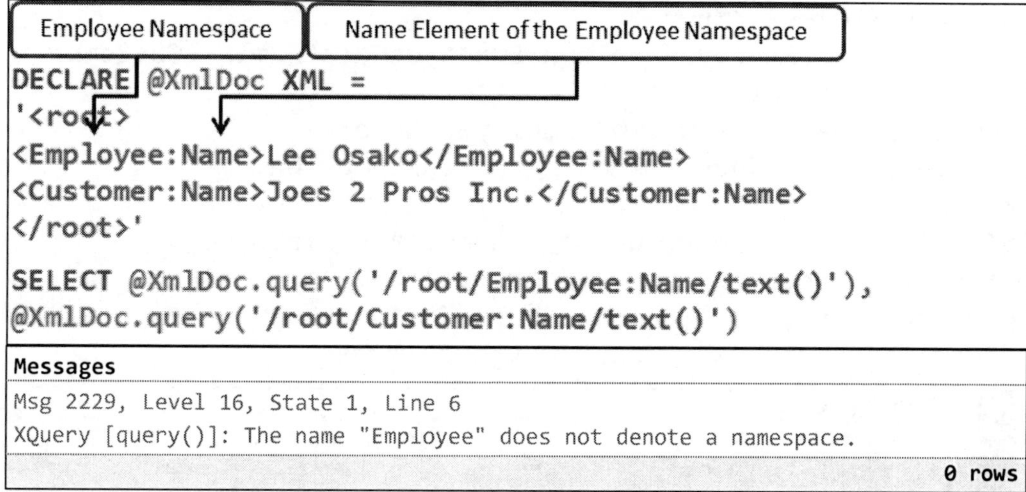

Figure 9.7 This shows the XQuery throws an error because Employee does not denote a namespace.

<Employee:> does not denote a namespace (Figure 9.7). Is it true that a namespace is what comes before the colon? It is true, but we have to declare it in the root of the XML to clarify these namespaces were intended and not an accident. Adding xmlns:Employee identifies the <Employee:> namespace. Next set the namespace equal to urn:EmployeeData. We will do the same thing to declare the Customer namespace. Add "xmlns:Customer" and set it equal to "urn:customerData" in the root element:

```
DECLARE @XmlDoc XML =
'<root xmlns:Employee = "urn:EmployeeData"
 xmlns:Customer = "urn:CustomerData" >
<Employee:Name>Lee Osako</Employee:Name>
<Customer:Name>Joes 2 Pros Inc.</Customer:Name>
</root>'
SELECT @XmlDoc.query('/root/Employee:Name/text()'),
 @XmlDoc.query('/root/Customer:Name/text()')
```

The XML namespace (xmlns) allows XQuery to use a namespace prefix. The xmlns must be declared in the XML stream and then specified by the consuming XQuery. The XQuery needs to know about the namespace. The <Employee:> namespace is currently named EmployeeData and the <Customer:> namespace is named customerData. For the XQuery to use the <Employee:> namespace in the XQuery, *declare namespace Employee = "urn:EmployeeData";* must be added to the XPath. And we must also add *declare namespace Customer = "urn:customerData";* for the <Customer:> Namespace.

```
DECLARE @XmlDoc XML =
'<root xmlns:Employee = "urn:EmployeeData" xmlns:Customer =
"urn:CustomerData" >
<Employee:Name>Lee Osako</Employee:Name>
<Customer:Name>Joes 2 Pros Inc.</Customer:Name>
</root>'
SELECT @XmlDoc.query('declare namespace Employee =
 "urn:EmployeeData"; /root/Employee:Name'),
@XmlDoc.query('declare namespace Customer =
 "urn:CustomerData"; /root/Customer:Name')
```

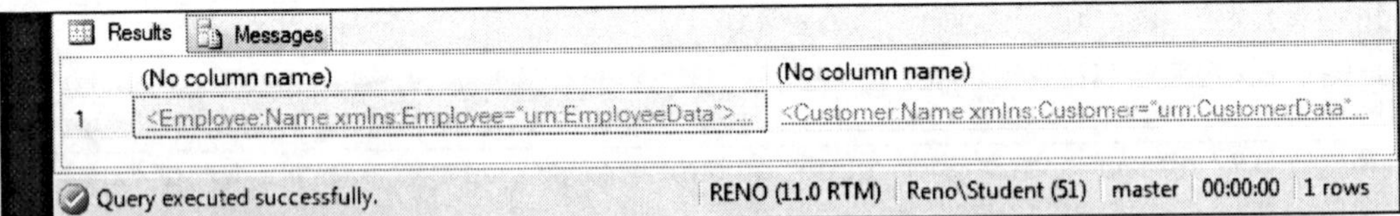

Figure 9.8 Declaring xmlns in the root of the XML allowed the XQuery to differentiate the Employee:Name from the Customer:Name at the same level in the XML.

The XQuery was able to consume the XML and separate the <Employee:Name > level from the <Customer:Name> level (Figure 9.8). After declaring a namespace in the root of the XML, its prefix can then be used in the XPath expression if you also tell the XPath expression to declare the same namespace. If we open the first link for EmployeeData we see "Lee Osako" wrapped in the name spaces tag:

```
<Employee:Name xmlns:Employee="urn:EmployeeData">
Lee Osako</Employee:Name>
```

Since we just want "Lee Osako", let's simply add the text() method to the end of the XPath of both XQueries.

```
DECLARE @XmlDoc XML =
'<root xmlns:Employee = "urn:EmployeeData" xmlns:Customer =
"urn:CustomerData">
<Employee:Name>Lee Osako</Employee:Name>
<Customer:Name>Joes 2 Pros Inc.</Customer:Name>
```

```
</root>'
SELECT @XmlDoc.query('declare Namespace Employee =
 "urn:EmployeeData"; /root/Employee:Name/text()'),
@XmlDoc.query('declare namespace Customer =
 "urn:CustomerData"; /root/Customer:Name/text()')
```

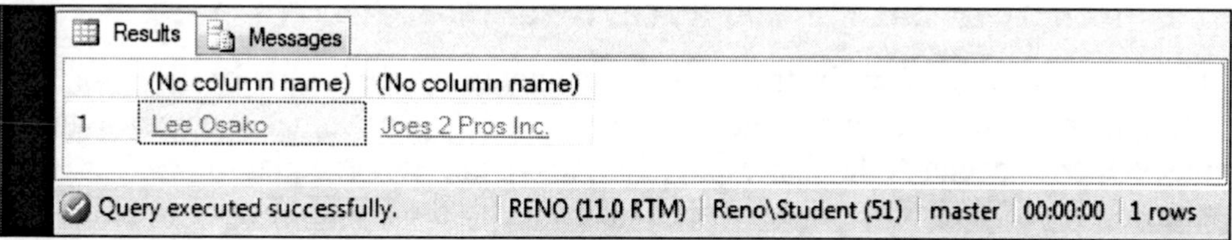

Figure 9.9 The text() method returned just the data contained in each namespace.

Adding the text() method to our XQuery allowed just "Lee Osako" and "Joes 2 Pros Inc." without the element data into the result set (Figure 9.9).

XQuery Multiple Elements in an XML Namespace

The XML from the previous section contained two <Name> elements that meant different things. It contains the <Employee:Name > element and the <Customer:Name> element:

```
<root xmlns:Employee = "urn:EmployeeData"
  xmlns:Customer = "urn:CustomerData">
 <Employee:Name>Lee Osako</Employee:Name>
 <Customer:Name>Joes 2 Pros Inc.</Customer:Name>
</root>
```

What if there are different types of employees? There may be warehouse employees, marketing employees, and sales employees. Let's add a <Type> element to the <Employee:> namespace and a <Type> element to the <Customer:> namespace. "Lee Osako" is in sales so after the <Employee:Name > namespace insert a new line for the <Employee:Type> namespace and between the tags put "Sales". Joes2Pros Inc. is a retail type customer so after the <Customer:Name> namespace insert a new line for the <Customer: > namespace and between the tags put "Retail" like the following example:

```
DECLARE @XmlDoc XML =
'<root xmlns:Employee = "urn:EmployeeData" xmlns:Customer =
"urn:CustomerData" >
<Employee:Name>Lee Osako</Employee:Name>
<Employee:Type>Sales</Employee:Type>
<Customer:Name>Joes 2 Pros Inc.</Customer:Name>
```

```
<Customer:Type>Retail</Customer:Type>
</root>'
SELECT @XmlDoc.query('declare namespace Employee =
 "urn:EmployeeData"; /root/Employee:Name/text()'),
@XmlDoc.query('declare namespace Customer =
 "urn:CustomerData"; /root/Customer:Name/text()')
```

There are two XQueries for the <Name> elements. There is one for the <Employee:Name > element and one for the <Customer:Name> element. Each of the XQueries declares the namespace Employee and sets it equal to urn:EmployeeData. The XQuery must also specify the XPath. For us to pull out the new <:type> elements with the SELECT statement we must add two more XQueries using the same process as the <:Name> elements. The xmlns:Employee and xmlns:Customer have already been declared in the root of the XML so this query should shred the XML just fine:

```
DECLARE @XmlDoc XML =
'<root xmlns:Employee = "urn:EmployeeData" xmlns:Customer =
"urn:CustomerData" >
<Employee:Name>Lee Osako</Employee:Name>
<Employee:Type>Sales</Employee:Type>
<Customer:Name>Joes 2 Pros Inc.</Customer:Name>
<Customer:Type>Retail</Customer:Type>
</root>'
SELECT @XmlDoc.query('declare namespace Employee =
 "urn:EmployeeData"; /root/Employee:Name/text()'),
@XmlDoc.query('declare namespace Employee =
 "urn:EmployeeData"; /root/Employee:Type/text()'),
@XmlDoc.query('declare namespace Customer =
 "urn:CustomerData"; /root/Customer:Name/text()'),
@XmlDoc.query('declare namespace Customer =
 "urn:CustomerData"; /root/Customer:Type/text()')
```

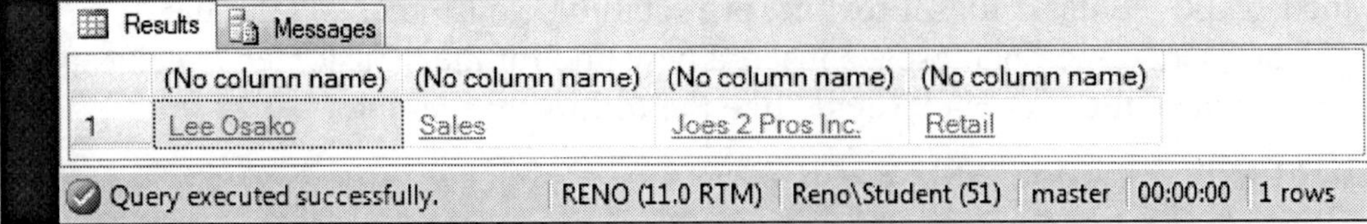

Figure 9.10 This used XQuery to pull out all the data form both the Employee and Customer namespaces.

An XML namespace can have multiple elements and using XQuery each element can be specified. In Figure 9.10 we see that "Lee Osako" is a Sales employee and the Customer Joes2Pros Inc. is a Retail type customer.

HTTP and URN Namespaces

For this section we will start by looking at the records from the Employee and [Grant] tables. We need to know which employee found each grant. Join the Employee table and the [Grant] table together using an INNER JOIN and correspond the tables using ON for the EmpID.

```
SELECT em.EmpID, em.FirstName, em.LastName, gr.GrantID,
gr.GrantName, gr.Amount
FROM Employee AS em INNER JOIN [Grant] AS gr
ON em.EmpID = gr.EmpID
```

Results | Messages

	EmpID	FirstName	LastName	GrantID	GrantName	Amount
1	7	David	Lonning	001	92 Purr_Scents %% team	4750.00
2	2	Barry	Brown	002	K-Land fund trust	15750.00
3	7	David	Lonning	003	Robert@BigStarBank.com	18100.00
4	4	David	Kennson	005	BIG 6's Foundation%	21000.00
5	3	Lee	Osako	006	TALTA_Kishan International	18100.00
6	10	Terry	O'Haire	007	Ben@MoreTechnology.com	41000.00

Query executed successfully. | RENO (11.0 RTM) | Reno\Student (51) | JProCo | 00:00:00 | 11 rows

Figure 9.11 This shows the Employee table joined to the [Grant] table on the EmpID.

Figure 9.11 shows us the employee that found each grant. It does not show us anything about the donation types. That data is stored in XML. To follow along you will need to load the Lab9.1Starter.sql file from the Joes 2 Pros Resources folder into Management Studio.

```
DECLARE @XmlDoc XML =
'<procure xmlns:Employee = "urn:Charity:Employee"
xmlns:Grant = "http://Joes2Pros.com/Donate">
<DonationType>Cash</DonationType>
<Employee:Name>Barry Brown</Employee:Name>
<Grant:Name>K-Land fund trust</Grant:Name>
</procure>'
SELECT @XmlDoc
```

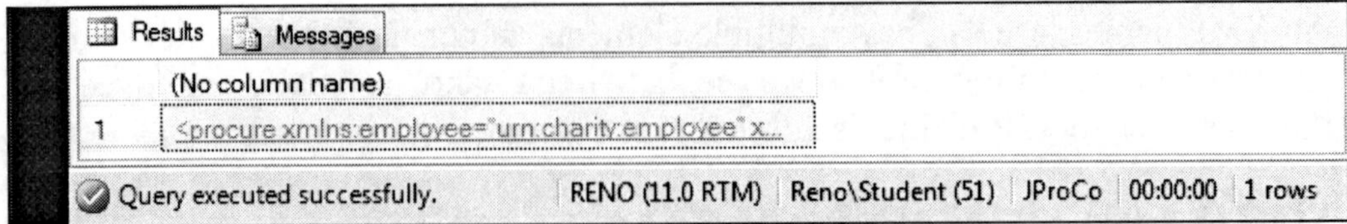

Figure 9.12 This shows the result from the C:\Joes2Pros\Resources\Lab9.1Starter.sql file.

If we open the link in Figure 9.12 we see the following XML:

```
<procure xmlns:Employee="urn:Charity:Employee"
xmlns:Grant="http://Joes2Pros.com/Donate">
 <DonationType>Cash</DonationType>
 <Employee:Name>Barry Brown</Employee:Name>
 <Grant:Name>K-Land fund trust</Grant:Name>
</procure>
```

This XML tells us the <Grant:Name> is K-Land fund trust, the <Employee:Name> who found that grant is Barry Brown. The <DonationType.> is "Cash". Using what we have learned so far in this chapter let's write a query that pulls out just the data from the DonationType. level using the text() method.

```
DECLARE @XmlDoc XML =
'<procure xmlns:Employee = "urn:Charity:Employee"
xmlns:Grant = "http://Joes2Pros.com">
<DonationType>Cash</DonationType>
<Employee:Name>Barry Brown</Employee:Name>
<Grant:Name>K-Land fund trust</Grant:Name>
</procure>'
SELECT @XmlDoc.query('/procure/DonationType/text()')
```

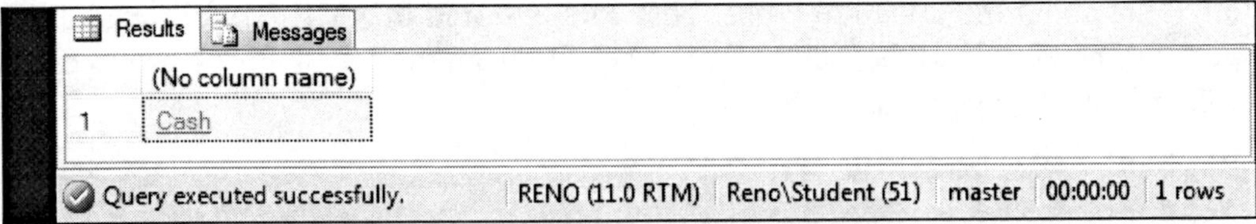

Figure 9.13 This shows the XQuery pulled out the DonationType. Cash without the element information.

In Figure 9.13 we see our XQuery was successful and pulled just the element data, cash. Our next goal is to pull out Barry Brown. The namespace has already been declared in the root. Let's start by adding another XQuery statement against the XmlDoc variable. Using the same process in a second XQuery against the XmlDoc variable, declare namespace employee equals "urn:charity:employee"; before the XPath and include the text() method to pullout only the data within the element tags.

```
DECLARE @XmlDoc XML =
'<procure xmlns:Employee = "urn:Charity:Employee"
xmlns:Grant = "http://Joes2Pros.com">
<DonationType>Cash</DonationType>
<Employee:Name>Barry Brown</Employee:Name>
<Grant:Name>K-Land fund trust</Grant:Name>
</procure>'
SELECT @XmlDoc.query('/procure/DonationType/text()'),
@XmlDoc.query('declare namespace Employee =
"urn:Charity:Employee"; /procure/Employee:Name/text()')
```

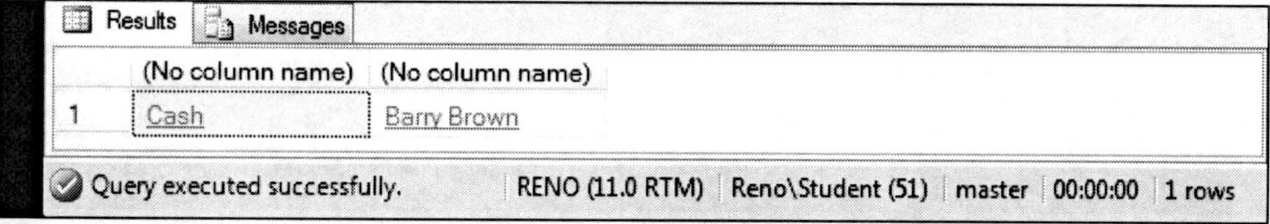

	(No column name)	(No column name)
1	Cash	Barry Brown

Figure 9.14 This shows Barry Brown was pulled out using the XML namespace in the XQuery.

In Figure 9.14 the query successfully pulled out the DonationType. element data and charity:employee element data. The declare statement in the XQuery is used to define the namespace to be used by that XPath. Let's continue and use the same technique to select the <Charity:Grant> element. On a new line we will add @XmlDoc query and in the parentheses declare the namespace <Grant:> equal to "http://Joes2Pros.com";. With the XPath and the text() method this query is ready to run.

```
DECLARE @XmlDoc XML =
'<procure xmlns:Employee = "urn:Charity:Employee"
xmlns:Grant = "http://Joes2Pros.com">
<DonationType>Cash</DonationType>
<Employee:Name>Barry Brown</Employee:Name>
<Grant:Name>K-Land fund trust</Grant:Name>
</procure>'
SELECT @XmlDoc.query('/procure/DonationType/text()'),
@XmlDoc.query('declare namespace Employee =
 "urn:Charity:Employee"; /procure/Employee:Name/text()'),
@XmlDoc.query('declare namespace grant =
 "http://Joes2Pros.com"; /procure/Grant:Name/text()')
```

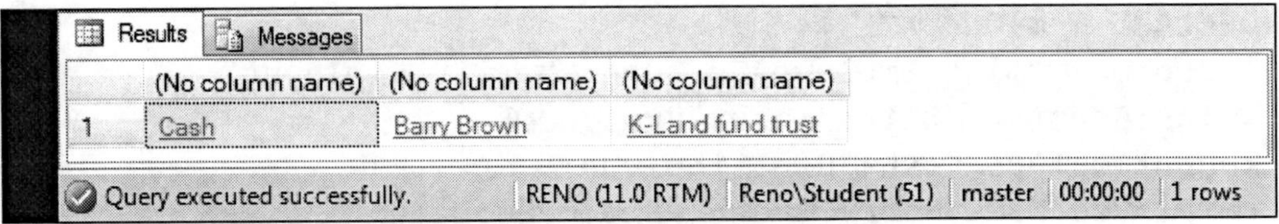

Figure 9.15 Our XQuery pulled out all the element data from the XML.

XML namespaces allow multiple simple names to be used with different prefixes such as <Grant:> and <Employee:>.

Lab 9.1: Using XML Namespaces

Lab Prep: Each lab has one or more Skill Checks. Start with Skill Check 1 and proceed until reaching the Points to Ponder section.

Before beginning this lab, verify that SQL Server 2012 is properly installed and operating. Before running the lab setup script for resetting the database (SQLQueries2012Vol5Chapter9.0-9.2Setup.sql), please make sure to close all query windows within SSMS. An open query window pointing to a database context can lock that database preventing it from updating when the script is executing. A simple way to assure all query windows are closed, is to exit out of SSMS, then open a new instance of SSMS, and lastly run the setup script.

Skill Check 1: Open the C:\Joes2Pros\Resources\Lab9.1SK1.sql file and pull out the text for all four fields. When done your results should resemble Figure 9.16.

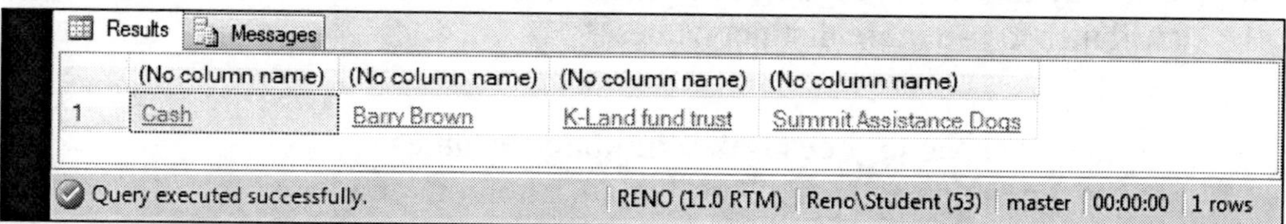

Figure 9.16 This shows the result of Skill Check 1.

Answer Code: The T-SQL code to this lab can be found in the downloadable files in a file named Lab9.1_Using_XML_namespaces.sql.

Points to Ponder - XML Namespaces

1. XQuery is great at using an XPath to specify the location of the needed data.
2. Sometimes XML tags like <Price> have many meanings like RetailPrice and Wholesale price.
3. XQuery can encounter an ambiguous path if looking for elements at the same level with the same name like the two elements seen in the XML below:

```
'<root>
<Name>Lee Osako</Name>
<Name>Joes 2 Pros Inc.</Name>
</root>'
```

4. One way to solve ambiguous Path names is differentiate all elements and attributes to use more distinct names.

```
'<root>
<EmployeeName>Lee Osako</EmployeeName>
<CustomerName>Joes 2 Pros Inc.</CustomerName>
</root>'
```

5. If company XML standards requires the use of simple duplicate element names that also have different meanings then namespace prefixes can be used.

```
'<root>
<Employee:Name >Lee Osako</Employee:Name >
<Customer:Name>Joes 2 Pros Inc.</customer:Name>
</root>'
```

6. XML Namespaces can help differentiate between the same name uses.
7. The XPath of the XQuery can only refer to the name of the Element and not the prefix. Therefore the <Employee:Name > element and the <Customer:Name> element use the same tag which causes ambiguity for your XQuery.
8. The XQuery can encounter an ambiguous path if looking for the <price> tag if the XML has two tags as seen here.
    - <retail:price>
    - <wholesale:price>

9. The namespace prefix for the following tag is “Retail” <retail:price>, the name of the tag is “Price”.

10. The XML namespace acts as a qualifier for XML elements and attributes names. For example the two price elements below have the same name but are more clearly defined with a different namespace as their prefix.

- <retail:price>
- <wholesale:price>

11. In this root element, xmlns means XML Namespaces. <root xmlns:Employee = "urn:empData">

12. The XML namespace allows XQuery to use a namespace prefix for a document.

13. The XML namespace must be declared in the XML stream and then specified by the consuming XQuery.

14. After you declare the namespace you can use its prefix in the XPath expression.

15. If the XQuery is not using the namespace in its XPath then the data is not consumable and you will get an error.

16. The XML namespace takes one of your prefixes and associates it with a URN (Uniform Resource Name) or URI (Uniform Resource Identifier) for the XML stream or document you are consuming.

17. You can use the declare statement in the XQuery to define the namespace used by your XPath.

18. XML namespaces allow you to pull multiple simple names with different prefixes like this:

- Employee:Name
- grant:name

19. After you declare the namespace you can use its prefix in the path expression.

WITH XMLNAMESPACES Clause

A few years ago I took skiing lessons at an indoor facility that was essentially a carpet mountain. With practice all summer long in my t-shirt and shorts I learned to ski. It was a lot of fun but would I enjoy the real skiing on the real snow when the winter season hit? Not being sure but wanting to try it, it made more sense to rent skis for the winter for $150 rather than buy them for $900.

Halfway through the first year, I went skiing so often that it made sense for me to get my own gear. By owning my own skis, ski bag, goggles, and warm winter gear I am ready to go as often as I like.

Also, it makes more sense to buy a season pass for a few hundred dollars rather than paying $40 each day that I go up. When you know you are going to use something over and over again it makes sense to set yourself up to be ready. Your preparation pays off with each use.

So if you have a namespace that has many element names, do you have to declare each field each time you use it? By using the WITH XMLNAMESPACES clause you can prepare to consume many elements from a common namespace without having to declare each field over and over.

Supporting Unicode in XML

To start this section first open the Lab9.2Starter.SQL file in the C:\Joes2Pros\Resources folder. This example uses three XML elements in two different namespaces. The employee in this XML stream has the name of Rick Morelan but the <First:Name> Rick appears in the Cyrillic writing Рик while the <Last:Name> uses Latin letters Morelan.

```
DECLARE @XmlDoc XML =
'<root xmlns:First = "urn:First:Name" xmlns:Last =
 "urn:Last:Name">
<First:Name>Рик</First:Name>
<First:WorkDay>1999-09-01 00:00:00.000</First:WorkDay>
<Last:Name>Morelan</Last:Name>
</root>'
SELECT @XmlDoc
```

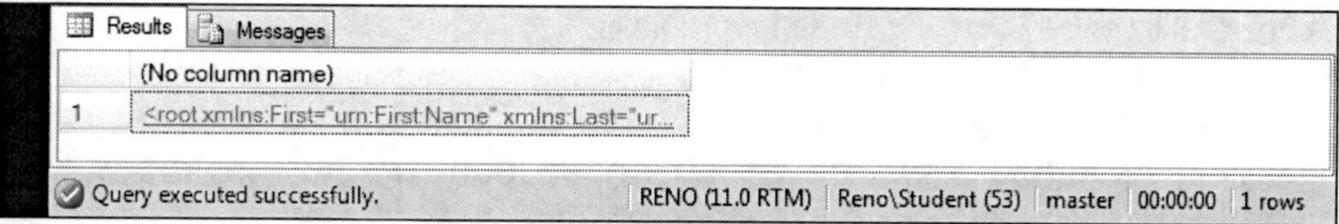

Figure 9.17 This shows the lab9.2Starter.sql file result.

When we open the link in Figure 9.17 we see the following XML:

```
<root xmlns:First="urn:First:Name"
  xmlns:Last="urn:Last:Name">
 <First:Name>???</First:Name>
 <First:WorkDay>1999-09-01 00:00:00.000</First:WorkDay>
 <Last:Name>Morelan</Last:Name>
</root>
```

Notice the <First:Name> text appears as question marks instead of the Cyrillic letters. To support international characters we have to use Unicode. All that is needed is an N before the XML stream. SQL will then be using Unicode supported characters.

```
DECLARE @XmlDoc XML =
N'<root xmlns:First = "urn:First:Name" xmlns:Last =
 "urn:Last:Name">
<First:Name>Рик</First:Name>
<First:WorkDay>1999-09-01 00:00:00.000</First:WorkDay>
<Last:Name>Morelan</Last:Name>
</root>'
SELECT @XmlDoc
```

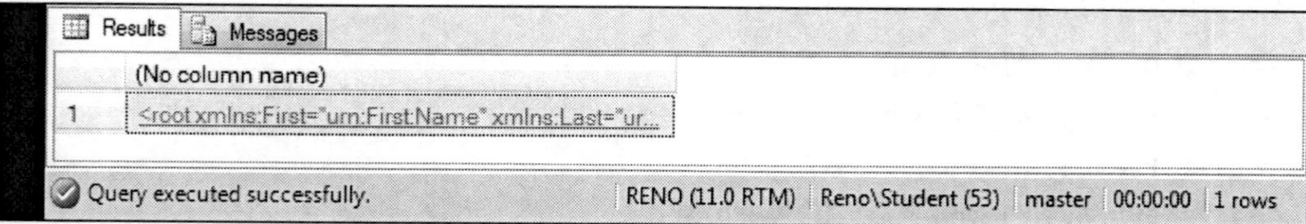

Figure 9.18 Uses Unicode to display the Cyrillic Рик for the First:Name Rick.

Open the link In Figure 9.18 and see that the Unicode N allowed the query to display international characters and the <First:Name> of Рик is displayed:

```
<root xmlns:First="urn:First:Name"
  xmlns:Last="urn:Last:Name">
 <First:Name>Рик</First:Name>
 <First:WorkDay>1999-09-01 00:00:00.000</First:WorkDay>
 <Last:Name>Morelan</Last:Name>
</root>
```

To support international characters use Unicode. The "N" prefix stands for National Language in the SQL-92 standard, and must be uppercase.

The WITH XMLNAMESPACES Clause

Let's start this section where we left off using international character supported Unicode with the XML prefix N:

```
DECLARE @XmlDoc XML =
N'<root xmlns:First = "urn:First:Name" xmlns:Last =
 "urn:Last:Name">
<First:Name>Рик</First:Name>
<First:WorkDay>1999-09-01 00:00:00.000</First:WorkDay>
<Last:Name>Morelan</Last:Name>
</root>'
SELECT @XmlDoc
```

Next we will consume this data with an XQuery statement. By now we should be well accustomed to writing an XQuery with a namespace. The difference will be that we must precede the declare statement of the query with the Unicode N. Declare the namespace and set it equal to "urn:First:Name" to match the declaration in the XML document.

```
DECLARE @XmlDoc XML =
N'<root xmlns:First = "urn:First:Name" xmlns:Last =
 "urn:Last:Name">
<First:Name>Рик</First:Name>
<First:WorkDay>1999-09-01 00:00:00.000</First:WorkDay>
<Last:Name>Morelan</Last:Name>
</root>'
SELECT @XmlDoc.query(N'declare namespace First =
"urn:First:Name"; /root/First:Name/text()');
```

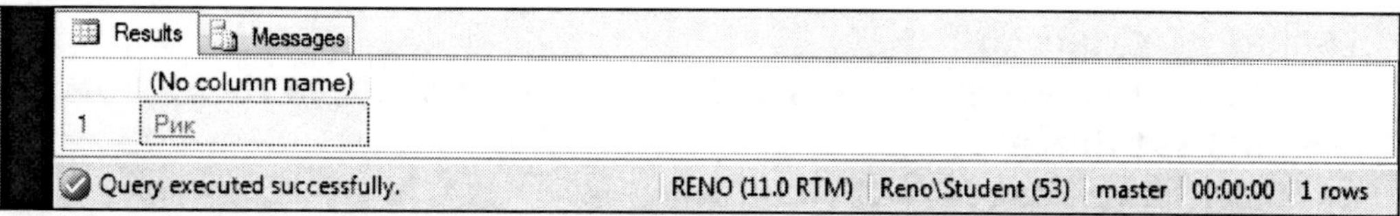

Figure 9.19 This shows the XQuery pulled out the <First:Name> of Рик using Unicode.

SQL Server can supply the XQuery with the namespace ahead of time by using the WITH XMLNAMESPACES clause. Start off by taking the declaration out of the XPath. Before the SELECT statement type WITH XMLNAMESPACES(). Inside the parentheses in single quotes add urn:First:Name and we will call this AS [First]. Finally add a semicolon to the end of the XML stream and this query is ready to run.

```
DECLARE @XmlDoc XML =
N'<root xmlns:First = "urn:First:Name" xmlns:Last =
  "urn:Last:Name">
 <First:Name>Рик</First:Name>
 <First:WorkDay>1999-09-01 00:00:00.000</First:WorkDay>
 <Last:Name>Morelan</Last:Name>
</root>';
WITH XMLNAMESPACES('urn:First:Name' AS [First])
SELECT @XmlDoc.query(N'/root/First:Name/text()');
```

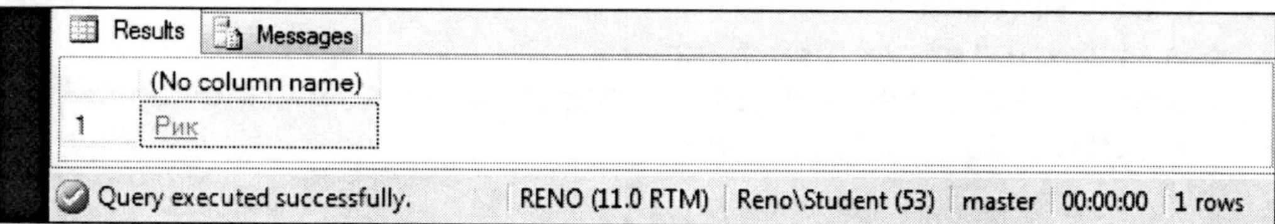

Figure 9.20 This shows we were able to pull the First:Name Рик using the WITH XMLNAMESPACES clause.

Рик is our <First:Name> in the XML string and Рик is what we got in our result (Figure 9.20). In SQL Server, you can supply your XQuery with the namespace ahead of time by using WITH XMLNAMESPACES.

Multiple Namespaces WITH XMLNAMESPACES

Take a look at the following code. It is very similar to the last example:

```
DECLARE @XmlDoc XML =
N'<root xmlns:First = "urn:First:Name" xmlns:Last =
  "urn:Last:Name">
 <First:Name>Lee</First:Name>
 <First:WorkDay>1999-09-01 00:00:00.000</First:WorkDay>
 <Last:Name>Osako</Last:Name>
</root>';
WITH XMLNAMESPACES('urn:First:Name' AS [First])
SELECT @XmlDoc.query(N'/root/First:Name/text()');
```

This code pulls out the named element from the <First:> namespace. What happens if we need to pull out multiple namespaces. Let's pull out both <First:Name> and <Last:Name> elements using the WITH XMLNAMESPACES clause. To declare the "Last" namespace, follow with a comma and in single quotes add urn:Last:Name and we will call this AS [Last]. Now that we have declared the namespace we need to call on it from the XQuery. Follow the first line of the SELECT statement with a comma and add a new line. Just like before, type @XmlDoc.query and inside the parentheses is the XPath for N'/root/Last:Name/text()';.

```
DECLARE @XmlDoc XML =
N'<root xmlns:First = "urn:First:Name" xmlns:Last =
  "urn:Last:Name">
 <First:Name>Lee</First:Name>
 <First:WorkDay>1999-09-01 00:00:00.000</First:WorkDay>
 <Last:Name>Osako</Last:Name>
</root>';
WITH XMLNAMESPACES('urn:First:Name' AS [First],
  'urn:Last:Name' AS [Last])
SELECT @XmlDoc.query(N'/root/First:Name/text()'),
 @XmlDoc.query(N'/root/Last:Name/text()') ;
```

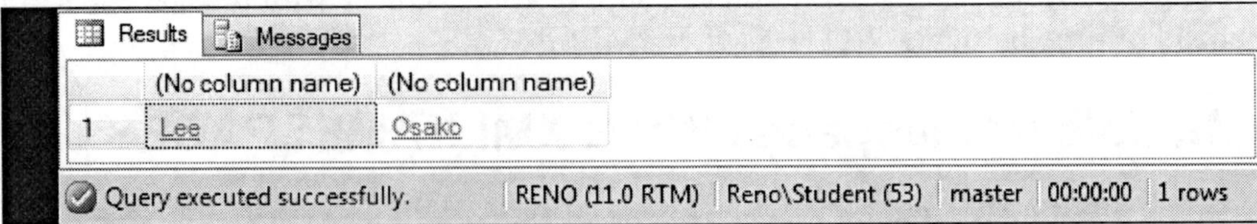

Figure 9.21 This shows WITH XMLNAMESPACES pulled out both Name elements.

In Figure 9.21 WITH XMLNAMESPACES successfully pulled out both the <:Name> elements from the XML string. The XML we are working with has three values. The second value in this XML string is the <First:WorkDay> element. The namespace <First:> has already been declared in the root of the

XML and in the WITH XMLNAMESPACES clause. All that is left is to call on it in the SELECT statement with one more XQuery just as before.

```
DECLARE @XmlDoc XML =
N'<root xmlns:First = "urn:First:Name" xmlns:Last =
  "urn:Last:Name">
 <First:Name>Lee</First:Name>
 <First:WorkDay>1999-09-01 00:00:00.000</First:WorkDay>
 <Last:Name>Osako</Last:Name>
</root>';
WITH XMLNAMESPACES('urn:First:Name' AS [First],
  'urn:Last:Name' AS [Last])
SELECT @XmlDoc.query(N'/root/First:Name/text()'),
 @XmlDoc.query(N'/root/Last:Name/text()'),
 @XmlDoc.query(N'/root/First:WorkDay/text()') ;
```

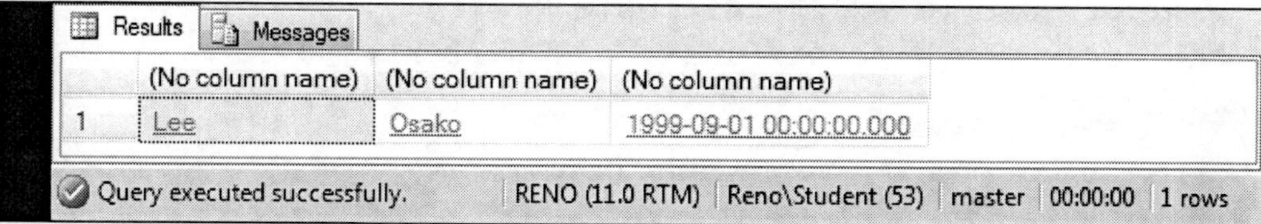

	(No column name)	(No column name)	(No column name)
1	Lee	Osako	1999-09-01 00:00:00.000

Figure 9.22 This shows the WITH XMLNAMESPACES clause allowed the XQuery to pull out three values from two namespaces.

In Figure 9.22 we were able to shred the XML using WITH XMLNAMESPACES and pull out <:Name> and <:WorkDay> from the <First:> namespace and <:Name> from the <Last:> namespace.

Multiple Test Values WITH XMLNAMESPACES

We left off in the last example with the following code.

```
DECLARE @XmlDoc XML =
N'<root xmlns:First = "urn:First:Name" xmlns:Last =
  "urn:Last:Name">
 <First:Name>Lee</First:Name>
 <First:WorkDay>1999-09-01 00:00:00.000</First:WorkDay>
 <Last:Name>Osako</Last:Name>
</root>';
WITH XMLNAMESPACES('urn:First:Name' AS [First],
  'urn:Last:Name' AS [Last])
SELECT @XmlDoc.query(N'/root/First:Name/text()'),
 @XmlDoc.query(N'/root/Last:Name/text()'),
 @XmlDoc.query(N'/root/First:WorkDay/text()') ;
```

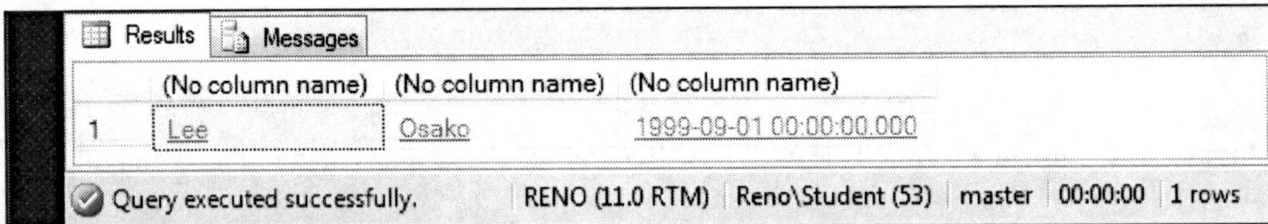

Figure 9.23 This shows the WITH XMLNAMESPACES clause allowed the XQuery to pull out three values from two namespaces.

We were able pull out three different fields from two different name spaces. We pulled out <:WorkDay> from the <First:> namespace, we pulled out <:Name> from the <First:> namespace, and we pulled out <:Name> from the <:last> namespace.

With one employee this works great. What happens if there are multiple employees? Look at the following code and notice we have added a new employee complete with <First:Name>, <First:WorkDay> and <Last:Name> elements. Both namespaces are declared and all three elements from both employees are called on in the SELECT statement. What result can we predict?

```
DECLARE @XmlDoc XML =
N'<root xmlns:First = "urn:First:Name" xmlns:Last =
  "urn:Last:Name">
 <First:Name>Lee</First:Name>
 <First:WorkDay>1999-09-01 00:00:00.000</First:WorkDay>
 <Last:Name>Osako</Last:Name>
 <First:Name>David</First:Name>
 <First:WorkDay>1996-03-16 00:00:00.000</First:WorkDay>
 <Last:Name>Kennson</Last:Name>
</root>';
WITH XMLNAMESPACES('urn:First:Name' AS [First],
  'urn:Last:Name' AS [Last])
SELECT @XmlDoc.query(N'/root/First:Name/text()'),
 @XmlDoc.query(N'/root/Last:Name/text()'),
 @XmlDoc.query(N'/root/First:WorkDay/text()');
```

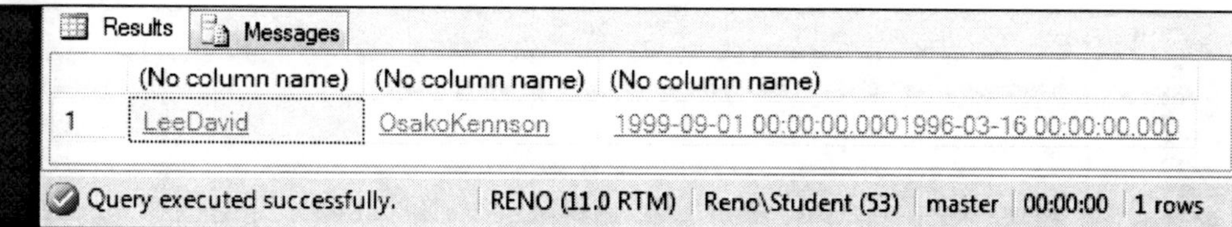

Figure 9.24 This shows the XQuery concatenated each element from the namespaces.

Figure 9.24 shows LeeDavid, OsakoKennson, and a concatenation of the two dates. The question is obvious. How are we going to differentiate the multiple values for each element of the namespace? Look at the SELECT statement and notice the entire XPath is contained within a set of parentheses. If we want to pull out the first employee which is “Lee Osako”, place a second set of parentheses around the actual path in the XQuery that does not include the text() method. Follow that with a [1] inside a set of brackets. The bracketed [1] directs the XQuery to the first employee. Follow this process for all three XQueries and we will pull out all the data from the first employee in the XML string.

```
DECLARE @XmlDoc XML =
N'<root xmlns:First = "urn:First:Name" xmlns:Last =
  "urn:Last:Name">
 <First:Name>Lee</First:Name>
 <First:WorkDay>1999-09-01 00:00:00.000</First:WorkDay>
 <Last:Name>Osako</Last:Name>
 <First:Name>David</First:Name>
 <First:WorkDay>1996-03-16 00:00:00.000</First:WorkDay>
 <Last:Name>Kennson</Last:Name>
</root>';
WITH XMLNAMESPACES('urn:First:Name' AS [First],
  'urn:Last:Name' AS [Last])
SELECT @XmlDoc.query(N'(/root/First:Name)[1]/text()'),
 @XmlDoc.query(N'(/root/Last:Name)[1]/text()'),
 @XmlDoc.query(N'(/root/First:WorkDay)[1]/text()');
```

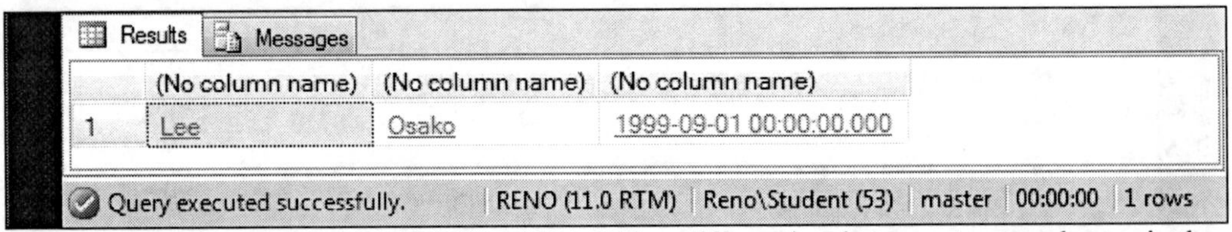

Results | Messages

	(No column name)	(No column name)	(No column name)
1	Lee	Osako	1999-09-01 00:00:00.000

Query executed successfully. | RENO (11.0 RTM) | Reno\Student (53) | master | 00:00:00 | 1 rows

Figure 9.25 This uses WITH XMLNAMESPACES to differentiate between two employees in the same namespaces level.

Lab 9.2: WITH XMLNAMESPACES Clause

Lab Prep: Each lab has one or more Skill Checks. Start with Skill Check 1 and proceed until reaching the Points to Ponder section.

Before beginning this lab, verify that SQL Server 2012 is properly installed and operating. Before running the lab setup script for resetting the database (SQLQueries2012Vol5Chapter9.0-9.2Setup.sql), please make sure to close all query windows within SSMS. An open query window pointing to a database context can lock that database preventing it from updating when the script is executing. A simple way to assure all query windows are closed, is to exit out of SSMS, then open a new instance of SSMS, and lastly run the setup script.

Skill Check1: Open the Lab9.2SK1.sql file found in the C:\Joes2Pros\Resources folder. The XML stream holds two records. The first record contains George Washington and the second John Adams. There are a total of six values. Write a query that pulls the text from the First and Last element of the <Name:> namespace for the first record, George Washington. When done your result should resemble the figure you see here.

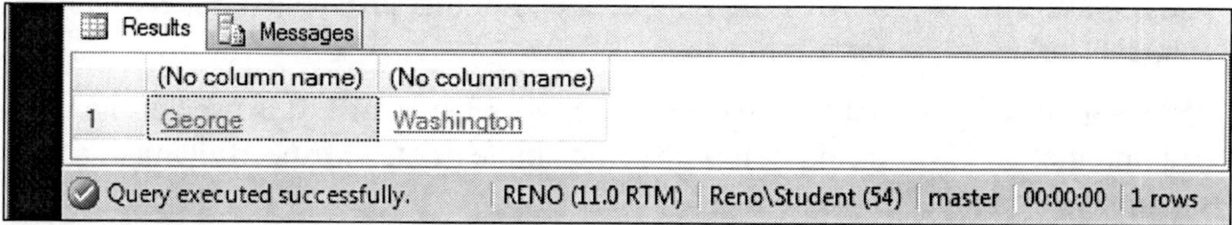

Figure 9.26 This shows the result from Skill Check 1.

Answer Code: The T-SQL code to this lab can be found in the downloadable files in a file named Lab9.2_WITH XMLNAMESPACES_Clause.sql.

Point to Ponder - WITH NAMESPACES

1. To specify Unicode to support international characters use the "N" prefix before the first single quotes.
2. The "N" stands for National Language in the SQL-92 standard, and must be uppercase.
3. XML Namespaces can help differentiate between the same name uses.
4. In SQL Server you can supply your XQuery with the namespace ahead of time by using the WITH XMLNAMESPACES clause.

Chapter Glossary

XPath: The XML path used to specify the location of the needed data within the XML.

XQuery: A query that uses an XPath to specify the location of the needed data.

XML Namespaces: An XML naming convention that provides uniquely named elements between the same name uses.

"N": Stands for National Language in the SQL-92 standard. It is used at the beginning of an XML string before the first single quotes to specify Unicode to support international characters.

WITH XMLNAMESPACES: A SQL clause that allows the namespace to be supplied to the XQuery ahead of time.

Review Quiz - Chapter Nine

1.) You have the following code that throws an error message:

```
DECLARE @XmlDoc XML =
'<root xmlns:Employee = "urn:EmployeeData">
<Employee:Name>Lee Osako</Employee:Name>
</root>'
SELECT @XmlDoc.query('/root/Employee:Name/text()')
```

What is the reason for the error?

O a. You need a capital N before the first single quote.

O b. The namespace is not declared or missing in the root.

O c. The namespace is not declared or missing in the XQuery.

2.) You have the following code:

```
DECLARE @XmlDoc XML =
N'<root xmlns:Last = "urn:Last:Name" >
<Last:Name>Morelan</Last:Name>
</root>'
SELECT @XmlDoc
```

What does the N before the first single quote mean?

O a. Namespace

O b. Unicode

O c. Indent

O d. Element

3.) What allows you to specify the XQuery namespaces ahead of time?

O a. WITH XMLNAMESPACES

O b. DECLARE

O c. <:>

Answer Key

1.) If you forget to specify N for Unicode you will not get an error, so (a) is wrong. The namespace is declared in the root but not the XQuery, so (b) is wrong, but (c) is the correct answer.

2.) To specify Unicode to support international characters, use the N prefix. This makes (b) correct.

3.) In SQL Server you can supply your XQuery with the namespace ahead of time by using the WITH XMLNAMESPACES clause, so (a) is correct.

Bug Catcher

To play the Bug Catcher game run the SQLQueries2012Vol5BugCatcher9.pps from the BugCatcher folder of the companion files found at www.Joes2Pros.com.

[THIS PAGE INTENTIONALLY LEFT BLANK.]

Chapter 10. XML Schemas & Processing

Do you know how to pack for the family vacation? Knowing ahead of time if it's a winter vacation or a summer vacation might make a big difference. Even if you don't know exactly what you are going to do each minute of the day you can prepare very well by knowing the overall theme. This theme to help us mostly be prepared ahead of time acts much like the XML processing instructions.

Sometimes we can set our own rules of what is allowed and not allowed. Making your own rules of dos and don'ts in SQL means using your own XML Schema design. This chapter will cover XML Schemas and some XML Pre-Processing.

READERNOTE:*Please run the SQLQueries2012Vol5Chapter10.0Setup.sql script in order to follow along with the examples in the first section of Chapter 10. All scripts mentioned in this chapter may be found at* ***www.Joes2Pros.com****.*

XML Prolog

Like most languages and technologies, XML is evolving and improving. If your XML was written many years ago it will still work in the more modern interpretation engines. The XML prolog provides some up front information about what to expect from the XML stream.

XML Prolog Version

Let's again look at the Lab9.2Starter.sql file. You'll find it in the C:\Joes2Pros\Resources folder. In Figure 10.1 we've got the first name which is the Cyrillic Рик (Rick), the workday which is in 1999 and the last name of Morelan.

```
DECLARE @XmlDoc XML =
'<root xmlns:first = "urn:First:Name" xmlns:last =
 "urn:Last:Name" >
<First:Name>Рик</First:Name>
<First:WorkDay>1999-09-01 00:00:00.000</First:WorkDay>
<Last:Name>Morelan</Last:Name>
</root>'
SELECT @XmlDoc
```

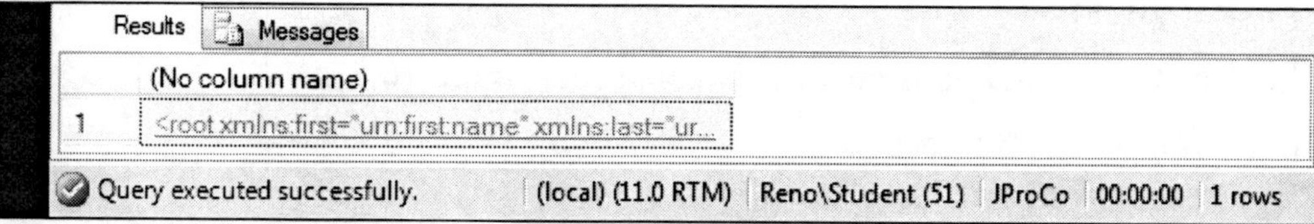

Figure 10.1 This shows the result from the Lab9.2Starter.sql file.

Take a look inside the link from Figure 10.1.

```
xmlresult1.xml*   SQLQuery1.sql - (lo...(Reno\Student (51))*
<root xmlns:first="urn:first:name" xmlns:last="urn:last:name">
  <first:name>???</first:name>
  <first:workday>1999-09-01 00:00:00.000</first:workday>
  <last:name>Morelan</last:name>
</root>
```

Figure 10.2 This shows the open link from Figure 10.1.

<Last:Name> Morelan shows up just fine and we see the workday no problem, but Рик did not come through. The Cyrillic Rick was replaced with question

marks. As we learned in Chapter 9 the Unicode can be supported by putting a capital N before the first single quote as seen in the follow code:

```
DECLARE @XmlDoc XML =
N'<root xmlns:first = "urn:First:Name" xmlns:last =
 "urn:Last:Name" >
<First:Name>Рик</First:Name>
<First:WorkDay>1999-09-01 00:00:00.000</First:WorkDay>
<Last:Name>Morelan</Last:Name>
</root>'
SELECT @XmlDoc
```

Next we are going to add the XML prolog. So far we have not used a prolog in any of our past XML examples in this book. The prolog is an optional processing instruction at the top of the XML stream. Processing instructions help give information to applications consuming the XML as to what XML standard to expect from the XML stream. The prolog will be in a tag following the Unicode N and inside the single quotes. The XML prolog has a question mark at each end of the tag:

```
<??>
```

Between the question marks let's type “xml version =” and in double quotes “1.0”. This 1.0 defines what version of XML is being used:

```
<?xml version="1.0"?>
```

Let's add this to our code and see what we get (Figure 10.3).

```
DECLARE @XmlDoc XML =
N'<?xml version="1.0"?>
<root xmlns:first = "urn:First:Name" xmlns:last =
"urn:Last:Name" >
<First:Name>Рик</First:Name>
<First:WorkDay>1999-09-01 00:00:00.000</First:WorkDay>
<Last:Name>Morelan</Last:Name>
</root>'
SELECT @XmlDoc
```

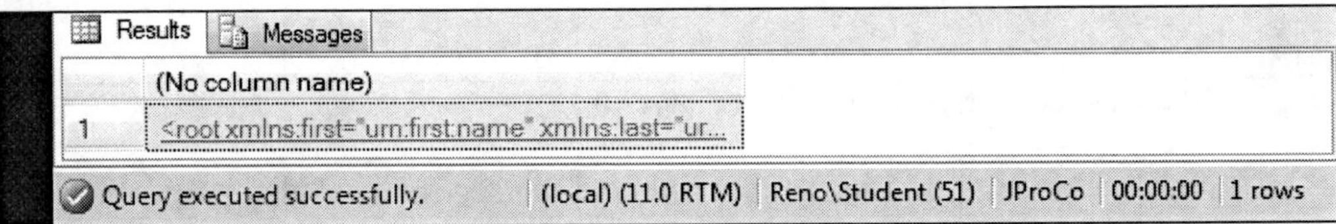

Figure 10.3 This shows the result from the Lab9.2Starter.sql file with the Unicode and XML prolog.

In Figure 10.4 we see the Cyrillic Rick, the first workday and the last name.

```
xmlresult3.xml*  xmlresult2.xml*  SQLQuery2.sql - RE...(Reno\Student (51))*
<root xmlns:First="urn:First:Name" xmlns:Last="urn:Last:Name">
  <First:Name>Рик</First:Name>
  <First:WorkDay>1999-09-01 00:00:00.000</First:WorkDay>
  <Last:Name>Morelan</Last:Name>
</root>
```

Figure 10.4 This shows the open link from Figure 10.3 with all three values.

XML is not very particular about white spaces. As a matter fact, if we put five spaces before the <root> and then we run it, the query runs the same (Figure 10.5).

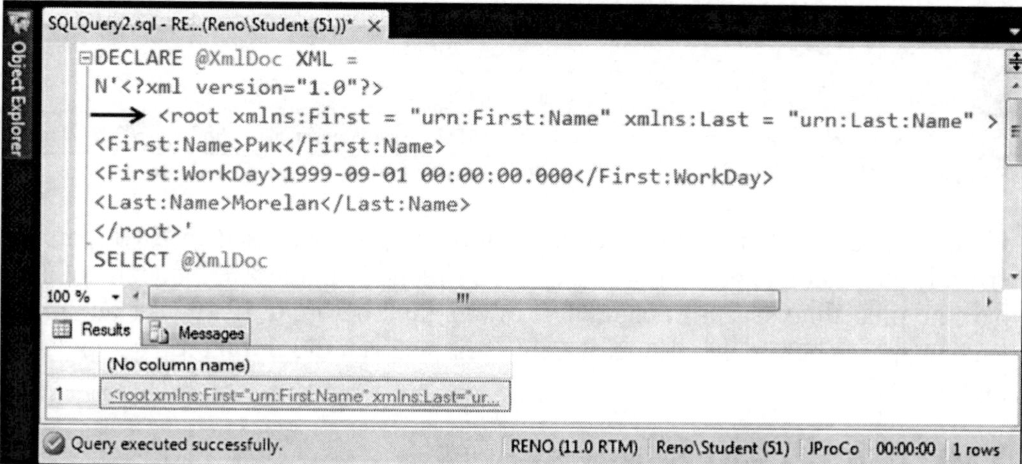

Figure 10.5 This shows indenting the root five spaces had no effect on the query.

Figure 10.5 show us that adding the five spaces in front of the root had no effect on the result.

```
xmlresult4.xml  SQLQuery2.sql - RE...(Reno\Student (51))*
<root xmlns:First="urn:First:Name" xmlns:Last="urn:Last:Name">
  <First:Name>Рик</First:Name>
  <First:WorkDay>1999-09-01 00:00:00.000</First:WorkDay>
  <Last:Name>Morelan</Last:Name>
</root>
```

Figure 10.6 This shows the open link from Figure 10.5.

The XML processing instruction in the prolog is enclosed within a set of bracket question mark tags. The target is placed inside the tag. Let's see how XML accepts whitespace before the prolog by adding five spaces before the opening tag of the prolog (Figure 10.7).

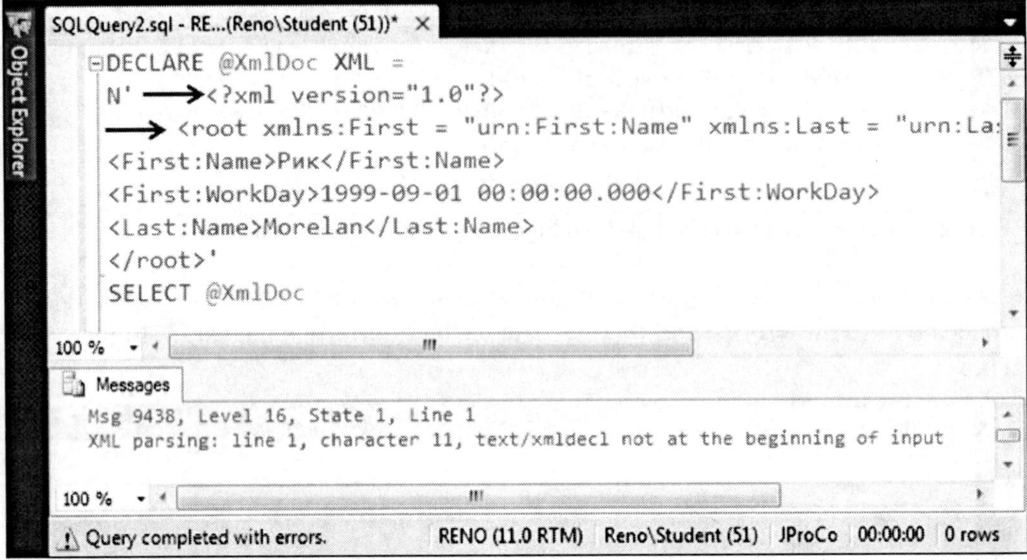

Figure 10.7 This shows white space in front of the prolog causes the query to throw an error.

Figure 10.7 shows that white space in front of the prolog caused an XML parsing error. If the prolog is present, it must be the first node in the XML document and have no preceding spaces or characters of any kind before it. If we take out all the leading spaces before the prolog, it will work just as it did in Figure 10.5 and Figure 10.6.

XML Prolog Encoding Specifier

Let's start with the Unicode supported XML stream conforming to the XML version 1.0 standard.

```
DECLARE @XmlDoc XML =
N'<?xml version="1.0"?>
<root xmlns:first = "urn:First:Name" xmlns:last =
  "urn:Last:Name" >
 <First:Name>Рик</First:Name>
 <First:WorkDay>1999-09-01 00:00:00.000</First:WorkDay>
 <Last:Name>Morelan</Last:Name>
</root>'
SELECT @XmlDoc
```

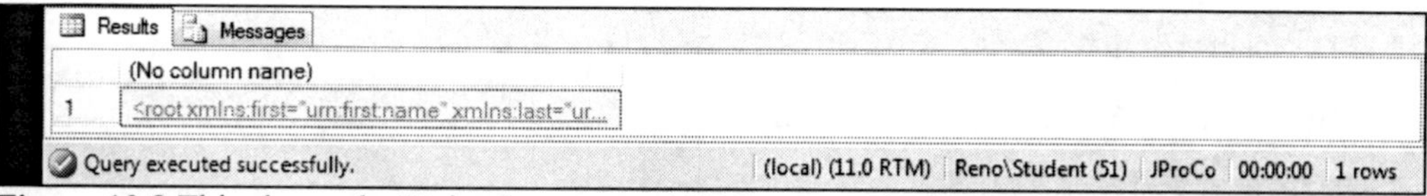

Figure 10.8 This shows the Unicode supported XML stream in the version 1.0 standard.

Remember what happened when we did not tell SQL to support Unicode? If we take out this N and we run it, the data shows three question marks instead of Рик.

```
DECLARE @XmlDoc XML =
'<?xml version="1.0"?>
<root xmlns:first = "urn:First:Name" xmlns:last =
  "urn:Last:Name" >
 <First:Name>Рик</First:Name>
 <First:WorkDay>1999-09-01 00:00:00.000</First:WorkDay>
 <Last:Name>Morelan</Last:Name>
</root>'
SELECT @XmlDoc
```

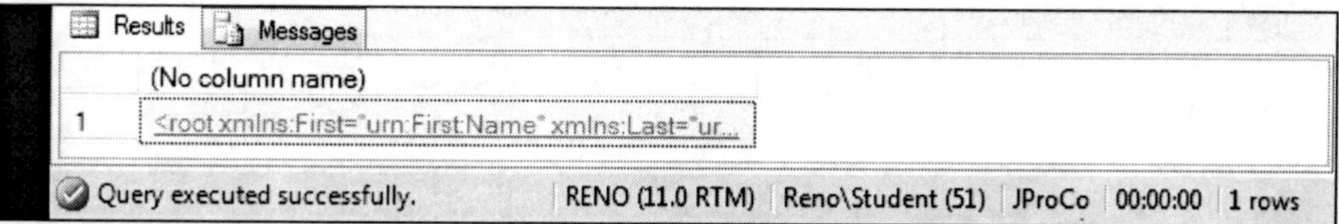

Figure 10.9 This shows the query without the Unicode supported XML.

xmlresult5.xml × SQLQuery2.sql - RE...(Reno\Student (51))*

Object Explorer

```
<root xmlns:First="urn:First:Name" xmlns:Last="urn:Last:Name">
  <First:Name>???</First:Name>
  <First:WorkDay>1999-09-01 00:00:00.000</First:WorkDay>
  <Last:Name>Morelan</Last:Name>
</root>
```

Figure 10.10 This shows international characters will not be displayed if Unicode is not supported.

Put the N back and the query will feed the Unicode encoded data in the XML and stream these characters. By default, XML supports Unicode encoded data.

To support all of the possible characters of the world, Unicode takes up more memory than ASCII letters. Unicode is 16-bits per letter, where ASCII is only eight. XML supports 16-bit Unicode by default. We can optionally put the encoding specifier we want in the prolog. To do this, add a space after the "1.0" in the prolog and set encoding equal to UTF-16 in quotes as shown here:

```
<?xml version="1.0" encoding = "UTF-16"?>
```

Put this in the XML and run the query.

```
DECLARE @XmlDoc XML =
N'<?xml version="1.0" encoding = "UTF-16"?>
<root xmlns:first = "urn:First:Name" xmlns:last =
  "urn:Last:Name" >
 <First:Name>Рик</First:Name>
 <First:WorkDay>1999-09-01 00:00:00.000</First:WorkDay>
 <Last:Name>Morelan</Last:Name>
</root>'
SELECT @XmlDoc
```

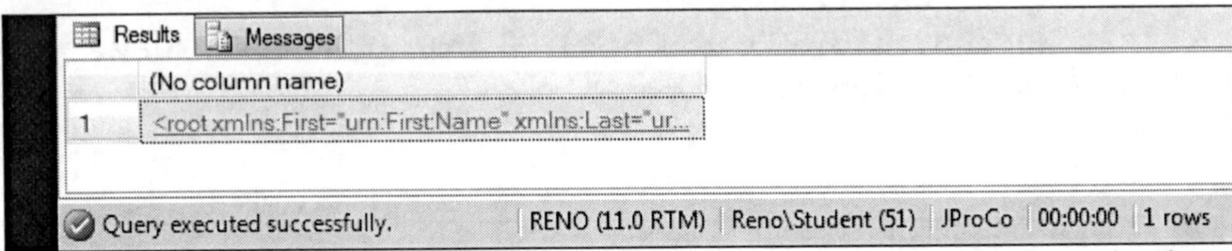

Figure 10.11 This shows the result of our query with the optional encoding specifier setting the Unicode to 16-bit.

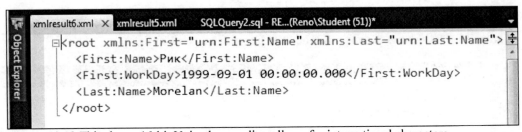

xmlresult6.xml × xmlresult5.xml SQLQuery2.sql - RE...(Reno\Student (51))*

Object Explorer

```
<root xmlns:First="urn:First:Name" xmlns:Last="urn:Last:Name">
  <First:Name>Рик</First:Name>
  <First:WorkDay>1999-09-01 00:00:00.000</First:WorkDay>
  <Last:Name>Morelan</Last:Name>
</root>
```

Figure 10.12 This shows 16-bit Unicode encoding allows for international characters.

Figure 10.11 and Figure 10.12 shows that if 16-bit is supported, Unicode will display international characters such as the Cyrillic Рик. Encoding instructions are known as the encoding specifier. The prolog can include either the XML version number, or encoding specifier or both. If the XML stream has no Unicode to be consumed then space consumption can be saved by choosing the UTF-8 encoding scheme.

```
DECLARE @XmlDoc XML =
N'<?xml version="1.0" encoding = "UTF-8"?>
<root xmlns:first = "urn:First:Name" xmlns:last =
  "urn:Last:Name" >
 <First:Name>Рик</First:Name>
 <First:WorkDay>1999-09-01 00:00:00.000</First:WorkDay>
 <Last:Name>Morelan</Last:Name>
</root>'
SELECT @XmlDoc
```

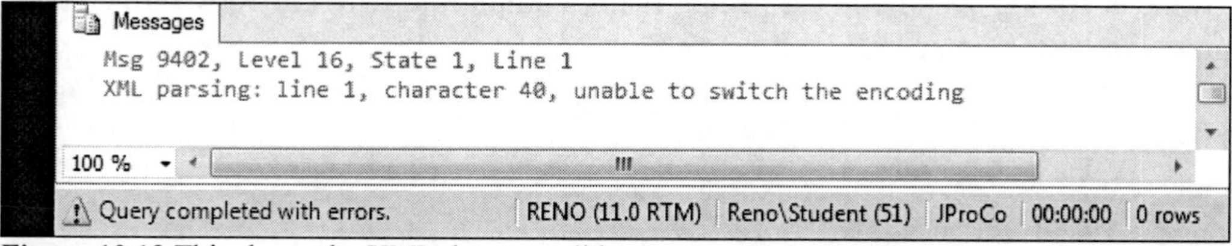

Figure 10.13 This shows the XML data type did not expect Unicode due to the encoding specifier.

In Figure 10.13 the stream caused an error because the prolog told the XML data type not to expect any Unicode, but we are in fact feeding it Unicode. Let's keep the 8-bit encoding and remove the N so we are not feeding it as Unicode XML.

```
DECLARE @XmlDoc XML =
'<?xml version="1.0" encoding = "UTF-8"?>
<root xmlns:first = "urn:First:Name" xmlns:last =
  "urn:Last:Name" >
 <First:Name>Рик</First:Name>
 <First:WorkDay>1999-09-01 00:00:00.000</First:WorkDay>
 <Last:Name>Morelan</Last:Name>
</root>'
SELECT @XmlDoc
```

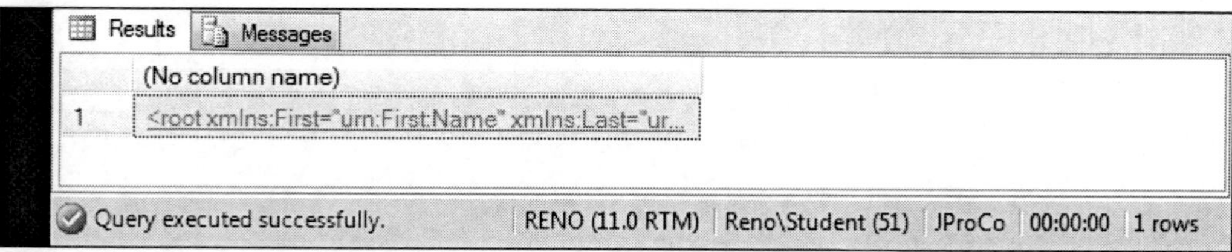

Figure 10.14 Removing the Unicode specifier N allowed the 8 bit encoding to run successfully.

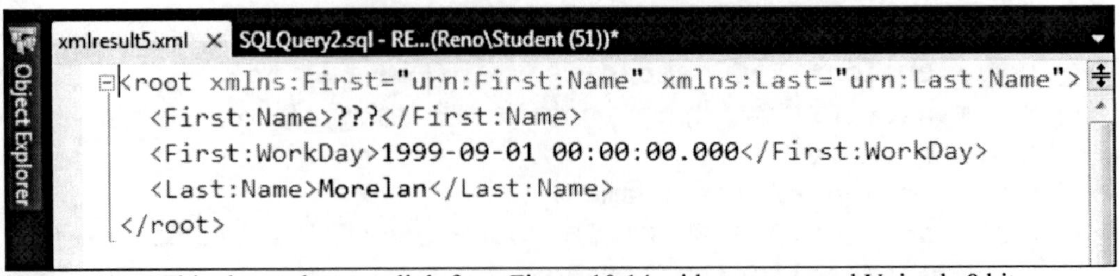

xmlresult5.xml × SQLQuery2.sql - RE...(Reno\Student (51))*

Object Explorer

```
<root xmlns:First="urn:First:Name" xmlns:Last="urn:Last:Name">
  <First:Name>???</First:Name>
  <First:WorkDay>1999-09-01 00:00:00.000</First:WorkDay>
  <Last:Name>Morelan</Last:Name>
</root>
```

Figure 10.15 This shows the open link from Figure 10.14 with unsupported Unicode 8 bit character type.

If the encoding scheme in the prolog is not compatible with the body of the XML it will result in an error.

Lab 10.1: XML Prolog

Lab Prep: Each lab has one or more Skill Checks. Start with Skill Check 1 and proceed until reaching the Points to Ponder section.

Before beginning this lab, verify that SQL Server 2012 is properly installed and operating. Before running the lab setup script for resetting the database (SQLQueries2012Vol5Chapter10.1Setup.sql), please make sure to close all query windows within SSMS. An open query window pointing to a database context can lock that database preventing it from updating when the script is executing. A simple way to assure all query windows are closed, is to exit out of SSMS, then open a new instance of SSMS, and lastly run the setup script.

Skill Check 1: Open the C:\Joes2Pros\Resources\Lab10.1SK1.sql file and correct the code to run without error. You are not allowed to change the encoding scheme in the prolog. When done the result should resemble Figure 10.16.

```
--Corrected Code
SELECT @XmlDoc
```

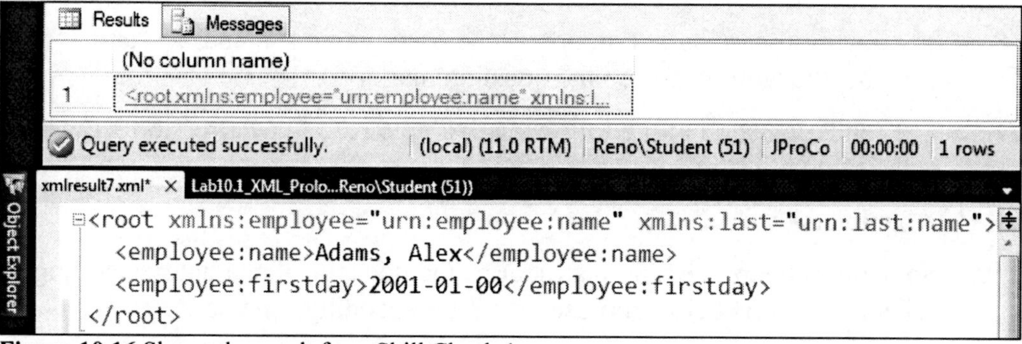

Figure 10.16 Shows the result from Skill Check 1.

Answer Code: The T-SQL code to this lab can be found in the downloadable files in a file named Lab10.1_XML_Prolog.sql.

Points to Ponder - XML Prolog

1. The Prolog is an optional processing instruction at the top of the XML stream.
2. Processing instructions help give information to applications consuming the XML as to the XML standard to expect from the stream.
3. The prolog includes the XML version number and can include encoding instructions known as an encoding specifier.
4. If the Prolog is present it must be the first node in the XML document and have no preceding spaces or characters of any kind.
5. By default XML supports Unicode encoded data.
6. To support all the possible characters of the world, Unicode takes more memory than ASCII letters. In fact, Unicode is 16-bits per letter where ASCII is only 8.
7. If the encoding scheme in the prolog is not compatible with the body of the XML then you get a parsing error message.
8. The XML processing instruction is enclosed within '<?' and '?>', and contains the target between the question marks.
9. The rendering style of the following example is for XML version 1.0 which is the standard:

   <?xml version="1.0"?>

10. Sometimes the processing instructions include a local character encoding scheme. The one below represents a 7-bit encoding scheme.

    <?xml version="1.0" encoding="UTF-7"?>

11. If there is a line above the root node (root element) then it is the prolog which is the processing instructions for the XML stream.

    <?xml version=”1.0”?>

XML Schema Definitions

If we are traveling to another country we might have some restrictions like not bringing any fruit. Packing fruit in your suitcase when you drive 50 kilometers to your relative's home is easy to do. It's also easy to pack fruit into your suitcase, but it's not allowed. In this case you can put further restrictions on what is possible by using an XML schema definition. This section will show how to create and use your own schema definitions to set your own company standards.

Valid XML (Review)

Sometimes you will have a valid XML stream that is not usable for your company standards. In this case let's say the JProCo Inc. company standards are that all XML is well-formed and <root> tags must be named <Hello World>.

```
DECLARE @XML1 XML = '<HelloWorld>1</HelloWorld>'
```

```
Messages
Command(s) completed successfully.
                                                          0 rows
```

Figure 10.17 This shows well-formed XML within company standards.

This first line works and is within our company standards. Let's add another almost identical variable called @XML2. This variable will have the value of 2.

```
DECLARE @XML2 XML = '<HelloWorld>2</HelloWorld>'
```

```
Messages
Command(s) completed successfully.
                                                          0 rows
```

Figure 10.18 This shows XML2 is also well-formed XML within company standards.

XML2 works great as well. Let's create the @XML3 variable but this time we will not use well-formed XML. Let's change just the ending tag to be <Goodbye World>.

```
DECLARE @XML3 XML = '<HelloWorld>3</GoodbyeWorld>'
```

```
Messages
Msg 9436, Level 16, State 1, Line 1
XML parsing: line 1, character 28, end tag does not match start tag
                                                          0 rows
```

Figure 10.19 This shows malformed XML. The ending tag must match the opening tag.

In Figure 10.19 we get an error. The @XML3 variable does not contain well-formed XML and is not a valid fragment. The XML data type makes sure the schema is either well-formed or a valid XML fragment.

Let's create the @XML4 variable. With this variable we are going to have well-formed XML but we're going to name the element as <GoodbyeWorld>.

```
DECLARE @XML4 XML = '<GoodbyeWorld>4</GoodbyeWorld>'
```

Messages
Command(s) completed successfully.
0 rows

Figure 10.20 This shows @XML4 works because it is well-formed but is not up to JProCo standards.

As we see in Figure 10.20 the code ran without error. The @XML4 variable is well-formed, but does not comply with company standards. Let's create one more variable called @XML5. We will keep the company naming standard but we will spell FIVE instead of the number 5.

```
DECLARE @XML5 XML = '<HelloWorld>Five</HelloWorld>'
```

Messages
Command(s) completed successfully.
0 rows

Figure 10.21 This shows @XML5 is well-formed and runs without error.

The @XML5 variable is well-formed and uses company naming standards, but is using an unapproved data type. JProCo only allows numbers in the element root text. The XML data type by itself will not enforce specific company naming standards or relationships within the XML stream.

Creating an XML Schema Definition

The JProCo company standards are that all XML root tags must be named <HelloWorld> and also only allows numbers in the root text node. Take a moment to look at these five XML variables:

```
DECLARE @XML1 XML = '<HelloWorld>1</HelloWorld>'
DECLARE @XML2 XML = '<HelloWorld>2</HelloWorld>'
DECLARE @XML3 XML = '<Hello>3</Hello>'
DECLARE @XML4 XML = '<GoodbyeWorld>4</GoodbyeWorld>'
DECLARE @XML5 XML = '<HelloWorld>Five</HelloWorld>'
```

We have changed @XML3 to now be well-formed. Notice that @XML1 and @XML2 fit our company standards. @XML3, @XML4, and @XML5 are well-formed but not up to company naming standards. All five statements run because they are valid XML. We want to prevent any XML that does not adhere to our company schema from running. An XML schema is a set of rules an XML stream must adhere to in order to be validated. Let's open a new query window but don't close the existing window since we will be coming back to these five variables very soon.

In a new query window let's create an XML schema definition that requires the root to be named <HelloWorld>, and the element text to be an integer data type:

```
<HelloWorld>1</HelloWorld>
```

To create the schema definition type CREATE XML SCHEMA COLLECTION WorldSchema AS. Next we will put the <root> node which is:

```
'<xsd:schema>
</xsd:schema>'
```

Here, xsd is commonly used and stands for XML schema definition. Next we will paste in the World Consortium web address for the XML namespace:

```
'<xsd:schema xmlns:xsd="http://www.w3.org/2001/XMLSchema">
</xsd:schema>'
```

In the body of the XML schema let's set the xsd:element equal to HelloWorld and set the type equal to xsd:int (integer).

```
CREATE XML SCHEMA COLLECTION WorldSchema
AS
'<xsd:schema xmlns:xsd="http://www.w3.org/2001/XMLSchema">
<xsd:element name="HelloWorld" type="xsd:int"/>
</xsd:schema>'
```

Messages
Command(s) completed successfully.
0 rows

Figure 10.22 This shows the WorldSchema was created successfully.

In Figure 10.22 we see that the WorldSchema was created successfully.

Back in the query window with our XML variables, we know @XML1 fits the company schema. To ensure it complies, pass it through the xsd schema we created.

```
DECLARE @XML1 XML(WorldSchema) ='<HelloWorld>1</HelloWorld>'
DECLARE @XML2 XML = '<HelloWorld>2</HelloWorld>'
DECLARE @XML3 XML = '<Hello>3</Hello>'
DECLARE @XML4 XML = '<GoodbyeWorld>4</GoodbyeWorld>'
DECLARE @XML5 XML = '<HelloWorld>Five</HelloWorld>'
```

Messages
Command(s) completed successfully.
0 rows

Figure 10.23 This shows the @XML1 variable complies and passed successfully through the company schema.

@XML1 does in fact comply with company standards and passed successfully through the WorldSchema (Figure 10.23). The xsd schema can be associated with one or more XML variables. So, let's parse the remaining XML variables with the same schema:

```
DECLARE @XML1 XML(WorldSchema) ='<HelloWorld>1</HelloWorld>'
DECLARE @XML2 XML(WorldSchema) ='<HelloWorld>2</HelloWorld>'
DECLARE @XML3 XML = '<Hello>3</Hello>'
DECLARE @XML4 XML = '<GoodbyeWorld>4</GoodbyeWorld>'
DECLARE @XML5 XML = '<HelloWorld>Five</HelloWorld>'
```

Messages
Command(s) completed successfully.
0 rows

Figure 10.24 This shows the @XML2 variable complies and passed successfully through the company schema.

The @XML2 variable passes through the XML schema successfully and is compliant with company standards. We suspect that @XML3 is not compliant. To test this out let's pass it through WorldSchema.

```
DECLARE @XML1 XML(WorldSchema) ='<HelloWorld>1</HelloWorld>'
DECLARE @XML2 XML(WorldSchema) ='<HelloWorld>2</HelloWorld>'
DECLARE @XML3 XML(WorldSchema) = '<Hello>3</Hello>'
DECLARE @XML4 XML = '<GoodbyeWorld>4</GoodbyeWorld>'
DECLARE @XML5 XML = '<HelloWorld>Five</HelloWorld>'
```

```
Messages
Msg 6913, Level 16, State 1, Line 1
XML Validation: Declaration not found for element 'Hello'. Location:
/*:Hello[1]
                                                              0 rows
```

Figure 10.25 This shows that the @XML3 variable does not comply and did not successfully pass through the schema.

When we try to assign @XML3 we get an error message. The element root <Hello> does not meet the schema definition and does not get passed to the variable. Let's try @XML4.

```
DECLARE @XML1 XML(WorldSchema) ='<HelloWorld>1</HelloWorld>'
DECLARE @XML2 XML(WorldSchema) ='<HelloWorld>2</HelloWorld>'
DECLARE @XML3 XML(WorldSchema) ='<Hello>3</Hello>'
DECLARE @XML4 XML(WorldSchema)=
 '<GoodbyeWorld>4</GoodbyeWorld>'
DECLARE @XML5 XML ='<HelloWorld>Five</HelloWorld>'
```

```
Messages
Msg 6913, Level 16, State 1, Line 1
XML Validation: Declaration not found for element 'GoodbyeWorld'. Location:
/*:GoodbyeWorld[1]
                                                              0 rows
```

Figure 10.26 This shows that the @XML4 variable does not comply and did not successfully pass through the schema.

The <GoodbyeWorld> root element does not meet the company naming specifications (Figure 10.26).

```
DECLARE @XML2 XML(WorldSchema) ='<HelloWorld>2</HelloWorld>'
DECLARE @XML3 XML(WorldSchema) ='<Hello>3</Hello>'
DECLARE @XML4 XML(WorldSchema) =
 '<GoodbyeWorld>4</GoodbyeWorld>'
DECLARE @XML5 XML(WorldSchema) =
 '<HelloWorld>Five</HelloWorld>'
```

```
Messages
Msg 6926, Level 16, State 1, Line 1
XML Validation: Invalid simple type value: 'Five'. Location: /*:HelloWorld[1]
                                                              0 rows
```

Figure 10.27 This shows that the @XML5 variable does not comply and did not successfully pass through the schema.

@XML5 does not work because "Five" does not meet the integer requirement. The @XML3, @XML4 and @XML5 statements threw an error. To create our own standard we are using typed XML. Untyped XML is valid XML but is not associated with any XML schema. To put it another way, typed XML is bound to an XML schema while untyped XML is simply valid XML.

Viewing XML Schema Definitions

We know the WorldSchema XML schema definition was created but how can its existence be verified? XML schema definitions can be found in the Object Explorer, under the *DatabaseName* (**JProCo**) > **Programmability** > **Types** > **XML Schema Collections** (Figure 10.28).

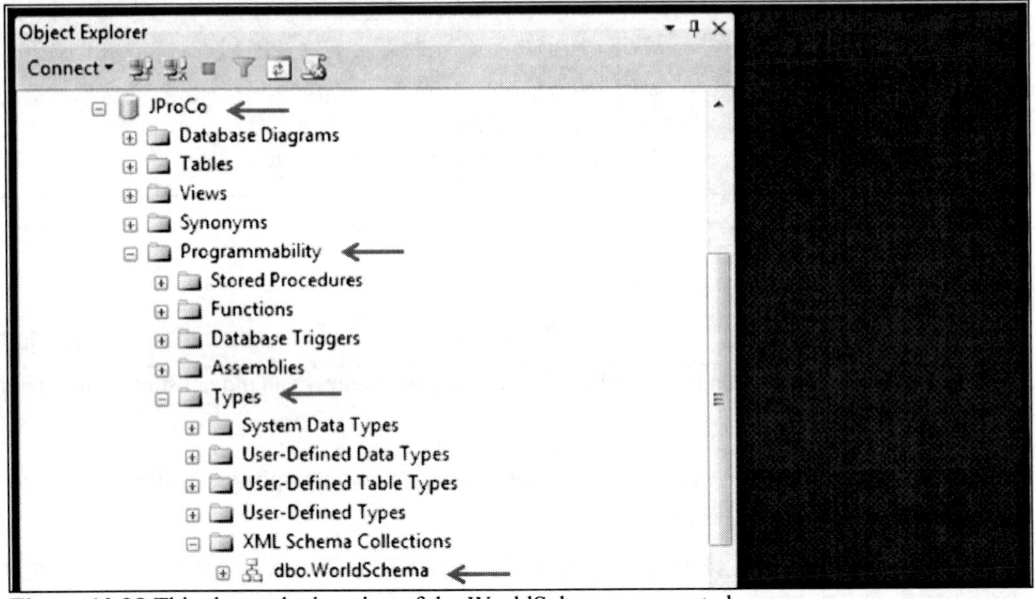

Figure 10.28 This shows the location of the WorldSchema we created.

In Figure 10.28 we can see dbo.WorldSchema in the Object Explorer. Another way to see the collection is with the sys.xml_schema_collections catalog view.

```
SELECT * FROM sys.xml_schema_collections
```

Results | Messages

	xml_collection_id	schema_id	principal_id	name	create_date	modify_date
1	1	4	NULL	sys	2009-04-13...	2012-02-10 ...
2	65536	1	NULL	WorldSchema	2012-10-24...	2012-10-24 ...

Query executed successfully. | RENO (11.0 RTM) | Reno\Student (51) | JProCo | 00:00:00 | 2 rows

Figure 10.29 The sys.xml_schema_collections shows the WorldSchema exists in the JProCo database.

The sys.xml_schema_collections catalog view shows the WorldSchema exists (Figure 10.29). If an XML schema is no longer needed, it can be dropped. To drop an XML schema type DROP XML SCHEMA COLLECTION followed by the name of the schema, WorldSchema, and then GO.

```
DROP XML SCHEMA COLLECTION WorldSchema
GO
```

Messages
Command(s) completed successfully.
0 rows

Figure 10.30 This shows WorldSchema was successfully dropped.

```
SELECT * FROM sys.xml_schema_collections
```

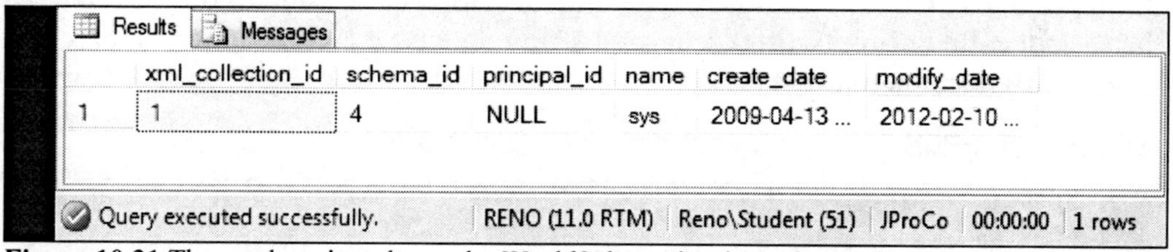

	xml_collection_id	schema_id	principal_id	name	create_date	modify_date
1	1	4	NULL	sys	2009-04-13 ...	2012-02-10 ...

Query executed successfully. | RENO (11.0 RTM) | Reno\Student (51) | JProCo | 00:00:00 | 1 rows

Figure 10.31 The catalog view shows the WorldSchema has been dropped.

If Figure 10.30 we see the schema was successfully dropped and in Figure 10.31 we notice WorldSchema is gone from the catalog view.

Lab 10.2: XML Schema Definitions

Lab Prep: Each lab has one or more Skill Checks. Start with Skill Check 1 and proceed until reaching the Points to Ponder section.

Before beginning this lab, verify that SQL Server 2012 is properly installed and operating. Before running the lab setup script for resetting the database (SQLQueries2012Vol5Chapter10.2Setup.sql), please make sure to close all query windows within SSMS. An open query window pointing to a database context can lock that database preventing it from updating when the script is executing. A simple way to assure all query windows are closed, is to exit out of SSMS, then open a new instance of SSMS, and lastly run the setup script.

Skill Check 1: Create a new schema collection in JProCo called SongSchema that has a root called <Songs> and accepts a string data type. When done you can check for your schema with:

```
SELECT * FROM sys.xml_schema_collections
```

Results | Messages

	xml_collection_id	schema_id	principal_id	name	create_date	modify_date
1	1	4	NULL	sys	2009-04-13...	2012-02-10...
2	65537	1	NULL	SongSchema	2012-10-24...	2012-10-24...

Query executed successfully. | RENO (11.0 RTM) | Reno\Student (54) | JProCo | 00:00:00 | 2 rows

Figure 10.32 This shows result from Skill Check 1.

Skill Check 2: Make each of the following XML typed XML using the SongSchema from Skill Check 1. Only let the XML that complies with the SongSchema pass through to the @XML variable.

```
DECLARE @XML1 XML = '<?xml version="1.0"?><Songs>Red-Red
 Wine</Songs>'

DECLARE @XML2 XML = '<?xml version="1.0"?><Songs>Manic
 Monday</Songs>'

DECLARE @XML3 XML = '<?xml version="1.0"?><Tunes>Manic
 Monday</Tunes>'
```

Answer Code: The T-SQL code to this lab can be found in the downloadable files in a file named Lab10.2_XML_Schema_Definitions.sql.

Points to Ponder - XML Schema Definitions

1. The XML data type makes sure the schema of the incoming stream is either a well-formed XML or a valid XML fragment.
2. The XML data type by itself will not enforce specific company naming standards or relationships within the XML stream.
3. An XML schema is a set of rules that an XML stream must adhere to in order to be validated.
4. XSD stands for XML Schema Definition.
5. XSD schemas can be associated with an XML variable or column from the XML schema collection.
6. XML Schema definitions can be found in Object Explorer under *DatabaseName* > **Programmability** > **Types** > **XML Schema Collections**.
7. XML Schema definitions can also be found from the sys.xml_schema_collections catalog view of each database.
8. Untyped XML is a valid XML but is not associated with an XML schema.
9. Typed XML is bound to an XML schema.
10. If you are not the one creating the XML data that you import and the design might change, that can break your import process. If you use the XSD for your import logic you can just use the new schema and the import can continue to work.
11. A schema from the XML schema collection is used to validate XML instances.
12. SQL Server uses an XML schema to validate XML instances.

Typed XML Columns

Inspector 12 is a made up character from the 1980s for the company Hanes. She has high quality standards, and only allows the best quality products to be approved. Any product passing through a very clear quality check point either gets rejected or approved. What do you call XML that passes through a schema check? That is known as typed XML.

XML Schema Definitions

As we learned in the last section, the schema definitions enforce a specific design for your XML. We used this to make sure an XML variable was measuring up to our standards. You can also use an XML Schema definition to make sure any field in your table that has the XML data type is typed XML.

XML Fields Revisited

Let's start out by creating a new table that will hold the XML. This table will need to have two fields, the first will be D_Id which will be an integer. The second field will be D_Data which will be XML (Figure 10.33).

```
CREATE TABLE DatabaseList
(D_Id INT,
D_Data XML)
GO
```

Messages
Command(s) completed successfully.
0 rows

Figure 10.33 The DatabaseList table was created successfully.

Let's insert two records into the DatabaseList table. The first record will have a D_Id of 1 and the XML will have a root tag called <Database>. Inside the tags let's add the text node of JProCo. The second record will have the D_Id field as 2 and this time we will name the root <db>. Let's put AdventureWorks as the text between the root tags.

```
INSERT INTO DatabaseList VALUES
 (1,'<Database>JProCo</Database>')

INSERT INTO DatabaseList VALUES
 (2,'<db>AdventureWorks</db>')
```

```
Messages

(1 row(s) affected)

(1 row(s) affected)

                                                    0 rows
```

Figure 10.34 This shows both records were inserted successfully.

```
SELECT * FROM DatabaseList
```

Results | Messages

	D_Id	D_Data
1	1	<Database>JProCo</Database>
2	2	<db>AdventureWorks</db>

Query executed successfully. | RENO (11.0 RTM) | Reno\Student (51) | JProCo | 00:00:00 | 2 rows

Figure 10.35 This shows the two records that were just inserted.

In the last section of this chapter SQL Server used an XML schema from the XML Schema collection to validate XML instances. Currently we have no validation on the D_Data field other than the XML data type making it valid XML. Since we are not using a schema on this, field D_Data is considered to be untyped XML.

Creating Typed XML Fields

Let's look at the two records in the DatabaseList table again.

```
SELECT * FROM DatabaseList
```

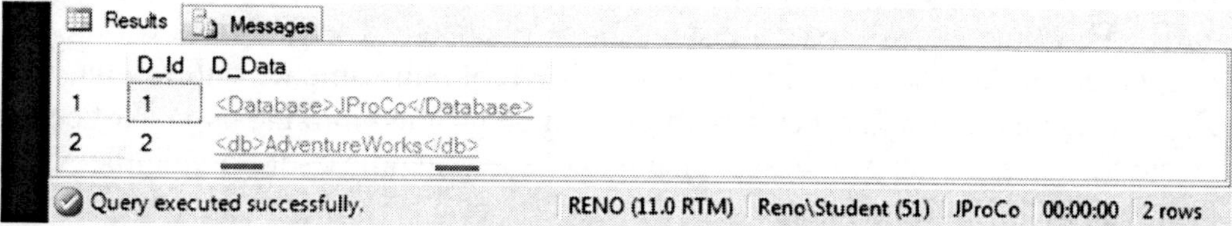

Figure 10.36 This shows the two records that were just inserted.

The JProCo schema should only allow the root to be called <Database>. There should be nothing else like <db> (Figure 10.36). Let's create an XML schema called JProCoSchema. First DROP the DatabaseList table so we can recreate it to be JProCoSchema compliant.

```
DROP TABLE DatabaseList
```

Messages
Command(s) completed successfully.
0 rows

Figure 10.37 The DatabaseList table was dropped successfully.

In a new query window, we will create the JProCoSchema schema definition. This time we will pick our namespace to be <xs:> instead of <xsd:>. We don't have to use the <xsd:> for our definition namespace. An often used nomenclature for namespace is <xs:> so we set the namespace name as <xs:>. Both xsd and xs are the most common and preferred namespace aliases.

```
CREATE XML SCHEMA COLLECTION JProCoSchema
AS
'<xs:schema xmlns:xs="http://www.w3.org/2001/XMLSchema">
<xs:element name="Database" type="xs:string"/>
</xs:schema>'
GO
```

Messages
Command(s) completed successfully.
0 rows

Figure 10.38 The JProCoSchema has been created successfully.

In Figure 10.38 we see that the JProCoSchema was created that require the root to be called <Database>.

In a new query window let's re-create the DatabaseList table that will hold our XML. This time we will have it use the JProCoSchema. The first field will be an integer as before. The second field will be XML but this time we will run the XML through our XML schema before it can be inserted into the table. Notice to create the table in this way the schema name is in parentheses following the XML data type in the D_Data line.

```
CREATE TABLE DatabaseList
(D_Id INT,
D_Data XML(JProCoSchema))
GO
```

Messages
Command(s) completed successfully.
0 rows

Figure 10.39 This shows the DatabaseList table (with JProCoSchema compliance built in) was created.

To test the schema let's insert the two records again. Insert them one at a time so we can clearly see what happens with each record.

```
INSERT INTO DatabaseList VALUES
 (1,'<Database>JProCo</Database>')
```

```
Messages

(1 row(s) affected)

                                                              0 rows
```

Figure 10.40 This shows the first record is compliant and was inserted without error.

The first record was inserted without error, the root of the XML was named <Database> and was found to be compliant by the JProCoSchema definition. The XML was passed back to be inserted into the DatabaseList table. Now attempt to insert the second record into the table. We already know that the root name <db> is not compliant. This INSERT throws the error you see in Figure 10.41.

```
INSERT INTO DatabaseList VALUES
(2,'<db>AdventureWorks</db>')
```

```
Messages
Msg 6913, Level 16, State 1, Line 2
XML Validation: Declaration not found for element 'db'. Location: /*:db[1]

                                                              0 rows
```

Figure 10.41 This shows the XML did not comply with the root element naming standard.

Just as we suspected, the JProCoSchema definition did not allow the XML data to pass through to the field. The XML we tried to send was well-formed but the root name <db> did not comply with the JProCo schema (Figure 10.41). An XML schema is not only capable of causing non-conforming XML variables to fail but can also keep XML fields compliant as long as the schema is used.

Lab 10.3: Typed XML Columns

Lab Prep: Each lab has one or more Skill Checks. Start with Skill Check 1 and proceed until reaching the Points to Ponder section.

Before beginning this lab, verify that SQL Server 2012 is properly installed and operating. Before running the lab setup script for resetting the database (SQLQueries2012Vol5Chapter10.3Setup.sql), please make sure to close all query windows within SSMS. An open query window pointing to a database context can lock that database preventing it from updating when the script is executing. A simple way to assure all query windows are closed, is to exit out of SSMS, then open a new instance of SSMS, and lastly run the setup script.

Skill Check 1: Alter the Employee table of the JProCo database to add a new typed XML field called EmpData. Be sure to use the JProCoSchema XML Schema definitions. When done the Employee table should resemble Figure 10.42.

```
SELECT * From Employee
```

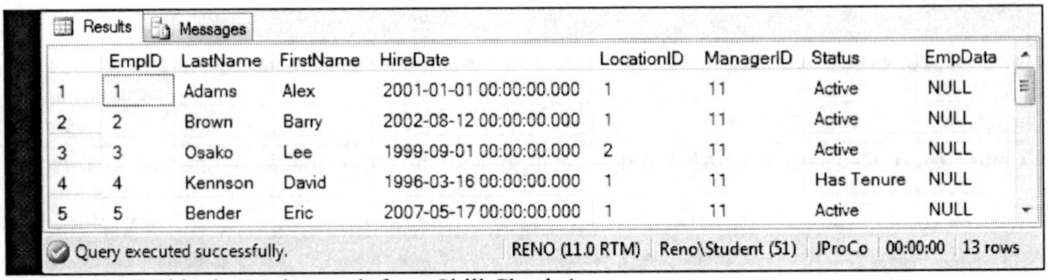

Results | Messages

	EmpID	LastName	FirstName	HireDate	LocationID	ManagerID	Status	EmpData
1	1	Adams	Alex	2001-01-01 00:00:00.000	1	11	Active	NULL
2	2	Brown	Barry	2002-08-12 00:00:00.000	1	11	Active	NULL
3	3	Osako	Lee	1999-09-01 00:00:00.000	2	11	Active	NULL
4	4	Kennson	David	1996-03-16 00:00:00.000	1	11	Has Tenure	NULL
5	5	Bender	Eric	2007-05-17 00:00:00.000	1	11	Active	NULL

Query executed successfully. | RENO (11.0 RTM) | Reno\Student (51) | JProCo | 00:00:00 | 13 rows

Figure 10.42 This shows the result from Skill Check 1.

Skill Check 2: Verify that Record 1 can be updated to Employee 1 through the Typed XML field. Then verify that record 2 cannot. After both updates the Employee table should resemble Figure 10.43.

```
SELECT * From Employee
```

Results | Messages

	EmpID	LastName	FirstName	HireDate	LocationID	ManagerID	Status	EmpData
1	1	Adams	Alex	2001-01-01 00:00:00.000	1	11	Active	<Database>JProCo</Database>
2	2	Brown	Barry	2002-08-12 00:00:00.000	1	11	Active	NULL
3	3	Osako	Lee	1999-09-01 00:00:00.000	2	11	Active	NULL
4	4	Kennson	David	1996-03-16 00:00:00.000	1	11	Has Tenure	NULL
5	5	Bender	Eric	2007-05-17 00:00:00.000	1	11	Active	NULL

Query executed successfully. RENO (11.0 RTM) Reno\Student (51) JProCo 00:00:00 13 rows

Figure 10.43 This shows the result from Skill Check 2.

Answer Code: The T-SQL code to this lab can be found in the downloadable files in a file named Lab10.3_Typed_XML_Columns.sql.

Points to Ponder - Typed XML Columns

1. You can create, modify and drop XML Schemas from the collection.
2. XML Schemas listed in the CREATE XML SCHEMA COLLECTION T-SQL statement are part of the newly created XML schema collection upon its creation.
3. To add more schemas to the collection you use the ALTER XML SCHEMA COLLECTION T-SQL statement.
4. To drop the schema collection use DROP XML SCHEMA COLLECTION *CollectionName*.
5. From the schema collection you can then create XML variables and columns to be associated with the schema collection.
6. The *ComplexType* element is known as a Complex element and defines an XML element with other elements and/or attributes children.
7. A Complex element can be empty by having no explicit ending tag like this example:

   <CurrentProduct ProductID="7"/>
8. An XML Schema (known as xsd) defines the elements and attributes of your XML data.
9. A simple element is an XML element that contains only text. It cannot contain any other elements or attributes.
10. Schema components can be elements, attributes, or type definitions.
11. The <schema> element of the xsd is always the root element.
12. The xsd:element can contain text but no child elements or attributes.
13. If you bind an XML column to a schema collection you can see the columns for that table in Object Explorer.
14. SELECT * FROM sys.xml_schemas_namespaces will show the schemas in your database.

Chapter Glossary

Typed XML: XML that is bound to an XML schema.

Untyped XML: XML that is not bound to any XML schema.

XML Schema: A set of rules that an XML stream must adhere to in order to be validated.

Review Quiz - Chapter Ten

1.) You have the following code that throws an error message:

```
DECLARE @XmlDoc XML =
N'   <?xml version="1.0"?>
  <root xmlns:first = "urn:First:Name" >
<First:Name>Рик</First:Name>
</root>'
SELECT @XmlDoc
```

What is the reason for the error?

O a. Cyrillic characters are not supported with Unicode.

O b. The trailing spaces before the root node are not allowed.

O c. The trailing spaces before the prolog are not allowed.

2.) The prolog contains the XML version number but can optionally also contain what?

O a. Encoding instructions.

O b. Namespace declarations.

3.) You have well-formed XML that is not using any XML schema definitions. What is another name for this type of XML?

O a. Typed XML.

O b. Untyped XML.

4.) You have the following code that assigns untyped XML to your @XML1 variable:

```
DECLARE @XML1 XML = '<Hello>1</Hello>'
```

You have an XML Schema called WorldSchema and want @XML1 to be typed XML. What code will do this?

O a. `DECLARE @XML1 XML(WorldSchema) = '<Hello>1</Hello>'`
O b. `DECLARE @XML1 XML AS (WorldSchema) = '<Hello>1</Hello>'`
O c. `DECLARE @XML1 XML = '<Hello>1</Hello>'(WorldSchema)`
O d. `DECLARE @XML1 XML = '<Hello>1</Hello>'AS (WorldSchema)`

Answer Key

1.) Cyrillic characters are supported by Unicode, so (a) is incorrect. SQL does not care about spaces before the <root> node, so (b) is incorrect. Trailing spaces before the prolog are not allowed, so (c) is the correct answer.

2.) Namespace declarations don't happen in the <root>, so (b) is incorrect. Encoding instructions can be added to the prolog, so (a) is the correct answer.

3.) XML that is using an XML schema definition is called typed XML. Untyped XML is XML that is not using any XML schema definition, so (b) is correct.

4.) XML(*schema*) = is the correct syntax to pass the variable through the xsd schema to create Typed XML, so (a) is correct.

Bug Catcher

To play the Bug Catcher game run the SQLQueries2012Vol5BugCatcher10.pps from the BugCatcher folder of the companion files found at www.Joes2Pros.com.

[THIS PAGE INTENTIONALLY LEFT BLANK.]

Chapter 11. XML Indexes

All types of indexes create a predictable order of data to make searching faster. We learned this in Volume 3. The book you are reading now counts up by page number as you flip to the right and down as you flip left. If this book was 400 pages and you were looking for page 390 you know to check the very last few pages. The Index at the back of the book is in alphabetical order and has important words to point to the page numbers. This means finding the word "prolog" will not take very long.

XML data can also be indexed for faster retrieval. This chapter will show the different types of XML queries and the different types of indexes to make those queries run faster.

READERNOTE:*Please run the SQLQueries2012Vol5Chapter10.0Setup.sql script in order to follow along with the examples in the first section of Chapter 10. All scripts mentioned in this chapter may be found at* ***www.Joes2Pros.com****.*

XQuery Variations

There are many different ways to query for XML data. Perhaps you want to retrieve the data based on an XPath to process that data. Maybe you would just like to verify that a specific XPath exists. You don't need the XML fragment but instead just need to know that it is there. Sometimes you don't even know your XPath but know that somewhere in your XML is a product that costs $56.85. Once the query finds a price of $56.85 the returned result should be the corresponding ProductName.

Your XQuery variations break down into three main areas of search:

- Searching by an exact or relative XML XPath.
- Searching for a specific value anywhere in the XML.
- Searching for a specific name anywhere in the XML.

Retrieving XML Fragments

Once you find the data you are looking for you often want to retrieve this XML data for further processing.

Standard XPath Revisited

Let's look at a table that contains some XML.

```
SELECT *
FROM CustomerActivity
```

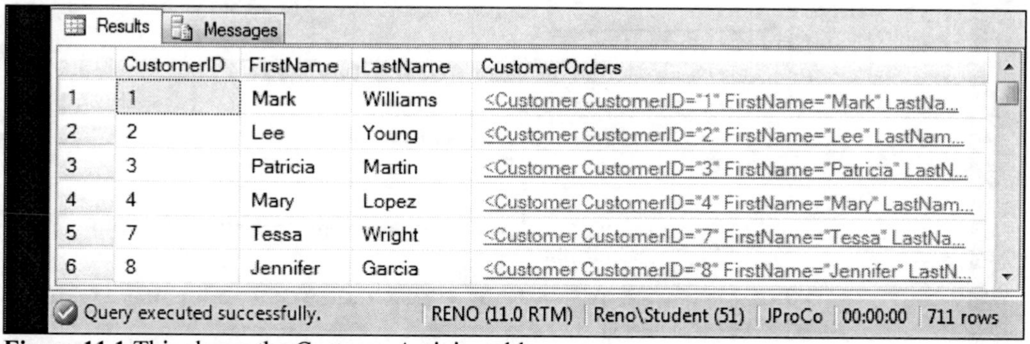

Results | Messages

	CustomerID	FirstName	LastName	CustomerOrders
1	1	Mark	Williams	<Customer CustomerID="1" FirstName="Mark" LastNa...
2	2	Lee	Young	<Customer CustomerID="2" FirstName="Lee" LastNam...
3	3	Patricia	Martin	<Customer CustomerID="3" FirstName="Patricia" LastN...
4	4	Mary	Lopez	<Customer CustomerID="4" FirstName="Mary" LastNam...
5	7	Tessa	Wright	<Customer CustomerID="7" FirstName="Tessa" LastNa...
6	8	Jennifer	Garcia	<Customer CustomerID="8" FirstName="Jennifer" LastN...

Query executed successfully. | RENO (11.0 RTM) | Reno\Student (51) | JProCo | 00:00:00 | 711 rows

Figure 11.1 This shows the CustomerActivity table.

The CustomerActivity table has 711 records, one for each customer who has placed an order. If we look at Customer number 1, Mark Williams, his orders appear in the XML in the CustomerOrders field. If we open that link we see the following:

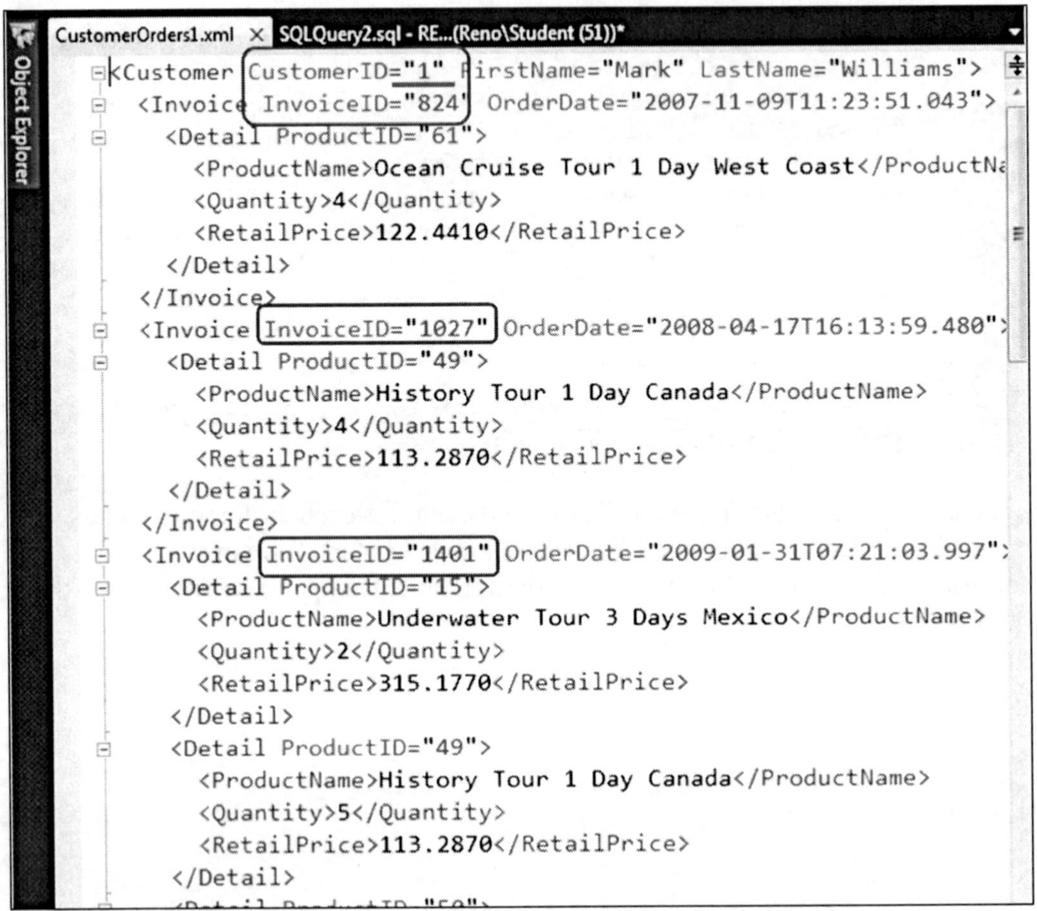

CustomerOrders1.xml × SQLQuery2.sql - RE...(Reno\Student (51))*

Object Explorer

```
<Customer CustomerID="1" FirstName="Mark" LastName="Williams">
  <Invoice InvoiceID="824" OrderDate="2007-11-09T11:23:51.043">
    <Detail ProductID="61">
      <ProductName>Ocean Cruise Tour 1 Day West Coast</ProductNa
      <Quantity>4</Quantity>
      <RetailPrice>122.4410</RetailPrice>
    </Detail>
  </Invoice>
  <Invoice InvoiceID="1027" OrderDate="2008-04-17T16:13:59.480">
    <Detail ProductID="49">
      <ProductName>History Tour 1 Day Canada</ProductName>
      <Quantity>4</Quantity>
      <RetailPrice>113.2870</RetailPrice>
    </Detail>
  </Invoice>
  <Invoice InvoiceID="1401" OrderDate="2009-01-31T07:21:03.997">
    <Detail ProductID="15">
      <ProductName>Underwater Tour 3 Days Mexico</ProductName>
      <Quantity>2</Quantity>
      <RetailPrice>315.1770</RetailPrice>
    </Detail>
    <Detail ProductID="49">
      <ProductName>History Tour 1 Day Canada</ProductName>
      <Quantity>5</Quantity>
      <RetailPrice>113.2870</RetailPrice>
    </Detail>
```

Figure 11.2 This shows the open XML with all of Customer 1's order information.

Here in Figure 11.2 we see customer 1 on invoice 824, and he ordered product 61. This customer also ordered products on invoices 1027 and 1401. On invoice 1401 there have been about 17 products ordered. This is a good example of a relational summary in the XML for all the activity of customer 1.

Next we are going to use XPath to ask for just the information we want. We will assume the company has asked us to drill down on a test analysis for CustomerID 1. We will drill down and find all the products that Customer 1 has ordered. The first step is to predicate for CustomerID 1 using the WHERE clause and to itemize the fields in the SELECT list.

```
SELECT CustomerID, FirstName, LastName, CustomerOrders
FROM CustomerActivity
WHERE CustomerID = 1
```

	CustomerID	FirstName	LastName	CustomerOrders
1	1	Mark	Williams	<Customer CustomerID="1" FirstName="Mark" LastNa...

Query executed successfully. RENO (11.0 RTM) Reno\Student (51) JProCo 00:00:00 1 rows

Figure 11.3 This shows a query of the CustomerActivity table for CustomerID 1.

Figure 11.3 shows our query has been narrowed down to just Mark Williams. The fields are all here but now they are explicitly listed. In the query window, drop CustomerOrders to its own line from the SELECT list and write an XQuery against it using an XPath. XPath refers to the syntax for identifying any part or parts of an XML document. We need to look for all the products that were ordered by customer 1.

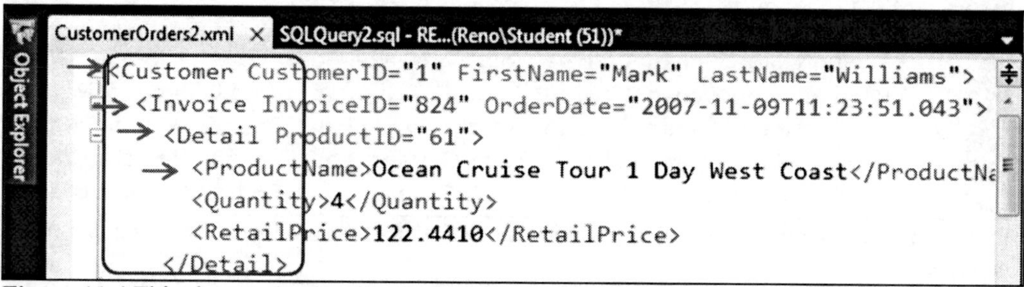

Figure 11.4 This shows what level to find the ProductName.

If we look at Figure 11.4 we can see at what level the <ProductName> is located:

/Customer/Invoice/Detail/ProductName

If the <ProductName> is what needs to be pulled out then we must instruct our query to find CustomerOrders at the fourth level. <Quantity> and <RetailPrice> are also located at the fourth level. For this example we are only going to specify the <ProductName>. In a set of single quotes add the path we found from the XML (Figure 11.4).

```
SELECT CustomerID, FirstName, LastName,
CustomerOrders.query('/Customer/Invoice/Detail/ProductName')
FROM CustomerActivity
WHERE CustomerID = 1
```

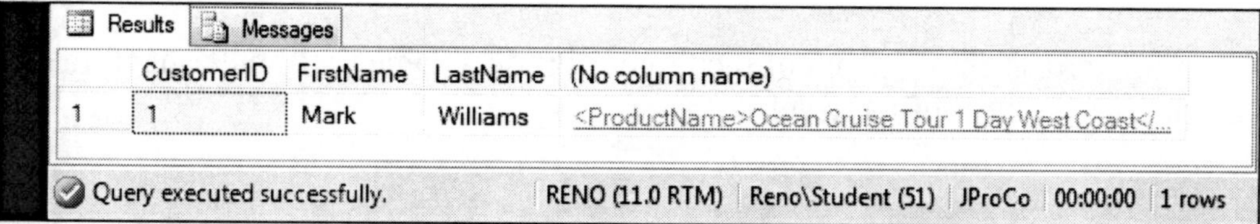

Figure 11.5 This shows the results of our query on CustomerID 1 with the drilled down XML.

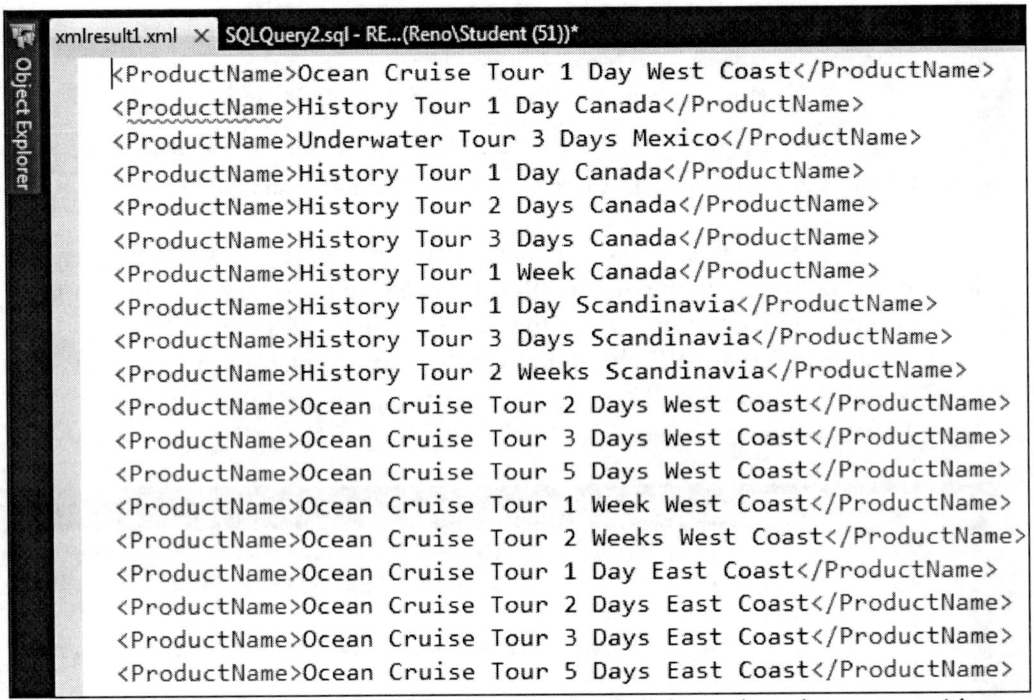
Object Explorer
xmlresult1.xml
SQLQuery2.sql - RE...(Reno\Student (51))*
<ProductName>Ocean Cruise Tour 1 Day West Coast</ProductName>
<ProductName>History Tour 1 Day Canada</ProductName>
<ProductName>Underwater Tour 3 Days Mexico</ProductName>
<ProductName>History Tour 1 Day Canada</ProductName>
<ProductName>History Tour 2 Days Canada</ProductName>
<ProductName>History Tour 3 Days Canada</ProductName>
<ProductName>History Tour 1 Week Canada</ProductName>
<ProductName>History Tour 1 Day Scandinavia</ProductName>
<ProductName>History Tour 3 Days Scandinavia</ProductName>
<ProductName>History Tour 2 Weeks Scandinavia</ProductName>
<ProductName>Ocean Cruise Tour 2 Days West Coast</ProductName>
<ProductName>Ocean Cruise Tour 3 Days West Coast</ProductName>
<ProductName>Ocean Cruise Tour 5 Days West Coast</ProductName>
<ProductName>Ocean Cruise Tour 1 Week West Coast</ProductName>
<ProductName>Ocean Cruise Tour 2 Weeks West Coast</ProductName>
<ProductName>Ocean Cruise Tour 1 Day East Coast</ProductName>
<ProductName>Ocean Cruise Tour 2 Days East Coast</ProductName>
<ProductName>Ocean Cruise Tour 3 Days East Coast</ProductName>
<ProductName>Ocean Cruise Tour 5 Days East Coast</ProductName>

Figure 11.6 This shows the open link from Figure 11.5 and all the products that customer 1 has ordered.

We have successfully pulled out all of the product names that CustomerID 1 has ever ordered. By specifying this specific level of the XPath, the XPath was a syntax for identifying the part of the XML we wanted to see.

Relative Level XPath

The last example worked great for our data because our product names are all at the fourth level. Sometimes there will be a taxonomy of products at different levels. What does that mean? Have you ever bought a product that contains other products? Microsoft Office is a good example. Inside the Product Office are other products that can be sold individually such as Excel, Word and PowerPoint. Maybe there's a fifth level product. If we know products reside at different levels and we need to pull out all products, we can use a relative XPath level:

//ProductName

Two forward slashes in front of the target <ProductName> will pull out all the products regardless of the level.

```
SELECT CustomerID, FirstName, LastName,
CustomerOrders.query('//ProductName')
FROM CustomerActivity
WHERE CustomerID = 1
```

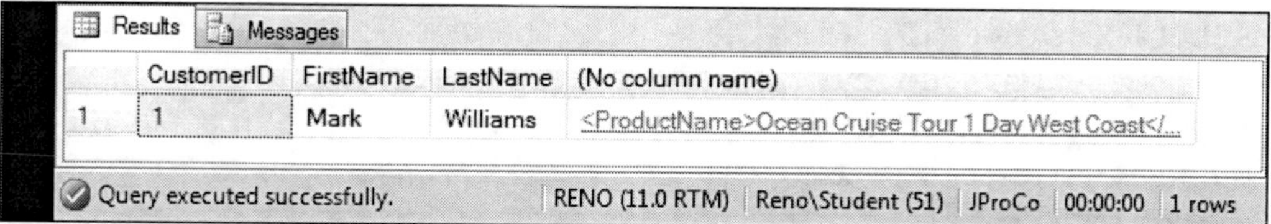

Figure 11.7 This shows the results of our query on CustomerID 1 with the drilled down XML using a relative XPath.

Using the double forward slash finds all the nodes named <ProductName> no matter where they are in the document. Let's modify our query to just pull out the text. Put a forward slash text() in the XPath.

```
SELECT CustomerID, FirstName, LastName,
CustomerOrders.query('//ProductName/text()')
FROM CustomerActivity WHERE CustomerID = 1
```

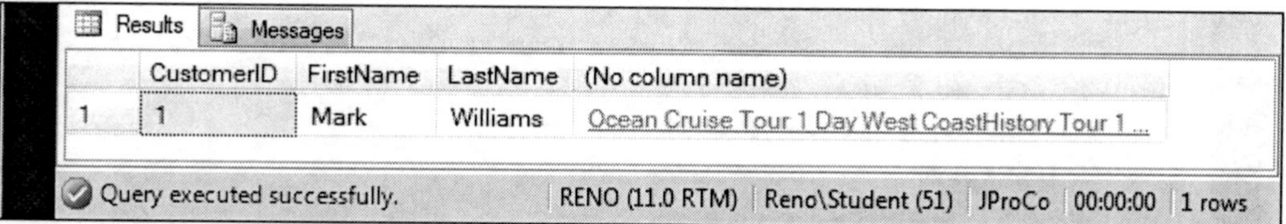

Figure 11.8 This shows the results of our query on CustomerID 1 with the drilled down XML using a relative XPath that specifies text only using the text() method.

By adding the text() method to the XPath, only the values stored in the XML will pass to the result.

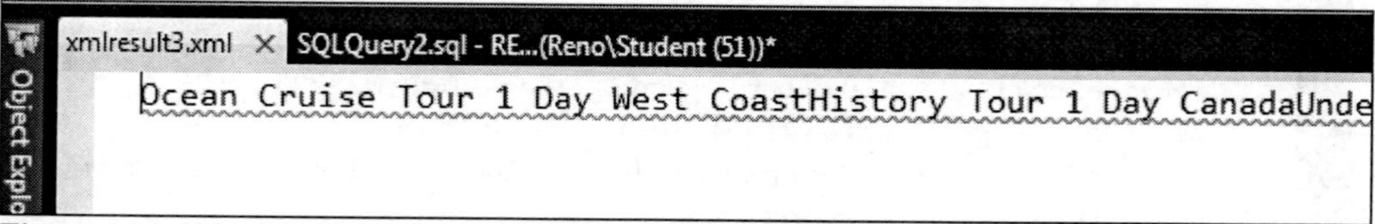

Figure 11.9 This shows the text only result from the XML link in Figure 11.8.

In Figure 11.8 we get all of our products that were purchased by CustomerID 1. Unfortunately they are run together since we have no separators. Prior to setting our query to text only, the values were separated in the result by XML tag information.

Absolute value XPath

Let's start this next sample by pulling all the XML data for CustomerID 1 To do that we will use single quote forward slash single quote:

```
SELECT CustomerID, FirstName, LastName,
CustomerOrders.query('/')
FROM CustomerActivity
WHERE CustomerID = 1
```

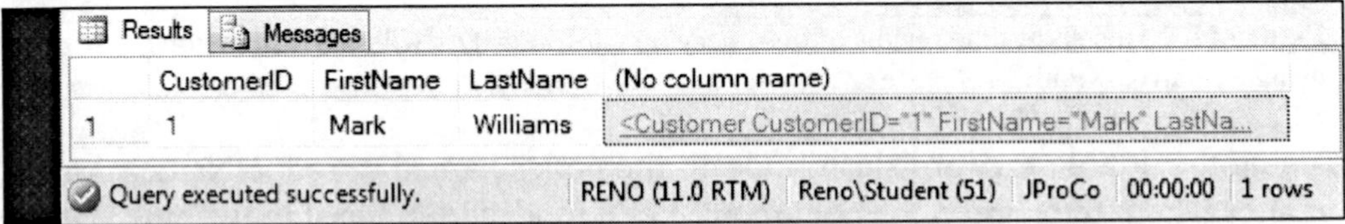

Figure 11.10 This shows the results of our query on CustomerID 1.

CustomerOrders1.xml × SQLQuery2.sql - RE...(Reno\Student (51))*

Object Explorer

```
<Customer CustomerID="1" FirstName="Mark" LastName="Williams">
  <Invoice InvoiceID="824" OrderDate="2007-11-09T11:23:51.043">
    <Detail ProductID="61">
      <ProductName>Ocean Cruise Tour 1 Day West Coast</ProductNa
      <Quantity>4</Quantity>
      <RetailPrice>122.4410</RetailPrice>
    </Detail>
  </Invoice>
  <Invoice InvoiceID="1027" OrderDate="2008-04-17T16:13:59.480">
    <Detail ProductID="49">
      <ProductName>History Tour 1 Day Canada</ProductName>
      <Quantity>4</Quantity>
      <RetailPrice>113.2870</RetailPrice>
    </Detail>
  </Invoice>
  <Invoice InvoiceID="1401" OrderDate="2009-01-31T07:21:03.997">
    <Detail ProductID="15">
      <ProductName>Underwater Tour 3 Days Mexico</ProductName>
      <Quantity>2</Quantity>
      <RetailPrice>315.1770</RetailPrice>
    </Detail>
    <Detail ProductID="49">
      <ProductName>History Tour 1 Day Canada</ProductName>
      <Quantity>5</Quantity>
      <RetailPrice>113.2870</RetailPrice>
    </Detail>
```

Figure 11.11 This shows the open XML with all of Customer 1's order information

In Figure 11.11 we see customer 1, Mark Williams, all of his invoices, and each invoice has varying amounts of data in Detail.

In the XPath of our query let's look at the detail level of the XML stream.

```
SELECT CustomerID, FirstName, LastName,
CustomerOrders.query('/Customer/Invoice/Detail')
FROM CustomerActivity
WHERE CustomerID = 1
```

	CustomerID	FirstName	LastName	(No column name)
1	1	Mark	Williams	<Detail ProductID="61"><ProductName>Ocean Cruise Tour 1 Day West ...

Query executed successfully. | (local) (11.0 RTM) | Reno\Student (53) | JProCo | 00:00:00 | 1 rows

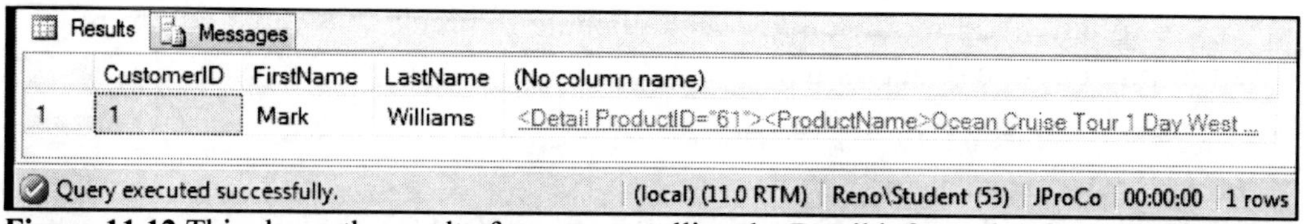

Figure 11.12 This shows the result of our query pulling the Detail information from the XML.

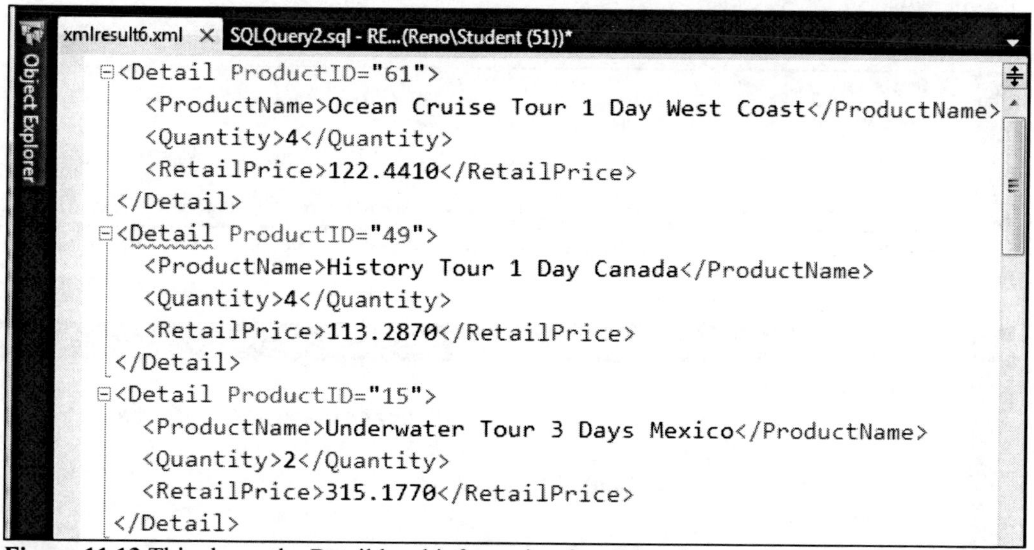

```
<Detail ProductID="61">
  <ProductName>Ocean Cruise Tour 1 Day West Coast</ProductName>
  <Quantity>4</Quantity>
  <RetailPrice>122.4410</RetailPrice>
</Detail>
<Detail ProductID="49">
  <ProductName>History Tour 1 Day Canada</ProductName>
  <Quantity>4</Quantity>
  <RetailPrice>113.2870</RetailPrice>
</Detail>
<Detail ProductID="15">
  <ProductName>Underwater Tour 3 Days Mexico</ProductName>
  <Quantity>2</Quantity>
  <RetailPrice>315.1770</RetailPrice>
</Detail>
```

Figure 11.13 This shows the Detail level information for all invoices.

Figure 11.13 shows all the details of all the purchases from all the invoices. We want to pull out every ProductID that has been ordered. The ProductIDs are not element text, they are attributes. ProductID is just one level below the <Detail> level. In the XPath add [ProductID] after the <Detail> level.

```
SELECT CustomerID, FirstName, LastName,
CustomerOrders.query('/Customer/Invoice/Detail[@ProductID]')
FROM CustomerActivity
WHERE CustomerID = 1
```

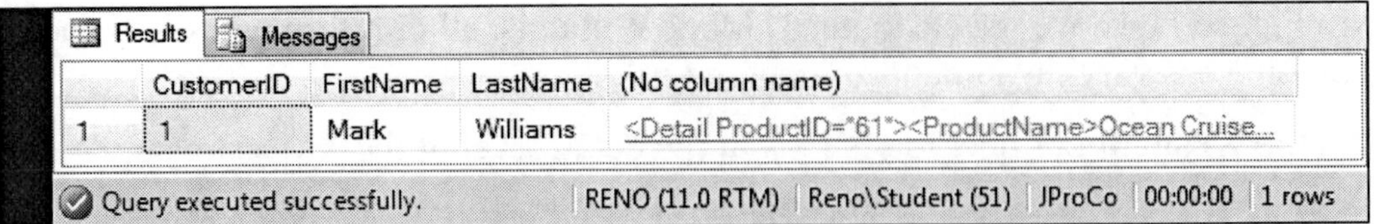

Figure 11.14 This shows the result from our query that pulls out all the details from all the ProductID values explicitly.

If you open the link in Figure 11.14 you will notice the same result as Figure 11.13. Explicitly adding the child-level attribute in brackets is most commonly used to pull out one exact value.

```
SELECT CustomerID, FirstName, LastName,
CustomerOrders.query
 ('/Customer/Invoice/Detail[@ProductID=57]')
FROM CustomerActivity
WHERE CustomerID = 1
```

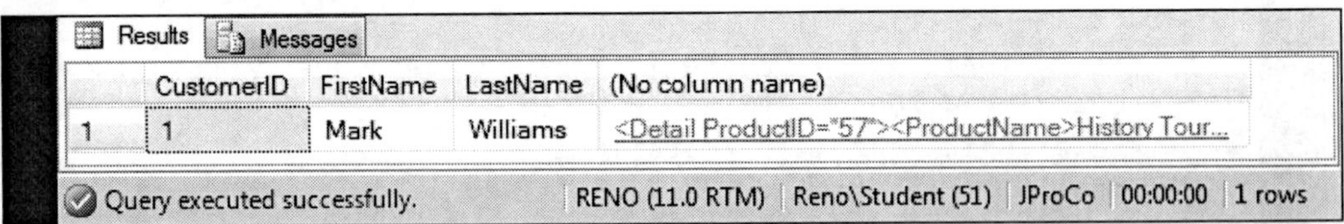

Figure 11.15 This shows the result from our query that pulls out all the details from ProductID number 57.

xmlresult12.xml × SQLQuery2.sql - RE...(Reno\Student (51))*

Object Explorer

```
<Detail ProductID="57">
  <ProductName>History Tour 3 Days Scandinavia</ProductName>
  <Quantity>1</Quantity>
  <RetailPrice>335.2050</RetailPrice>
</Detail>
```

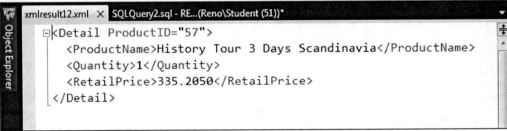

Figure 11.16 This shows the <Detail> level information for ProductID 57.

Figure 11.16 shows us that CustomerID 1 purchased product 57 and shows all the details available about that purchase.

XPath Contains String Function

Take a look at the following query.

```
SELECT CustomerID, FirstName, LastName,
CustomerOrders.query
 ('/Customer/Invoice/Detail/ProductName/text()')
FROM CustomerActivity
WHERE CustomerID = 1
```

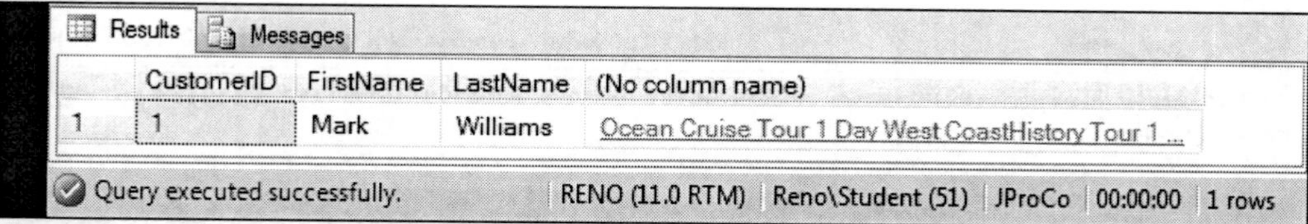

	CustomerID	FirstName	LastName	(No column name)
1	1	Mark	Williams	Ocean Cruise Tour 1 Day West CoastHistory Tour 1 ...

Figure 11.17 This shows the results of our query on CustomerID 1 with text only using the text() method.

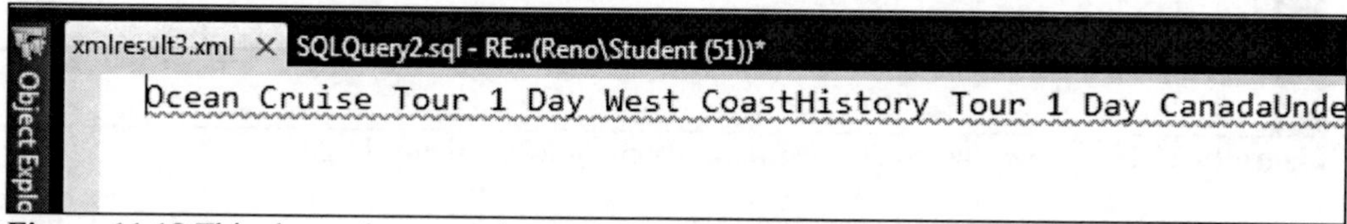

Figure 11.18 This shows the text only result from the XML link in Figure 11.17

Just like before in Figure 11.9, all of the text data is run together. Text is not a very useful way to pull out node sets. Text is more useful in searching, or to query for data. If you scroll to the right you can see many products for Canadian and Scandinavian tourists.

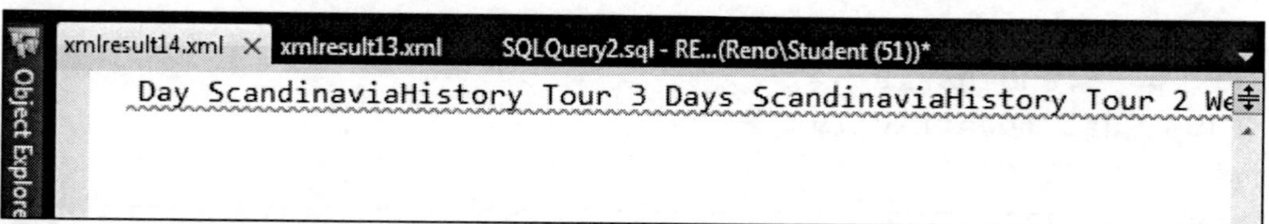

Figure 11.19 This shows the "History Tour 3 Days Scandinavia" product.

Figure 11.18 is scrolled to the right we find a product called History Tour 3 Days Scandinavia (Figure 11.19). Let's modify our query to pull that exact product by name, rather than position or value. Just after the text, add a set of square brackets containing a dot, which means the current position and set it equal to the product name in double quotes.

```
SELECT CustomerID, FirstName, LastName,
CustomerOrders.query
 ('/Customer/Invoice/Detail/ProductName/
 text() [. = "History Tour 3 Days Scandinavia"]')
FROM CustomerActivity
WHERE CustomerID = 1
```

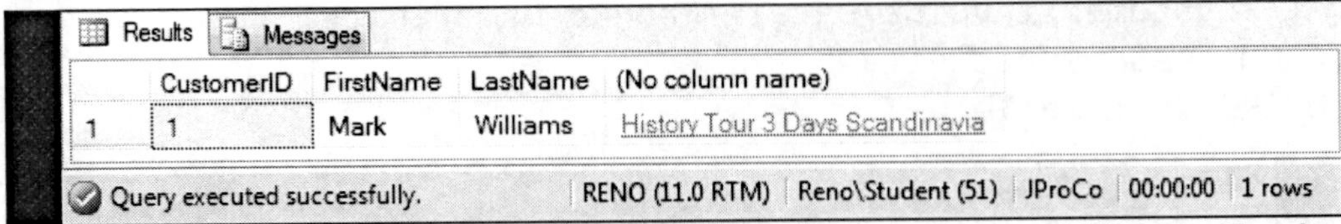

Figure 11.20 This shows the result for our query looking for the product named "History Tour 3 days Scandinavia".

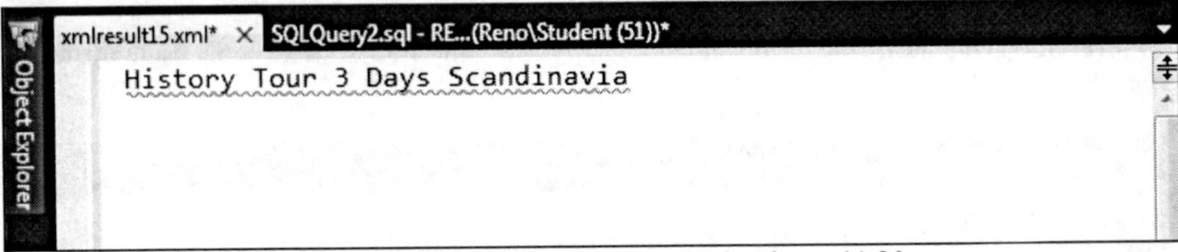

Figure 11.21 This shows the product we were searching for in Figure 11.20.

And in Figure 11.21 we see the query found the product we were looking for. The query in Figure 11.20 will only find an exact match. If we misspelled "Scandinavia" our query would not have found it. Is this the only Scandinavian tour that this customer has gone on? Let's search for the word "Scandinavia".

```
SELECT CustomerID, FirstName, LastName,
CustomerOrders.query
 ('/Customer/Invoice/Detail/ProductName/text()
 [. = "Scandinavia"]')
FROM CustomerActivity
WHERE CustomerID = 1
```

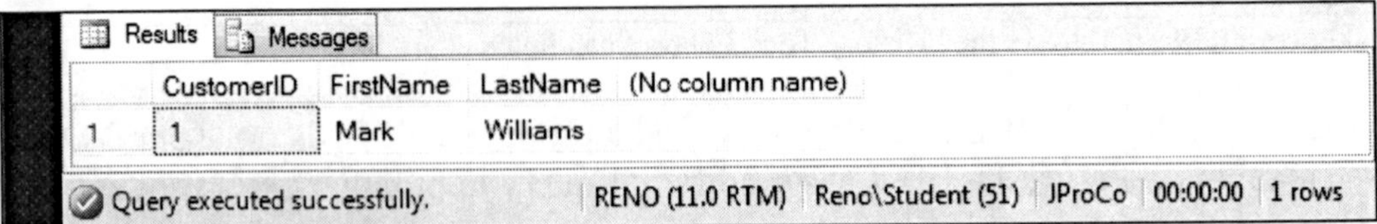

Figure 11.22 This shows the query returned nothing for "Scandinavia".

There is not trip named "Scandinavia" so our query returned nothing (Figure 11.22). What can we do to find a ProductName that contains Scandinavia? Instead

of the "Dot equals" use the word "contains" and then in parentheses put dot comma and "Scandinavia":
[contains(.,"Scandinavia")]

Let's make this change to our query and see what we get.

```
SELECT CustomerID, FirstName, LastName,
CustomerOrders.query('/Customer/Invoice/Detail/ProductName/t
ext()[contains(.,"Scandinavia")]')
FROM CustomerActivity
WHERE CustomerID = 1
```

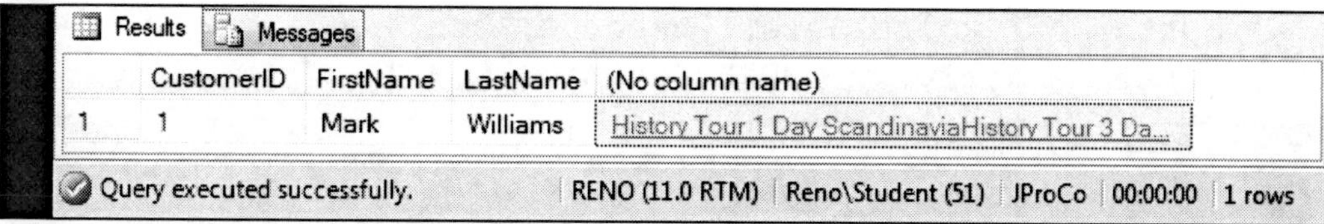

Figure 11.23 This shows the result for our query for the word "Scandinavia" contained in ProductName.

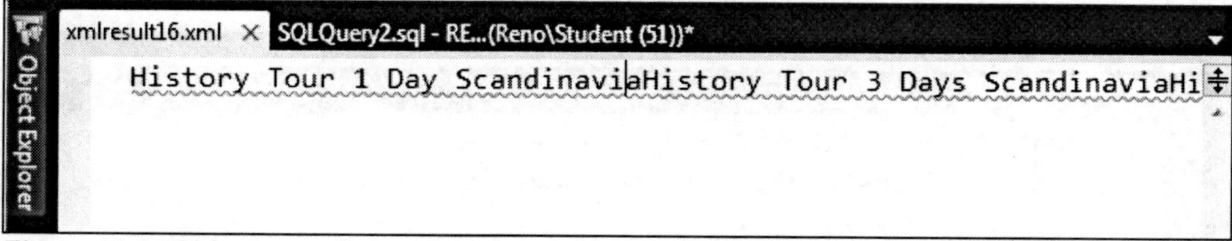

Figure 11.24 This shows all the trips customer 1 took in Scandinavia.

Figure 11.24 listed all of the Scandinavian trips that this customer has taken.

Predicating on XML Data

Even though customer 1 has ordered many products with a lot of <Detail> information, he has not ordered everything. What happens if we try and pull <Detail> for ProductID 16 from CustomerOrders?

```
SELECT CustomerID, FirstName, LastName,
CustomerOrders.query
 ('/Customer/Invoice/Detail[@ProductID=16]')
FROM CustomerActivity
WHERE CustomerID = 1
```

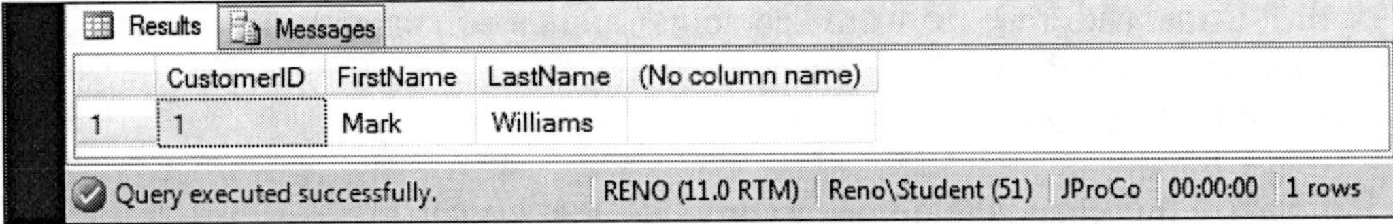

	CustomerID	FirstName	LastName	(No column name)
1	1	Mark	Williams	

Figure 11.25 This shows customer 1 has never ordered Product 16.

This customer has never ordered product 16 (Figure 11.25). Let's change our XPath to find a product this customer has ordered.

```
SELECT CustomerID, FirstName, LastName,
CustomerOrders.query
 ('/Customer/Invoice/Detail[@ProductID=57]')
FROM CustomerActivity WHERE CustomerID = 1
```

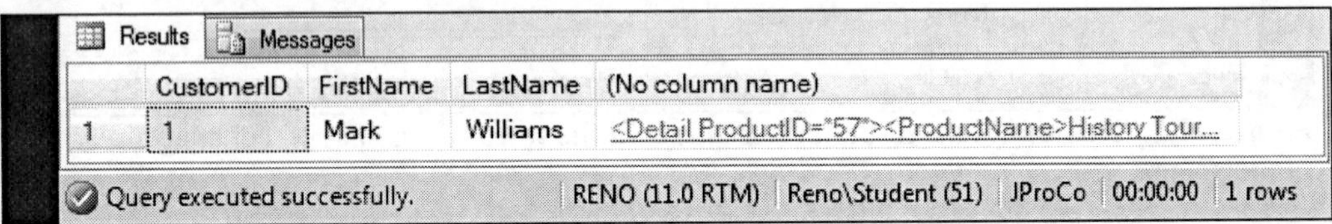

	CustomerID	FirstName	LastName	(No column name)
1	1	Mark	Williams	<Detail ProductID="57"><ProductName>History Tour...

Figure 11.26 This shows Customer 1 did order product 57.

```
<Detail ProductID="57">
  <ProductName>History Tour 3 Days Scandinavia</ProductName>
  <Quantity>1</Quantity>
  <RetailPrice>335.2050</RetailPrice>
</Detail>
```

Figure 11.27 This shows all the Detail information for ProductID 57.

We know that if the query returns nothing, the customer did not order the product. If the query returns XML data then the product was purchased. What if we only want to know if the product exists or not? We have been using the query method. If there is no need for additional data and we don't want to see the <Details>, we need to use the exist method. CustomerOrders.query changes to CustomerOrders.exist. With the exist method, if our result shows a 1, our search criteria exists in the XML (Figure 11.28), while a 0 means that it doesn't exist in the XML.

```
SELECT CustomerID, FirstName, LastName ,
CustomerOrders.exist
 ('/Customer/Invoice/Detail[@ProductID=57]')
FROM CustomerActivity
WHERE CustomerID = 1
```

Results | Messages

	CustomerID	FirstName	LastName	(No column name)
1	1	Mark	Williams	1

Query executed successfully. | RENO (11.0 RTM) | Reno\Student (51) | JProCo | 00:00:00 | 1 rows

Figure 11.28 This shows a 1 indicating that ProductID 57 exists in the XML.

```
SELECT CustomerID, FirstName, LastName ,
CustomerOrders.exist
 ('/Customer/Invoice/Detail[@ProductID=16]')
FROM CustomerActivity
WHERE CustomerID = 1
```

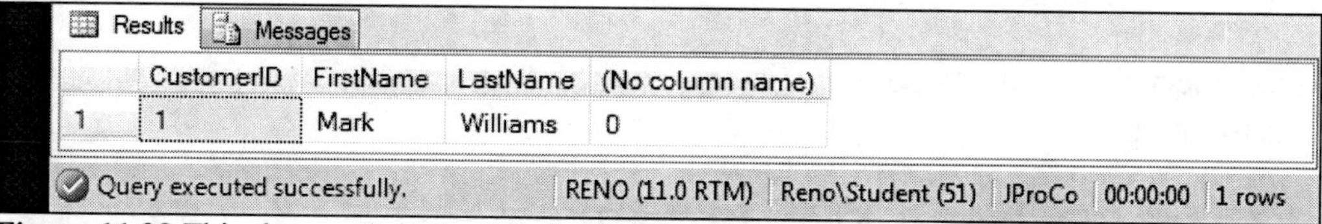

Results | Messages

	CustomerID	FirstName	LastName	(No column name)
1	1	Mark	Williams	0

Query executed successfully. | RENO (11.0 RTM) | Reno\Student (51) | JProCo | 00:00:00 | 1 rows

Figure 11.29 This shows a 0, indicating that ProductID 16 does not exist in the XML.

The XQueries XPath syntax can do a combination of searching XML, retrieving XML, or both. Let's check if the specific trip "History Tour 1 Day" Canada exists.

```
SELECT CustomerID, FirstName, LastName,
CustomerOrders.exist
 ('/Customer/Invoice/Detail/ProductName/text()
 [. = "History Tour 1 Day Canada"]')
FROM CustomerActivity
WHERE CustomerID = 1
```

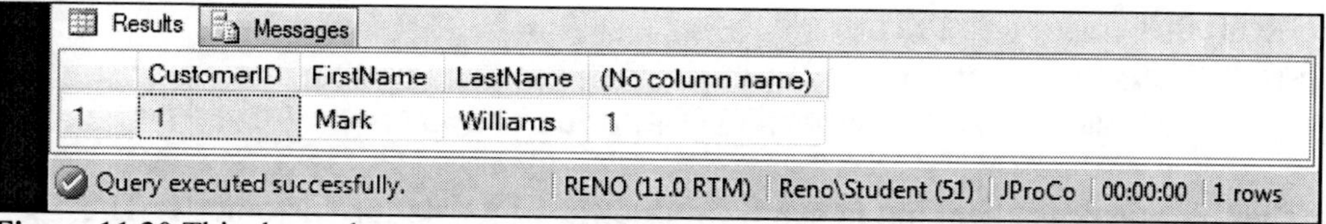

Results | Messages

	CustomerID	FirstName	LastName	(No column name)
1	1	Mark	Williams	1

Query executed successfully. | RENO (11.0 RTM) | Reno\Student (51) | JProCo | 00:00:00 | 1 rows

Figure 11.30 This shows the query returned a 1 indicating that "History Tour 1 Day Canada" exists.

Figure 11.30 returned a one, so the "History Tour 1 Day Canada" does exist in the XML. Have they done "History Tour 5 day Canada"?

```
SELECT CustomerID, FirstName, LastName,
CustomerOrders.exist
 ('/Customer/Invoice/Detail/ProductName/text()
 [. = "History Tour 55 Day Canada"]')
FROM CustomerActivity
WHERE CustomerID = 1
```

	CustomerID	FirstName	LastName	(No column name)
1	1	Mark	Williams	0

Query executed successfully. | RENO (11.0 RTM) | Reno\Student (51) | JProCo | 00:00:00 | 1 rows

Figure 11.31 This shows a 0, so they have not purchased a 55 day Canada trip.

Our query returned a 0, so no "History Tour 55 Day Canada" was purchased by customer 1.

Searching Many XML Instances

Take a moment and look at these two very similar queries. They both have the XPath, looking for ProductID 57 to exist.

```
SELECT CustomerID, FirstName, LastName,
CustomerOrders.exist
  ('/Customer/Invoice/Detail[@ProductID=57]')
FROM CustomerActivity
WHERE CustomerID = 1
```

```
SELECT CustomerID, FirstName, LastName,
CustomerOrders.query('/Customer/Invoice/Detail/ProductName')
FROM CustomerActivity
WHERE CustomerOrders.exist
 ('/Customer/Invoice/Detail[@ProductID=57]') = 1
```

The first query is checking to see if ProductID 57 exists for customer 1. The second query wants to know who else has ordered this product. To do this we moved the "exist" to the WHERE clause. By doing this we will find all of the records where a customer has ordered ProductID 57.

```
SELECT CustomerID, FirstName, LastName,
CustomerOrders.query('/Customer/Invoice/Detail/ProductName')
FROM CustomerActivity
WHERE CustomerOrders.exist
 ('/Customer/Invoice/Detail[@ProductID=57]') = 1
```

	CustomerID	FirstName	LastName	(No column name)
1	1	Mark	Williams	<ProductName>Ocean Cruise Tour 1 Day West Coast</...
2	13	Linda	Hernandez	<ProductName>History Tour 3 Days Canada</Product...
3	21	Carol	Thompson	<ProductName>History Tour 1 Day Scandinavia</Prod...
4	57	Sandra	Allen	<ProductName>History Tour 1 Day Canada</ProductN...
5	96	Richard	Thompson	<ProductName>Ocean Cruise Tour 2 Weeks Mexico</...
6	123	George	Wilson	<ProductName>History Tour 1 Day Canada</ProductN...

Query executed successfully. | RENO (11.0 RTM) | Reno\Student (51) | JProCo | 00:00:00 | 47 rows

Figure 11.32 This shows we found 47 customers that have ordered ProductID 57.

Figure 11.32 shows the query found 47 different customers that have ordered ProductID 57. We can also use this to see who ordered a specific product by name.

```
SELECT CustomerID, FirstName, LastName,
CustomerOrders.query('/Customer/Invoice/Detail/ProductName')
FROM CustomerActivity
WHERE CustomerOrders.exist
 ('/Customer/Invoice/Detail/ProductName/text()
 [. = "History Tour 1 Day Canada"]') = 1
```

	CustomerID	FirstName	LastName	(No column name)
1	1	Mark	Williams	<ProductName>Ocean Cruise Tour 1 Day West Coast</...
2	3	Patricia	Martin	<ProductName>Underwater Tour 1 Day Scandinavia</P...
3	8	Jennifer	Garcia	<ProductName>Ocean Cruise Tour 1 Day Mexico</Pro...
4	9	Linda	Adams	<ProductName>Underwater Tour 2 Weeks East Coast</...
5	11	Kimberly	Taylor	<ProductName>History Tour 3 Days Canada</ProductN...
6	12	Helen	Hernandez	<ProductName>History Tour 2 Days Canada</ProductN...

Query executed successfully. | RENO (11.0 RTM) | Reno\Student (51) | JProCo | 00:00:00 | 269 rows

Figure 11.33 This shows 269 customers have ordered the "History Tour 1 Day Canada" trip.

269 people have ordered the History Tour 1 Day Canada product (Figure 11.33). How many people have ordered any type of Canadian product? We need to change the XPath to the contains syntax.

```
SELECT CustomerID, FirstName, LastName,
CustomerOrders.query('/Customer/Invoice/Detail/ProductName')
FROM CustomerActivity
WHERE CustomerOrders.exist
 ('/Customer/Invoice/Detail/ProductName/text()
 [contains(.,"Canada")]') = 1
```

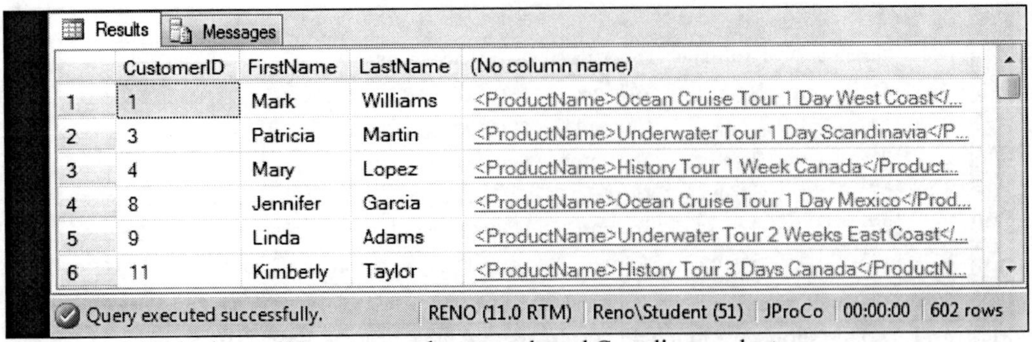

Results | Messages

	CustomerID	FirstName	LastName	(No column name)
1	1	Mark	Williams	<ProductName>Ocean Cruise Tour 1 Day West Coast</...
2	3	Patricia	Martin	<ProductName>Underwater Tour 1 Day Scandinavia</P...
3	4	Mary	Lopez	<ProductName>History Tour 1 Week Canada</Product...
4	8	Jennifer	Garcia	<ProductName>Ocean Cruise Tour 1 Day Mexico</Prod...
5	9	Linda	Adams	<ProductName>Underwater Tour 2 Weeks East Coast</...
6	11	Kimberly	Taylor	<ProductName>History Tour 3 Days Canada</ProductN...

Query executed successfully. | RENO (11.0 RTM) | Reno\Student (51) | JProCo | 00:00:00 | 602 rows

Figure 11.34 This shows 602 customers have purchased Canadian products.

602 customers have purchased some sort of product that has the word Canada in the name (Figure 11.34).

Lab 11.1: XQuery Variations

Lab Prep: Each lab has one or more Skill Checks. Start with Skill Check 1 and proceed until reaching the Points to Ponder section.

Before beginning this lab, verify that SQL Server 2012 is properly installed and operating. Before running the lab setup script for resetting the database (SQLQueries2012Vol5Chapter11.1Setup.sql), please make sure to close all query windows within SSMS. An open query window pointing to a database context can lock that database preventing it from updating when the script is executing. A simple way to assure all query windows are closed, is to exit out of SSMS, then open a new instance of SSMS, and lastly run the setup script.

Skill Check 1: Write a query from the dbo.MusicHistory table that predicates for MusicTypeID 3 and pulls out all the text from the MusicDetails file where the WriterName contains the letter "R". Show the MusicTypeName field and the correct XPath of the MusicDetails field in your result set. When done your result should resemble the figure you see here.

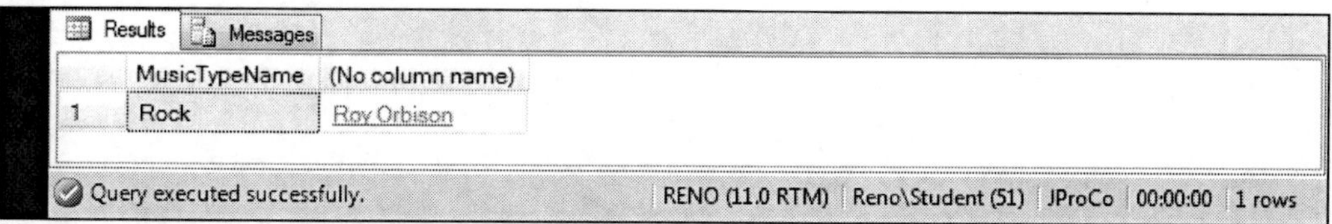

Figure 11.35 This shows the result from Skill Check 1.

Skill Check 2: Write a query against the dbo.MusicHistory table and show all fields. Use the EXIST method in the WHERE clause to find all the records that have a WriterName text of "Neil Diamond". When done your result should resemble the figure you see here.

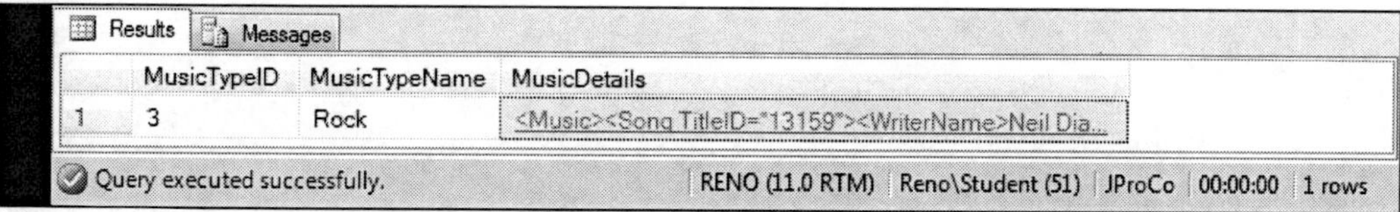

Figure 11.36 This shows the result from Skill Check 2.

Answer Code: The T-SQL code to this lab can be found in the downloadable files in a file named Lab11.1_XQuery_Variations.sql.

Points to Ponder - XQuery Variations

1. XQueries use the XPath syntax to do a combination of searching XML, retrieving XML or both.
2. Common XQuery uses are usually one of the following three types:
    - Searching XML and retrieving an XML fragment based on a given XPath.
    - Searching for an XML node by its property or name to see that value.
    - Searching for an XML node value and retrieving the name or property.

Primary XML Indexes

Saying that XML has data inside of data based on how many levels it goes down is like saying SQL can do joins for as many tables as it has. In other words, XML is often like many joined tables put into one data stream. So too is a query with many joins turned into one tabular stream. We know how to put clustered indexes on tables to make them go faster.

How do Primary XML indexes work? They are very similar to clustered indexes for a table with some more complexities. The Primary XML index has a row for every node in each XML stream. If you have two records in your table then there are two XML streams to have indexed. Each XML stream within each row of a table that has XML is called an XML instance. If you have 12 records in your table then the XML field in that table would have 12 XML instances. Each instance will have many rows (one for each node).

Comparing XML Query Types

The previous section of this chapter showed a lot of different ways to query XML using XPath and XQuery. Here are two examples:

```
--Query1: Pulls out entire XML

SELECT CustomerID, FirstName, LastName,
CustomerOrders.query('/Customer')
FROM CustomerActivity
WHERE CustomerID = 1

--Query2: Pulls out XML Fragment

SELECT CustomerID, FirstName, LastName,
CustomerOrders.query
 ('/Customer/Invoice/Detail[@ProductID=57]')
FROM CustomerActivity
WHERE CustomerID = 1
```

Different XML queries in SQL Server do different things. For example, Query1 pulls out the entire XML starting at the <root> for record 1. We see everything for record 1 in this result set (Figure 11.37, Figure 11.38).

Results | Messages

	CustomerID	FirstName	LastName	(No column name)
1	1	Mark	Williams	<Customer CustomerID="1" FirstName="Mark" LastNa...

Query executed successfully. | RENO (11.0 RTM) | Reno\Student (51) | JProCo | 00:00:00 | 1 rows

Figure 11.37 This shows the result from Query1.

xmlresult18.xml | SQLQuery2.sql - RE...(Reno\Student (51))*

```
<Customer CustomerID="1" FirstName="Mark" LastName="Williams">
  <Invoice InvoiceID="824" OrderDate="2007-11-09T11:23:51.043">
    <Detail ProductID="61">
      <ProductName>Ocean Cruise Tour 1 Day West Coast</ProductN
      <Quantity>4</Quantity>
      <RetailPrice>122.4410</RetailPrice>
    </Detail>
  </Invoice>
  <Invoice InvoiceID="1027" OrderDate="2008-04-17T16:13:59.480"
    <Detail ProductID="49">
      <ProductName>History Tour 1 Day Canada</ProductName>
      <Quantity>4</Quantity>
      <RetailPrice>113.2870</RetailPrice>
    </Detail>
```

Figure 11.38 This shows the open link from Figure 11.37.

The second query also pulls out data from customer 1, but it's only looking for product number 57. It's showing all of the times that customer 1 has ordered product number 57 (Figure 11.39, Figure 11.40).

Results | Messages

	CustomerID	FirstName	LastName	(No column name)
1	1	Mark	Williams	<Detail ProductID="57"><ProductName>History Tour...

Query executed successfully. | RENO (11.0 RTM) | Reno\Student (51) | JProCo | 00:00:00 | 1 rows

Figure 11.39 This shows the result from Query2.

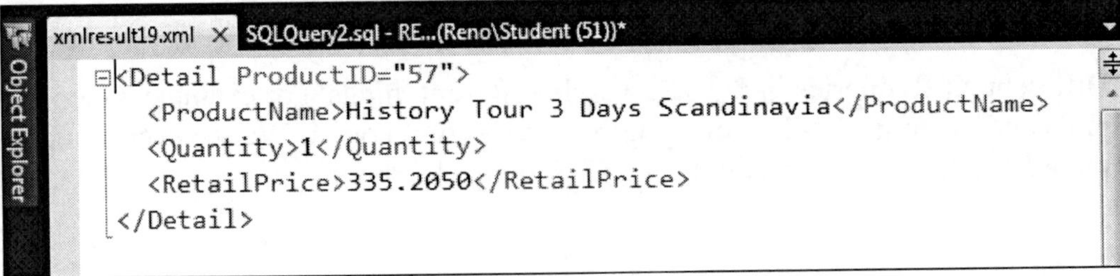

Figure 11.40 This shows the open link from Figure 11.39.

There's one instance of product 57 being ordered by customer 1 (Figure 11.40). Both queries pull out XML data. The first one pulled out the entire XML and the second pulled out a fragment of the XML. Some SQL XML queries won't pull out XML at all. The code below shows a few examples:

```
--Query3: Does not return XML it only searches the XML

SELECT CustomerID, FirstName
CustomerOrders
FROM CustomerActivity

WHERE CustomerOrders.exist
 ('/Customer/Invoice/Detail[@ProductID=57]') = 1

--Query4: Same as Query 3 but by name.

SELECT CustomerID, FirstName, LastName
FROM CustomerActivity
WHERE CustomerOrders.exist
 ('/Customer/Invoice/Detail/ProductName/text()
 [. = "History Tour 3 Days Scandinavia"]') = 1
```

Query3 and Query4 are going to give us the exact same tabular data in our result set. They are both using XPath with an XML field, but they are not going to return XML in the result set. Both Query3 and Query4 are searching to see if a certain XML pattern exists for records in the table. Let's focus on Query3. Query3 asks to show all of the records in the CustomerID, FirstName and LastName fields of anybody who's ordered product number 57.

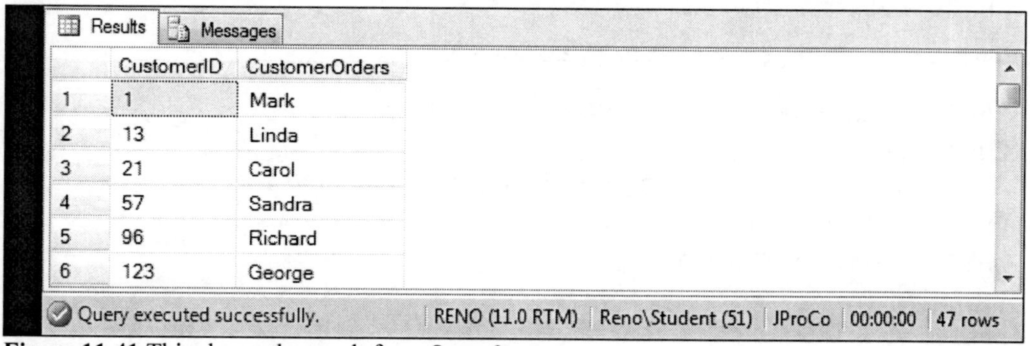

Results | Messages

	CustomerID	CustomerOrders
1	1	Mark
2	13	Linda
3	21	Carol
4	57	Sandra
5	96	Richard
6	123	George

Query executed successfully. | RENO (11.0 RTM) | Reno\Student (51) | JProCo | 00:00:00 | 47 rows

Figure 11.41 This shows the result from Query3.

If you have not already figured it out, ProductID 57 is called the "History Tour 3 Days Scandinavia". Query4 is going to find the exact same records because it is querying for ProductID 57 in a different way. Query4 is not querying by ProductID, but by ProductID 57 by its ProductName value.

Results | Messages

	CustomerID	CustomerOrders
1	1	Mark
2	13	Linda
3	21	Carol
4	57	Sandra
5	96	Richard
6	123	George

Query executed successfully. | RENO (11.0 RTM) | Reno\Student (51) | JProCo | 00:00:00 | 47 rows

Figure 11.42 This shows the result from Query4.

The query optimizer can traverse the XML entirely for XML queries, but there are benefits to parsing out the XML internally, based on the type of query that's going to be run. Queries searching for XML or retrieving XML can have XML indexes created for faster retrieval.

Adding a PRIMARY XML INDEX

We have four different XML queries against our CustomerActivity table that seem to be working just fine. These four queries are listed below:

```
--Query1: Pulls out entire XML

SELECT CustomerID, FirstName, LastName,
CustomerOrders.query('/Customer')
FROM CustomerActivity
WHERE CustomerID = 1

--Query2: Pulls out XML Fragment

SELECT CustomerID, FirstName, LastName,
CustomerOrders.query
 ('/Customer/Invoice/Detail[@ProductID=57]')
FROM CustomerActivity
WHERE CustomerID = 1

--Query3: Does not return XML it only searches the XML

SELECT CustomerID, FirstName
CustomerOrders
FROM CustomerActivity

WHERE CustomerOrders.exist
 ('/Customer/Invoice/Detail[@ProductID=57]') = 1
```

```
--Query4: Same as Query 3 but by name.
SELECT CustomerID, FirstName, LastName
FROM CustomerActivity
WHERE CustomerOrders.exist
 ('/Customer/Invoice/Detail/ProductName/text()
 [. = "History Tour 3 Days Scandinavia"]') = 1
```

Even though each of these queries runs without errors, they can be optimized and made to run faster. Where exactly is the XML data for each of these four queries?

```
     SELECT CustomerID, FirstName, LastName,
  →    CustomerOrders.Query('/Customer')
→    FROM CustomerActivity
     WHERE CustomerID = 1

     --Query2: Pulls out XML Fragment
```

Figure 11.43 This shows the location of the XML data.

The XML is stored in the CustomerOrders field of the CustomerActivity table (Figure 11.43). Before an XML index can be created we must know where our XML data is located. Let's create a primary XML index called PXML_CustomerActivity on the CustomerActivity table and CustomerOrders field.

```
CREATE PRIMARY XML INDEX PXML_CustomerActivity
ON CustomerActivity(CustomerOrders)
GO
```

```
Messages
Msg 6332, Level 16, State 201, Line 1
Table 'CustomerActivity' needs to have a clustered primary key with less than
16 columns in it in order to create a primary XML index on it.
                                                                       0 rows
```

Figure 11.44 This shows the CREATE command threw an error.

The CustomerActivity table needs to have a clustered primary key with less than 16 columns in it (Figure 11.44). Take a look at the design of the CustomerActivity table. In Object Explorer expand **Databases** > **JProCo** > **Tables** > **dbo.CustomerActivity > Columns**.

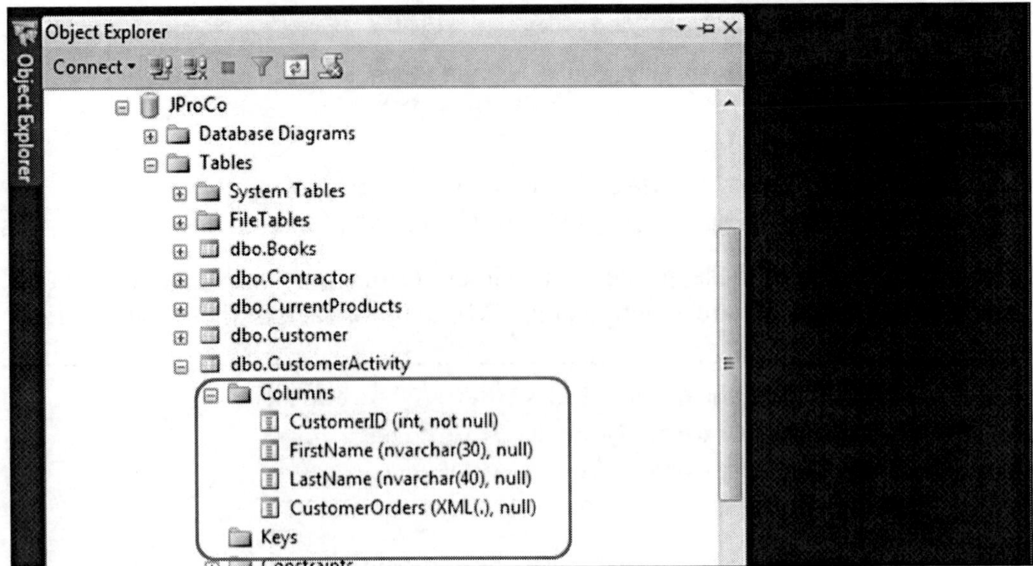

Figure 11.45 This shows the CustomerActivity table currently has no primary key.

Notice in Figure 11.45 there is no primary key. You cannot create a primary XML index on a table that doesn't have a primary key. Let's alter the CustomerActivity table and add a constraint call PK_CustomerActivity_CustomerID. We will put the primary key on the CustomerID field of the CustomerActivity table.

```
ALTER TABLE CustomerActivity
ADD CONSTRAINT PK_CustomerActivity_CustomerID PRIMARY
KEY(CustomerID)
GO
```

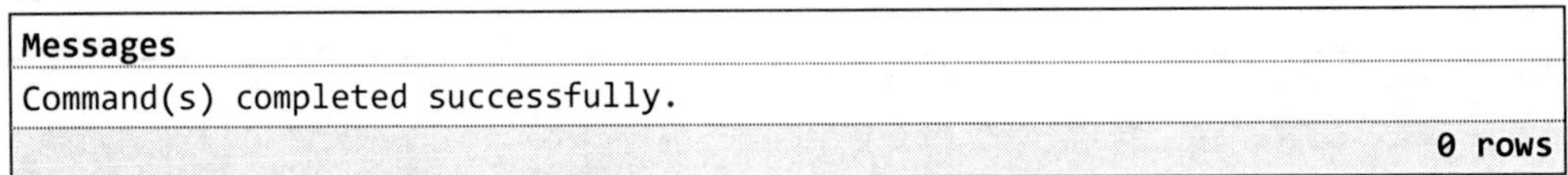

Figure 11.46 This shows the primary key was successfully created.

Let's verify in Figure 11.47 that the primary key has been created.

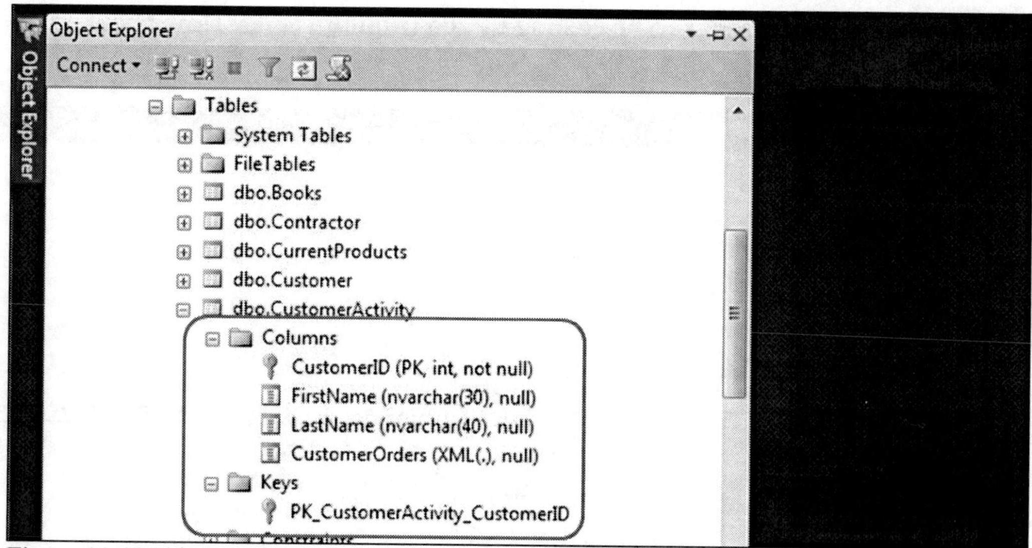

Figure 11.47 This shows the primary key was created successfully.

It looks like we're ready to create the XML index. How much faster will this make our query? Let's create a baseline. Before we create this XML index, let's see how fast Query1 runs, and let's ask for the actual execution plan. Hover your mouse over the left most icon in the execution plan diagram.

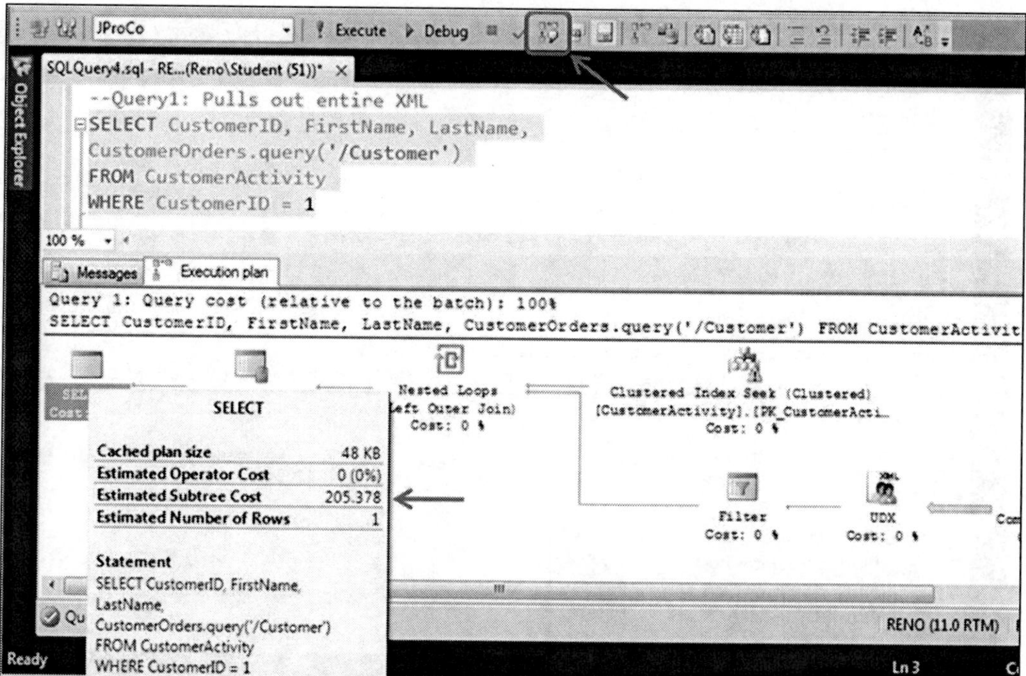

Figure 11.48 This shows the "Estimated Subtree Cost" at 205 and identifies the icon for the execution plan.

Our execution plan appears to be costing us 205 (Figure 11.48). How about Query2?

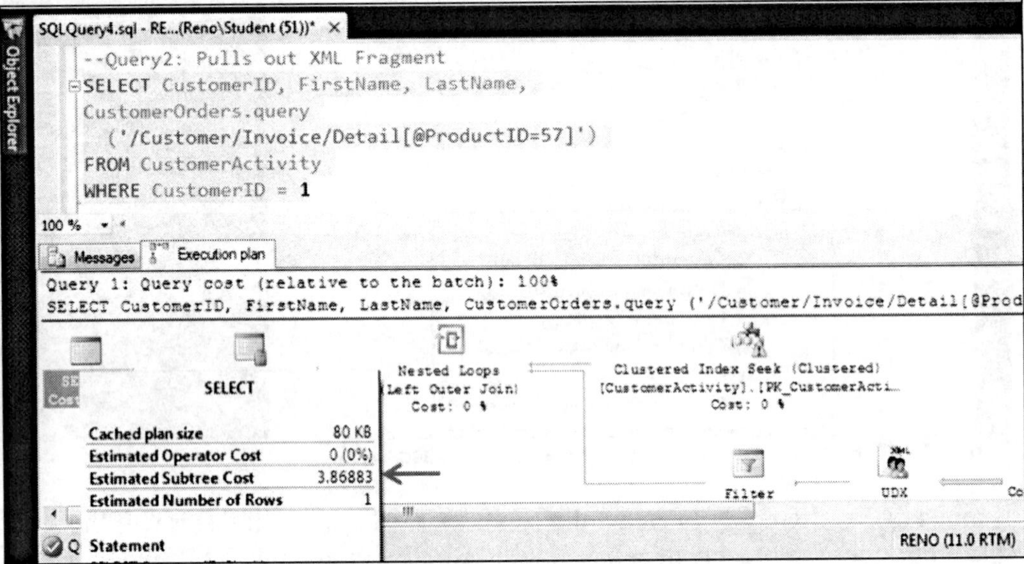

Figure 11.49 This shows the "Estimated Subtree Cost" of 3.86.

The execution plan says Query2 is costing us about 3.86 (Figure 11.49).

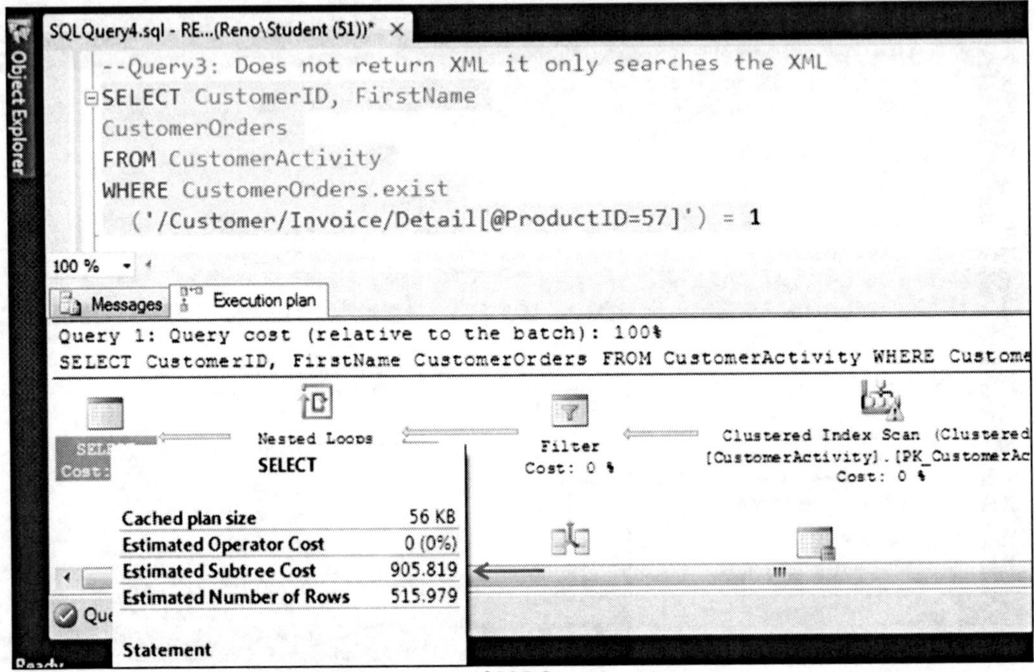

Figure 11.50 This shows Query3 has a cost of 905.8

Query3 is coming at a cost of 905 (Figure 11.50).

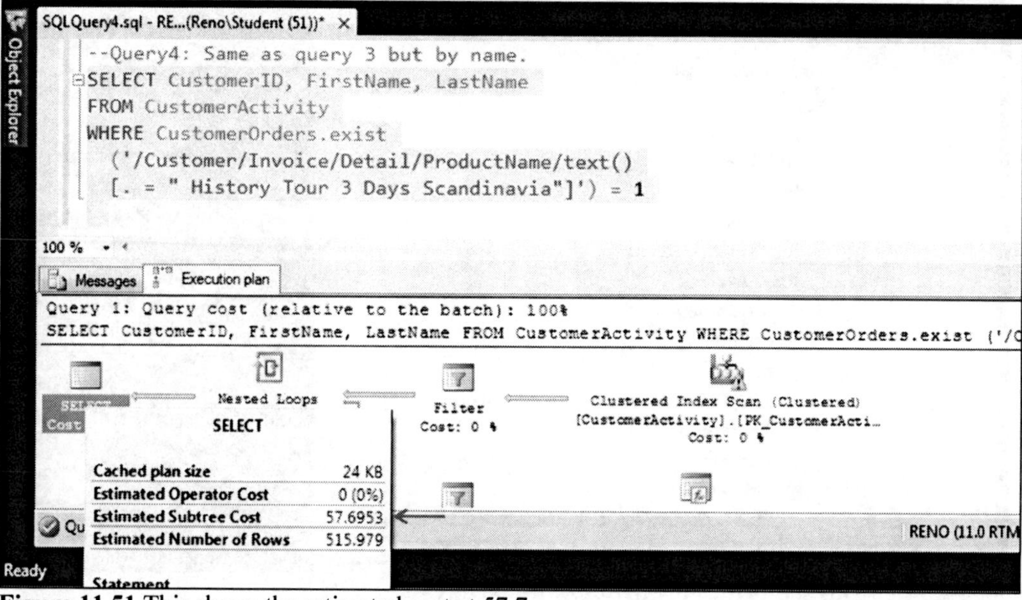

Figure 11.51 This shows the estimated cost at 57.7.

The baseline for Query4 is costing 57.7. Now that we have a baseline cost for each query let's create the XML index.

```
CREATE PRIMARY XML INDEX PXML_CustomerActivity
ON CustomerActivity(CustomerOrders)
GO
```

Messages
Command(s) completed successfully.
0 rows

Figure 11.52 This shows the PRIMARY XML INDEX was created successfully.

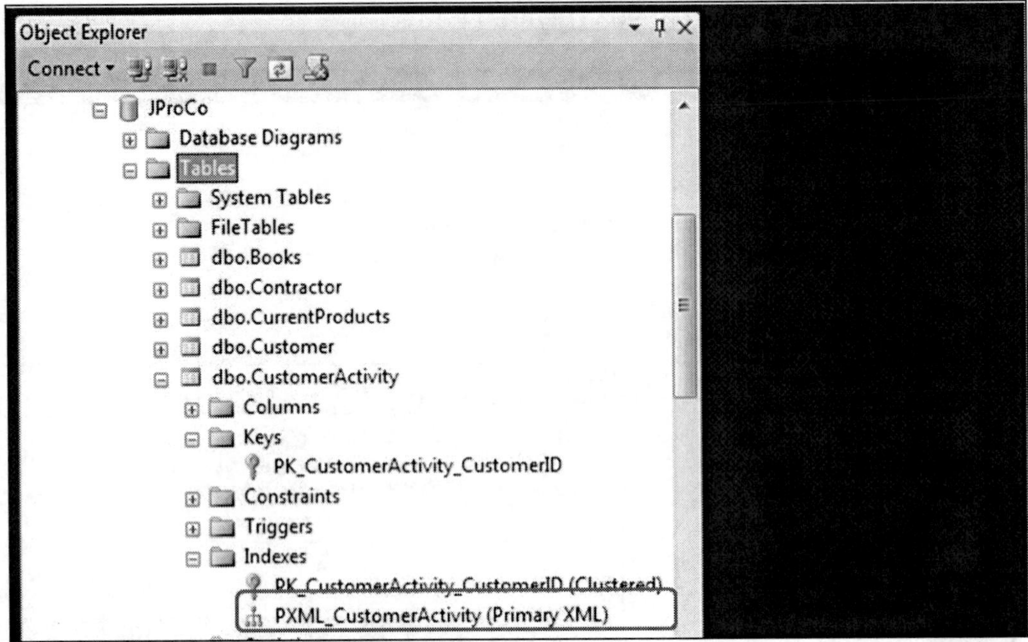

Figure 11.53 This shows the PRIMARY XML INDEX was created.

Checking Performance

Now that we have verified we have created the PRIMARY XML INDEX (Figure 11.53) we are ready to check the cost of the same four queries.

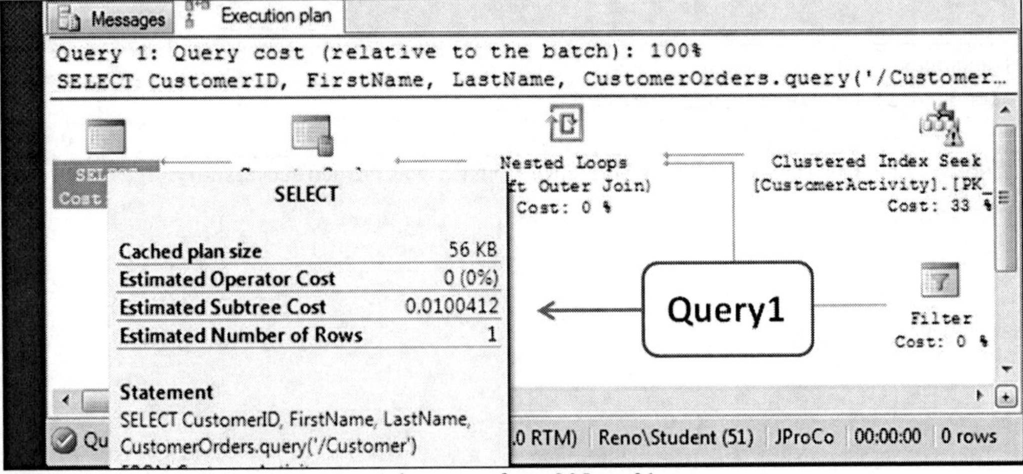

Figure 11.54 This shows Query1 cost has gone from 205 to .01.

Query1 cost went from 205 down to .01 (Figure 11.54).

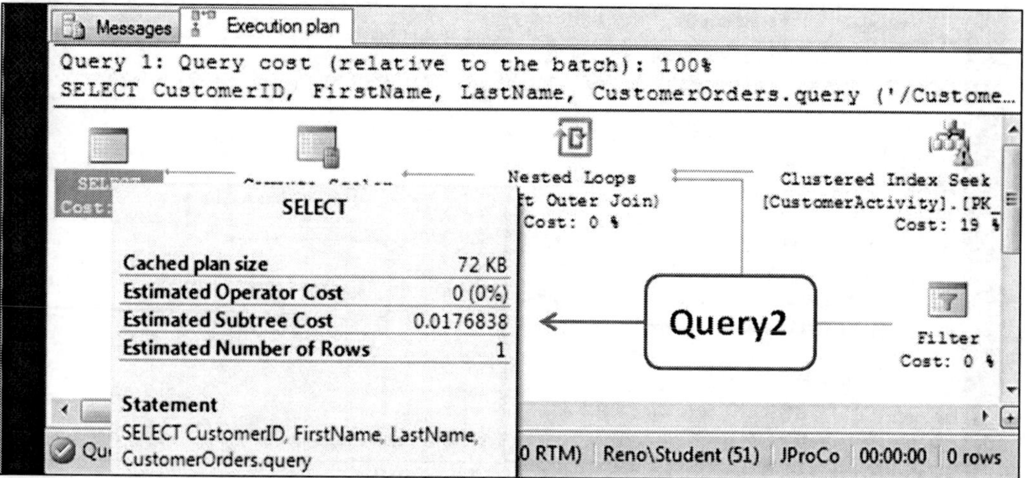

Figure 11.55 This shows Query2 cost went from 3.86 to .017.

Query2's cost went from 3.86 down to .017 (Figure 11.55).

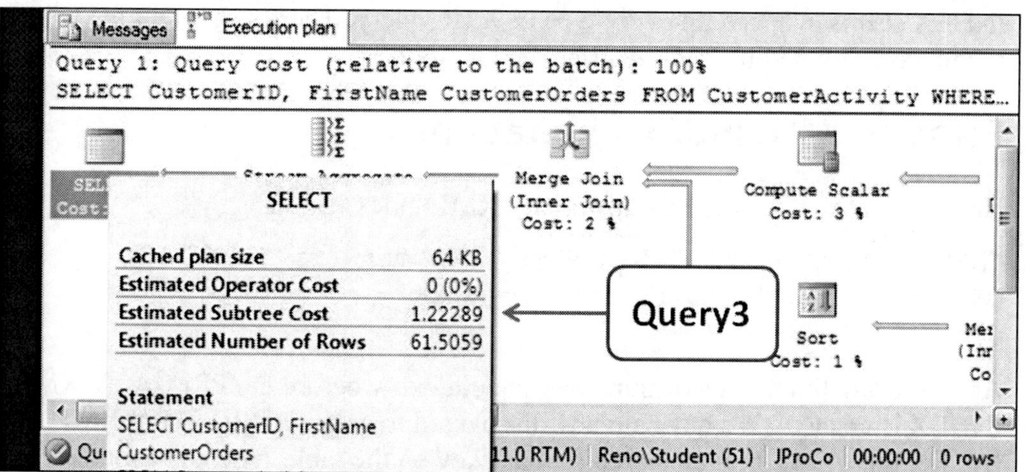

Figure 11.56 This shows Query3 cost went from 905.8 to 1.22

Cost for Query3 dropped from 905 to 1.22 (Figure 11.56).

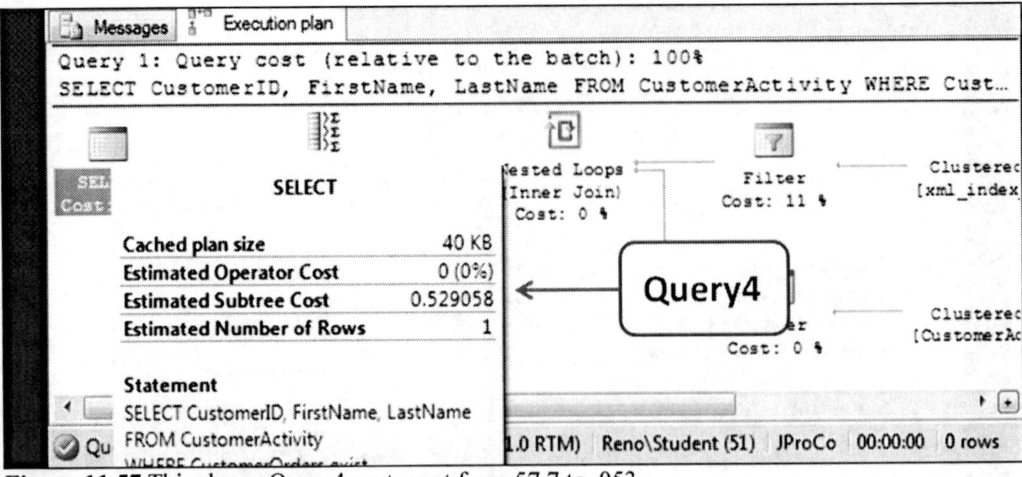

Figure 11.57 This shows Query4 cost went from 57.7 to .053.

Query4 had an "Estimated Subtree Cost" of 57.7 during the baseline test and 0.053 with the PRIMARY XML INDEX. As we can see the PRIMARY XML INDEX seems to speed up every type of XML query. There's never a time where it will slow down your XML queries on this field.

Primary XML Index Limitations

Here's the code that created our primary XML index:

```
CREATE PRIMARY XML INDEX PXML_CustomerActivity
ON CustomerActivity(CustomerOrders)
GO
```

Are there any limitations or things we should know before the PRIMARY XML INDEX is created? We have already discovered to create a PRIMARY XML INDEX there must be a clustered primary key on the table. There is another limitation. Let's try to create another XML index on the same field. This time we will name this new field CustomerActivity2.

```
CREATE PRIMARY XML INDEX PXML_CustomerActivity2
ON CustomerActivity(CustomerOrders)
GO
```

Messages
Msg 6331, Level 16, State 201, Line 1 Primary XML Index 'PXML_CustomerActivity' already exists on column 'CustomerOrders' on table 'CustomerActivity', and multiple Primary XML Indexes per column are not allowed.
0 rows

Figure 11.58 This shows you can only have one PRIMARY XML INDEX for each XML column.

Figure 11.58 shows a PRIMARY XML INDEX already exists on this table. So each XML column in the table is limited to having one PRIMARY XML INDEX. Another limitation is that an XML index can only be created on a column that is using the XML data type that doesn't already have an XML index. Many secondary indexes are possible which we will explore a little later in this chapter.

Lab 11.2: Primary XML Indexes

Lab Prep: Each lab has one or more Skill Checks. Start with Skill Check 1 and proceed until reaching the Points to Ponder section.

Before beginning this lab, verify that SQL Server 2012 is properly installed and operating. Before running the lab setup script for resetting the database (SQLQueries2012Vol5Chapter11.2Setup.sql), please make sure to close all query windows within SSMS. An open query window pointing to a database context can lock that database preventing it from updating when the script is executing. A simple way to assure all query windows are closed, is to exit out of SSMS, then open a new instance of SSMS, and lastly run the setup script.

Skill Check 1: Add a Primary XML Index called PXML_MusicHistory_MusicTypeID to the MusicDetails field of the dbo.MusicHistory table. When done you should see the primary key and XML index in the Object Explorer as shown in Figure 11.59.

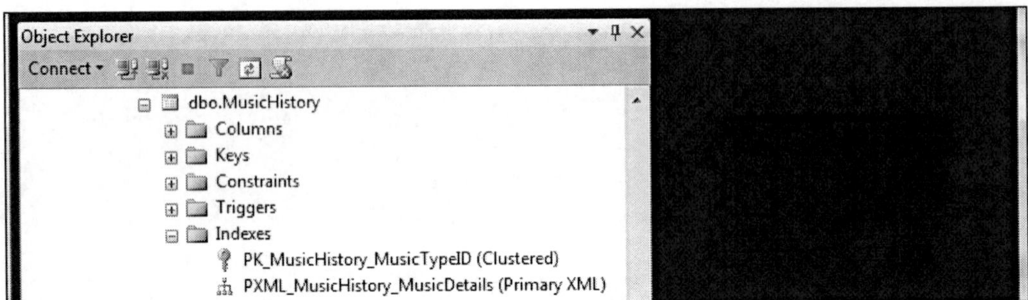

Figure 11.59 This shows the result of Skill Check1.

Answer Code: The T-SQL code to this lab can be found in the downloadable files in a file named Lab11.2PrimaryXML_Indexes.sql.

Points to Ponder - Primary XML Indexes

1. The query optimizer can traverse the XML column entirely for XML queries but there are benefits to parsing out the XML into internally indexed columns and rows for faster retrieval.
2. A primary XML index can only be created if a clustered primary key exists on the table.
3. An XML Index can only be created if the table has a primary XML index.
4. The primary XML index on a column is clustered on the internal node table of the XML for use by secondary indexes.
5. If you retrieve the entire XML then the indexes will not be used since it's faster to scan the XML than separating out the parts and putting it all back together.
6. Each row in a table with an XML column is a new XML instance.
7. The primary XML index creates one row for every node in the XML instance.
8. Each XML column is limited to having one primary XML index but you can have many secondary XML indexes.
9. You can only create an XML index on a column that is using the XML data type.

Secondary XML Indexes

The primary XML index takes every node (including values and tag names) and organizes them in an easy to search way. What if you only search for values and never search for element names? A smaller index with only values would take even less time to search. Think of secondary XML indexes as mini copies of the primary XML index that are specialized and lightweight for the type of querying you might do on your XML data. This section will explore the different types of secondary XML indexes.

FOR XML PATH

Take a look at the following query that returns XML or an XML fragment.

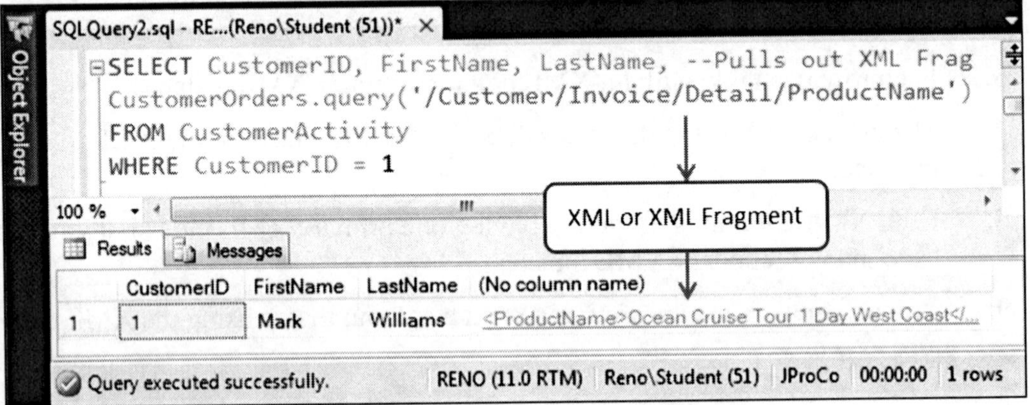

Figure 11.60 This shows a query that returns XML or an XML fragment.

We're looking for all products customer 1 has ordered.

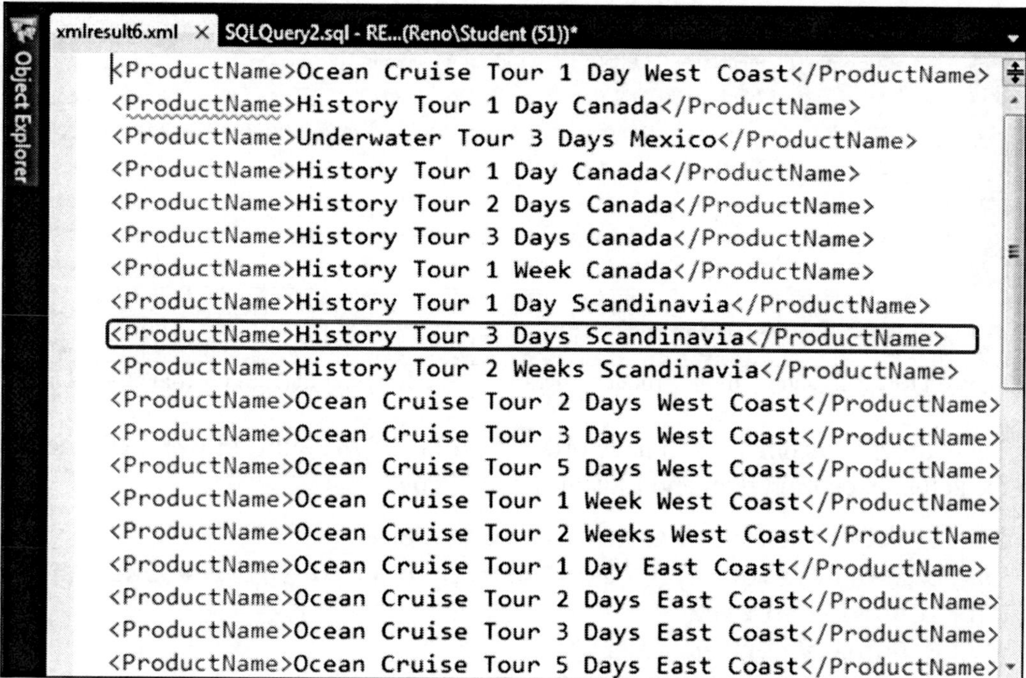

Figure 11.61 This shows all the products ordered by customer 1.

Make a special note of the "History Tour 3 Day Scandinavia". In the last section we learned this was the same as ProductID 57. When someone orders ProductID 57, what other products do they also tend to order? Customer number 1 did order this product but he is not the only customer to order ProductID 57. Let's write a query that returns all the XML of all the products ordered by customers who have also ordered ProductID 57.

We need to change the WHERE clause to WHERE CustomerOrders.exist() and in the parentheses add the XPath of /Customer/Invoice/Detail followed by the @ProductID of 57. The exist() function will return a 0 if the object does not exist and a 1 if it does. So let's add "= 1" to only return records if it exists in the XML.

```
SELECT CustomerID, FirstName, LastName,
CustomerOrders.query('/Customer/Invoice/Detail/ProductName')
FROM CustomerActivity
WHERE CustomerOrders.exist
 ('/Customer/Invoice/Detail/@ProductID[.="57"]') = 1
```

Results | Messages

	CustomerID	FirstName	LastName	(No column name)
1	1	Mark	Williams	<ProductName>Ocean Cruise Tour 1 Day West Coast</...
2	13	Linda	Hernandez	<ProductName>History Tour 3 Days Canada</ProductN...
3	21	Carol	Thompson	<ProductName>History Tour 1 Day Scandinavia</Produ...
4	57	Sandra	Allen	<ProductName>History Tour 1 Day Canada</ProductNa...
5	96	Richard	Thompson	<ProductName>Ocean Cruise Tour 2 Weeks Mexico</P...
6	123	George	Wilson	<ProductName>History Tour 1 Day Canada</ProductNa...

Query executed successfully. | RENO (11.0 RTM) | Reno\Student (51) | JProCo | 00:00:00 | 47 rows

Figure 11.62 This shows all the product orders for every customer that has ordered product 57.

There are 47 customers who have ordered product 57 (Figure 11.62). Let's include the actual execution plan and look at the total cost.

```
SELECT CustomerID, FirstName, LastName,
CustomerOrders.query('/Customer/Invoice/Detail/ProductName')
FROM CustomerActivity
WHERE CustomerOrders.exist
 ('/Customer/Invoice/Detail/@ProductID[.="57"]') = 1
```

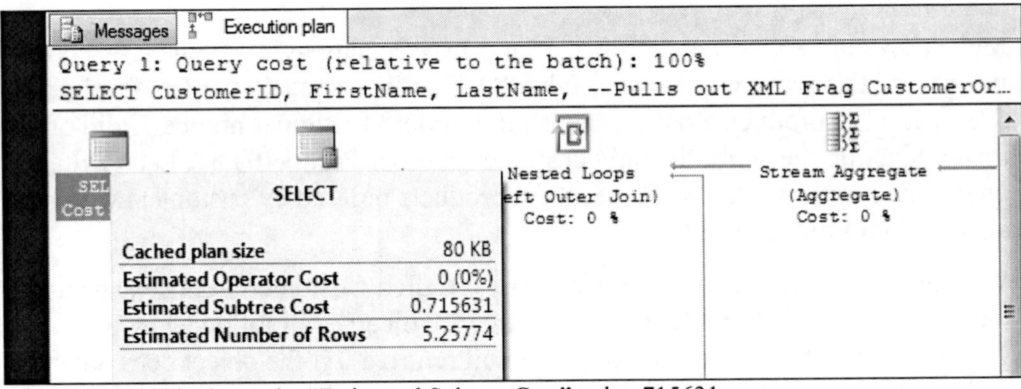

Figure 11.63 This shows the "Estimated Subtree Cost" to be .715631.

It looks like our total cost is just under 0.72. This query is looking for an exact path with an exact value and will return certain fragments of the XML when found. If the query is searching for, or retrieving XML based on a path, we can actually build a secondary index on top of the primary XML index.

The secondary index specializes in XML fragments within a path. Let's create a secondary XML index and call it IXML_CustomerActivity_Path and we'll base that on the CustomerActivity table on the CustomerOrders field. We need to call on the primary index by USING XML INDEX PXML_CustomerActivity . Finally, specify that this secondary XML index specializes in finding exact paths and fragments.

```
CREATE XML INDEX IXML_CustomerActivity_Path
ON CustomerActivity(CustomerOrders)
USING XML INDEX PXML_CustomerActivity FOR PATH
GO
```

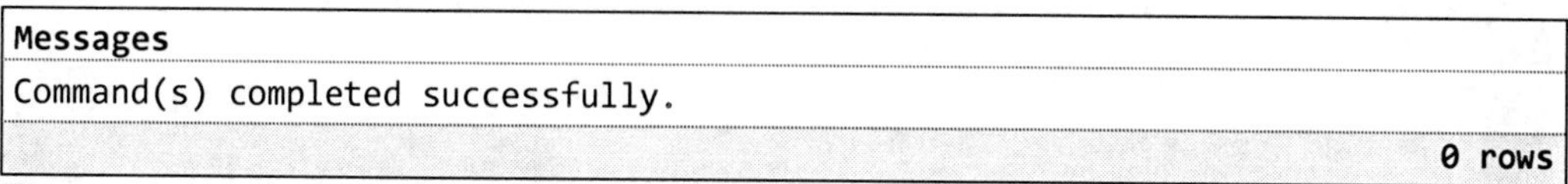

Messages
Command(s) completed successfully.
0 rows

Figure 11.64 This shows the secondary index IXML_CustomerActivity_Path was created successfully.

We have successfully created the secondary XML Index (Figure 11.64). If we run the query in Figure 11.63 let's check and see if we have reduced the "Estimated Subtree Cost".

```
SELECT CustomerID, FirstName, LastName,
CustomerOrders.query('/Customer/Invoice/Detail/ProductName')
FROM CustomerActivity
WHERE CustomerOrders.exist
 ('/Customer/Invoice/Detail/@ProductID[.="57"]') = 1
```

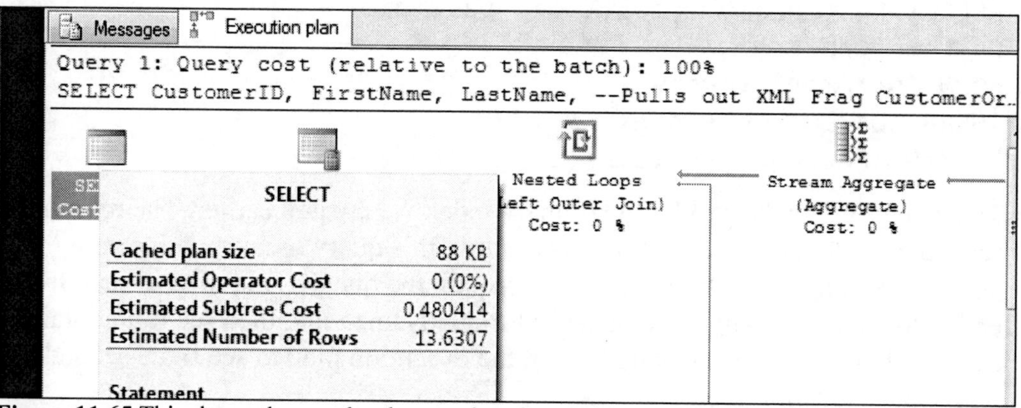

Figure 11.65 This shows the cost has been reduced to .480414.

The execution plan looks a little different and the total cost has gone from .72 to .48. Also, if we look a little closer at the plan, we see that it actually used the secondary XML in gathering this information.

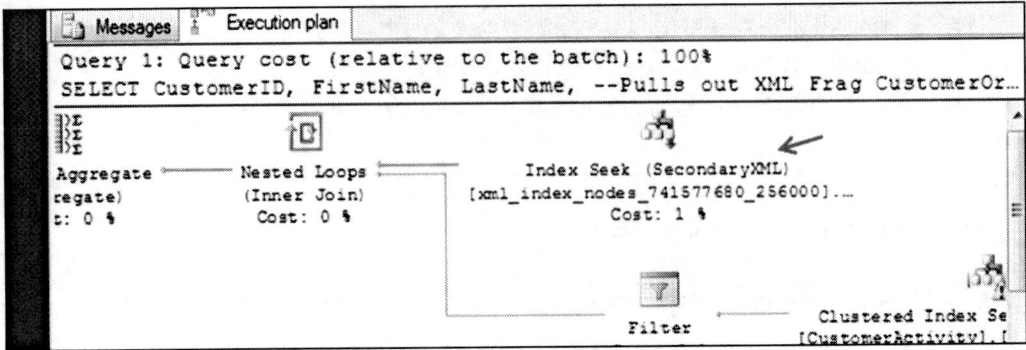

Figure 11.66 This shows the secondary index was used in the execution plan.

The creation of this secondary XML index worked and facilitated the execution of this query.

FOR XML PROPERTY

Take a moment and look at the following query. This query will not benefit from an XML path index.

```
SELECT CustomerID, FirstName, LastName,
CustomerOrders
FROM CustomerActivity
WHERE CustomerOrders.exist
 ('//ProductName[contains(.,"Mexico")]') = 1
```

This query will be helped by the primary index we created earlier. The reason the secondary path index will not help is because this query uses a relative path (//) and not an exact path. By using a relative path the query is required to search the entire document for any node named <ProductName> and then see if it contains Mexico. Let's run this code and look at the execution plan to see if the secondary XML index is being used.

```
SELECT CustomerID, FirstName, LastName,
CustomerOrders
FROM CustomerActivity
WHERE CustomerOrders.exist
 ('//ProductName[contains(.,"Mexico")]') = 1
```

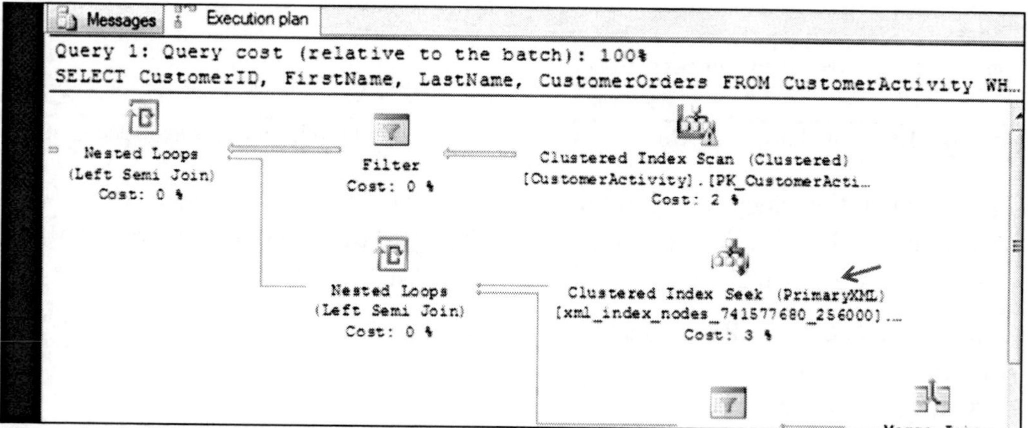

Figure 11.67 This shows the query used the primary XML Index.

The speed of execution was already improved by the primary index, but the secondary index was not used in the execution plan. The relative path required it to search data point by data point from the primary XML index. The primary XML index contains every node and the level relationships to other nodes. This query is just looking for the node name and does not care about level.

If we did not need all the tree structure to run the query and the XML could be listed in a flat invisible table with every value in every node, then it could be searched rather rapidly as long as we don't care what level the value is in. The XPath in the query above uses a relative path so the level the data is in does not matter. What kind of secondary XML would search for such a value or a property?

The FOR PROPERTY secondary XML index will pre-list all the values and properties without storing the levels. This is useful for an exist query that does not need to return any XML structure back.

We will create this index the same way we created the FOR PATH index. Let's name the FOR PROPERTY index IXML_CustomerActivity_Property. We will put it on the CustomerActivity table for the CustomerOrders field. A secondary index is only possible if a primary XML index already exists. For this reason we have to specify the name of the primary XML index that was created. Lastly we want this index specified to be optimized for searching by property.

```
CREATE XML INDEX IXML_CustomerActivity_Property
ON CustomerActivity(CustomerOrders)
USING XML INDEX PXML_CustomerActivity FOR PROPERTY
GO
```

Messages
Command(s) completed successfully.
0 rows

Figure 11.68 This shows the IXML_CustomerActivity_Property index was created successfully.

If we look at the execution plan for our query cost we can see it used to be 7.99 and is now 7.96. The FOR PROPERTY index sped this small query up just a little. Larger XML instances would benefit even more.

```
SELECT CustomerID, FirstName, LastName,
CustomerOrders
FROM CustomerActivity
WHERE CustomerOrders.exist
 ('//ProductName[contains(.,"Mexico")]') = 1
```

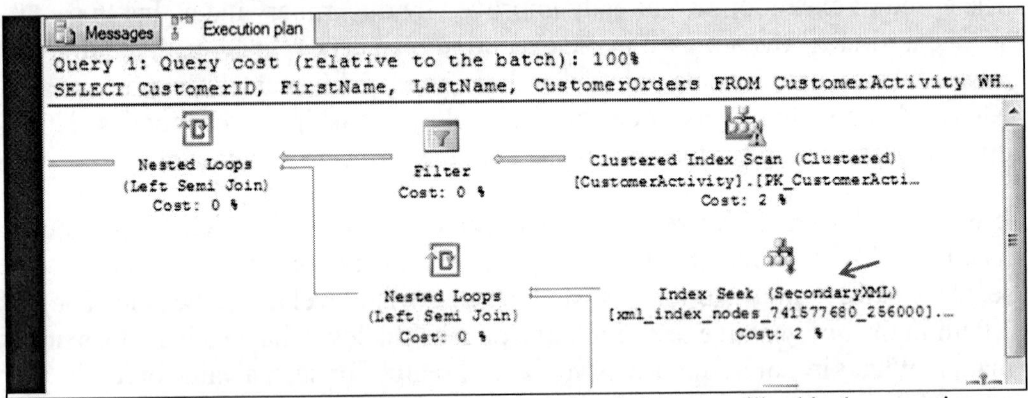

Figure 11.69 This shows the FOR PROPERTY secondary index was utilized in the execution plan.

Notice the property index benefited the use of this query. The secondary XML index is listed in the execution plan.

FOR XML VALUE

Take a look at the following query that is searching for an exact text node value.

```
SELECT CustomerID, FirstName, LastName, CustomerOrders
FROM CustomerActivity
WHERE CustomerOrders.exist
 ('/Customer/Invoice/Detail/ProductName/text()
 [. = " History Tour 3 Days Scandinavia"]') = 1
```

The best tool to make this run faster is to use an XML secondary index that is optimized for finding exact values. Just like before, we need to use CREATE XML INDEX IXML. This is a secondary XML index optimized for values so this time we will name it IXML_CustomerActivity_Value. Let's base this index on the value of the customer orders field in the CustomerActivity table. This is a secondary index so it too needs to leverage off of the primary XML index. Lastly we need to specify that this index is optimized for finding values by typing FOR VALUE.

```
CREATE XML INDEX IXML_CustomerActivity_Value
ON CustomerActivity(CustomerOrders)
USING XML INDEX PXML_CustomerActivity FOR VALUE
GO
```

Messages
Command(s) completed successfully.
0 rows

Figure 11.70 This shows the IXML_CustomerActivity_Value secondary index was created.

```
SELECT CustomerID, FirstName, LastName, CustomerOrders
FROM CustomerActivity
WHERE CustomerOrders.exist
 ('/Customer/Invoice/Detail/ProductName/text()
 [. = " History Tour 3 Days Scandinavia"]') = 1
```

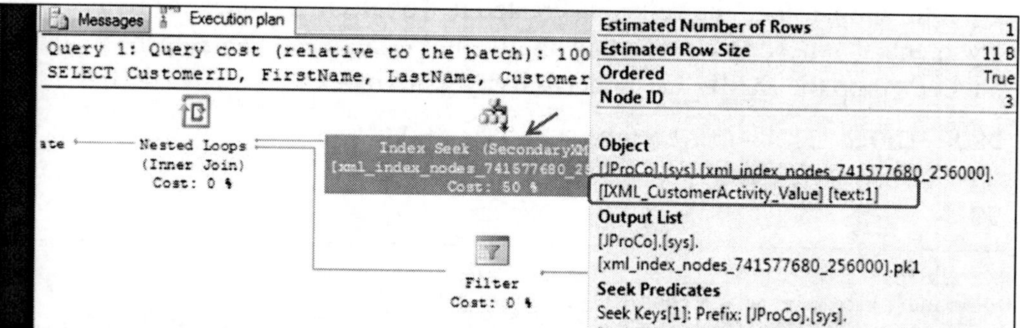

Figure 11.71 This shows the query uses the IXML_CustomerActivity_Value index.

Notice in Figure 11.71 the query used the IXML_CustomerActivity_Value index in the execution plan.

Dropping XML Indexes

Here we have the code that created our three secondary XML indexes:

```
CREATE XML INDEX IXML_CustomerActivity_Path
ON CustomerActivity(CustomerOrders)
USING XML INDEX PXML_CustomerActivity FOR PATH
GO

CREATE XML INDEX IXML_CustomerActivity_Property
ON CustomerActivity(CustomerOrders)
USING XML INDEX PXML_CustomerActivity FOR PROPERTY
GO

CREATE XML INDEX IXML_CustomerActivity_Value
ON CustomerActivity(CustomerOrders)
USING XML INDEX PXML_CustomerActivity FOR VALUE
GO
```

Figure 11.72 This shows the code that created the three secondary indexes.

If we no longer need an index how do we remove it? The code to DROP an index is a little simpler than the code that created it. To DROP an index the two arguments that need to be specified are the index name and the table the index is on. Let's drop the IXML_CustomerActivity_Path index.

```
DROP INDEX IXML_CustomerActivity_Path
ON CustomerActivity
GO
```

Messages
Command(s) completed successfully.
0 rows

Figure 11.73 This shows the FOR PATH index was dropped successfully.

Next we can drop the secondary XML index we created that was optimized for property XQueries that we named IXML_CustomerActivity_Property.

```
DROP INDEX IXML_CustomerActivity_Property
ON CustomerActivity
GO
```

Messages
Command(s) completed successfully.
0 rows

Figure 11.74 This shows the FOR PROPERTY index was dropped successfully.

Last but not least let's drop the IXML_CustomerActivity_Value secondary XML index by using DROP INDEX.

```
DROP INDEX IXML_CustomerActivity_Value
ON CustomerActivity
GO
```

Messages
Command(s) completed successfully.
0 rows

Figure 11.75 This shows the FOR VALUE index was dropped successfully.

All three secondary XML indexes created in this chapter have now been dropped.

Lab 11.3: Secondary XML Indexes

Lab Prep: Each lab has one or more Skill Checks. Start with Skill Check 1 and proceed until reaching the Points to Ponder section.

Before beginning this lab, verify that SQL Server 2012 is properly installed and operating. Before running the lab setup script for resetting the database (SQLQueries2012Vol5Chapter11.3Setup.sql), please make sure to close all query windows within SSMS. An open query window pointing to a database context can lock that database preventing it from updating when the script is executing. A simple way to assure all query windows are closed, is to exit out of SSMS, then open a new instance of SSMS, and lastly run the setup script.

Skill Check 1: Create a secondary XML index on the MusicDetails field of the MusicHistory table that is optimized to return XML fragments based on an absolute XPath. When done you should see the XML index in the Object Explorer as shown in the figure you see here.

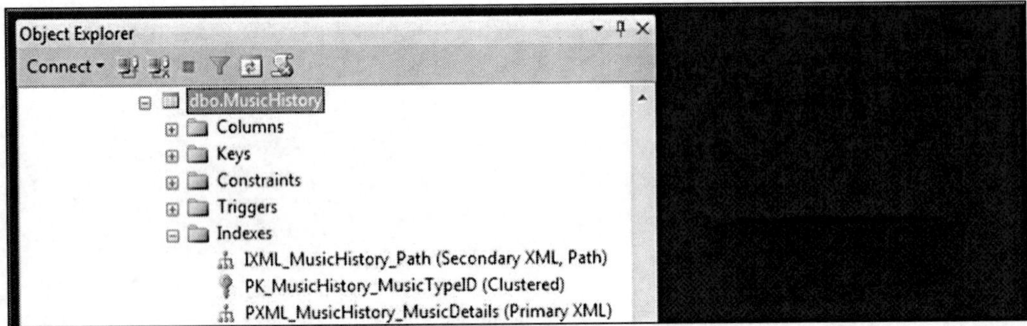

Figure 11.76 This shows the result from Skill Check 1.

Answer Code: The T-SQL code to this lab can be found in the downloadable files in a file named Lab11.3SecondaryXML_Indexes.sql.

Points to Ponder - Secondary XML Indexes

1. There are three kinds of secondary indexes PATH, PROPERTY, or VALUE.
   - FOR PATH
   - FOR PROPERTY
   - FOR VALUE
2. The PATH, PROPERTY, and VALUE indexes are specialized and designed to help certain XQuery statements.
3. The PATH secondary XML index is useful for XPath query expressions on the XML column looking to retrieve XML fragments or to find the existence and exact XML path.
4. The VALUE secondary XML index is useful when you query for unknown attribute names. Works great with finding values with contains()
5. The PROPETRY secondary XML index is useful when you know the name of the element or attribute but don't care about the exact level. It is also useful if you have the element name and the are looking for the text() value with [.=] .

Chapter Glossary

FOR PATH: A type of secondary XML index optimized for retrieving an XML fragment based on a given XPath.

FOR XML PROPERTY: A type of secondary XML index optimized for retrieving the name or property.

FOR XMLVALUE: A type of secondary XML index optimized for querying an XML node based on its property or name to see that value.

XML Instance: One XML stream in one row of a table that has an XML field.

Primary XML Index: Has a row for every node in each XML stream.

Secondary XML: A specialized XML index to make specific types of XQueries run even faster than the primary XML Index.

Estimated Subtree Cost: The total cost of one specific query.

Review Quiz - Chapter Eleven

1.) You have the following code:

```
SELECT CustomerID, FirstName, LastName,
CustomerOrders.query('//ProductName/text()')
FROM CustomerActivity
WHERE CustomerID = 1
```

Which ProductName nodes will be returned?

O a. ProductName text from the root level only.

O b. ProductName text from the top-level only.

O c. ProductName text from any level below the root.

O d. ProductName text from any level.

2.) A primary XML index can only be created on an XML field if…

O a. The XML is typed XML.

O b. The XML field has a clustered primary key.

O c. The table has a clustered primary key.

3.) You have the following code which throws an error:

```
CREATE PRIMARY XML INDEX PXML_CustomerActivity
ON CustomerActivity(CustomerName)
GO
```

What is one possible reason this code would throw an error?

O a. There are no secondary indexes on this table.

O b. There are no secondary indexes on this filed.

O c. There are no XML schemas on this field.

O d. The CustomerName field is not an XML data type.

4.) You have the following code:

```
SELECT CustOrders.query('/Cust/Invoice)
FROM CustActivity
WHERE CustOrders.exist('/Cust/Invoice/@ID[.="4563"]') = 1
```

Currently you have a primary XML index that is benefiting query execution speed. You want to create a secondary XML index to make this type of query even faster. Which type of secondary XML index will help the most?

O a. FOR PATH

O b. FOR VALUE

O c. FOR PRPOERTY

5.) You have the following code:

```
SELECT *
FROM ProductLibrary
WHERE Prod.exist('/Inc/ProdName/text()[.="Gum Bears"]')
= 1
```

Currently you have a primary XML index that is benefiting query execution speed. You want to create a secondary XML index to make this type of query even faster. Which type of secondary XML index will help the most?

O a. FOR PATH

O b. FOR VALUE

O c. FOR PRPOERTY

Answer Key

1.) Two forward slashes in front of the target ProductName will pull out all the products regardless of the level, so (d) is the correct answer.

2.) A PRIMARY XML INDEX can only be created if a clustered Primary key exists on the table, so (c) is the correct answer.

3.) Each XML column in the table is limited to having one PRIMARY XML INDEX. Another limitation is that an XML index can only be created on a column that is using the XML data type that doesn't already have an XML index, so (d) is correct.

4.) FOR VALUE is an XML secondary index that is optimized for finding exact values, so (b) is incorrect. The FOR PROPERTY secondary XML index will pre-list all the values and properties without storing the levels. This is useful for an exist query that does not need to return any XML structure back, so (c) is incorrect. (a) is correct, this pulls out XML and only FOR PATH retains the XML structure.

5.) FOR PATH retains the XML structure, so (a) is incorrect. FOR PROPERTY disregards all element level metadata, so (c) is incorrect. This is searching for a text value and not needing the XML returned so FOR VALUE is the fastest, so (b) is correct.

Bug Catcher

To play the Bug Catcher game run the SQLQueries2012Vol5BugCatcher11.pps from the BugCatcher folder of the companion files found at www.Joes2Pros.com.

Chapter 12. Final Thoughts

Thomas Alva Edison was one of the greatest inventors in history. He sold 1,093 US patents, plus many more in the UK, France and Germany. He is known for so many inventions, many of which we cannot live without. For example: electric lights, recorded music, motion pictures! He has inventions everywhere! Thomas Edison was a great thinker and is also remembered through is timeless and meaningful quotes. He has given us a motto for learning: "Many of life's failures are experienced by people who didn't realize how close they were to success when they gave up." This book is all about finishing what was started. At this point writing queries correctly is no problem. As a Joes2Pros student you will find you can write queries better than many people in industry. You have made it through every Skill Check, Bug Catching game, Points to Ponder, and Review Quiz. You may have even boosted your learning experience by watched all the related videos. With all of this are you done? Are your SQL skills perfect yet? Absolutely not.

So the question remains, what is on the other side of the SQL Server coin? Luckily for us both sides of the SQL Server coin are bright. The first side is SQL Server developer, the other is SQL administrator. The developer does a great job writing queries, but if they are not properly deployed problems will ensue. Queries have to be deployed properly, and the server has to be maintained. Developers make mistakes but they shouldn’t affect performance. When the mistakes happen, there should be policies in place to prevent disasters.

When a query is deployed on one server, who controls the mechanisms that allow it to be used on another server? As the amount of data grows, you need the query to be running on multiple servers and be able to pull the same data out. Now is the time to understand applications. It is valuable to understand how to have SQL Server running optimally with proper file groups. The data should be placed as optimally as possible. There will be cases to add more memory, to catch offending queries, to know when indexes are no longer useful. There will be scenarios where you need to know if your data is safe so your query runs fine when you need it the next time. There will be cases when disasters happen.

You’re SQL Career

These are all things you need to learn. Understanding both sides of the SQL coin make you a much more valuable employee. Be proud that you have mastered writing queries. The next step should be to build your value and learn database administration. From here it is time to make sure you understand backup, recovery, index management, replication, file placement, partitioning, Always On, and other features of the SQL administrator. Be sure to look for the next series of Joes2Pros books: Joes to Pros: SQL Server Administrator. We promise to take you on the same journey. With the completion of Joes to Pros: SQL Server Administrator you will have mastered both sides of the SQL coin. Your future is bright, your opportunities are limitless. When the coin flips, you will never have to worry. "Heads or tails?" - In your case it doesn't matter, you will win either way.

And we come back to Thomas Edison. He didn't stop with one invention; he continued inventing more. In the same way, you have just finished Joes2Pros SQL Queries, go to next level, and build your value as an employee. Learn from Thomas Edison continue learning, continue writing new queries, continue upgrading yourself - We will see you in next series!

Index

Lightning Source UK Ltd.
Milton Keynes UK
UKOW010335220313

207981UK00003B/146/P